Methods of Argument

An Anthology of Readings

Deborah H. Holdstein

Danielle Aquiline

New York   Oxford
OXFORD UNIVERSITY PRESS

Oxford University Press is a department of the University of Oxford.
It furthers the University's objective of excellence in research, scholarship,
and education by publishing worldwide. Oxford is a registered trade mark of
Oxford University Press in the UK and certain other countries.

Published in the United States of America by Oxford University Press
198 Madison Avenue, New York, NY 10016, United States of America.

© 2019 by Oxford University Press

For titles covered by Section 112 of the US Higher Education
Opportunity Act, please visit www.oup.com/us/he for the latest
information about pricing and alternate formats.

All rights reserved. No part of this publication may be reproduced, stored in
a retrieval system, or transmitted, in any form or by any means, without the
prior permission in writing of Oxford University Press, or as expressly permitted
by law, by license, or under terms agreed with the appropriate reproduction
rights organization. Inquiries concerning reproduction outside the scope of the
above should be sent to the Rights Department, Oxford University Press,
at the address above.

You must not circulate this work in any other form
and you must impose this same condition on any acquirer.

Library of Congress Cataloging-in-Publication Data

Names: Holdstein, Deborah H., 1952- editor. | Aquiline, Danielle, editor.
Title: Methods of argument : an anthology of readings / [edited by Deborah H.
    Holdstein and Danielle Aquiline].
Description: New York, NY : Oxford University Press, [2019]
Identifiers: LCCN 2018038622
Subjects: LCSH: College readers. | English language—Rhetoric. | Persuasion
    (Rhetoric) | Report writing.
Classification: LCC PE1417 .M4825 2019 | DDC 808/.0427—dc23 LC
record available at https://lccn.loc.gov/2018038622
(print) | ISBN 9780190855727 (online ebook) |
    ISBN 9780190855710 (paperback)

9 8 7 6 5 4 3 2 1

Printed by LSC Communications, Inc., United States of America

To Reinhard Holdstein and Henia Freifeld Holdstein,
survivors and optimists.

CONTENTS

CHAPTER 4: *Higher Ground*

CHAPTER 5: *Ethics*

CONTENTS ALPHABETICALLY BY AUTHOR

CONTENTS BY GENRE

NONFICTION

The Book

The selections in *Methods of Argument* model directly or by implication an array of arguments and techniques. More precisely, not only is this a volume that models a variety of methods by which a range of authors argue points of view or create images that suggest particular positions, but it also is a reader that represents complex approaches to forms of argument and "ways of arguing." For our students, the object is the same: to respond to complex images and texts, in writing and discussion, with responsible, well-supported arguments and points of view.

While truthful reasoning, opinions, and arguments have always been essential to citizenship and have been the mark of a responsible thinker and writer, the current (and likely long-term) climate of "fake news" presents an even greater challenge to effective and truthful argument and students' ability to analyze which viewpoints are credible and which are not. When one adds to this the notion of "alternative facts," we find a timely and even more compelling context within which to offer the opportunity to craft logical and well-reasoned arguments and to support them with solid, appropriate evidence.

Methods of Argument—which stands alone or works well as an accompaniment to *Who Says?: The Writer's Research*—showcases both classic and contemporary essays and images from a wide range of sources and writers, arguing both by presentation and explicitly through its structural features that many of the selections, including those that might not be seen as overt forms of "argument," nonetheless present or imply points of view that are worthy of analysis, discussion, and writing.

Methods of Argument includes the following features:

- **Headnotes** provide biographical details and context to orient students who may be unfamiliar with or interested in learning more about an author or subject.

- **"Reflecting and Discussing" Questions** prompt students to engage more deeply with the piece itself and explore the arguments within it.
- **"Connecting and Writing" Questions** provide complex, contemporary, intriguing prompts for students to analyze a piece's themes and respond to them in detail through writing.
- **Cross-referential writing questions** engage students in comparative discussion of the selections.

Most importantly, *Methods of Argument* illustrates the value of analysis and questioning, not only in the classroom, but also as part of one's life experiences. As students question and challenge these readings and the issues they raise—and in turn question their assumptions about and perspectives on the world—they will be able to apply these abilities to other complex issues, whether in print, in conversation, or on the Internet and social media.

Methods of Argument affirms that there are few simple answers when we interact with a complex universe, offering student thinkers and writers the opportunity to address and question others' viewpoints and their own, whether to reinforce and strengthen them or, perhaps, to change them. At its best, argument results in invigorating conversation and lively, well-wrought, and accountably argued writing. It's essential that students be clear, reasoned, and fair when explaining why they feel the way they do about certain issues—and that they understand and appreciate the views of others. *Methods of Argument* asks that its readers and writers take well-reasoned positions on subjects, eschewing neutrality, as neutrality often masks a position taken in a passive way.

ACKNOWLEDGMENTS

We thank our editors at Oxford University Press for their ongoing support, and we especially thank Garon Scott for his consistent presence and important institutional memory.

We also each thank our respective institutions: Columbia College Chicago and Oakton Community College.

An expected part of the process of writing and publishing a textbook involves the participation of a number of reviewers in academe from a variety of institutions throughout the United States. We thank the following for their thoughtful work: Chad Barbour, Lake Superior State University; Heather Braun, University of Akron; Mary Bulkot, Cayuga Community College; Judith Coleman, Delta State University; Anthony Cooke, Emory University; Deborah Cordonnier, Rider University; Sarah Cote, Alfred University; Jason DePolo, North Carolina A&T State University; Annette Lovrien Duncan, Carthage College; Gina Firenzi, San Jose State University; Richard Groper, California State University, Los Angeles; Steffen Guenzel, University of Central Florida; Tara Hembrough, Southeastern Oklahoma State University; Melvin G. Hill, University of Tennessee at Martin; Laura Jessup, Southern Oregon University; Adam Kaiserman, College of the Canyons; Susan Peterson, Curry College; Aimee Pozorski, Central Connecticut State University; William Quirk, Rider University; Yelizaveta Renfro, Westfield State University; Lisa Robeson, Ohio Northern University; Emily Jo Scalzo, Ball State University; Wilma J. Shires, Southeastern Oklahoma State University; Margot Soven, La Salle University; John B. Stoker, Kent State University at Ashtabula; Paige Talbot, South Seattle College; and Susan Wright, Campbellsville University.

Finally, Deborah H. Holdstein thanks her husband, Jay Boersma, for his ongoing partnership, constructive critiques, and divine presence; and her children, Emily Gilman and David Gilman, for being particularly bright lights in her life. Danielle Aquiline thanks her wife, Sona Aquiline, for being her partner in all things, but most especially in raising two wild and joyful sons, Finn Aquiline and Elias Aquiline.

What Is Argument?

We often hear speakers or writers who argue a particular opinion or point of view. In most arenas of life, it is essential that one's arguments be accountable, responsible, credible, and truthful. There is a good deal at stake in arguing well and appropriately: one's credibility, one's ability to engage in civil and factually persuasive discourse, and the perception of one's *ethos* (a concept we will discuss later) are all on the line.

Although the word *argument* often makes us think of fights we have with parents, friends, and others, the word itself isn't always negative, and it is not at all negative in this case. For instance, persuading your parents or someone else that you should be allowed to use the car to drive 150 miles to a music festival is one form of argument— a "fight." So is getting angry at your brother because he called "shotgun." However, these are not the kind of arguments we're talking about. But explaining to to your sibling, logically and persuasively, using facts, why you should get to sit in the front passenger seat *could* be an example of effective argument, if, for example, you were to contend that your legs are longer, you'll be giving directions to the driver and monitoring the GPS, or that you've been put in charge of the radio.

Academic argument, or any credible argument, for that matter, is an evidence-based defense of an opinion or a position. There are different ways to fashion an argument, but most arguments include at least three critical elements: the claim, the reasons, and the evidence.

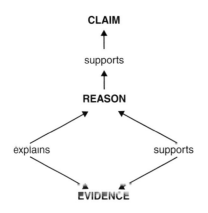

The Claim

The claim stakes out the argument—that is, it is a clearly defined position on a particular subject. Often, the claim is explicit, readily identified through the a piece of writing's title or introductory paragraph; other times, it is implicit, and as a reader you have to "read between the lines" or analyze even more carefully than you would otherwise to decide what the author is trying to argue.

Think, for instance, of a television advertisement for yogurt. The explicit claim is "buy our product." Many of these ads feature women who are athletic or athletic-looking (wearing spandex and the like) and almost alarmingly excited about eating yogurt that comes in a variety of flavors. A tagline such as "It's so good—it tastes just like cheesecake!" belies the implied message that yogurt is good, it is (sort of) healthy, and by purchasing and eating it, you will become more like the spandex-wearing women in the advertisement (or, if you're already like them, it will keep you that way).

As you can see, even in this fairly innocent advertisement, it's as important to pay attention to the implicit claim as to the explicit one. Why, you might ask yourself, are certain arguments made? What is the evidence for those arguments?

The Reasons

In traditional argument, the reasons should support the claim. They explain the rationale for the argument. In more academic or journalistic styles of writing, reasons are often stated close to the start of paragraphs within the body of the text, with evidence given to further support the claim.

Consider our original example of riding shotgun in the car, with the following claim: "I should sit in the front seat this time." Chances are, if you made this argument to your sibling, his or her response would be, "Why?" The reasons often answer that question. Why should we buy that yogurt? Why should I sit in the front seat? To answer the latter, we might say, "Because it would be more comfortable for me." But the evidence would be "my legs are longer," and so forth.

The Evidence

As we just outlined, the evidence truthfully and factually substantiates the reason. It is what turns a statement of opinion into a well-supported argument.

In some cases, you will look for evidence to substantiate *established reasons*—you know that something is either good or bad, but you don't know why. For instance, you know school should be canceled during a snowstorm, but you don't readily have any data about the number of car accidents that occur during severely inclement weather. Similarly, you probably know that you shouldn't smoke. Why? It's bad for your health. This is a reason that might prompt someone to ask, "How do you know?" The evidence would explain how you came to that conclusion—health studies regarding the link between smoking and disease, for example.

Often, an argument's reasons and evidence are conflated; that is, they are confused. Some writers (or politicians) may present an opinion and give reasons for it but omit, either intentionally or inadvertently, important evidence to back up the claim, making their argument inappropriate or lacking in accountability. Therefore, it's important that your reasons for an argument be backed up with evidence.

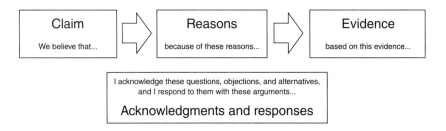

The Rhetorical Situation—Or, Some Things to Consider When Analyzing (or Writing) an Argument

As defined by Aristotle, *rhetoric* is the art of persuasion. And the situation in which arguments are made will help to determine the shape, style, and effectiveness of the argument.

What we say or argue and how we formulate our arguments will often depend on a number of factors, including but not limited to the speaker or writer, the audience, the topic, the purpose, and the mode (or medium or method of arguing, whether direct or implied). The rhetorical situation should be considered when you read others' texts or images and when you write your own, well-argued point of view.

The Speaker or Writer

Who is making the argument? What is his or her position? Does this position affect his or her credibility? What is his or her relationship to the audience?

The Audience

Who will read this argument? What can be assumed about the audience's knowledge of the subject? Does the audience already have an opinion about the stated or implied point of view? What is the audience's relationship to both the topic and the speaker or writer? What will the writer need to do to persuade an audience that might have a point of view that differs from that of the speaker/writer? How is an audience "complex"—that is, how is it possible to have more diverse audiences than the author might have originally considered? How does one address that type of situation?

The Topic

What is the argument? How does the topic (and the audience) influence the writer/speaker's tone, language, and strategy for arguing? What background information and evidence are necessary for the argument to be successful?

The Purpose

Is there a specific call to action as a result of this argument? Does the speaker/writer want the audience to behave, think, or act differently now or in the future? How effective is the evidence in achieving the desired result? What might the speaker/writer have done differently?

The Mode (or the Medium or the Method)

What is the way in which the speaker/writer makes the argument? Does there seem to be an occasion for this writing or speaking? What is it (television address, newspaper article, blog piece, image, advertisement, poem, etc.)? How do these different "occasions" influence the strategies used to persuade the audience? Why are these strategies necessary?

Ethos, Pathos, and Logos

Aristotle's definition of rhetoric also relies on three concepts that represent the various forms of appeal that can be made as part of an argument. We can persuade our audience(s) in many ways, through a variety of means. Our assessment of the rhetorical situation influences how we employ these forms of appeal. For instance, some speakers will influence audiences through logic, facts, and by encouraging

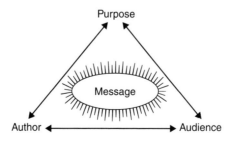

a sense of community; others might influence the same audience by cultivating fear, guilt, and a sense of isolation. While both approaches might be effective, it is essential that we eschew the latter.

Ethos appeals to an audience (or set of audiences) using the author's own credibility and established expertise. However, ethos is still dependent upon the author's use of factual and accountable arguments. Authors can establish ethos, but they can also damage it by using spurious or false facts or arguments.

So, returning to the more innocent example of your desire to sit shotgun in the family car, you might say to your sibling that you've earned the right to sit in the front seat because you are the one who planned the trip. Or, alternatively, you could say that you should sit in the front seat because (a) you're better looking, and (b) your parents like you better. The latter would not make for credible ethos, and your audience—your sibling—probably wouldn't be too receptive to that argument.

Pathos appeals to an audience using emotion. This is potentially a more dangerous form of appeal, and it is often all too effective when abused by the speaker or writer. You have likely fallen victim to some emotional appeals yourself—for instance, late-night infomercials about abandoned puppies. (We know we have.) While these emotional appeals can sometime be backed by factual truths, we must be cautious not to fall for emotional appeals alone. Even the most emotional appeal about abandoned animals usually features what appear to be fact-based appeals as well. ("In October, there were _____ homeless kittens in El Paso who needed homes.")

Logos appeals to an audience using logic or reason, and it goes hand-in-hand with appropriate employment of the other strategies we have just discussed. Logos-based appeals could include both quantitative data from reliable sources and logical arguments from other, more qualitative, types of reliable sources. Part of your task in arguing your own point of view is to determine which resources are credible.

Going back to the advertisement about yogurt, a company employing a logos-based appeal might suggest that you buy its yogurt because it has 30 percent more protein than competitive brands. (Of course, said company would have to also establish its credibility, its ethos, as a reliable and truthful source.)

Again, the trick—increasingly difficult these days—is to analyze and determine which sources are credible and which are misleading. Just because a resource representing itself as truthful seems to make a logical, fact-based argument doesn't necessarily mean it can be trusted. Facts can be misused and misrepresented; sometimes, you will read something that, while presenting itself as fact, is an out-and-out lie. (Consider, for instance, the 2017 and ongoing controversy surrounding fake news on Facebook and Twitter.)

Being Part of the Discussion

As we said at the start, there is a lot at stake in being able to argue well and truthfully and being able to read and understand the arguments (implied or otherwise) of others.

Any text you read or argument you make will be in the context of a larger discussion that, potentially, could have been going on for decades. That is, none of these discussions happens in a vacuum: for instance, Kennedy's 1961 inaugural address can be read on its own as well as within the context of preceding speeches. Our ability to respond to it logically depends on our understanding of its context, of the situation in which it was written, how it connects to what came before it, how it has influenced what has come after it, and the rhetorical strategies and arguments within the speech itself. Even arguments about the detrimental effects of current technologies echo arguments made about radio, television, and the movies.

What good arguments do is acknowledge, either explicitly or implicitly, the many other voices to which they respond. This is important to keep in mind as you read, and, of course, as you write. It's also important to put yourself in the position of the writer, especially if you think you might disagree with that writer's point of view. This will not only help you to better understand the writer's argument but will help you fashion the most *effective* ways to respond to that argument. You can't argue effectively against a particular point of view unless you fully understand what you're arguing against, as we think the readings in this volume illustrate.

Keep in mind that not every text, especially in this volume, will have an *explicit*, *obvious* argument. Many times, the argument will be implied, and it will be up to you to analyze and determine what that argument is. However, your own argument about what a particular piece is about should use evidence from that text, as well as any relevant contextual information you can find in an accountable source.

Therefore, when writing in response to these arguments or others, remember that you are taking part in an ongoing, possibly longstanding, discussion. Framing your own argument as part of an ongoing conversation (e.g., "Although Mary Wollstonecraft argues that . . ., other writers of the time, including . . . argue that . . ." or, "Malcolm Gladwell asserts that . . ., which confirms my belief that . . ., especially when one looks at the works of . . .") can be a helpful, appropriate, and effective way to create a structure by which you argue your point of view. But this is just one of many possibilities.

While accountable, well-reasoned points of view have always been an essential part of our civic lives, the recent political and social climate of "fake news" and "alternative facts" makes our own analysis of news and our own abilities to respond to arguments more timely and compelling than ever. The contents of this book offer the opportunity to analyze explicit and implicit arguments and to argue one's own perspective on them accountably and effectively.

The Myth of Neutrality and More About This Book

It's all too easy to claim to be neutral on various subjects. In that very neutrality, however, some of us actually take a position. That is, by choosing not to take a stand, we actually take one in a passive, potentially damaging way. But a very basic concern for all of us is the way we believe we should lead our lives: how we should treat others, how we should respond to difficult moral decisions, what choices we should make regarding faith, and many other issues. The readings in this collection often ask you directly or by implication to take a position on complex issues. Once you take that position, it's essential that you defend it not only persuasively, but also truthfully and factually.

The wide-ranging selections in this text include personal essays, academic essays (writing from sources), poetry, op-ed pieces, short stories, cartoons, and photography. Their range demonstrates that the challenging questions that confront us can be voiced and examined through a variety of forms and genres. The questions asked across these readings have been raised across many centuries, cultures, and spiritual traditions, and the diverse array of perspectives that the readings offer reflect upon each broad question.

Each reading is prefaced by a brief headnote that provides you with the opportunity to think about issues of authority and ethos. Following each reading, you will find questions for "Reflecting and Discussing," which prompt you to consider both the rhetorical strategies and choices the author makes as well as to reflect upon and respond to larger issues of ethics and values. After that, the "Connecting and Writing" questions may be used as prompts for journal writing or contextual research, or as the basis for in-class or extended essays.

Each piece included in this book makes an argument, or several arguments. Reading, analyzing, discussing, and writing about these very diverse pieces offers the opportunity to craft your own positions and to argue for or against these ideas credibly and persuasively.

METHODS OF ARGUMENT

RACE AND IDENTITY

Constructs of race and identity might help to define us, but they can also limit us. Discussions of these constructs are of necessity rather messy and have been at the center of public discourse for a long time—especially of late.

How to Tame a Wild Tongue

Gloria Anzaldúa (1942–2004)

A scholar of Chicana culture, a celebrated writer, and a feminist and poet, Gloria Anzaldúa worked tirelessly for social justice. Anzaldúa was the recipient of numerous awards, including the National Endowment for the Arts Fiction Award, the Lesbian Rights Award, and the Sappho Award of Distinction. Born and raised in the Rio Grande Valley of South Texas, her work focuses on identity, racism, feminism, and inclusionary politics. Her best-known book is Borderlands *(1987), a book that spans multiple genres, from which this excerpt is taken.*

"We're going to have to control your tongue," the dentist says, pulling out all the metal from my mouth. Silver bits plop and tinkle into the basin. My mouth is a motherlode.

The dentist is cleaning out my roots. I get a whiff of the stench when I gasp. "I can't cap that tooth yet, you're still draining," he says.

"We're going to have to do something about your tongue," I hear the anger rising in his voice. My tongue keeps pushing out the wads of cotton, pushing back the drills, the long thin needles. "I've never seen anything as strong or as stubborn," he says. And I think, how do you tame a wild tongue, train it to be quiet, how do you bridle and saddle it? How do you make it lie down?

> *Who is to say that robbing a people of its language*
> *is less violent than war?*
> —RAY GWYN SMITH

I remember being caught speaking Spanish at recess—that was good for three licks on the knuckles with a sharp ruler. I remember being sent to the corner of the classroom for "talking back" to the Anglo teacher when all I was trying to do was tell her how to pronounce my name. "If you want to be American, speak 'American.' If you don't like it, go back to Mexico where you belong."

"I want you to speak English. *Pa' hallar buen trabajo tienes que vaber hablar el inglés bien. Qué vale toda tu educación si todavía hablas inglés con un* 'accent,'"[1] my mother would say, mortified that I spoke English like a Mexican. At Pan American University, I, and all Chicano students were required to take two speech classes. Their purpose: to get rid of our accents.

Attacks on one's form of expression with the intent to censor are a violation of the First Amendment. *El Anglo con cara de inocente nos arrancó la lengua.*[2] Wild tongues can't be tamed, they can only be cut out.

Overcoming the Tradition of Silence

> *Abogadas, escupimos el oscuro.*
> *Peleando con nuestra propia sombra*
> *el silencio nos seputta.*[3]

En boca cerrada no entran moscas. "Flies don't enter a closed mouth" is a saying I kept hearing when I was a child. *Ser habladora* was to be a gossip and a liar, to talk too much. *Muchachitas bien criadas,*[4] well-bred girls don't answer back. *Es una falta de respeto*[5] to talk back to one's mother or father. I remember one of the sins I'd recite to the priest in the confession box the few times I went to confession: talking back to my mother, *hablar pa' 'tras, repelar.*[6] *Hocicona, repelona, chismosa,*[7] having a big mouth, questioning, carrying tales are all signs of being *mal criada.*[8] In my culture they are all words that are derogatory if applied to women—I've never heard them applied to men.

The first time I heard two women, a Puerto Rican and a Cuban, say the word "*nosotras,*"[9] I was shocked. I had not known the word existed. Chicanas use *nosotros*[10]

---

1   "In order to find a good job, you have to know how to speak English well. Of what value is your education if you still speak English with an 'accent.'"
2   The Anglo with an innocent face tore our tongue out.
3   "Choked, we spit out darkness / Fighting with our own shadow / The silence buries us."
4   Well-bred little girls.
5   It is not respectful.
6   To talk back, to argue.
7   Chatterer, arguer, gossip.
8   Ill bred girl.
9   We (fem.).
10 We (masc.).

whether we're male or female. We are robbed of our female being by the masculine plural. Language is a male discourse.

> And our tongues have become
> dry the wilderness has
> dried out our tongues and
> we have forgotten speech.
> —Irena Klepfisz

Even our own people, other Spanish speakers *nos quieren poner candados en la boca*.[11] They would hold us back with their bag of *reglas de academia*.[12]

> *Oyé como ladra: el lenguaje de la frontera*[13]
> *Quien tiene boca se equivoca*.[14]
> —MEXICAN SAYING

"*Pocho*, cultural traitor, you're speaking the oppressor's language by speaking English, you're ruining the Spanish language," I have been accused by various Latinos and Latinas. Chicano Spanish is considered by the purist and by most Latinos deficient, a mutilation of Spanish.

But Chicano Spanish is a border tongue which developed naturally. Change, *evolución, enriquecimiento de palabras nuevas por invención o adopción* have created variants of Chicano Spanish, *un nuevo lenguaje. Un lenguaje que corresponde a un modo de vivir*.[15] Chicano Spanish is not incorrect, it is a living language.

For a people who are neither Spanish nor live in a country in which Spanish is the first language; for a people who live in a country in which English is the reigning tongue but who are not Anglo; for a people who cannot entirely identify with either standard (formal, Castillian) Spanish nor standard English, what recourse is left to them but to create their own language? A language which they can connect their identity to, one capable of communicating the realities and values true to themselves—a language with terms that are neither *español ni inglés*,[16] but both. We speak a patois, a forked tongue, a variation of two languages.

Chicano Spanish sprang out of the Chicanos' need to identify ourselves as a distinct people. We needed a language with which we could communicate with ourselves, a secret language. For some of us, language is a homeland closer than the Southwest—for many Chicanos today live in the Midwest and the East. And because

---

11   Want to put locks on our mouths.
12   Academic rules.
13   Hear how the dog barks: language of the frontier.
14   "He who has a mouth makes mistakes."
15   Evolution, enrichment of new words through invention and adoption . . . a new language. A language that corresponds to a way of life.
16   Spanish nor English.

we are a complex, heterogeneous people, we speak many languages. Some of the languages we speak are:

1. Standard English
2. Working class and slang English
3. Standard Spanish
4. Standard Mexican Spanish
5. North Mexican Spanish dialect
6. Chicano Spanish (Texas, New Mexico, Arizona and California have regional variations)
7. Tex-Mex
8. *Pachuco* (called *caló*)

My "home" tongues are the languages I speak with my sister and brothers, with my friends. They are the last five listed, with 6 and 7 being closest to my heart. From school, the media and job situations, I've picked up standard and working class English. From Mamagrande Locha and from reading Spanish and Mexican literature, I've picked up Standard Spanish and Standard Mexican Spanish. From *los recién llegados*, Mexican immigrants, and *braceros*,[17] I learned the North Mexican dialect. With Mexicans I'll try to speak either Standard Mexican Spanish or the North Mexican dialect. From my parents and Chicanos living in the Valley, I picked up Chicano Texas Spanish, and I speak it with my mom, younger brother (who married a Mexican and who rarely mixes Spanish with English), aunts and older relatives.

With Chicanas from *Nuevo México* or *Arizona* I will speak Chicano Spanish a little, but often they don't understand what I'm saying. With most California Chicanas I speak entirely in English (unless I forget). When I first moved to San Francisco, I'd rattle off something in Spanish, unintentionally embarrassing them. Often it is only with another Chicana *tejana*[18] that I can talk freely.

Words distorted by English are known as anglicisms or *pochismos*. The *pocho* is an anglicized Mexican or American of Mexican origin who speaks Spanish with an accent characteristic of North Americans and who distorts and reconstructs the language according to the influence of English. Tex-Mex, or Spanglish, comes most naturally to me. I may switch back and forth from English to Spanish in the same sentence or in the same word. With my sister and my brother Nune and with Chicano *tejano* contemporaries I speak in Tex-Mex.

From kids and people my own age I picked up *Pachuco*. *Pachuco* (the language of the zoot suiters) is a language of rebellion, both against Standard Spanish and Standard English. It is a secret language. Adults of the culture and outsiders cannot understand it. It is made up of slang words from both English and Spanish. *Ruca* means girl or woman, *vato* means guy or dude, *chale* means no, *simón* means yes, *churro* is sure, talk is *periquiar*, *pigionear* means petting, *que gacho* means how nerdy, *ponte águila* means watch out, death is called *la pelona*. Through lack of practice and not having others who can speak it, I've lost most of the *Pachuco* tongue.

---

17 *Los recién llegados*: recent arrivals; *braceros*: laborers.
18 Texan (fem.).

Chicano Spanish

Chicanos, after 250 years of Spanish/Anglo colonization have developed significant differences in the Spanish we speak. We collapse two adjacent vowels into a single syllable and sometimes shift the stress in certain words such as *maíz/maiz, cohete/cuete*.[19] We leave out certain consonants when they appear between vowels; *lado/lao, mojado/mojao*.[20] Chicanos from South Texas pronounce *f* as *j* as in *jue* (*fue*).[21] Chicanos use "archaisms," words that are no longer in the Spanish language, words that have been evolved out. We say *semos, truje, haiga, ansina,* and *naiden*.[22] We retain the "archaic" *j*, as in *jalar*,[23] that derives from an earlier *h* (the French *halar* or the Germanic *halon* which was lost to standard Spanish in the 16th century), but which is still found in several regional dialects such as the one spoken in South Texas. (Due to geography, Chicanos from the Valley of South Texas were cut off linguistically from other Spanish speakers. We tend to use words that the Spaniards brought over from Medieval Spain. The majority of the Spanish colonizers in Mexico and the Southwest came from Extremadura—Hernán Cortés was one of them—and Andalucía. Andalucians pronounce *ll* like a *y*, and their *d*'s tend to be absorbed by adjacent vowels: *tirado*[24] becomes *tirao*. They brought *el lenguaje popular, dialectos y regionalismos*).[25]

Chicanos and other Spanish speakers also shift *ll* to *y* and *z* to *s*. We leave out initial syllables, saying *tar* for *estar, toy* for *estoy, hora* for *ahora* (*cubanos* and *puertorriqueños*[26] also leave out initial letters of some words). We also leave out the final syllable such as *pa* for *para*. The intervocalic *y*, the *ll* as in *tortilla, ella, botella*, gets replaced by *tortia* or *tortiya, ea, botea*. We add an additional syllable at the beginning of certain words: *atocar* for *tocar, agastar* for *gastar*. Sometimes we'll say *lavaste las vacijas*, other times *lavates* (substituting the *ates* verb endings for the *aste*).[27]

We use anglicisms, words borrowed from English: *bola* from ball, *carpeta* from carpet, *máchina de lavar* (instead of *lavadora*) from washing machine. Tex-Mex argot, created by adding a Spanish sound at the beginning or end of an English word such as *cookiar* for cook, *watchar* for watch, *parkiar* for park, and *rapiar* for rape, is the result of the pressures on Spanish speakers to adapt to English.

We don't use the word *vosotros/as* or its accompanying verb form. We don't say *claro* (to mean yes), *imagínate*, or *me emociona*,[28] unless we picked up Spanish from Latinas, out of a book, or in a classroom. Other Spanish-speaking groups are going through the same, or similar, development in their Spanish.

---

19 *Maiz*: corn; *cohete*: rocket.
20 *Lado*: side; *mojado*: wet.
21 Went.
22 *Semos*: we are; *truje*: brought; *haiga*: there is; *ansina*: that (adj.); *naiden*: nobody.
23 To pull.
24 Thrown.
25 Popular language, dialects, and regionalism.
26 *Estar*: to be; *estoy*: I am; *ahora*: now; *cubanos, puertorriqueños*: Cubans, Puerto Ricans.
27 *Para*: for; *trotilla, ella, botella*: tortilla, she, bottle; *tocar*: to touch; *gastar*: to spend; *lavaste las vacijas*: did you wash the dishes (*vacijas* is Texan).
28 *Vosotros/as*: you (plural, formal); *imagínate*: imagine; *me emociona*: I am moved.

Linguistic Terrorism

> *Deslenguadas. Somos los del español deficiente.*[29] We are your linguistic night-
> mare, your linguistic aberration, your linguistic *mestisaje*, the subject of your
> *burla*. Because we speak with tongues of fire we are culturally crucified. Racially,
> culturally and linguistically somos *huérfanos*[30]—we speak an orphan tongue.

Chicanas who grew up speaking Chicano Spanish have internalized the belief that we
speak poor Spanish. It is illegitimate, a bastard language. And because we internalize how our language has been used against us by the dominant culture, we use our
language differences against each other.

Chicana feminists often skirt around each other with suspicion and hesitation.
For the longest time I couldn't figure it out. Then it dawned on me. To be close to
another Chicana is like looking into the mirror. We are afraid of what we'll see there.
Pena. Shame. Low estimation of self. In childhood we are told that our language is
wrong. Repeated attacks on our native tongue diminish our sense of self. The attacks
continue throughout our lives.

Chicanas feel uncomfortable talking in Spanish to Latinas, afraid of their censure. Their language was not outlawed in their countries. They had a whole lifetime of being immersed in their native tongue; generations, centuries in which
Spanish was a first language, taught in school, heard on radio and TV, and read in
the newspaper.

If a person, Chicana or Latina, has a low estimation of my native tongue, she also
has a low estimation of me. Often with *mexicanas y latinas* we'll speak English as a
neutral language. Even among Chicanas we tend to speak English at parties or conferences. Yet, at the same time, we're afraid the other will think we're *agringadas*[31] because we don't speak Chicano Spanish. We oppress each other trying to out-Chicano
each other, vying to be the "real" Chicanas, to speak like Chicanos. There is no one
Chicano language just as there is no one Chicano experience. A monolingual Chicana
whose first language is English or Spanish is just as much a Chicana as one who
speaks several variants of Spanish. A Chicana from Michigan or Chicago or Detroit
is just as much a Chicana as one from the southwest. Chicano Spanish is as diverse
linguistically as it is regionally.

By the end of this century, Spanish speakers will comprise the biggest minority
group in the U.S., a country where students in high schools and colleges are encouraged to take French classes because French is considered more "cultured." But for a
language to remain alive it must be used. By the end of this century English, and not
Spanish, will be the mother tongue of most Chicanos and Latinos.

So, if you want to really hurt me, talk badly about my language. Ethnic identity is twin
skin to linguistic identity—I am my language. Until I can take pride in my language,
I cannot take pride in myself. Until I can accept as legitimate Chicano Texas Spanish,

---

29 Loose tongues. We are those with deficient Spanish.
30 *Mestisaje*: hybrid; *burla*: joke; *somos huérfanos*: we are orphans.
31 Foreigners, like "gringos."

Tex-Mex and all the other languages I speak, I cannot accept the legitimacy of myself. Until I am free to write bilingually and to switch codes without having always to translate, while I still have to speak English or Spanish when I would rather speak Spanglish, and as long as I have to accommodate the English speakers rather than having them accommodate me, my tongue will be illegitimate.

I will no longer be made to feel ashamed of existing. I will have my voice: Indian, Spanish, white. I will have my serpent's tongue—my woman's voice, my sexual voice, my poet's voice. I will overcome the tradition of silence.

> My fingers
> move sly against your palm
> Like women everywhere, we speak in code . . .
> —Melanie Kaye/Kantrowitz

REFLECTING AND DISCUSSING

1. The title of the piece references the "wild tongue," an image and metaphor to which Anzaldúa returns throughout the excerpt. How does the tongue serve as a metaphor throughout the essay? What might be the larger contexts in which the metaphor of the tongue is relevant?
2. How do the structure and languages of this essay affect your reading of it? What are the effects of these stylistic choices? Why do you think Anzaldúa chose to write the essay in this way?
3. What, overall, is Anzaldúa's argument? How would various audiences respond to that argument? Are both Spanish and non-Spanish speakers likely to respond in the same way or differently? Why?

CONNECTING AND WRITING

1. The final section of this essay is called "Linguistic Terrorism," and in it, Anzaldúa writes, "So, if you really want to hurt me, talk badly about my language." Who is the terrorist here? Why do you think so, and what is the impact of this "terrorism"? Is "silence" part of this "terrorism"? Why or why not?
2. It has been said that this excerpt reveals the tension between the desire to assimilate, to be part of a dominant culture, and the need to have a "secret language" and to retain and honor one's own culture and background. How does Anzaldúa reveal and highlight this tension? Is it resolved? Why or why not?

"I Don't See Color": Then You Don't See Me!

Sam Louie (?)

Sam Louie is a practicing psychotherapist and mental health counselor whose work and training center around issues of shame, trauma, and addiction. He is also a first-generation Chinese American from Hong Kong who grew up in Seattle. Louie's own experience makes him "keenly aware of the role of multicultural sensitivity," according to Louie's website. This piece originally appeared on the website of Psychology Today *in 2016.*

When well-meaning people with good intentions say, "I don't see color," an ethnic minority will internalize that as meaning, "You don't see me." Part of the problem with our country's desire to be "post-racial" and color-blind in terms of seeing the inherent worth of an individual regardless of skin color, is that you can dismiss all the concerns, experiences, and real-world issues of racism that plague this country from both an individual and larger societal level.

I was reminded of this when attending a race and faith training and hearing people from different ethnic minorities speak their truth. Discrimination, prejudice, and stereotypes are the ones most people in white America are familiar with and maybe even tired of hearing us talk about them. But there are also the more subtle issues of microaggressions and the inherent stress of trying to assimilate to a white, mainstream culture that is oftentimes ignorant of these stressors.

Micro aggressions are a good place to start as these are defined as the everyday verbal, nonverbal, and environmental slights, or insults, whether intentional or unintentional, which communicate hostile, derogatory, or negative messages to people based solely on their marginalized group membership.

Some examples of microaggressions include:

- "Where are you from?"
- "You speak such good English."
- "You're not really Black."
- "You're not really eating that are you?"
- "What are you?"
- "There is only one race, the human race!"
- "I'm not racist, I have several _____ (Black, Asian, Latino) friends."
- "Why do you have to be so loud?!"
- "Why do you have to be so quiet."
- "You're a credit to your race."

Beyond the microaggressions, stereotypes, and other forms of overt racism that we can see and name, there's the stress of just being ethnic in America which many people would like to downplay including myself.

For many years, I denied the stress and emotional, psychological, and spiritual impact this had on me. This may sound like a foreign concept to the dominant culture so I'll give some personal examples.

For example, being Asian-American is an identity that I've been sensitive to for as long as I can remember. Part of this is the desire to fit in with both Black culture and white mainstream America. Growing up in a predominantly African-American neighborhood, I knew I was different so I did what I could to try and assimilate as quickly as possible lest you get teased (it didn't matter the teasing still happened).

Assimilation meant "proving I was American" so much so that I chose to speak English when parents or relatives talked to us in public, all done in an effort to garner acceptance from society. Hiding Asian food or ditching it altogether became normative due to teasing. This became so insidious, I distanced myself and excluded my two younger brothers from hanging out with me, thinking my chances to get accepted might be threatened if they were around (the impact from this remains a story of brokenness).

Growing up Asian also meant if you are in white neighborhoods, malls, restaurants, or other public areas, your "ethnic antenna" goes up. It doesn't stop just because I'm an adult now and we live in a more culturally diverse and aware society. The antenna stays vigilant as a means to warn me of any incoming threat, suspicion or rejection from others. One thought that's often running through an ethnic person's mind in a majority setting is, "How much of this is because of my race or culture?"

I can remember going out in large numbers (6 or more) as a group of Asian-Americans starting in my teenage years and wondering what white customers saw when they noticed us. More specifically, I wondered internally, "Am I accepted here?" This doesn't end simply with the passage of time because there are reminders that we are not welcome or continually perceived as foreign. Two years ago on our annual camping trip to Eastern Washington (a predominantly white part of the state), a boat cruised by our campsite pointing and shouting, "There's China!"

Other incidents can involve incidents of inclusion or exclusion. If you're hired, you wonder did race play a role and will other employees ask themselves similar questions. If you're not hired, you wonder how much was related to your race?

I remember my first job interview was at an all-black staffed McDonald's where I didn't get the job and wondered if it was due to being Asian. I went further away to a white community and applied at an all-white employed car wash and didn't get that job either wondering the same question. I ended up getting a bagger position at a Chinese grocery store where I was teased for not knowing how to speak Chinese well. So in all these formative years, the question of how to fit in and what to do to fit in and find a place of acceptance remained central, although mostly on either a subconscious or reflexive, survival mechanism level.

When I graduated from high school and went to college, I wondered if my admission was based on Affirmative action. My white friends in the dorm would talk about how Affirmative action took away spots from them and also questioned my need to join an Asian-American student club, by citing the double-standard that they couldn't start an all-white club without getting accused of racism. As a young man, I had no answers to those questions but meekly tried to blend in and apologized for race being such an issue.

But paradoxically white friends had free rein to criticize and disparage r&b music and judgments about people like myself who listened to it. One friend even asked me pointedly, "Why do you listen to that?! Have you heard the lyrics, it's all about sex . . . now why don't you listen to this song" (playing some white grunge artist).

What kind of toll does this have on an ethnic person's identity or psyche? For many, it can mean denying your cultural preferences or at least denying the truth of your personhood in public, thus stripping the very essence of a person's core and individuality all in an effort to conform to societal mainstream ideals, tastes, or styles in an effort to make mainstream America feel more "comfortable" with us.

This isn't intended to make white America feel guilty or ashamed because just as we are proud of our ethnic ancestry and culture, you should be equally proud of being Caucasian. Once again, there's nothing wrong with being white. But what we do ask is some measure of empathy, understanding, and acknowledgment that life in the U.S. is difficult already, let alone the additional challenges where race is an integral part of an ethnic minority's identity.

REFLECTING AND DISCUSSING

1. How would Louie respond to arguments claiming that our country is "postracial"?
2. How does Louie define microaggressions? Do his examples cause you to reexamine the ways in which you have responded to issues of race?
3. Overall, do you agree with the notion that it is most appropriate to "see color"? Why or why not?

CONNECTING AND WRITING

1. In the early twentieth century, immigrants were pushed to "become American" and to assimilate into a vast, dominant cultural (and religious) "melting pot" in, as Louie phrases it, an "effort to make mainstream America feel more 'comfortable.'" This philosophy has changed to a good extent. Consult sources that help you compare attitudes about assimilation, its importance, and the liabilities that accompany it. What conclusions do you draw?
2. Writing about internalizing racism, Louie asks, "What kind of toll does this have on an ethnic person's identity or psyche?" Consult sources to assess the impact of "othering" and analyze, compare, and contrast another source with Louie's arguments. Which sources seem most effective in these instances? Why? Be specific.

Two Ways to Belong in America

Bharati Mukherjee (1940–2017)

Mukherjee was a native of Calcutta, India, but grew up in both India and Europe. She traveled to the United States to attend the Iowa Writers' Workshop, where she earned her MFA in 1963. Mukherjee was most well known for her fiction, but she also published several books of nonfiction, including Regionalism in Indian Perspective *(1992) and* Political Culture and

Leadership in India *(1991). This piece was originally published in the* New York Times *in response to a movement in the U.S. Congress to take benefits away from resident aliens (legal immigrants) in the United States.*

This is a tale of two sisters from Calcutta, Mira and Bharati, who have lived in the United States for some 35 years, but who find themselves on different sides in the current debate over the status of immigrants. I am an American citizen and she is not. I am moved that thousands of long-term residents are finally taking the oath of citizenship. She is not.

Mira arrived in Detroit in 1960 to study child psychology and pre-school education. I followed her a year later to study creative writing at the University of Iowa. When we left India, we were almost identical in appearance and attitude. We dressed alike, in saris; we expressed identical views on politics, social issues, love, and marriage in the same Calcutta convent-school accent. We would endure our two years in America, secure our degrees, then return to India to marry the grooms of our father's choosing.

Instead, Mira married an Indian student in 1962 who was getting his business administration degree at Wayne State University. They soon acquired the labor cer-tifications necessary for the green card of hassle-free residence and employment.

Mira still lives in Detroit, works in the Southfield, Mich., school system, and has become nationally recognized for her contributions in the fields of pre-school edu-cation and parent-teacher relationships. After 36 years as a legal immigrant in this country she clings passionately to her Indian citizenship and hopes to go home to India when she retires.

In Iowa City in 1963, I married a fellow student, an American of Canadian parent-age. Because of the accident of his North Dakota birth, I bypassed labor-certification requirements and the race-related "quota" system that favored the applicant's coun-try of origin over his or her merit. I was prepared for (and even welcomed) the emo-tional strain that came with marrying outside my ethnic community. In 33 years of marriage, we have lived in every part of North America. By choosing a husband who was not my father's selection, I was opting for fluidity, self-invention, blue jeans, and T-shirts, and renouncing 3,000 years (at least) of caste-observant, "pure culture" marriage in the Mukherjee family. My books have often been read as unapologetic (and in some quarters overenthusiastic) texts for cultural and psychological "mon-grelization." It's a word I celebrate.

Mira and I have stayed sisterly close by phone. In our regular Sunday morning conversations, we are unguardedly affectionate. I am her only blood relative on this continent. We expect to see each other through the looming crises of aging and ill health without being asked. Long before Vice President Gore's "Citizenship U.S.A." drive, we'd had our polite arguments over the ethics of retaining an overseas citizen-ship while expecting the permanent protection and economic benefits that come with living and working in America.

Like well-raised sisters, we never said what was really on our minds, but we prob-ably pitied one another. She, for the lack of structure in my life, the erasure of Indian-ness, the absence of an unvarying daily core. I, for the narrowness of her perspective, her uninvolvement with the mythic depths or the superficial pop culture of this so-ciety. But, now, with the scapegoatings of "aliens" (documented or illegal) on the increase, and the targeting of long-term legal immigrants like Mira for new scrutiny and new self-consciousness, she and I find ourselves unable to maintain the same polite discretion. We were always unacknowledged adversaries, and we are now, more than ever, sisters.

"I feel used," Mira raged on the phone the other night. "I feel manipulated and discarded. This is such an unfair way to treat a person who was invited to stay and work here because of her talent. My employer went to the I.N.S. and petitioned for the labor certification. For over 30 years, I've invested my creativity and professional skills into the improvement of this country's preschool system. I've obeyed all the rules, I've paid my taxes, I love my work, I love my students, I love the friends I've made. How dare America now change its rules in midstream? If America wants to make new rules curtailing benefits of legal immigrants, they should apply only to immigrants who arrive after those rules are already in place."

To my ears, it sounded like the description of a long-enduring, comfortable yet loveless marriage, without risk or recklessness. Have we the right to demand, and to expect, that we be loved? (That, to me, is the subtext of the arguments by immigration advocates.) My sister is an expatriate, professionally generous and creative, socially courteous and gracious, and that's as far as her Americanization can go. She is here to maintain an identity, not to transform it.

I asked her if she would follow the example of others who have decided to become citizens because of the anti-immigration bills in Congress. And here, she surprised me. "If America wants to play the manipulative game, I'll play it, too," she snapped. "I'll become a U.S. citizen for now then change back to India when I'm ready to go home. I feel some kind of irrational attachment to India that I don't to America. Until all this hysteria against legal immigrants, I was totally happy. Having my green card meant I could visit any place in the world I wanted to and then come back to a job that's satisfying and that I do very well."

In one family, from two sisters alike as peas in a pod, there could not be a wider divergence of immigrant experience. America spoke to me—I married it—I embraced the demotion from expatriate aristocrat to immigrant nobody, surrendering those thousands of years of "pure culture," the saris, the delightfully accented English. She retained them all. Which of us is the freak?

Mira's voice, I realize, is the voice not just of the immigrant South Asian community but of an immigrant community of the millions who have stayed rooted in one job, one city, one house, one ancestral culture, one cuisine, for the entirety of their productive years. She speaks for greater numbers than I possibly can. Only the fluency of her English and the anger, rather than fear, born of confidence from her education, differentiate her from the seamstresses, the domestics, the technicians, the shop owners, the millions of hard-working but effectively silenced documented immigrants as well as their less fortunate "illegal" brothers and sisters.

Nearly 20 years ago, when I was living in my husband's ancestral homeland of Canada, I was always well-employed but never allowed to feel part of the local Quebec or larger Canadian society. Then, through a Green Paper that invited a national referendum on the unwanted side effects of "nontraditional" immigration, the government officially turned against its immigrant communities, particularly those from South Asia. I felt then the same sense of betrayal that Mira feels now. I will never forget the pain of that sudden turning, and the casual racist outbursts the Green Paper elicited. That sense of betrayal had its desired effect and drove me, and thousands like me, from the country.

Mira and I differ, however, in the ways in which we hope to interact with the country that we have chosen to live in. She is happier to live in America as expatriate Indian than as an immigrant American. I need to feel like a part of the community I have adopted (as I tried to feel in Canada as well). I need to put roots down, to vote and make the difference that I can. The price that the immigrant willingly pays, and that the exile avoids, is the trauma of self-transformation.

REFLECTING AND DISCUSSING

1. Mukherjee presents her perspective and that of her sister. With whom do you agree most? Is there a middle ground between the two? What would that middle ground be?

2. In remembering her move from Canada to the United States, Mukherjee writes that her "sense of betrayal had its desired effect and drove me, and thousands like me, from the country." How does this immigrant narrative, published in 1996, compare to those heard today? What was the betrayal then, and what is the betrayal now?

3. How does the last sentence of the essay take on additional significance today? What is the "trauma of self-transformation"?

CONNECTING AND WRITING

1. Immigration and citizenship continue to be fraught topics in the United States and elsewhere. What is the author's central argument? How does she make her points through personal experience—her own and her sister's? Are they effective? Why or why not?

2. Using credible sources such as the *New York Times*, the *Wall Street Journal*, and the *Washington Post*, find several articles or editorials on different "sides" of the current debate on immigration. Compare and contrast them. What do you conclude? Use evidence from the articles to back up your points.

Just Walk on By: A Black Man Ponders His Ability to Alter Public Space

Brent Staples (1951–   )

Brent Staples grew up in a small town outside of Philadelphia. He earned the MA and Ph.D. in psychology from the University of Chicago. An editorial writer for the New York Times *and the author of numerous articles, Staples's books include* Parallel Time: Growing Up in Black and

White *(2000) and* An American Love Story *(1999). In this 1986 essay from* Ms. *magazine,
Staples describes walking in the city as a tall Black man, an experience that resonates with current
concerns about racial stereotypes and profiling.*

My first victim was a woman—white, well dressed, probably in her early twenties. I came upon her late one evening on a deserted street in Hyde Park, a relatively affluent neighborhood in an otherwise mean, impoverished section of Chicago. As I swung onto the avenue behind her, there seemed to be a discreet, uninflammatory distance between us. Not so. She cast back a worried glance. To her, the youngish black man—a broad six feet two inches with a beard and billowing hair, both hands shoved into the pockets of a bulky military jacket—seemed menacingly close. After a few more quick glimpses, she picked up her pace and was soon running in earnest. Within seconds she disappeared into a cross street.

That was more than a decade ago. I was 23 years old, a graduate student newly arrived at the University of Chicago. It was in the echo of that terrified woman's footfalls that I first began to know the unwieldy inheritance I'd come into—the ability to alter public space in ugly ways. It was clear that she thought herself the quarry of a mugger, a rapist, or worse. Suffering a bout of insomnia, however, I was stalking sleep, not defenseless wayfarers. As a softy who is scarcely able to take a knife to raw chicken—let alone hold it to a person's throat—I was surprised, embarrassed, and dismayed all at once. Her flight made me feel like an accomplice in tyranny. It also made it clear that I was indistinguishable from the muggers who occasionally seeped into the area from the surrounding ghetto. That first encounter, and those that followed signified that a vast unnerving gulf lay between nighttime pedestrians—particularly women—and me. And I soon gathered that being perceived as dangerous is a hazard in itself. I only needed to turn a corner into a dicey situation, or crowd some frightened, armed person in a foyer somewhere, or make an errant move after being pulled over by a policeman. Where fear and weapons meet—and they often do in urban America—there is always the possibility of death.

In that first year, my first away from my hometown, I was to become thoroughly familiar with the language of fear. At dark, shadowy intersections in Chicago, I could cross in front of a car stopped at a traffic light and elicit the thunk, thunk, thunk, thunk of the driver—black, white, male, or female—hammering down the door locks. On less traveled streets after dark, I grew accustomed to but never comfortable with people who crossed to the other side of the street rather than pass me. Then there were the standard unpleasantries with police, doormen, bouncers, cab drivers, and others whose business it is to screen out troublesome individuals before there is any nastiness.

I moved to New York nearly two years ago and I have remained an avid night walker. In central Manhattan, the near-constant crowd cover minimizes tense one-on-one street encounters. Elsewhere—visiting friends in SoHo, where sidewalks are narrow and tightly spaced buildings shut out the sky—things can get very taut indeed.

Black men have a firm place in New York mugging literature. Norman Podhoretz in his famed (or infamous) 1963 essay, "My Negro Problem—and Ours," recalls growing up in terror of black males; they were "tougher than we were, more ruthless," he writes—and as an adult on the Upper West Side of Manhattan, he continues, he cannot constrain his nervousness when he meets black men on certain streets. Similarly, a decade later, the essayist and novelist Edward Hoagland extols a New York where once "Negro bitterness bore down mainly on other Negroes." Where some see mere panhandlers, Hoagland sees "a mugger who is clearly screwing up his nerve to do more than just ask for money." But Hoagland has "the New Yorker's quickhunch posture for broken-field maneuvering," and the bad guy swerves away.

I often witness that "hunch posture," from women after dark on the warrenlike streets of Brooklyn where I live. They seem to set their faces on neutral and, with their purse straps strung across their chests bandolier style, they forge ahead as though bracing themselves against being tackled. I understand, of course, that the danger they perceive is not a hallucination. Women are particularly vulnerable to street violence, and young black males are drastically overrepresented among the perpetrators of that violence. Yet these truths are no solace against the kind of alienation that comes of being ever the suspect, against being set apart, a fearsome entity with whom pedestrians avoid making eye contact.

It is not altogether clear to me how I reached the ripe old age of 22 without being conscious of the lethality nighttime pedestrians attributed to me. Perhaps it was because in Chester, Pennsylvania, the small, angry industrial town where I came of age in the 1960s, I was scarcely noticeable against a backdrop of gang warfare, street knifings, and murders. I grew up one of the good boys, had perhaps a half-dozen fist fights. In retrospect, my shyness of combat has clear sources.

Many things go into the making of a young thug. One of those things is the consummation of the male romance with the power to intimidate. An infant discovers that random flailings send the baby bottle flying out of the crib and crashing to the floor. Delighted, the joyful babe repeats those motions again and again, seeking to duplicate the feat. Just so, I recall the points at which some of my boyhood friends were finally seduced by the perception of themselves as tough guys. When a mark cowered and surrendered his money without resistance, myth and reality merged— and paid off. It is, after all, only manly to embrace the power to frighten and intimidate. We, as men, are not supposed to give an inch of our lane on the highway; we are to seize the fighter's edge in work and in play and even in love; we are to be valiant in the face of hostile forces.

Unfortunately, poor and powerless young men seem to take all this nonsense literally. As a boy, I saw countless tough guys locked away; I have since buried several, too. They were babies, really—a teenage cousin, a brother of 22, a childhood friend in his mid-twenties—all gone down in episodes of bravado played out in the streets. I came to doubt the virtues of intimidation early on. I chose, perhaps even unconsciously, to remain a shadow—timid, but a survivor.

The fearsomeness mistakenly attributed to me in public places often has a perilous flavor. The most frightening of these confusions occurred in the late 1970s and early 1980s when I worked as a journalist in Chicago. One day, rushing into the office of a magazine I was writing for with a deadline story in hand, I was mistaken for a burglar. The office manager called security and, with an ad hoc posse, pursued me through the labyrinthine halls, nearly to my editor's door. I had no way of proving who I was. I could only move briskly toward the company of someone who knew me.

Another time I was on assignment for a local paper and killing time before an interview. I entered a jewelry store on the city's affluent Near North Side. The proprietor excused herself and returned with an enormous red Doberman pinscher straining at the end of a leash. She stood, the dog extended toward me, silent to my questions, her eyes bulging nearly out of her head. I took a cursory look around, nodded, and bade her good night. Relatively speaking, however, I never fared as badly as another black male journalist. He went to nearby Waukegan, Illinois, a couple of summers ago to work on a story about a murderer who was born there. Mistaking the reporter for the killer, police hauled him from his car at gunpoint and but for his press credentials would probably have tried to book him. Such episodes are not uncommon. Black men trade tales like this all the time.

In "My Negro Problem—And Ours," Podhoretz writes that the hatred he feels for blacks makes itself known to him through a variety of avenues—one being his discomfort with that special brand of "paranoid touchiness" to which he says blacks are prone. No doubt he is speaking here of black men. In time, I learned to smother the rage I felt as so often being taken for a criminal. Not to do so would surely have led to madness—via that special "paranoid touchiness" that so annoyed Podhoretz at the time he wrote the essay.

I began to take precautions to make myself less threatening. I move about with care, particularly late in the evening. I give a wide berth to nervous people on subway platforms during the wee hours, particularly when I have exchanged business clothes for jeans. If I happen to be entering a building behind some people who appear skittish, I may walk by, letting them clear the lobby before I return, so as not to seem to be following them. I have been calm and extremely congenial on those rare occasions when I've been pulled over by the police.

And on late-evening constitutionals along streets less traveled by, I employ what has proved to be an excellent tension-reducing measure: I whistle melodies from Beethoven and Vivaldi and the more popular classical composers. Even steely New Yorkers hunching toward nighttime destinations seem to relax, and occasionally they even join in the tune. Virtually everybody seems to sense that a mugger wouldn't be warbling bright, sunny selections from Vivaldi's *Four Seasons*. It is my equivalent of the cowbell that hikers wear when they know they are in bear country.

REFLECTING AND DISCUSSING

1. "My first victim was a woman—white, well dressed, probably in her early twenties." Why would Staples choose to start his essay this way? What is the effect of describing the woman as his "victim"?

2. In the middle of the essay, the author begins a paragraph by saying that "many things go into the making of a young thug." What are those many things? Discuss Staples's ideas about how young "thugs" are made. What is the effect of using the word "thug"?

3. This essay was published several decades ago. What is its relevance to current times? Would this essay be different if it were written today? How so—or how not?

CONNECTING AND WRITING

1. Throughout his essay, Staples depicts himself as a force to be feared and others as his victims. However, the metaphor he invokes at the end of the cowbell worn by hikers in bear country reverses this scenario. Why does Staples seem to contradict himself in this way? Explore the relationship between victims and predators in this essay. What is the effect of this metaphor? How does it shape the argument Staples is making?

2. "Where fear and weapons meet—and they often do in urban America—there is always the possibility of death." Why does Staples include this statement in his essay? Consider Staples's analysis of the relationship among fear, weapons, and death alongside more current analyses. Are they similar? Different? How so?

"Filipineza" Doesn't Mean "Servant": Notes of Witness from an Immigrant Daughter

Melissa R. Sipin (1988–   )

Filipino American writer Melissa Sipin primarily works in fiction. Born and raised in California, Sipin has received fellowships from Poets and Writers, Inc., Kundiman, the Sewanee Writers' Conference, and the Voices of our Nation (VONA) Writers' Conference. Her work has appeared in Washington Square, Glimmer Train, Eleven Eleven Magazine, *and the* Tidal Basin Review. *She is coeditor of an anthology on Filipino myths entitled* Kuwento: Lost Things *(2014). This piece originally appeared on* Salon.com *in 2017.*

> If I became the brown woman mistaken
> for a shadow, please tell your people I'm a tree.
> —from "Filipineza" by Bino A. Realuyo

One Family, Two Mail Order Brides

When I first met my beloved stepmother, it was on a computer screen. Her tinged-brown face was shrouded by the limelight's glow. We stood in my family's old blue house on Neptune Avenue, the one that was inevitably foreclosed in 2009 and sat on the southern edges of Los Angeles, near the streets of Compton. Carson, for all that I have known it, has always been a Filipinotown, and my father, an immigrant, an ex-meth addict, son of a war hero, a stricken gambler, but also the parent-who-never-left, hovered above me, with that bright smile filled with dentured teeth. *This is my anak*, my father said. A surging hello followed. There, my future stepmother stood before me, boxed in the laptop's glaring glow. A baby was in her arms, waving. I said hello back, warmly. *This is your girlfriend, daddy?* I said. He nodded back. Proud. His fading hair shimmering in the sunlight that knifed in through the window. His wrinkled face, his whitened skin bleached by papaya soap products from Manila, all beaming, bursting, with love.

That blue house on Neptune Avenue was the only house my father ever tried to buy. My paternal grandmother and adoptive mother, Pacita, whom I called Mama, Lola, *mine*, sold the very first house she bought in America on Javelin Street to bail my father out of jail. The house was bought with a mortgage by my aunt, my uncle's third wife and a hard-working nurse who arrived from the Philippines when I was around nine years old. Even back then, it was rumored that my uncle, a jolly-faced man who wore "FBI" shirts—*Female Body Inspector*—and only adored action films because all other films with too much talking in them were what he called "chick flicks," had bought my aunt on the internet. That he had agreed to marry another Filipina, seas away from her, but at the end of it all, she got cold feet. So, whatever dating service my uncle had used sent him another one, a Filipina he did not love. But they married, in the heat of Vegas, anyway. And she became one with our family, us calling her "tita," our aunt, an addition to our ever-growing, huge, big, fat Filipino family.

The arrangement was that my aunt would buy the house with a mortgage, because my father couldn't get one due to his shitty credit, and that my father would use those mortgage payments as rent. Eventually, after the mortgage would be paid in full, my aunt and uncle would give us this powdered-blue house on Neptune Avenue. My uncle would joke: anak, *you're so beautiful! I'm your favorite uncle, right? What street do you live on again? Ah-ha, I knew you were from out of space!* It was his ironic way of showing love, this uncle who was my second father, who called me *anak* though I was not his child.

My aunt, just like my stepmother who would enter our lives years later, was a mail order bride. She was not a slave, but she was trafficked. She was hardworking. She did the housework impeccably and without fail and she cooked and cleaned and worked without complaining. She wanted to come to America and take the hard-earned money she gained from working overtime and late-night shifts and send it all back home, to her *familia*, to her beloveds.

In the end, my aunt banked my father's monthly rent payments. She never paid the mortgage. She took that money and ran away to the other side of town, which wasn't very far. She divorced my uncle, who had a penchant for other women, just like my grandfather. We got the notice that the home we were living in, with its white carpeted floors, the pictures of us as children on the walls and arrayed in the china cabinet, the hospital bed that could rise up and down my grandmother owned, and the kitchen stove—the first stove I learned how to really cook on—would be foreclosed in a week. During that time, I was finishing my last semester in college, the first one in my family to do so, and the news took me by surprise, shook me with fear and shock, made me afraid that my father, half-brother and I might end up homeless. It made me feel stupid and foolish for thinking I was like those other college kids, who always had a home to return to, a house and a room to hold all their childhood things, their first pictures and drawings and clothes and shoes and all the things loved and held dear.

Our home was lost because my aunt needed to escape, needed to run away. This is the irony of Filipino families: the way we construct them allows us to abuse and maltreat each other, and even allows us to enslave our own blood.

Despite this, in spite of losing the first house I allowed to feel like home, I thought: but who could blame her? Chastise her for leaving, for stealing my father's money, for doing what she needed to do to survive—just like my birthmother? No one can.

I think of my stepmother, whom I call nanay, *my* mother, a name I never called my own birthmother, and I feel the same contentious emotions. The difference is that my nanay loves my father. They joke. They laugh. They chase each other around their small apartment and fall down tickling each other. They kiss, they make love, they hold hands while walking down the street, he takes her on dates, she cooks dinner, and they watch *Bones* together religiously, crying and laughing whenever the characters they love fail or succeed. My nanay is not like my aunt, not like Lola Eudocia "Cosiang" Pulido, the grandmother who was enslaved by the Tizon family for 56 years.

But the same racist socioeconomic, imperialist and classist forces that led to Lola Eudocia's enslavement also pushed both my aunt and nanay to marry my uncle and father as mail order brides.

I am not here to absolve Alex Tizon, his family, mother, father, or great-grandfather, the upper and middle classes of the Philippines, or even my father. They and Tizon cannot be absolved: He was complicit, they are complicit, we are complicit by virtue of living and paying taxes in America that fuel the neoliberal and foreign policies that create these industries of modern-day slavery. This is why the industries of memory have lauded Tizon's piece in the *Atlantic*, and it is lauded because of the very reasons that gave critics of his essay their knee-jerked and triggered reactions: his essay, by virtue of the *Atlantic*'s power and reach, conforms to the single story of the Filipino as victim (and only victim) and as oppressor of his own people.

"Filipineza": Maid, Servant, Caregiver, Domestic Help

In the 1990s, a dictionary in Greece defined the word "Filipineza," the Greek word for Filipina, as "domestic worker from the Philippines or a person who performs non-essential auxiliary tasks." In 2014, a textbook for elementary students in Hong Kong named an activity "Racial Harmony," where they drew cute pictures of different ethnicities which prompted the students to fill in the blanks.

A picture of a blond-haired man with blue eyes had a thought bubble next to him: "I am _____. I am an English teacher."

A picture of a woman with black hair and a kimono said: "I am _____. I have a sushi restaurant in Hong Kong."

A picture of another woman with black hair dressed in a red cheongsam said: "I am _____. Shanghai is my hometown."

Finally, another image of a woman, also with black hair but dressed in a simple yellow shirt, said: "I am _____. I am a domestic helper in Hong Kong."

Across the globe, the Filipina is translated as maid. As servant. As caregiver. As domestic help. This comes from the industries of memory and how the Filipino is erased, without measure, constantly. It is why we are known as the Forgotten Minority.

This is why, I believe, I have heard Filipino Americans demanding to sue the Tizon family and to disown any Tizon sympathizer; why I have heard Filipino Americans and Asian Americans from upper and middle classes criticize non-Filipino Americans for tying threads between Eudocia's honorific, "lola," and the term, "mammy," a word given to enslaved domestic caretakers by their white masters. There are many parallels, many intersections, and we ought and need to see these connections, honor and mourn them. But we must also be acute and specific in these comparisons, for we cannot equate "lola" to "mammy." To equate how Philippine feudalistic slavery operates—which has been rooted in and perpetuated by U.S. imperialism—with the devastating mass genocide of American chattel slavery is to do a disservice to those who have suffered from these cycles of oppression, massacres and enslavement. We must give each their own degree of mourning and resistance.

We cannot talk about the Philippine society without the acknowledgement of the Philippine-American War (which by its very name causes a mistranslation; it was an insurrection, a fight for freedom against an invading army) and our own genocide. We cannot talk about Philippine enslavement without first recognizing that to categorize it within an American framework is imperialist: It is reductive to say all slavery is the same (i.e., "all slavery operates the same," rather than "slavery, objectively, in all cultures, is morally wrong"), and that reductive thinking is based on Westernized Enlightenment thought.

The reason that "lola" could hypothetically be used for an enslaved person in a Philippine family is because the construction of that family is based on the psychological terms of kapwa (sense of togetherness, the need to be one, the need to be the same), awa (pity), utang na loob (reciprocal indebtedness) and hiya (shame). These words can't translate properly into English, but I feel them in my body, I know them every time I kiss a relative "hello" or "good-bye." These constructions of family are based in indigenous thought, not Westernized thought. It is just as cruel to label your slave with an honorific such as "lola" as the condescension of "mammy." Lola—like anak, which roughly translates to "my child"—means "my grandmother," and these psychological terms express how the Filipino family operates in a framework of hierarchal possession. It is similar to what my birthmother once said to me, after she threw a flurry of insults at me and my sister on a Facebook message, disowned me for the x-nth time, and confessed that she didn't know how to be a mother when her *own* mother sold her when she was only 15 years old: *If I gave you life, carried you in my womb for nine months, then I can give you death.*

Sometimes I don't know how my body holds onto so much grief. It is like I am in a perpetual state of grieving.

The Rapes of Our Grandmothers

Here is a fact:

The Philippines is one of the largest labor exporters in the world with 6,000 Filipinos—60% women—leaving the country every single day to work, because of rampant poverty, joblessness, and landlessness. Lured to apply for positions that do not exist, promised legal status and wages, and instead becoming undocumented, drowning in debt, and isolated in a foreign country—thousands of OFWs end up working in virtual slavery. Recruiters and employment agencies take advantage of their workers, by charging exorbitant fees and loans and threatening their workers with deportation or physical violence to the workers and their families. Living in fear and with no place to go, many OFWs endure the discrimination, abuse, and exploitation in order to survive.

—Gabriela *USA*

Here is another one:

When I search Google for the term "Lila Pilipina (League for Filipino Grandmothers)" I come up with a slew of articles. They portray the fight for redress for the Filipina Comfort Women—the lolas who were captured during WWII and raped repeatedly, instituted in sexual slavery. They were mostly girls, 13, 14, 15 years old. They were raped more than 20 times a night. Their families were massacred in front of them. Beaten by the butt of the gun. Slashed open with the bayonet. They were girls. They were women. They were as young as 12 years old. Now they are lolas, grandmothers, who are fighting for recognition, for an official, government-sanctioned apology, proof that what they suffered was not erased, was not forgotten. Japan refuses. They instead issue a blanket apology and give reparations to the Philippine government, funds the grandmothers have still not received.

Funds that my own grandmother did not receive.

She was a hostage, a prisoner of war, because my grandfather, Major Diego Sipin, was a wanted guerrilla fighter and one of the heroes of the Battle of Bessang Pass. She was held in a garrison in Agoo, La Union, Philippines, a seaside town on the Lingayen Gulf hit right after the attack on Pearl Harbor, for more than six months during the war. She gave birth in captivity. This is a cemented truth, something no one can counter or erase. My eldest aunt, to the silence of my familia, is the only sibling out of 11 who did not inherit my grandfather's looks.

Out of the 200 Filipino Comfort Women who came forward after 50 years of silence, none had a child of the "enemy's." Most of them, estimated to be more than 1,000, perished in the "comfort" stations, these militarized and forced brothels. In my own contours, I estimate more—because our islands were enemy territory and the Imperial Army retaliated with brutal ferocity, especially those who were part of or supported the guerrillas. According to the Asian Women's Fund, a quasi-public organization established by the Japanese government with state and privatized donations created as redress, but only *if* the lolas accepted an ambiguous apology, the Imperial Army did not only have official "comfort" stations in the Philippines; they had countless makeshift garrisons turned into rooms of mass rape, ones that were not organized into "militarized brothels" and were not visited by Japanese doctors. The systematic mass rape the Filipino women suffered was an instrument of warfare and scorched-earth policy, much like the Bosnian mass rapes that grabbed international attention in the 1990s.

Was my grandmother a Comfort Woman? It is possible. The Imperial Army was mercilessly brutal to any person who was suspected to be connected to the guerrillas. It is also possible that she was the sole woman to give birth in this captivity whose baby survived.

I can only imagine, only witness the bottomless cavern within my own body; I want to stop the grieving, I want to stop the erasure, I want to remember. I want to witness and speak. I need to remember.

And yet.

Something impedes me, a gate, a lock, like the one my grandmother once placed on the outside of my girlhood room that I shared with my sister.

I wonder what will happen if I let it slip. Let that golden key dangle. I wonder how much I would fall. I've done it many times before; have seen the brink, the edge, of my grief. Psychologists call it dissociation, dysphoria. Suicidal ideation. I need to go slow; I want to stop the triggers, the voices shouting over mine. Over my nanay's, my birthmother's, my lola's, my family's. And yet. All I hear is that cacophony, that mixture of missionary complexes and erasure.

Tomorrow, I wonder if Lola Eudocia will be remembered. Tomorrow, I wonder if my own grandmother, a woman who must have suffered the most one can suffer and lived, would be remembered, too.

The Colonized Become Their Colonizers

I ask myself now: What does it mean to become family? Familia? Pamilya? What are these terms but a representation of the bonds we hold with one another? They are lies. They are true. They are what we are left with, what we have. Should I call my birth-mother Mother? *My* mother? Nanay? That is what nanay means. What lola means: *my* grandmother.

Here is a truth: Lola Eudocia unfortunately did become part of Alex Tizon's family, because despite her lower class, she was still considered a Filipino citizen in their eyes. In contrast, chattel slavery never allowed the enslaved to become one with the family, because those who were enslaved were considered less than human. It is here where the difference lies, and it is imperative to point this out.

The white supremacy that fueled chattel slavery is also what fueled America to conquer the Pacific, to massacre over 1.4 million Filipinos and make the Philippines theirs:

> There was nothing wrong that profit motive and gain should be the only reason for American expansion into the Pacific.
>
> —Theodore Roosevelt, *June 24, 1900*

> We make no hypocritical pretense of being interested in the Philippines solely on account of others. While we regard the welfare of these people as a sacred trust, we regard the welfare of the American people first. We see our duty to ourselves as well as to others. We believe in the trade expansion.
>
> —Senator Henry Cabot Lodge, *June 1900*

> It has been charged that our conduct of the war has been cruel. Senators, it has been the reverse. . . . Senators must remember that we are not dealing with Americans or Europeans. We are dealing with Orientals. We are dealing with Orientals who are Malays. We are dealing with Malays instructed in Spanish methods. They mistake kindness for weakness, forbearance for fear. It could not be otherwise unless you could erase hundreds of years of savagery . . .
>
> —Albert J. Beveridge, *January 9, 1900*

The difference is stark: Filipinos have become the embodiment of their colonizer by enslaving their own people; white Americans, through their racist mythos of manifest destiny, enslaved and conquered and massacred those they believed were not human. We must find the parallels, we must find the intersections, but we must not allow Westernized, reductive thought to conflate these two systems of oppression—to do so is another erasure, and erasure is the crux of trauma for Filipinos. It is what catalyzed our migrations, both forced and voluntary.

This erasure is important to say aloud. It is because of the Philippine Insurrection, because of the over 300 years of subjugation by the Spanish, that the feudalistic and racist system of domestic servitude, katulongs and kasambahays continues to exist and thrive; it is this forgetting, this un-memory, this erasure that allows the Philippine populace to shroud their past and embody the colonizer that has colonized them. Simply put: The novelist Bob Shacochis once said the identity of war is "the genesis of a nation's soul." Even the name of our genocide is written in mistranslation—the Philippine-American War—as if these two countries were on equal footing. Let me repeat: It was an insurrection against an invading army. And it was an invasion that eventually succeeded because General Aguinaldo and the ilustrados wound up conspiring with the Americans to gain privileges and control during the U.S.'s rule, just as their ancestors conspired with the Spanish. The Philippines is a nation defined by its oppression, by its corroboration for complicity.

Through this erasure, this anti-memory, our old dictator Ferdinand Marcos and our new dictator in-the-making Rodrigo Duterte, who has just declared martial law in Mindanao and has threatened to extend it to the Visayas and Luzon, were created. They promised us they would be the strong-man we needed against all oppressors, and yet. Their promises were and are masked and wrapped up by their collusion with the United States, so that they could maintain their power and control. Marcos was supported by Reagan and Nixon. Duterte is supported by Trump. This is not by coincidence. This is because this is how oppression operates, according to Paulo Freire's *Pedagogy of the Oppressed*—through conquest, divide and rule, manipulation and cultural invasion.

This is our erasure: Our fight for freedom, our insurrection against the invading American army, is not taught either in American schools or Philippine schools; 1.4 million Filipinos died as a result of this invasion through water torture, concentration camps, famine, diseases and public massacres. And yet. The colonizer has us believe that America is the land of the free and the bounty. The colonizer has us believe that our island's resources are theirs to conquer and keep—for the sake of expansion. The colonizer has us believe that the way they enslave is exactly how we enslave, and thus who are we to complain of our sufferings, our traumas, our complicity, when we are just like them?

Intergenerational Trauma

I will end with this: This past weekend, one of the Dulay matriarchs, my great-aunt, who became a surrogate mother to me after my own grandmother passed and knew and remembered so much about the war (she was 15 years old when the Japanese Imperial Army bombed the Island of Corregidor), was laid into the earth near her sister.

Ever since Alex Tizon's essay came out, I've finally come to understand the intense class, hierarchal, and often racist class dynamics that my own family operates in, and especially the intense class anxiety I grew up with and still often feel, especially around the rich side of my family. Just because my nails were not painted, I felt poor. Just because my teeth never had braces and aren't straight, I felt poor. Lesser, of no value. My familia reaches over 300 in Los Angeles, and the main matriarch, my other grand aunt, married a white real estate tycoon and took over his company while employing most of my family members scattered between the freeways. The wealth disparity in my family is vast—my great-aunt, to give you a sense of her wealth, donated $13.5 million to the hospital I was born in, where many of my relatives were. My side and those who work for her and/or live in her apartment complexes, like my father, are regulated to the "help" side of the familia; it's the katulong system working within America's capitalism. We are not slaves, but we answer the beck-and-call of my great-aunt and of her son.

You want to tell me that slavery is slavery. You want to tell me that slavery is the same everywhere. But this is what I believe you are saying: Slavery, morally, is and will always be, no matter what, wrong. It is objectively evil in all cultures, like rape. How it exists is objectively and will always be evil and based upon the superiority complexes of the oppressor class—and therein lies the intersections, the parallels, the ravaged truth: The master's egotism is rooted in his enslavement of the oppressed.

But I also believe this is a truth: How slavery operates, by culture, country, and nation-state, is different. It bleeds and finds its way into our lives and cuts the very core of our bonds and our ability to love and see each other. The consequences, the devastating ruptures of familial bonds and love, are the same: they are knifed by the trauma, by the intergenerational trauma. They mirror the other.

My inay is not a slave, is not an indentured servant, but she was trafficked. My aunt is not a slave, is not an indentured servant, but she was trafficked. My birthmother, who abandoned me the day after I was born, is not a slave, is not an indentured servant, but she was sold—*by her own mother*. Modern-day slavery is filtered through this system of human trafficking.

And yet.

When I am near her, *my* inay, *my* stepmother, she fixes my dress, my hair, my messed-up lipstick with her fingers, like she were my real mother. I ask her if she misses her family back home, if they, too, want to come here, and she tells me, *It is okay anak. Here, I can help them more. But they want to stay there, and I want to be with your father.*

My father, through the hard work of my familia, is finally a citizen. My inay, who migrated here legally, will soon, too, become a U.S. citizen.

Her children are my age. I meet them, too, on the computer screen. Next year, my husband and I will make a pilgrimage to Metro Manila to meet my stepsiblings for the very first time. Though we are thousands of miles and oceans away from each other, we laugh and talk and smile as if we were familia.

I know there are many nonprofit orgs fighting for the rights of my titas, my lolas, those from families like mine. Damayan Migrant Workers Association, Gabriela USA, Lila Pilipina, and so many more—they are on the frontlines, like Gabriela Silang, and they are fighting to dispel modern-day slavery in its most current, most vicious insti-tutionalized form. I know this is not enough. I know my familia is lucky; that not all families are like mine, not all are kind, that they do not operate in the same clannish, overly protective way the matriarchs in my family do.

For me, I have to go back. To the faces of my nanay's children on the computer screen. To the countless faces that filled the church at my grand-aunt's funeral, all those who were my relatives, all of them blood, all of them kin. Because despite the forces that continue to enslave and oppress us, the truth is, despite it all, despite everything, despite what bonds slavery has severed, what bonds trauma has sliced and knifed with merciless brutality, is that, yes, this is a truth: *we are.*

REFLECTING AND DISCUSSING

1. Where does the word "filipineza" come from? What does it mean? What are its connotations? How does Sipin redefine the word?
2. How does Sipin situate her own personal narrative within the larger context of Fili-pino immigration? How does she use her story to argue a point of view?
3. How does Sipin argue that the "colonized become their colonizers"? What specific examples does she provide? Are they persuasive? Why or why not?

CONNECTING AND WRITING

1. "We cannot talk about the Philippine society without the acknowledgement of the Philippine-American War (which by its very name causes a mistranslation; it was an insurrection, a fight for freedom against an invading army) and our own genocide." Research this war. How does your research either confirm or refute Sipin's assertion that calling this conflict a war is a "mistranslation"?
2. How does Sipin define "intergenerational trauma"? Research this concept as it might apply to another immigrant group—even if that term isn't explicitly used—and articulate a point of view, using Sipin and other sources to back up your points.

Dinosaurs in the Hood

Danez Smith (1989–   )

Among the best-known contemporary African American poets, Danez Smith's work addresses current issues related to race and sexuality. He has received fellowships from the Poetry Founda-tion and the McKnight Foundation, and he was a National Endowment for the Arts Fellow in 2017. Smith has also found success in national poetry slam competitions, and his work is often noted for bridging the gap between the page and the stage. Smith has been a National Book Award finalist, and three collections of his poetry have been published: [Insert] Boy *(2014),* Black Movie *(2015), and* Don't Call Us Dead: Poems *(2017). The following poem is from* Black Movie.

Let's make a movie called *Dinosaurs in the Hood*.
Jurassic Park meets *Friday* meets *The Pursuit of Happyness*.
There should be a scene where a little black boy is playing
with a toy dinosaur on the bus, then looks out the window
& sees the T. Rex, because there has to be a T. Rex.

Don't let Tarantino direct this. In his version, the boy plays
with a gun, the metaphor: black boys toy with their own lives,
the foreshadow to his end, the spitting image of his father.
Fuck that, the kid has a plastic Brontosaurus or Triceratops
& this is his proof of magic or God or Santa. I want a scene

where a cop car gets pooped on by a pterodactyl, a scene
where the corner store turns into a battle ground. Don't let
the Wayans brothers in this movie. I don't want any racist shit
about Asian people or overused Latino stereotypes.
This movie is about a neighborhood of royal folks —

children of slaves & immigrants & addicts & exiles — saving their town
from real-ass dinosaurs. I don't want some cheesy yet progressive
Hmong sexy hot dude hero with a funny yet strong commanding
black girl buddy-cop film. This is not a vehicle for Will Smith
& Sofia Vergara. I want grandmas on the front porch taking out raptors

with guns they hid in walls & under mattresses. I want those little spitty,
screamy dinosaurs. I want Cicely Tyson to make a speech, maybe two.
I want Viola Davis to save the city in the last scene with a black fist afro pick
through the last dinosaur's long, cold-blood neck. But this can't be
a black movie. This can't be a black movie. This movie can't be dismissed

because of its cast or its audience. This movie can't be a metaphor
for black people & extinction. This movie can't be about race.
This movie can't be about black pain or cause black people pain.
This movie can't be about a long history of having a long history with hurt.
This movie can't be about race. Nobody can say nigga in this movie

who can't say it to my face in public. No chicken jokes in this movie.
No bullets in the heroes. & no one kills the black boy. & no one kills
the black boy. & no one kills the black boy. Besides, the only reason
I want to make this is for that first scene anyway: the little black boy
on the bus with a toy dinosaur, his eyes wide & endless

his dreams possible, pulsing, & right there.

REFLECTING AND DISCUSSING

1. Analyze the language and diction of this poem. What effect do they have? Taken together, what is the poem about?
2. Smith is noted for his use of irony and sarcastic tone. Define "irony" and "sarcasm" and analyze their use in the poem. What effect do they have on your reading of this poem?
3. Make note of the references to popular culture. What are they? To what extent is one's appreciation of the poem dependent on "getting" the references? Do you believe this dependence will affect the longevity of this poem? Why or why not?

CONNECTING AND WRITING

1. Reread the sixth stanza of Smith's poem and observe the way(s) it seems to respond to a long history of black archetypes in film. Research the characters and archetypes in the films Smith mentions and argue a point of view that aligns or contrasts with Smith's view in the poem.
2. The poem begins and ends with the character of the "little black boy." How is the boy a metaphor for the essential argument of the poem? What does he symbolize? Why is the dinosaur important? What argument is Smith making by including this character?

Killing Like They Do in the Movies

Justin Reed (1989–   )

Justin Reed is a self-professed "three-time high school expellee and ex-college dropout" who eventually earned an MFA in poetry from Washington University in St. Louis. He is a Cave Canem Fellow, an award from the preeminent organization supporting young African American poets. Reed's first poetry collection, Indecency, *was published by Coffee House Press (2018). His work has appeared in the* Kenyon Review, *the* Boston Review, *and* Lambda Literary. *The following piece was published online as part of the newsmagazine* Catapult.

"Black ghosts dangle in all the corners of my horror flicks lately."

1. Digging Beneath My Uncle's Feet

In 1996, I knew nothing of the word "lynch," only that it was also the last name of a girl in my grade whom none of us talked to.

They found Uncle Craig hanging from a tree on McKeever Road. I remember that his skin was darker than most of the skin I had seen, remember thinking later that his body and the tree must have shared a darkness. Crooked silhouette of limbs and fingers and trunks, all that Carolina morning burning holes through it. I shouldn't have been able to beautify that image. I want to take to task my mind's archive of envisioned, consumable violence.

At seven, I knew only what it was: a hanging. Not who, not why, and not since when.

A chain of associations drags me out of sleep. I dreamed someone tattooed on my forearm a talismanic pentagram. I somehow surface recalling the gruesome kills of Michael Myers throughout the *Halloween* franchise. All the white teenage girls, strangled or bleeding out, and then Tyra Banks: gutted and hanging by the neck from a wire. I demand a metaphor for how these scenes are imagined—how dust and waste and forgotten things might collect in the bed of a huge river, how I could pick up a small stone formed from centuries of this and wonder about its weight in my palm, the color contrast, and never question the river, what cut across it, sank through it, floated on its surface.

It's not that Michael Myers had never strung up a body before *Halloween: Resurrection* (2002). On the contrary, it was by then the killer's hallmark to suspend his victims, cocking his head in odd curiosity or appraisal of his work. It's that Banks's Blackness, her Black woman body silent in the center of the room, reveals the grotesque as no curio but a well-known wound. I've been failing to write a poem that ends with the lines *this body didn't teach you all / you know about gore, but damn / if it didn't try.*

I haven't thought about Uncle Craig in I don't know how long, had forgotten ever having known someone who was lynched, and this lapse is what troubles me when I throw back the sheets. I ask my mother for details, and she calls from work, and yeah it had to be about '96 because that was the year after Daddy died and left her with two sons and the year my sister was born, and she wants to send me pictures of Craig's daughter's daughter, who is beautiful and in one picture is holding my baby niece, and our girls are always beautiful, but yeah, Momma doesn't think they ever found who did it, doesn't think they were really looking, no use in me being mad about it now, she's gotta go visit Craig's wife Aunt Deborah in Columbia and see the new granddaughter, and she's gonna send me all these pictures of the beautiful girls.

2. We Live on Elm Street

Wes Craven died. Brain cancer. Violent, but relatively goreless, considering. Features and images went up online to commemorate what Craven had given us. I wonder if maybe lately I don't have much grief left on reserve for famous white men, or if I have trouble mourning in general, but in a predictable mix of homage and nostalgia, that evening I decided to watch *A Nightmare on Elm Street* (1984), Craven's classic franchise-starter in which razor-fingered Freddy Krueger stalks the dreams of four archetypal suburban kids.

I rarely think of Craven, but I can easily visualize many of the kill scenes that made him famous and his killers infamous. I keep a mental library of the kills. I often call on them while writing poems as though for a diction of fantasized violence, a showcase of its pronunciations. This is what Craven and his counterparts have given me.

A few minutes into the film I began to dread the rest of it. Each scene seemed to climb toward the least red death in the film—that of Rod, the first victim's dark, "rough-edged," pretty-faced boyfriend, the prime suspect in her death; Rod, whom Freddy—existing somewhere between nightmare and poltergeist—hangs by a bed sheet in what will appear to the always-ain't-seen-nothin' cops to be an otherwise-empty jail cell.

It's a bloodless kill. It looks to the adults like a simple guilt-fueled suicide. Meanwhile, I barely register it as the scene of a film. My ears fumble the dialogue. My eyes take in the images from the laptop screen, but my mind is digressing, recycling props kaleidoscopically, replacing Rod with Sandra Bland. That I can color in the glue-and-scissors details around Bland's death with a scene as outrageous and inventive as this one irritates me. The story from the Waller County jail has as many holes, cuts, edits, and special effects as Craven's slasher. Black ghosts dangle in all the corners of my horror flicks lately, even when I am not looking.

Upon discovering Rod's body, the heroine Nancy shrieks the beginning of her long frustration. She knows what's killing her friends, what's coming after her. Knowing makes her crazy. Disrupting everyone else's resistance to knowing makes her the problem.

3. Everybody Knows Your Name

When I enter the bar, its walls are talking loudly amongst themselves, the way a dead woods might always be filled with falling trees regardless of whether an eavesdropping ear would hear. One wall has its mouth full of Josephine Baker and all her feathers. Another holds Miles Davis in the dark throat of its holler, his trumpet paused mid-rapture. There are others, bound in frames, jazzing up the space. All the patrons are white. Their beer voices slap up the Black talent and bounce back. I come like a gap in a white caravan and grit my teeth against the din of it. Down an aisle of stools and minimalist tables, a vintage-looking man plays a vintage-looking piano, grinning at the skinny woman thinly singing another jazz standard, her hair in a vintage-looking bun. A young New Yorker sits across from me and gets bored with my pointing out how white spaces have "this thing" for making ornament of non-white strife and achievement—which are often difficult to tell apart. I'm also bored. I'm trying to understand this nearly ubiquitous need for the Negro edge. Bodies dangling like festive decorations, tricking the light. Somehow I've become a conduit for haunting—a needle pushed across the black cut, which spins even when I don't want to lower my nose to it because maybe tonight my spine needs respite from the violent signals of memory and literacy. How hopeful. Not this night. *What happens when I'm not here? What am I assumed to cosign when I am here?* These are two different questions with similar answers. Sometimes, when I say I'm bored, I mean bored into. White nostalgia in the age of the hipster bar is a dense sulfuric stink. For one reason or another, I keep inhaling. I order a pizza and neat whiskeys.

4. Who Kills Casey Becker

We are introduced to a blonde, and the plot seems likely to center on her. She is stalked and attacked, but her blondeness and surplus lines of dialogue are supposed to save her. She dies around twelve minutes in, murdered in the most violent way.

The violent murder of a blonde who spoke frequently suggests that no one is safe. Craven's *Scream*, credited with revitalizing the slasher subgenre in 1996, follows a formula previously deployed in *A Nightmare on Elm Street*. I can trace the tradition back to Hitchcock's *Psycho*.

Some nights, when I want to slip inside the guilty space between guaranteed discomfort and the foreknowledge of it, I turn on the movie just to watch this paradigm-shifting first scene. The killing of Casey Becker in *Scream* was momentous. It marked the end of Craven's hiatus from big-box-office horror. It marked Drew Barrymore's return to prominence. It established the Ghostface Killer—that easily laughable horror symbol—as a significant addition to the lineage of masked murderers. It brought the Michael Myers tradition back to the unsuspecting suburbs, where high school girls are often home alone and anyone, especially their boyfriends, could be the home-invading butcher. It's as if in the imagination of Smalltown, USA, few other perils exist.

The killing of Casey Becker was historic. It's difficult to see the scene—her body disemboweled, dragged, and hanged from a large tree with the rope of a swing—as existing outside of American history, as created anywhere but in the continuum of a societal id that can't forget what it's seen its own hands do, that merely shuffles the moving parts of memory.

There being no Black characters in *Scream* and so few in its contemporaries illustrates a dissonance, the rasp of an unintended truth. These films imagine the extremities of white cultural depravity and brutality but do so in an America where only whiteness factors (and is in fact not "white" but some agreed-upon glare of homogeneity convinced of its comfort). This arrangement falls back quickly on psychosis-as-motive, in which the mysteries of mental disorder and individual deviance are alibis for the whites-only fantasy. The artifice of chance is the drama. In the case of *Scream*, the logic seems presented like so: "These two white teens are psychological anomalies *and* their killing spree of other white teens is an isolated incident *although* all of their parents are always circumstantially absent *and* there will be a sequel in which another white man terrorizes the very same white people . . ."

5. My Other Education

I was a queer and skinny child whose dominant emotion was fear. While other boys practiced succeeding at masculinity, thrashing and breaking their bodies in hours of commune, I hung back and cultivated a knowledge of exits, of how to get out alive, how to avoid entry. I was probably sitting on the floor, legs in a bow, safe from my cousins' game of tackle football in the front yard, when my aunt and uncle put a rented copy of *Scream* in the VCR.

When I was a fifth- or sixth-grader in after-school care, Momma had an HBO subscription and I had a habit of unwrapping the aluminum foil from the school's afternoon snacks, folding and shaping it into a hook circa Ben Willis of *I Know What You Did Last Summer*, and smuggling the flimsy prop out of the cafeteria and onto the playground, where I stalked my classmates throughout the plastic foil. I daydreamed of drafting a horror novel but only got as far as the cover image. I filled sketchbooks with color-penciled movie posters for teen slashers that existed and some that I hoped soon would. My drawings were decent. My illustration of the new playground had graced the school yearbook cover. One of my tornado scenes, inspired by Jan de Bont's 1996 special-effects montage *Twister*, had aired on the morning news. In third grade, my post-*Titanic* sketches of nude women had stirred some quiet controversy among the faculty, but in the end the principal was lenient, even impressed, having found the renderings "tasteful." I managed to keep the slasher sketches to myself until middle school, when all the low-boiling parts of me wanted to be acted out. My crosshatched knives stabbed no bodies but hovered in white space, dripping potential.

6. The Punch Line

I'm a queer and skinny adult whose flesh has known more blades than fists, whose mind knows the MOs of Bundy, Dahmer, Gacy, Ramirez, and others, who is still a bit bolstered by being able to stomach certain information without a cringe.

One study purports that Black people are believed to feel pain to a lesser degree than whites. Another supports the existence of racial PTSD. Another: the physiological effects of racism can substantially shorten a life. What Black bodies perhaps know: You can spend a long lifetime performing the role of a retort, a punch line. I want to make of this an if-then statement, a colored optimism. My poetry students are optimistic about clichés. They hypothesize that *if* an artist acknowledges the cliché and/or transforms it just enough, *then* an audience can more readily accept the cliché.

In 1997, singer Brandy played the lead role in Rodgers & Hammerstein's *Cinderella*. The cast—portraying mixed-race families, royal and common—still (humorously) perplexes people on IMDb message boards. The year after, Brandy was Karla Wilson in *I Still Know What You Did Last Summer*, a sequel for which the filmmakers seem to have taken a cue from *Scream 2* and included Black characters in the supporting cast *and* allowed them to survive more than half the action.

Scream 2 cast Omar Epps, Jada Pinkett, Elise Neal, and Duane Martin. In the first minute, Pinkett's Maureen delivers the line: "All I'm saying is the horror genre's historical for excluding the African-American element," and the sequel laughs loudly at its predecessor. Epps's Phil jokes about "an all-Black movie," and Craven maybe giggles a little at himself. (His directing credit immediately preceding *Scream* had been *Vampire in Brooklyn*, which grossed less than its budget and boasted a predominantly Black cast.) Martin's character Joel—a source of comic relief—is the only one of the four who survives *Scream 2*; the others suffer together a total of at least thirteen stab wounds, Phil and Maureen having been targeted, it turns out, because their names loosely replicated those of white characters who died in the original *Scream*.

Karla Wilson is the best college friend of *Last Summer* veteran Julie James, played by Jennifer Love Hewitt. Julie runs a lot but lives again, as does her partner Ray. Unlike her partner Tyrell, Karla—having fallen backward through the glass ceiling of a bedroom, having fallen backward through the glass roof of a greenhouse, having fallen backward through a glass door and played dead—also lives, limping into the penultimate scene.

7. She Is (Beside) Herself

My first and only real conversation with my great-grandmother, the truest stoic I ever knew, was a warning after she caught wind that I "went around" with white girls. Perhaps she recalled how this would've ended in the early part of the century she had lived, had witnessed. The consistent drama of horror seems to be its nestling inside the trope of preying on and violating innocence, which is the domain ruled by young white women, if ruling is a way of being puppeteered. I wonder if Uncle Craig was somebody's Black friend, or if I should mention that Aunt Deborah could pass as white.

In her poem "The Jailer," Sylvia Plath writes *He has been burning me with cigarettes, / Pretending I am a negress with pink paws. / I am myself. That is not enough.* I hold these lines like a grudge. Plath's speaker wants to level an indictment against the shadowy man who has imprisoned, abused, *drugged and raped* her. A numeration of injustices. To be burned with cigarettes—*what holes this papery day is already full of!*—is apparently a violence that a Black woman traditionally vests. Unambiguously, "paws" belong to an animal. *I am myself*, as if the rapist's imagining the inhuman Black body in the speaker's stead lubricates his brutality. He is deluded, unappeasable. The poem swells with the desperation of this moment. *I am myself.* For whom is that not enough?

8. Spectacle / Sport

Consider the state-sanctioned hubs of public humiliation and mutilation. Gladiator death-matches, Crusades, the Inquisition, the evolution of legal public execution including lynching, from the advent of television into continuously looped video clips of police shootings—all as if there's a consistent desire to access carnage from the safe distance of a spectator. Less than a century out of Jim Crow, I doubt it's difficult to argue that a public imagination lingers with the same appetite for gore that lynchings—their rape, dragging, shooting, castration, hanging, burning, and displayed decay—once sated. Now it leeches elsewhere.

The physical kill. The imaginary kill. The execution that is "nigger." The amateur porn subgenre of race-play. I tell a friend *No, I won't let a man call me that, fucking or not*, but I've watched a Black man enjoy exactly this somewhere on MyVidster, three-fourfive times now. When the white boys slap the hog-tied Rogan Hardy and call him "nigger," their jaws glitch over the strange shape of the word, their faces momentarily funhoused away from human, the eyelids receding, whites waxing cartoonish. I watch and a heated radius expands. I've been sweating the matters of agency and impulse. My friend responds *but it's fantasy*—which it is, for everyone except the actors: the man whose mouth makes the killing and the one whose body approximates a corpse. But maybe, I concede, even for them.

9. Unmaking the Monster

I try to elude the burden. Then I attempt to share it. I remember how I got here, who sent me, the single sentence that propels me.

"What white people have to do is try to find out in their own hearts why it was necessary to have the nigger in the first place." James Baldwin poses this challenge on a PBS-segment of Henry Morgenthau III's "The Negro and the American Promise" in 1963. "Cause I'm not a nigger," he continues. "I'm a man. But if you think I'm a nigger, it means you need it." Skip to 2011: In Chapter 7 ("Black Is Back!") of *Horror Noire: Blacks in American Horror Films from the 1890s to Present*, Robin R. Means Coleman analyzes Craven's 1991 cult favorite *The People Under the Stairs*, "in which the 'hood and the suburbs stood in confrontation against each other . . . with the 'hood proving victorious." She writes of the white slumlords in the film:

> The couple, then, represent a bundle of horrible taboos: (1) food (forced cannibalism); (2) death (they murder the two thieves); and (3) incest (among themselves and with their "daughters"). Central to the narrative of their taboos is that these are horrors easily hidden behind wealth and Whiteness; two positions of power which mean one would seldom be suspected of, or can get a pass for, evil.

Coleman has, by this point in the chapter, already made legible a few ills of *Candyman* (1992), a supernatural slasher that is perhaps more candid about its leaning on the myth of Black monstrosity than it means to be, practically in syzygy with *King Kong* and, Coleman argues, *The Birth of a Nation*. But *Candyman*'s eponymous hook-handed haint is only the Vader-mask to its messy racial mush-mouth.

The Candyman is the vengeful spirit of a lynched man, Daniel Robitaille, mutilated for his miscegenation. His bloody acts manifest his desire to seduce the live white Helen to her death. His trail of impoverished Black victims from the Cabrini-Green projects seems peripheral to this bizarre infatuation. Helen debuts as a (bored and scorned and) curious grad student in Chicago. After hearing the legend of Candyman, she's taken in by a headline: "Cause of Death, What Killed Ruthie Jean? Life in the Projects." Her arrival in "the 'hood" from the highway's good side, looking for sources to inflate her thesis on urban legends, is cute and exploitative. What killed Ruthie Jean is more enigmatic and enticing than what usually kills the all-Black residents of Cabrini-Green, where, according to Helen and her friend Bernadette, every day a kid gets shot. Around seventeen minutes in:

> BERNADETTE: I just want you to think, okay? The gangs hold this whole neighborhood hostage.
> HELEN: Okay, let's just turn around then. Let's just go back and we can write a nice little boring thesis regurgitating all the usual crap about urban legends.

In recent months I've been gradually collecting notes for the practice of centering Blackness. The Candyman is a distraction. Décor. I fold him aside. Helen needs this haunting. Her whiteness and access to a predominantly white institution of higher education have failed to elude the risk of mediocrity. Whatever is lurking in the gutted Cabrini-Green projects, whatever killed Ruthie Jean, can save Helen from disappointing namelessness. In a stasis-intrusion model of plot, little dissimilates the intrusion of Candyman (who appears only to her) into Helen's high-story-condo life from Helen's intrusion into Cabrini-Green—where most of the blood in the film is shed—except that nobody seems to hallucinate Helen, or the corpses made in her presence.

When I view the images of mobs huddled under hanged men, of Michael Brown's half-fetal body four hours facedown and cops at compass points, I want to talk about necessity. I want to ask, *What do you need? Do you know?* What did the landscape of Darlington, South Carolina, need with Craig's darkness? What does the urge toward mass murder need with anomalous madness? It seems that forms of atrocity have no use for the semantics of mental fitness. Darren Wilson hallucinated a demon and a body dropped. What did he need? What does ritual human sacrifice need with a god?

10. Grace and Mercy

One of the most insidious facets of Dylann Roof's massacre of the Emanuel AME Church in Charleston, South Carolina, is the matter of setting: The Black church is a testament to and tomb of America's sustained racist violence, a memorial of the pillaged spirit poorly substituted with religion. Its insistence on the power of healing forgiveness is unwavering because what else. There is always something to forgive, to get over.

I was brought up in these places. My grandma can be found in one three or four days a week. Even on the phone she has a suffocating hopefulness. All that she survives she does so "by God's good grace." I'm still not irreverent enough to tell her that her God and our Black lives are irreconcilable to me. I want to call more often. I wish she would just pray at home.

I'm anxious, ambivalent about the re-presentations of daily horrors—man shot down, gun planted; woman pulled from car, her pregnant body slammed—because I neither trust America to live with its own memory nor trust myself not to forget to live. I mean I might try to forget in order to live. I might try. I'm often afraid. I'm not above trying.

There's a scene in *I Still Know What You Did Last Summer*, after a hurricane hits and the body pile first peaks, when Julie—who took this vacation in the Bahamas in an effort to move on from the murders of the previous year—finally reveals to her friends that they're all going to die and the who and the why.

> KARLA: How could you not tell me the whole story? I'm your best friend!
> JULIE: I just wanted it to be over. I didn't wanna involve anybody else.
> KARLA: Well, it's too late for that now.

They all stand in a downpour, distraught, on a useless pier.

REFLECTING AND DISCUSSING

1. What is the structure of this essay? How is this particular structure effective? Discuss Reed's use of first-person narrative interwoven with critique.
2. In discussing Nancy, the heroine in *A Nightmare on Elm Street* (1984), Reed writes, "She knows what's killing her friends, what's coming after her. Knowing makes her crazy. Disrupting everyone else's resistance to knowing makes her the problem."

Reed implicitly draws a parallel between her and Black figures who are "disrupting everyone else's resistance." What parallels are drawn between Nancy and Reed's life in the communities he discusses?

3. How do you respond to the title of this piece? Who is the "they"? How do you know?

CONNECTING AND WRITING

1. Reed delineates the history of Black characters in horror films, or the absence thereof. Research a history of Black characters in the horror film genre. Do such archetypes exist, as Reed argues? If so, what are they? Use Reed's article and other credible resources to support your point of view.

2. Reed's essay can accurately be described as "multi-genre." What does this mean? Write an essay in which you articulate the ways in which Reed argues effectively using a variety of genres, crafting a thesis from the general theme of Black characters being either absent from horror movies or presented unfairly in them.

QUESTION

How do the writers in this section reconcile their individual identities within a larger American context? Choose at least two of these pieces to make an effective argument and to support your points.

2 TECHNOLOGY AND MEDIA

E lectronically, we are more connected to one another than ever before, and yet some would argue that we have lost our more fundamental connections to one another. The articles in this section give witness to the influence of technological devices and media in our lives.

Be a Gamer, Change the World

Jane McGonigal (1977–   )

Jane McGonigal earned a Ph.D. in performance studies from the University of California at Berkeley. She is now a world-renowned game designer and advocate for the positive use of digital media, believing that game designers are "on a humanitarian mission." Her games have been featured in the New York Times, *the* Economist, *and the* Wall Street Journal, *and on NPR. She is also director of games research and development at the Institute for the Future in Palo Alto, California, and the author of a best-selling book,* Reality Is Broken: Why Games Make Us Better and How They Can Change the World *(2011).*

W e often think of immersive computer and videogames—like *FarmVille, Guitar Hero* and *World of Warcraft*—as "escapist," a kind of passive retreat from reality. Many critics consider such games a mind-numbing waste of time, if not a corrupting influence. But the truth about games is very nearly the opposite. In today's society, they consistently fulfill genuine human needs that the real world fails to satisfy. More than that, they may prove to be a key resource for solving some of our most pressing real world problems.

Hundreds of millions of people around the globe are already devoting larger and larger chunks of time to this alternate reality. Collectively, we spend three billion hours a week gaming. In the United States, where there are 183 million active gamers, videogames took in about $15.5 billion last year. And though a typical gamer plays for just an hour or two a day, there are now more than five million "extreme" gamers in the U.S. who play an average of 45 hours a week. To put this in perspective, the number of hours that gamers world-wide have spent playing *World of Warcraft* alone adds up to 5.93 million years.

These gamers aren't rejecting reality entirely, of course. They have careers, goals, schoolwork, families and real lives that they care about. But as they devote more of their free time to game worlds, they often feel that the real world is missing something.

Gamers want to know: Where in the real world is the gamer's sense of being fully alive, focused and engaged in every moment? The real world just doesn't offer up the same sort of carefully designed pleasures, thrilling challenges and powerful social bonding that the gamer finds in virtual environments. Reality doesn't motivate us as effectively. Reality isn't engineered to maximize our potential or to make us happy.

Those who continue to dismiss games as merely escapist entertainment will find themselves at a major disadvantage in the years ahead, as more gamers start to harness this power for real good. My research over the past decade at the University of California, Berkeley, and the Institute for the Future has shown that games consistently provide us with the four ingredients that make for a happy and meaningful life: satisfying work, real hope for success, strong social connections and the chance to become a part of something bigger than ourselves.

We get these benefits from our real lives sometimes, but we get them almost every time we play a good game. These benefits are what positive psychologists call intrinsic rewards—we don't play games to make money, improve our social status, or achieve any external signposts of success. And these intrinsic rewards, studies at the University of Pennsylvania, Harvard and U.C. Berkeley have shown, provide the foundation for optimal human experience.

In a good game, we feel blissfully productive. We have clear goals and a sense of heroic purpose. More important, we're constantly able to see and feel the impact of our efforts on the virtual world around us. As a result, we have a stronger sense of our own agency—and we are more likely to set ambitious real-life goals. One recent study found, for example, that players of *Guitar Hero* are more likely to pick up a real guitar and learn how to play it.

When we play, we also have a sense of urgent optimism. We believe whole-heartedly that we are up to any challenge, and we become remarkably resilient in the face of failure. Research shows that gamers spend on average 80% of their time failing in game worlds, but instead of giving up, they stick with the difficult challenge and use the feedback of the game to get better. With some effort, we can learn to apply this resilience to the real-world challenges we face.

Games make it easy to build stronger social bonds with our friends and family. Studies show that we like and trust someone better after we play a game with them—even if they beat us. And we're more likely to help someone in real life after we've helped them in an online game. It's no wonder that 40% of all user time on Facebook is spent playing social games. They're a fast and reliable way to strengthen our connection with people we care about.

Today's videogames are increasingly created on an epic scale, with compelling stories, sweeping mythologies and massive multiplayer environments that produce feelings of awe and wonder. Researchers on positive emotion have found that whenever we feel awe or wonder, we become more likely to serve a larger cause and to collaborate selflessly with others.

With so much blissful productivity and urgent optimism, stronger social bonds and extreme cooperation, it's not surprising that so many players feel that they become the best version of themselves in games. That's one of the reasons I believe we can take the benefits of games a step further. We can harness the power of game design to tackle real-world problems. We can empower gamers to use their virtual-world strengths to accomplish real feats. Indeed, when game communities have been matched with challenging real-world problems, they have already proven themselves capable of producing tangible, potentially world-changing results.

In 2010, more than 57,000 gamers were listed as co-authors for a research paper in the prestigious scientific journal *Nature*. The gamers—with no previous background in biochemistry—had worked in a 3D game environment called Foldit, folding virtual proteins in new ways that could help cure cancer or prevent Alzheimer's. The game was developed by scientists at the University of Washington who believed that gamers could outperform supercomputers at this creative task—and the players proved them right, beating the supercomputers at more than half of the game's challenges.

More recently, more than 19,000 players of EVOKE, an online game that I created for the World Bank Institute, undertook real-world missions to improve food security, increase access to clean energy and end poverty in more than 130 countries. The game focused on building up players' abilities to design and launch their own social enterprises.

After 10 weeks, they had founded more than 50 new companies—real businesses working today from South Africa and India to Buffalo, N.Y. My favorite is Libraries Across Africa, a new franchise system that empowers local entrepreneurs to set up free community libraries. It also creates complementary business opportunities for selling patrons refreshments, WiFi access and cellphone time. The first is currently being tested in Gabon.

These examples are just the beginning of what is possible if we take advantage of the power of games to make us better and change the world. Those who understand this power will be the people who invent our future. We can create rewarding, transformative games for ourselves and our families; for our schools, businesses and neighborhoods; for an entire industry or an entirely new movement.

We can play any games we want. We can create any future we can imagine. Let the games begin.

REFLECTING AND DISCUSSING

1. "Could games like *Guitar Hero* cure cancer and end poverty?" While this may seem like a lofty goal, how does the author argue that games could potentially have positive impacts? Do you agree or disagree? Why?

2. McGonigal says that "reality isn't engineered to maximize our potential or to make us happy." Do you agree with this view of reality? What might be the strengths and pitfalls of this argument?

3. McGonigal illustrates how daily time is spent among eight- to eighteen-year-olds, who have over the past several decades moved away from reading books, magazines,

and newspapers for pleasure to nearly double the time they spend playing video games. One might assume that this is a negative development, but how might McGonigal argue differently? Do you buy her argument?

CONNECTING AND WRITING

1. McGonigal's perspective is a minority perspective, as there have been many critiques of video games and their effects. Find one of these critiques in a credible source and compare its arguments with McGonigal's, crafting a thesis that comes to a conclusion about the two and using the two articles for evidence.

2. The author references her research at Berkeley and work done at the Institute for the Future on creating "good games" that may actually help players solve world problems. Do some further research on at least one of the games developed by McGonigal or her peers and write an essay in which you explore the impact of these games and whether their potentially positive effects outweigh the negative influences of excessive gaming.

How Technology Hijacks People's Minds—From a Magician and Google's Design Ethicist

Tristan Harris (1984–   )

Tristan Harris previously served as a design ethicist at Google and now leads Time Well Spent, an organization created to "transform the race for attention so it aligns with our best interests." He is a well-known speaker and contributor on information technology, with work often focusing on the intersection of ethics and technology. A frequent TED Talk speaker, Harris's work has been featured on 60 Minutes, *Bill Maher's* Real Time, *and PBS's* NewsHour. *Harris humorously promises that this essay, published on his personal blog in May 2016, will not "hijack" more than fifteen minutes of the reader's time.*

> *"It's easier to fool people than to convince them that they've been fooled."*
> —UNKNOWN.

I'm an expert on how technology hijacks our psychological vulnerabilities. That's why I spent the last three years as a Design Ethicist at Google caring about how to design things in a way that defends a billion people's minds from getting hijacked.

When using technology, we often focus *optimistically* on all the things it does for us. But I want to show you where it might do the opposite.

Where does technology exploit our minds' weaknesses?

I learned to think this way when I was a magician. Magicians start by looking for *blind spots, edges, vulnerabilities* and *limits* of people's perception, so they can influence what people do without them even realizing it. Once you know how to push people's buttons, you can play them like a piano.

And this is exactly what product designers do to your mind. They play your psychological vulnerabilities (consciously and unconsciously) against you in the race to grab your attention.

I want to show you how they do it.

Hijack #1: If You Control the Menu, You Control the Choices

Western Culture is built around ideals of individual choice and freedom. Millions of us fiercely defend our right to make "free" choices, while we ignore how those choices are manipulated upstream by menus we didn't choose in the first place.

This is exactly what magicians do. They give people the illusion of free choice while architecting the menu so that they win, no matter what you choose. I can't emphasize enough how deep this insight is.

When people are given a menu of choices, they rarely ask:

- "what's not on the menu?"
- "why am I being given *these options* and not others?"
- "do I know the menu provider's goals?"
- "is this menu *empowering* for my original need, or are the choices actually a distraction?" (e.g. an overwhelmingly array of toothpastes)

For example, imagine you're out with friends on a Tuesday night and want to keep the conversation going. You open Yelp to find nearby recommendations and see a list of bars. The group turns into a huddle of faces staring down at their phones *comparing bars*. They scrutinize the photos of each, comparing cocktail drinks. Is this menu still relevant to the original desire of the group?

It's not that bars aren't a good choice, it's that Yelp substituted the group's original question ("where can we go to keep talking?") with a different question ("what's a bar with good photos of cocktails?") all by shaping the menu.

Moreover, the group falls for the illusion that Yelp's menu represents a *complete set of choices* for where to go. While looking down at their phones, they don't see the park across the street with a band playing live music. They miss the pop-up gallery on the other side of the street serving crepes and coffee. Neither of those show up on Yelp's menu.

The more choices technology gives us in nearly every domain of our lives (information, events, places to go, friends, dating, jobs)—*the more we assume that our phone is always the most empowering and useful menu to pick from. Is it?*

The "most empowering" menu is different than the menu that has the most choices. But when we blindly surrender to the menus we're given, it's easy to lose track of the difference:

- "Who's free tonight to hang out?" becomes a menu of *most recent people who texted us* (who we could ping).
- "What's happening in the world?" becomes a menu of news feed stories.
- "Who's single to go on a date?" becomes a menu of faces to swipe on Tinder (instead of local events with friends, or urban adventures nearby).
- "I have to respond to this email" becomes a menu of *keys to type a response* (instead of empowering ways to communicate with a person).

When we wake up in the morning and turn our phone over to see a list of notifications—it frames the experience of "waking up in the morning" around a menu of "all the things I've missed since yesterday."

By shaping the menus we pick from, technology hijacks the way we perceive our choices and replaces them with new ones. But the closer we pay attention to the options we're given, the more we'll notice when they don't actually align with our true needs.

Hijack #2: Put a Slot Machine in a Billion Pockets

If you're an app, how do you keep people hooked? Turn yourself into a slot machine.

The average person checks their phone 150 times a day. Why do we do this? Are we making *150 conscious choices?*

One major reason why is the #1 psychological ingredient in slot machines: **intermittent variable rewards**.

If you want to maximize addictiveness, all tech designers need to do is link a user's action (like pulling a lever) with a *variable reward*. You pull a lever and immediately receive either an enticing reward (a match, a prize!) or nothing. Addictiveness is maximized when the rate of reward is most variable.

Does this effect really work on people? Yes. **Slot machines make more money in the United States than baseball, movies, and theme parks combined**. Relative to other kinds of gambling, people get "problematically involved" with slot machines **3–4x faster** according to NYU professor Natasha Dow Schull, author of *Addiction by Design*.

But here's the unfortunate truth—several billion people have a slot machine their pocket:

- When we pull our phone out of our pocket, we're *playing a slot machine* to see what notifications we got.
- When we pull to refresh our email, we're *playing a slot machine* to see what new email we got.
- When we swipe down our finger to scroll the Instagram feed, we're *playing a slot machine* to see what photo comes next.
- When we swipe faces left/right on dating apps like Tinder, we're *playing a slot machine* to see if we got a match.
- When we tap the # of red notifications, we're *playing a slot machine* to what's underneath.

Apps and websites sprinkle intermittent variable rewards all over their products because it's good for business.

But in other cases, slot machines emerge by accident. For example, there is no malicious corporation behind *all of email* who consciously chose to make it a slot machine. No one profits when millions check their email and nothing's there. Neither did Apple and Google's designers *want* phones to work like slot machines. It emerged by accident.

But now companies like Apple and Google have a responsibility to reduce these effects by *converting intermittent variable rewards into less addictive, more predictable ones* with better design. For example, they could empower people to set predictable times during the day or week for when they want to check "slot machine" apps, and correspondingly adjust when new messages are delivered to align with those times.

Hijack #3: Fear of Missing Something Important (FOMSI)

Another way apps and websites hijack people's minds is by inducing a "1% chance you could be missing something important."

If I convince you that I'm a channel for important information, messages, friendships, or potential sexual opportunities—it will be hard for you to turn me off, unsubscribe, or remove your account—because (aha, I win) you might miss something important:

- This keeps us subscribed to newsletters even after they haven't delivered recent benefits ("what if I miss a future announcement?")
- This keeps us "friended" to people with whom we haven't spoken in ages ("what if I miss something important from them?")
- This keeps us swiping faces on dating apps, even when we haven't even met up with anyone in a while ("what if I miss that *one hot match* who likes me?")
- This keeps us using social media ("what if I miss that important news story or fall behind what my friends are talking about?")

But if we zoom into that fear, we'll discover that it's unbounded: *we'll always miss something important* at any point when we stop using something.

- There are magic moments on Facebook we'll miss by not using it for the 6th hour (e.g. an old friend who's visiting town *right now*).
- There are magic moments we'll miss on Tinder (e.g. our dream romantic partner) by not swiping our 700th match.
- There are emergency phone calls we'll miss if we're not connected 24/7.

But living moment to moment with the fear of missing something isn't how we're built to live.

And it's amazing how quickly, once we let go of that fear, we wake up from the illusion. When we unplug for more than a day, unsubscribe from those notifications, or go to Camp Grounded—the concerns we thought we'd have don't actually happen.

We don't miss what we don't see.

The thought, "what if I miss something important?" is generated *in advance of unplugging, unsubscribing, or turning off*—not after. Imagine if tech companies recognized that, and helped us proactively tune our relationships with friends and businesses in terms of what we define as "time well spent" for our lives, instead of in terms of what we might miss.

Hijack #4: Social Approval

We're all vulnerable to **social approval**. The need to belong, to be approved or appreciated by our peers is among the highest human motivations. But now our social approval is in the hands of tech companies.

When I get tagged by my friend Marc, I imagine him making a *conscious choice* to tag me. But I don't see how a company like Facebook orchestrated his doing that in the first place.

Facebook, Instagram or SnapChat can manipulate how often people get tagged in photos by automatically suggesting all the faces people should tag (e.g. by showing a box with a 1-click confirmation, "Tag Tristan in this photo?").

So when Marc tags me, *he's actually responding to Facebook's suggestion*, not making an independent choice. But through design choices like this, *Facebook controls the multiplier for how often millions of people experience their social approval on the line.*

The same happens when we change our main profile photo—Facebook knows that's a moment when we're *vulnerable to social approval: "what do my friends think of my new pic?"* Facebook can rank this higher in the news feed, so it sticks around for longer and more friends will like or comment on it. Each time they like or comment on it, we'll get pulled right back.

Everyone innately responds to social approval, but some demographics (teenagers) are more vulnerable to it than others. That's why it's so important to recognize how powerful designers are when they exploit this vulnerability.

Hijack #5: Social Reciprocity (Tit-for-Tat)

- You do me a favor—I owe you one next time.
- You say, "thank you"—I have to say "you're welcome."
- You send me an email—it's rude not to get back to you.
- You follow me—it's rude not to follow you back (especially for teenagers).

We are *vulnerable to needing to reciprocate others' gestures*. But as with Social Approval, tech companies now manipulate how often we experience it.

In some cases, it's by accident. *Email, texting and messaging apps are social reciprocity factories.* But in other cases, companies exploit this vulnerability on purpose.

LinkedIn is the most obvious offender. LinkedIn wants as many people creating social obligations for each other as possible, because each time they reciprocate (by accepting a connection, responding to a message, or endorsing someone back for a skill) they have to come back to linkedin.com where they can get people to spend more time.

Like Facebook, LinkedIn exploits an asymmetry in perception. When you receive an invitation from someone to connect, you imagine that person making a *conscious choice* to invite you, when in reality, they likely unconsciously responded to LinkedIn's list of suggested contacts. In other words, LinkedIn turns your *unconscious impulses* (to "add" a person) into new social obligations that millions of people feel obligated to repay. All while they profit from the time people spend doing it.

Imagine millions of people getting interrupted like this throughout their day, running around like chickens with their heads cut off, reciprocating each other—all designed by companies who profit from it.

Welcome to social media.

Imagine if technology companies had a responsibility to minimize social reciprocity. Or if there was an independent organization that represented the public's interests—an industry consortium or an FDA for tech—that monitored when technology companies abused these biases?

Hijack #6: Bottomless Bowls, Infinite Feeds, and Autoplay

Another way to hijack people is to keep them consuming things, even when they aren't hungry anymore.

How? Easy. *Take an experience that was bounded and finite, and turn it into a bottomless flow that keeps going.*

Cornell professor Brian Wansink demonstrated this in his study showing you can trick people to keep eating soup by giving them a bottomless bowl that automatically refills as they eat. With bottomless bowls, people eat 73% more calories than those with normal bowls and underestimate how many calories they ate by 140 calories.

Tech companies exploit the same principle. News feeds are purposely designed to auto-refill with reasons to keep you scrolling, and purposely eliminate any reason for you to pause, reconsider or leave.

It's also why video and social media sites like Netflix, YouTube or Facebook *autoplay* the next video after a countdown instead of waiting for you to make a conscious choice (in case you won't). A huge portion of traffic on these websites is driven by autoplaying the next thing.

Tech companies often claim that "we're just making it easier for users to see the video *they want* to watch" when they are actually serving their business interests. And you can't blame them, because increasing "time spent" is the currency they compete for.

Instead, imagine if technology companies empowered you to *consciously bound your experience* to align with what would be "time well spent" for you. Not just bounding the *quantity* of time you spend, but the *qualities* of what would be "time well spent."

Hijack #7: Instant Interruption vs. "Respectful" Delivery

Companies know that messages *that interrupt people immediately are more persuasive at getting people to respond* than messages delivered asynchronously (like email or any deferred inbox).

Given the choice, Facebook Messenger (or WhatsApp, WeChat or SnapChat for that matter) would *prefer to design their messaging system to interrupt recipients immediately (and show a chat box)* instead of helping users respect each other's attention.

In other words, interruption is good for business.

It's also in their interest to heighten the feeling of urgency and social reciprocity. For example, Facebook automatically *tells the sender when you "saw" their message, instead of letting you avoid disclosing whether you read it* ("now that you know I've seen the message, I feel even more obligated to respond").

By contrast, Apple more respectfully lets users toggle "Read Receipts" on or off.

The problem is, maximizing interruptions in the name of business creates a tragedy of the commons, ruining global attention spans and causing billions of unnecessary interruptions each day. This is a huge problem we need to fix with shared design standards (potentially, as part of Time Well Spent).

Hijack #8: Bundling Your Reasons with Their Reasons

Another way apps hijack you is by taking *your reasons* for visiting the app (to perform a task) and *make them inseparable from the app's business reasons* (maximizing how much we consume once we're there).

For example, in the physical world of grocery stores, the #1 and #2 most popular reasons to visit are pharmacy refills and buying milk. But grocery stores want to maximize how much people buy, so they put the pharmacy and the milk at the back of the store.

In other words, they make the thing customers want (milk, pharmacy) inseparable from what the business wants. If stores were truly organized to support people, they would put the most popular items in the front.

Tech companies design their websites the same way. For example, when you want to look up a Facebook event happening tonight (your reason) the Facebook app doesn't allow you to access it without first landing on the news feed (their reasons), and that's on purpose. *Facebook wants to convert every reason you have for using Facebook, into their reason which is to maximize the time you spend consuming things.*

Instead, imagine if . . .

- Twitter gave you a *separate way* to post a tweet than having to see their news feed.
- Facebook gave a *separate way* to look up Facebook Events going on tonight, without being forced to use their news feed.
- Facebook gave you a *separate way* to use Facebook Connect as a passport for creating new accounts on 3rd party apps and websites, without being forced to install Facebook's entire app, news feed and notifications.

In a Time Well Spent world, there is always a *direct way* to get what you want *separately* from what businesses want. Imagine a digital "bill of rights" outlining design standards that forced the products used by billions of people to let them navigate directly to what they want without needing to go through intentionally placed distractions.

Hijack #9: Inconvenient Choices

We're told that it's enough for businesses to "make choices available."

- "If you don't like it you can always use a different product."
- "If you don't like it, you can always unsubscribe."
- "If you're addicted to our app, you can always uninstall it from your phone."

Businesses naturally want to make the choices *they want you to make easier, and the choices they don't want you to make harder.* Magicians do the same thing. You make it easier for a spectator to pick the thing you want them to pick, and harder to pick the thing you don't.

For example, NYTimes.com lets you "make a free choice" to cancel your digital subscription. But instead of just doing it when you hit "Cancel Subscription," they *send you an email with information on how to cancel your account by calling a phone number* that's only open at certain times.

Instead of viewing the world in terms of *availability of choices*, we should view the world in terms of *friction required to enact choices.* Imagine a world where choices were labeled with how difficult they were to fulfill (like coefficients of friction) and there was an independent entity—an industry consortium or non-profit—that labeled these difficulties and set standards for how easy navigation should be.

Hijack #10: Forecasting Errors, "Foot in the Door" Strategies

Lastly, apps can exploit people's inability to forecast the consequences of a click.

People don't intuitively forecast the *true cost of a click* when it's presented to them. Sales people use "foot in the door" techniques by asking for a small innocuous request to begin with ("just one click to see which tweet got retweeted") and escalate from there ("why don't you stay awhile?"). Virtually all engagement websites use this trick.

Imagine if web browsers and smartphones, the gateways through which people make these choices, were truly watching out for people and helped them forecast the consequences of clicks (based on real data about what benefits and costs it actually had)?

That's why I add "Estimated reading time" to the top of my posts. When you put the "true cost" of a choice in front of people, you're treating your users or audience with dignity and respect. In a Time Well Spent internet, choices could be framed in terms of projected cost and benefit, so people were empowered to make informed choices by default, not by doing extra work.

Summary and How We Can Fix This

Are you upset that technology hijacks your agency? I am too. I've listed a few techniques but there are literally thousands. Imagine whole bookshelves, seminars, workshops and trainings that teach aspiring tech entrepreneurs techniques like these. Imagine hundreds of engineers whose job every day is to invent new ways to keep you hooked.

The ultimate freedom is a free mind, and we need technology that's on our team to help us live, feel, think and act freely.

We need our smartphones, notifications, screens and web browsers to be exoskeletons for our minds and interpersonal relationships that put our values, not our impulses, first. People's time is valuable. And we should protect it with the same rigor as privacy and other digital rights.

REFLECTING AND DISCUSSING

1. The essay begins, "I'm an expert on how technology hijacks our psychological vulnerabilities. That's why I spent the last three years as a Design Ethicist at Google." In what ways does Harris's decision to establish his credibility early on inform the way you approach his argument (if it does)? Discuss.
2. Harris's original essay includes a variety of photographs and screen captures. How effective is the piece without these images? Explain. If you were to add images to the piece, what images would you choose, and why?
3. Harris asks, rhetorically, "Where does technology exploit our minds' weakness?" Using evidence from the essay and your own experience, how might you answer this question?

CONNECTING AND WRITING

1. Analyze your own overengagement with technology through the lens of Harris's arguments. Craft a thesis to argue a point of view about the hijacking of your own mind and the ways in which Harris's essay supports your contentions.
2. "Hijack #1" argues that "if you control the menu, you control the choices." Harris goes on to say, "This is exactly what magicians do. They give people the illusion of free choice while architecting the menu so that they win, no matter what you choose." Explore this comparison and analyze a form of technology with which you interact regularly. Does the issue about "free choice" still hold? Why or why not? Use specific examples to back up your points.
3. Consider Harris's quoting of a Cornell University professor's research about the bottomless bowl of soup. Harris argues that tech companies similarly exploit this principle. What might be a solution to this problem? Take a look at the site *Time Well Spent* and similar resources. Write an essay in which you explore the validity of the solutions Harris (and/or others) proposes to this problem and what further solutions could be proposed to discourage "bottomless" technology.

The Information: How the Internet Gets Inside Us

Adam Gopnik (1956–   )

Writer and essayist Adam Gopnik's work spans multiple genres, including memoir, fiction, children's literature, and art criticism. From 1987 to 1995, he was the art critic for the New Yorker *and later went on to become the magazine's Paris correspondent, an experience that led to the publication of his well-known book* Paris to the Moon *(2000). Gopnik has received three national awards for his magazine writing, is a regular contributor to BBC radio, and has won a George Polk Award for magazine reporting.*

When the first Harry Potter book appeared, in 1997, it was just a year before the universal search engine Google was launched. And so Hermione Granger, that charming grind, still goes to the Hogwarts library and spends hours and hours working her way through the stacks, finding out what a basilisk is or how to make a love potion. The idea that a wizard in training might have, instead, a magic pad where she could inscribe a name and in half a second have an avalanche of news stories, scholarly articles, books, and images (including images she shouldn't be looking at) was a Quidditch broom too far. Now, having been stuck with the library shtick, she has to go on working the stacks in the Harry Potter movies, while the kids who have since come of age nudge their parents. "Why is she doing that?" they whisper. "Why doesn't she just Google it?"

That the reality of machines can outpace the imagination of magic, and in so short a time, does tend to lend weight to the claim that the technological shifts in communication we're living with are unprecedented. It isn't just that we've lived one technological revolution among many; it's that our technological revolution is the big social revolution that we live with. The past twenty years have seen a revolution less in morals, which have remained mostly static, than in means: you could already say "fuck" on HBO back in the eighties; the change has been our ability to tweet or IM or text it. The set subject of our novelists is information; the set obsession of our dons is what it does to our intelligence.

The scale of the transformation is such that an ever-expanding literature has emerged to censure or celebrate it. A series of books explaining why books no longer matter is a paradox that Chesterton would have found implausible, yet there they are, and they come in the typical flavors: the eulogistic, the alarmed, the sober, and the gleeful. When the electric toaster was invented, there were, no doubt, books that said that the toaster would open up horizons for breakfast undreamed of in the days of burning bread over an open flame; books that told you that the toaster would bring an end to the days of creative breakfast, since our children, growing up with uniformly sliced bread, made to fit a single opening, would never know what a loaf of their own was like; and books that told you that sometimes the toaster would make breakfast better and sometimes it would make breakfast worse, and that the cost for finding this out would be the price of the book you'd just bought.

All three kinds appear among the new books about the Internet: call them the Never-Betters, the Better-Nevers, and the Ever-Wasers. The Never-Betters believe that we're on the brink of a new utopia, where information will be free and democratic, news will be made from the bottom up, love will reign, and cookies will bake themselves. The Better-Nevers think that we would have been better off if the whole thing had never happened, that the world that is coming to an end is superior to the one that is taking its place, and that, at a minimum, books and magazines create private space for minds in ways that twenty-second bursts of information don't. The Ever-Wasers insist that at any moment in modernity something like this is going on, and that a new way of organizing data and connecting users is always thrilling to some and chilling to others—that something like this is going on is exactly what makes it a modern moment. One's hopes rest with the Never-Betters; one's head with the Ever-Wasers; and one's heart? Well, twenty or so books in, one's heart tends to move toward the Better-Nevers, and then bounce back toward someplace that looks more like home.

Among the Never-Betters, the N.Y.U. professor Clay Shirky—the author of *Cognitive Surplus* and many articles and blog posts proclaiming the coming of the digital millennium—is the breeziest and seemingly most self-confident. "Seemingly," because there is an element of overdone provocation in his stuff (So people aren't reading Tolstoy? Well, Tolstoy *sucks*) that suggests something a little nervous going on underneath. Shirky believes that we are on the crest of an ever-surging wave of democratized information: the Gutenberg printing press produced the Reformation, which produced the Scientific Revolution, which produced the Enlightenment, which produced the Internet, each move more liberating than the one before. Though it may take a little time, the new connective technology, by joining people together in new communities and in new ways, is bound to make for more freedom. It's the *Wired* version of Whig history: ever better, onward and upward, progress unstopped. In John Brockman's anthology *Is the Internet Changing the Way You Think?*, the evolutionary psychologist John Tooby shares the excitement—"We see all around us transformations in the making that will rival or exceed the printing revolution"—and makes the same extended parallel to Gutenberg: "Printing ignited the previously wasted intellectual potential of huge segments of the population. . . . Freedom of thought and speech—where they exist—were unforeseen offspring of the printing press."

Shirky's and Tooby's version of Never-Betterism has its excitements, but the history it uses seems to have been taken from the back of a cereal box. The idea, for instance, that the printing press rapidly gave birth to a new order of information, democratic and bottom-up, is a cruel cartoon of the truth. If the printing press *did* propel the Reformation, one of the biggest ideas it propelled was Luther's newly invented absolutist anti-Semitism. And what followed the Reformation wasn't the Enlightenment, a new era of openness and freely disseminated knowledge. What followed the Reformation was, actually, the Counter-Reformation, which used the same means—i.e., printed books—to spread ideas about what jerks the reformers were, and unleashed a hundred years of religious warfare. In the seventeen-fifties, more than two centuries later, Voltaire was still writing in a book about the horrors of those other books that urged burning men alive in auto-da-fé. Buried in Tooby's little parenthetical—"where they exist"—are millions of human bodies. If ideas of democracy and freedom emerged at the end of the printing-press era, it wasn't by some technological logic but because of parallel inventions, like the ideas of limited government and religious tolerance, very hard won from history.

Of course, if you stretch out the time scale enough, and are sufficiently casual about causes, you can give the printing press credit for anything you like. But all the media of modern consciousness—from the printing press to radio and the movies— were used just as readily by authoritarian reactionaries, and then by modern totalitarians, to reduce liberty and enforce conformity as they ever were by libertarians to expand it. As Andrew Pettegree shows in his fine new study, *The Book in the Renaissance*, the mainstay of the printing revolution in seventeenth-century Europe was not dissident pamphlets but royal edicts, printed by the thousand: almost all the new media of that day were working, in essence, for kinglouis.gov.

Even later, full-fledged totalitarian societies didn't burn books. They burned *some* books, while keeping the printing presses running off such quantities that by the mid-fifties Stalin was said to have more books in print than Agatha Christie. (Recall that in *1984* Winston's girlfriend works for the Big Brother publishing house.) If you're going to give the printed book, or any other machine-made thing, credit for all the good things that have happened, you have to hold it accountable for the bad stuff, too. The Internet *may* make for more freedom a hundred years from now, but there's no historical law that says it has to.

Many of the more knowing Never-Betters turn for cheer not to messy history and mixed-up politics but to psychology—to the actual expansion of our minds. The argument, advanced in Andy Clark's *Supersizing the Mind* and in Robert K. Logan's *The Sixth Language*, begins with the claim that cognition is not a little processing program that takes place inside your head, Robby the Robot style. It is a constant flow of information, memory, plans, and physical movements, in which as much thinking goes on out there as in here. If television produced the global village, the Internet produces the global psyche: everyone keyed in like a neuron, so that to the eyes of a watching Martian we are really part of a single planetary brain. Contraptions don't change consciousness; contraptions are part of consciousness. We may not act better than we used to, but we sure think differently than we did.

Cognitive entanglement, after all, is the rule of life. My memories and my wife's intermingle. When I can't recall a name or a date, I don't look it up; I just ask her. Our machines, in this way, become our substitute spouses and plug-in companions. Jerry Seinfeld said that the public library was everyone's pathetic friend, giving up its books at a casual request and asking you only to please return them in a month or so. Google is really the world's Thurber wife: smiling patiently and smugly as she explains what the difference is between eulogy and elegy and what the best route is to that little diner outside Hackensack. The new age is one in which we have a know-it-all spouse at our fingertips.

But, if cognitive entanglement exists, so does cognitive exasperation. Husbands and wives deny each other's memories as much as they depend on them. That's fine until it really counts (say, in divorce court). In a practical, immediate way, one sees the limits of the so-called "extended mind" clearly in the mob-made Wikipedia, the perfect product of that new vast, supersized cognition: when there's easy agreement, it's fine, and when there's widespread disagreement on values or facts, as with, say, the origins of capitalism, it's fine, too; you get both sides. The trouble comes when one side is right and the other side is wrong and doesn't know it. The Shakespeare authorship page and the Shroud of Turin page are scenes of constant conflict and are packed with unreliable information. Creationists crowd cyberspace every bit as effectively as evolutionists, and extend their minds just as fully. Our trouble is not the over-all absence of smartness but the intractable power of pure stupidity, and no machine, or mind, seems extended enough to cure that.

The books by the Better-Nevers are more moving than those by the Never-Betters for the same reason that Thomas Gray was at his best in that graveyard: loss is always the great poetic subject. Nicholas Carr, in *The Shallows*, William Powers, in *Hamlet's BlackBerry*, and Sherry Turkle, in *Alone Together*, all bear intimate witness to a sense that the newfound land, the ever-present BlackBerry-and-instant-message world, is one whose price, paid in frayed nerves and lost reading hours and broken attention, is hardly worth the gains it gives us. "The medium does matter," Carr has written. "As a technology, a book focuses our attention, isolates us from the myriad distractions that fill our everyday lives. A networked computer does precisely the opposite. It is designed to scatter our attention. . . . Knowing that the depth of our thought is tied directly to the intensity of our attentiveness, it's hard not to conclude that as we adapt to the intellectual environment of the Net our thinking becomes shallower."

These three Better-Nevers have slightly different stories to tell. Carr is most concerned about the way the Internet breaks down our capacity for reflective thought. His testimony about how this happened in his own life is plangent and familiar, but he addles it a bit by insisting that the real damage is being done at the neurological level, that our children are having their brains altered by too much instant messaging and the like. This sounds impressive but turns out to be redundant. Of course the changes are in their brains; where else would they be? It's the equivalent of saying that playing football doesn't just affect a kid's fitness; it changes the muscle tone that creates his ability to throw and catch footballs.

Powers's reflections are more family-centered and practical. He recounts, very touchingly, stories of family life broken up by the eternal consultation of smartphones and computer monitors:

> Somebody excuses themselves for a bathroom visit or a glass of water and doesn't return. Five minutes later, another of us exits on a similarly mundane excuse along the lines of "I have to check something.". . . Where have all the humans gone? To their screens of course. Where they always go these days. The digital crowd has a way of elbowing its way into everything, to the point where a family can't sit in a room together for half an hour without somebody, or everybody, peeling off. . . . As I watched the Vanishing Family Trick unfold, and played my own part in it, I sometimes felt as if love itself, or the acts of heart and mind that constitute love, were being leached out of the house by our screens.

He then surveys seven Wise Men—Plato, Thoreau, Seneca, the usual gang—who have something to tell us about solitude and the virtues of inner space, all of it sound enough, though he tends to overlook the significant point that these worthies were not entirely in favor of the kinds of liberties that we now take for granted and that made the new dispensation possible. (He knows that Seneca instructed the Emperor Nero, but sticks in a footnote to insist that the bad, fiddling-while-Rome-burned Nero asserted himself only after he fired the philosopher and started to act like an Internet addict.)

Similarly, Nicholas Carr cites Martin Heidegger for having seen, in the mid-fifties, that new technologies would break the meditational space on which Western wisdoms depend. Since Heidegger had not long before walked straight out of his own meditational space into the arms of the Nazis, it's hard to have much nostalgia for this version of the past. One feels the same doubts when Sherry Turkle, in *Alone Together*, her touching plaint about the destruction of the old intimacy-reading culture by the new remote-connection-Internet culture, cites studies that show a dramatic decline in empathy among college students, who apparently are "far less likely to say that it is valuable to put oneself in the place of others or to try and understand their feelings." What is to be done? Other Better-Nevers point to research that's supposed to show that people who read novels develop exceptional empathy. But if reading a lot of novels gave you exceptional empathy university English departments should be filled with the most compassionate and generous-minded of souls, and, so far, they are not.

One of the things that John Brockman's collection on the Internet and the mind illustrates is that when people struggle to describe the state that the Internet puts them in they arrive at a remarkably familiar picture of disassociation and fragmentation. Life was once whole, continuous, stable; now it is fragmented, multi-part, shimmering around us, unstable and impossible to fix. The world becomes Keats's "waking dream," as the writer Kevin Kelly puts it.

The odd thing is that this complaint, though deeply felt by our contemporary Better-Nevers, is identical to Baudelaire's perception about modern Paris in 1855, or Walter Benjamin's about Berlin in 1930, or Marshall McLuhan's in the face of three-channel television (and Canadian television, at that) in 1965. When department stores had Christmas windows with clockwork puppets, the world was going to pieces; when the city streets were filled with horse-drawn carriages running by bright-colored posters, you could no longer tell the real from the simulated; when people were listening to shellac 78s and looking at color newspaper supplements, the world had become a kaleidoscope of disassociated imagery; and when the broadcast air was filled with droning black-and-white images of men in suits reading news, all of life had become indistinguishable from your fantasies of it. It was Marx, not Steve Jobs, who said that the character of modern life is that everything falls apart.

We must, at some level, *need* this to be true, since we think it's true about so many different kinds of things. We experience this sense of fracture so deeply that we ascribe it to machines that, viewed with retrospective detachment, don't seem remotely capable of producing it. If all you have is a hammer, the saying goes, everything looks like a nail; and, if you think the world is broken, every machine looks like the hammer that broke it.

It is an intuition of this kind that moves the final school, the Ever-Wasers, when they consider the new digital age. A sense of vertiginous overload is the central experience of modernity, they say; at every moment, machines make new circuits for connection and circulation, as obvious-seeming as the postage stamps that let nineteenth-century scientists collaborate by mail, or as newfangled as the Wi-Fi connection that lets a sixteen-year-old in New York consult a tutor in Bangalore. Our new confusion is just the same old confusion.

Among Ever-Wasers, the Harvard historian Ann Blair may be the most ambitious. In her book *Too Much to Know: Managing Scholarly Information Before the Modern Age*, she makes the case that what we're going through is like what others went through a very long while ago. Against the cartoon history of Shirky or Tooby, Blair argues that the sense of "information overload" was not the consequence of Gutenberg but already in place before printing began. She wants us to resist "trying to reduce the complex causal nexus behind the transition from Renaissance to Enlightenment to the impact of a technology or any particular set of ideas." Anyway, the crucial revolution was not of print but of paper: "During the later Middle Ages a staggering growth in the production of manuscripts, facilitated by the use of paper, accompanied a great expansion of readers outside the monastic and scholastic contexts." For that matter, our minds were altered less by books than by index slips. Activities that seem quite twenty-first century, she shows, began when people cut and pasted from one manuscript to another; made aggregated news in compendiums; passed around précis. "Early modern finding devices" were forced into existence: lists of authorities, lists of headings.

Everyone complained about what the new information technologies were doing to our minds. Everyone said that the flood of books produced a restless, fractured attention. Everyone complained that pamphlets and poems were breaking kids' ability to concentrate, that big good handmade books were ignored, swept aside by printed works that, as Erasmus said, "are foolish, ignorant, malignant, libelous, mad." The reader consulting a card catalogue in a library was living a revolution as momentous, and as disorienting, as our own. The book index was the search engine of its era, and needed to be explained at length to puzzled researchers—as, for that matter, did the Hermione-like idea of "looking things up." That uniquely evil and necessary thing the comprehensive review of many different books on a related subject, with the necessary oversimplification of their ideas that it demanded, was already around in 1500, and already being accused of missing all the points. In the period when many of the big, classic books that we no longer have time to read were being written, the general complaint was that there wasn't enough time to read big, classic books.

Blair's and Pettegree's work on the relation between minds and machines, and the combination of delight and despair we find in their collisions, leads you to a broader thought: at any given moment, our most complicated machine will be taken as a model of human intelligence, and whatever media kids favor will be identified as the cause of our stupidity. When there were automatic looms, the mind was like an automatic loom; and, since young people in the loom period liked novels, it was the cheap novel that was degrading our minds. When there were telephone exchanges, the mind was like a telephone exchange, and, in the same period, since the nickelodeon reigned, moving pictures were making us dumb. When mainframe computers arrived and television was what kids liked, the mind was like a mainframe and television was the engine of our idiocy. Some machine is always showing us Mind; some entertainment derived from the machine is always showing us Non-Mind.

Armed with such parallels, the Ever Wasers smile condescendingly at the Better-Nevers and say, "Of course, some new machine is always ruining everything. We've all been here before." But the Better-Nevers can say, in return, "What if the Internet is actually doing it?" The hypochondriac frets about this bump or that suspicious freckle and we laugh—but sooner or later one small bump, one jagged-edge freckle, will be the thing for certain. Worlds really do decline. "Oh, they always say that about the barbarians, but every generation has its barbarians, and every generation assimilates them," one Roman reassured another when the Vandals were at the gates, and next thing you knew there wasn't a hot bath or a good book for another thousand years.

And, if it was ever thus, how did it ever get to be thus in the first place? The digital world is new, and the real gains and losses of the Internet era are to be found not in altered neurons or empathy tests but in the small changes in mood, life, manners, feelings it creates—in the texture of the age. There is, for instance, a simple, spooky sense in which the Internet is just a loud and unlimited library in which we now live— as if one went to sleep every night in the college stacks, surrounded by pamphlets and polemics and possibilities. There is the sociology section, the science section, old sheet music and menus, and you can go to the periodicals room anytime and read old issues of the *New Statesman*. (And you can whisper loudly to a friend in the next carrel to get the hockey scores.) To see that that is so is at least to drain some of the melodrama from the subject. It is odd and new to be living in the library; but there isn't anything odd and new about the library.

Yet surely having something wrapped right around your mind is different from having your mind wrapped tightly around something. What we live in is not the age of the extended mind but the age of the inverted self. The things that have usually lived in the darker recesses or mad corners of our mind—sexual obsessions and con-spiracy theories, paranoid fixations and fetishes—are now out there: you click once and you can read about the Kennedy autopsy or the Nazi salute or hog-tied Swedish flight attendants. But things that were once external and subject to the social rules of caution and embarrassment—above all, our interactions with other people—are now easily internalized, made to feel like mere workings of the id left on its own. (I've felt this myself, writing anonymously on hockey forums: it is easy to say vile things about Gary Bettman, the commissioner of the N.H.L., with a feeling of glee rather than with a sober sense that what you're saying should be tempered by a little truth and reflection.) Thus the limitless malice of Internet commenting: it's not newly unleashed anger but what we all think in the first order, and have always in the past socially restrained if only thanks to the look on the listener's face—the monstrous music that runs through our minds is now played out loud.

A social network is crucially different from a social circle, since the function of a social circle is to curb our appetites and of a network to extend them. Everything once inside is outside, a click away; much that used to be outside is inside, experienced in solitude. And so the peacefulness, the serenity that we feel away from the Internet, and which all the Better-Nevers rightly testify to, has less to do with being no longer harried by others than with being less oppressed by the force of your own inner life. Shut off your computer, and your self stops raging quite as much or quite as loud.

It is the wraparound presence, not the specific evils, of the machine that oppresses us. Simply reducing the machine's presence will go a long way toward alleviating the disorder. Which points, in turn, to a dog-not-barking-in-the-nighttime detail that may be significant. In the Better-Never books, television isn't scanted or ignored; it's celebrated. When William Powers, in *Hamlet's BlackBerry*, describes the deal his family makes to have an Unplugged Sunday, he tells us that the No Screens agreement doesn't include television: "For us, television had always been a mostly communal experience, a way of coming together rather than pulling apart." ("Can you please turn off your damn computer and come watch television with the rest of the family," the dad now cries to the teen ager.)

Yet everything that is said about the Internet's destruction of "interiority" was said for decades about television, and just as loudly. Jerry Mander's *Four Arguments for the Elimination of Television*, in the nineteen-seventies, turned on television's addictive nature and its destruction of viewers' inner lives; a little later, George Trow proposed that television produced the absence of context, the disintegration of the frame—the very things, in short, that the Internet is doing now. And Bill McKibben ended his book on television by comparing watching TV to watching ducks on a pond (advantage: ducks), in the same spirit in which Nicholas Carr leaves his computer screen to read *Walden*.

Now television is the harmless little fireplace over in the corner, where the family gathers to watch *Entourage*. TV isn't just docile; it's positively benevolent. This makes you think that what made television so evil back when it was evil was not its essence but its omnipresence. Once it is not everything, it can be merely something. The real demon in the machine is the tirelessness of the user. A meatless Monday has advantages over enforced vegetarianism, because it helps release the pressure on the food system without making undue demands on the eaters. In the same way, an unplugged Sunday is a better idea than turning off the Internet completely, since it demonstrates that we can get along just fine without the screens, if only for a day.

Hermione, stuck in the nineties, never did get her iPad, and will have to manage in the stacks. But perhaps the instrument of the new connected age was already in place in fantasy. For the Internet screen has always been like the palantír in Tolkien's *Lord of the Rings*—the "seeing stone" that lets the wizards see the entire world. Its gift is great; the wizard can see it all. Its risk is real: evil things will register more vividly than the great mass of dull good. The peril isn't that users lose their knowledge of the world. It's that they can lose all sense of proportion. You can come to think that the armies of Mordor are not just vast and scary, which they are, but limitless and undefeatable, which they aren't.

REFLECTING AND DISCUSSING

1. Why do you think Gopnik chose to make "The Information" the first part of his title? Is it deliberately ambiguous? Why? What effect does this choice have on the reader?
2. "But, if cognitive entanglement exists, so does cognitive exasperation." How might Gopnik define these terms? How are they related to an overall (and excessive) reliance on the Internet?
3. What is the relationship between the Better-Nevers and the Never-Betters? How does this evoke our relationship with books and our relationship with the Internet?

CONNECTING AND WRITING

1. "Thoughts are bigger than the things that deliver them. Our contraptions may shape our consciousness, but it's our consciousness that shapes our credos." Delineate what you believe to be the implications of Gopnik's argument. If he doesn't explicitly pose solutions to the problems he outlines, what do you think they would be? How are such solutions implied? Use specific examples from the essay.

2. Gopnik references three specific books with arguments that parallel his (those by Carr, Powers, and Turkle). Referencing at least part of one of these books, analyze the similarities or differences in the authors' arguments and explore how they make the same arguments differently—or similarly. Be sure to come to your own point of view, using evidence from the different works to back up your overall point.

Is Facebook Making Us Lonely?

Stephen Marche (1976–   )

Stephen Marche is a Canadian writer and a columnist for numerous publications, including Esquire *and the* Atlantic Monthly. *The author of several books, including* The Hunger of the Wolf *(2015),* How Shakespeare Changed Everything *(2012), and* Shining at the Bottom of the Sea *(2007), Marche holds a doctorate in early modern drama from the University of Toronto. This article, originally published in 2012 in the* Atlantic Monthly, *is seen as an early, significant critique of social media.*

Yvette Vickers, a former *Playboy* playmate and B-movie star, best known for her role in *Attack of the 50 Foot Woman*, would have been 83 last August, but nobody knows exactly how old she was when she died. According to the Los Angeles coroner's report, she lay dead for the better part of a year before a neighbor and fellow actress, a woman named Susan Savage, noticed cobwebs and yellowing letters in her mailbox, reached through a broken window to unlock the door, and pushed her way through the piles of junk mail and mounds of clothing that barricaded the house. Upstairs, she found Vickers's body, mummified, near a heater that was still running. Her computer was on too, its glow permeating the empty space.

The *Los Angeles Times* posted a story headlined "Mummified Body of Former Playboy Playmate Yvette Vickers Found in Her Benedict Canyon Home," which quickly went viral. Within two weeks, by Technorati's count, Vickers's lonesome death was already the subject of 16,057 Facebook posts and 881 tweets. She had long been a horror-movie icon, a symbol of Hollywood's capacity to exploit our most basic fears in the silliest ways; now she was an icon of a new and different kind of horror: our growing fear of loneliness. Certainly she received much more attention in death than she did in the final years of her life. With no children, no religious group, and no immediate social circle of any kind, she had begun, as an elderly woman, to look elsewhere for companionship. Savage later told *Los Angeles* magazine that she had searched Vickers's phone bills for clues about the life that led to such an end. In the months before her grotesque death, Vickers had made calls not to friends or family but to distant fans who had found her through fan conventions and Internet sites.

Vickers's web of connections had grown broader but shallower, as has happened for many of us. We are living in an isolation that would have been unimaginable to our ancestors, and yet we have never been more accessible. Over the past three decades, technology has delivered to us a world in which we need not be out of contact for a fraction of a moment. In 2010, at a cost of $300 million, 800 miles of fiber-optic cable was laid between the Chicago Mercantile Exchange and the New York Stock Exchange to shave three milliseconds off trading times. Yet within this world of instant and absolute communication, unbounded by limits of time or space, we suffer from unprecedented alienation. We have never been more detached from one another, or lonelier. In a world consumed by ever more novel modes of socializing, we have less and less actual society. We live in an accelerating contradiction: the more connected we become, the lonelier we are. We were promised a global village; instead we inhabit the drab cul-de-sacs and endless freeways of a vast suburb of information.

At the forefront of all this unexpectedly lonely interactivity is Facebook, with 845 million users and $3.7 billion in revenue last year. The company hopes to raise $5 billion in an initial public offering later this spring, which will make it by far the largest Internet IPO in history. Some recent estimates put the company's potential value at $100 billion, which would make it larger than the global coffee industry— one addiction preparing to surpass the other. Facebook's scale and reach are hard to comprehend: last summer, Facebook became, by some counts, the first Web site to receive 1 trillion page views in a month. In the last three months of 2011, users generated an average of 2.7 billion "likes" and comments every day. On whatever scale you care to judge Facebook—as a company, as a culture, as a country—it is vast beyond imagination.

Despite its immense popularity, or more likely because of it, Facebook has, from the beginning, been under something of a cloud of suspicion. The depiction of Mark Zuckerberg, in *The Social Network*, as a bastard with symptoms of Asperger's syndrome, was nonsense. But it felt true. It felt true to Facebook, if not to Zuckerberg. The film's most indelible scene, the one that may well have earned it an Oscar, was the final, silent shot of an anomic Zuckerberg sending out a friend request to his ex-girlfriend, then waiting and clicking and waiting and clicking—a moment of superconnected loneliness preserved in amber. We have all been in that scene: transfixed by the glare of a screen, hungering for response.

When you sign up for Google+ and set up your Friends circle, the program specifies that you should include only "your real friends, the ones you feel comfortable sharing private details with." That one little phrase, *Your real friends*—so quaint, so charmingly mothering—perfectly encapsulates the anxieties that social media have produced: the fears that Facebook is interfering with our real friendships, distancing us from each other, making us lonelier; and that social networking might be spreading the very isolation it seemed designed to conquer.

Facebook arrived in the middle of a dramatic increase in the quantity and intensity of human loneliness, a rise that initially made the site's promise of greater connection seem deeply attractive. Americans are more solitary than ever before. In 1950, less than 10 percent of American households contained only one person. By 2010, nearly 27 percent of households had just one person. Solitary living does not guarantee a life of unhappiness, of course. In his recent book about the trend toward living alone, Eric Klinenberg, a sociologist at NYU, writes: "Reams of published research show that it's the quality, not the quantity of social interaction, that best predicts loneliness." True. But before we begin the fantasies of happily eccentric singledom, of divorcées dropping by their knitting circles after work for glasses of Drew Barrymore pinot grigio, or recent college graduates with perfectly articulated, Steampunk-themed,

300-square-foot apartments organizing croquet matches with their book clubs, we should recognize that it is not just isolation that is rising sharply. It's loneliness, too. And loneliness makes us miserable.

We know intuitively that loneliness and being alone are not the same thing. Solitude can be lovely. Crowded parties can be agony. We also know, thanks to a growing body of research on the topic, that loneliness is not a matter of external conditions; it is a psychological state. A 2005 analysis of data from a longitudinal study of Dutch twins showed that the tendency toward loneliness has roughly the same genetic component as other psychological problems such as neuroticism or anxiety.

Still, loneliness is slippery, a difficult state to define or diagnose. The best tool yet developed for measuring the condition is the UCLA Loneliness Scale, a series of 20 questions that all begin with this formulation: "How often do you feel . . . ?" As in: "How often do you feel that you are 'in tune' with the people around you?" And: "How often do you feel that you lack companionship?" Measuring the condition in these terms, various studies have shown loneliness rising drastically over a very short period of recent history. A 2010 AARP survey found that 35 percent of adults older than 45 were chronically lonely, as opposed to 20 percent of a similar group only a decade earlier. According to a major study by a leading scholar of the subject, roughly 20 percent of Americans—about 60 million people—are unhappy with their lives because of loneliness. Across the Western world, physicians and nurses have begun to speak openly of an epidemic of loneliness.

The new studies on loneliness are beginning to yield some surprising preliminary findings about its mechanisms. Almost every factor that one might assume affects loneliness does so only some of the time, and only under certain circumstances. People who are married are less lonely than single people, one journal article suggests, but only if their spouses are confidants. If one's spouse is not a confidant, marriage may not decrease loneliness. A belief in God might help, or it might not, as a 1990 German study comparing levels of religious feeling and levels of loneliness discovered. Active believers who saw God as abstract and helpful rather than as a wrathful, immediate presence were less lonely. "The mere belief in God," the researchers concluded, "was relatively independent of loneliness."

But it is clear that social interaction matters. Loneliness and being alone are not the same thing, but both are on the rise. We meet fewer people. We gather less. And when we gather, our bonds are less meaningful and less easy. The decrease in confidants—that is, in quality social connections—has been dramatic over the past 25 years. In one survey, the mean size of networks of personal confidants decreased from 2.94 people in 1985 to 2.08 in 2004. Similarly, in 1985, only 10 percent of Americans said they had no one with whom to discuss important matters, and 15 percent said they had only one such good friend. By 2004, 25 percent had nobody to talk to, and 20 percent had only one confidant.

In the face of this social disintegration, we have essentially hired an army of replacement confidants, an entire class of professional carers. As Ronald Dworkin pointed out in a 2010 paper for the Hoover Institution, in the late '90s, the United States was home to 2,500 clinical psychologists, 30,000 social workers, and fewer than 500 marriage and family therapists. As of 2010, the country had 77,000 clinical psychologists, 192,000 clinical social workers, 400,000 nonclinical social workers, 50,000 marriage and family therapists, 105,000 mental-health counselors, 220,000 substance-abuse counselors, 17,000 nurse psychotherapists, and 30,000 life coaches. The majority of patients in therapy do not warrant a psychiatric diagnosis. This raft of psychic servants is helping us through what used to be called regular problems. We have outsourced the work of everyday caring.

We need professional carers more and more, because the threat of societal breakdown, once principally a matter of nostalgic lament, has morphed into an issue of public health. Being lonely is extremely bad for your health. If you're lonely, you're more likely to be put in a geriatric home at an earlier age than a similar person who isn't lonely. You're less likely to exercise. You're more likely to be obese. You're less likely to survive a serious operation and more likely to have hormonal imbalances. You are at greater risk of inflammation. Your memory may be worse. You are more likely to be depressed, to sleep badly, and to suffer dementia and general cognitive decline. Loneliness may not have killed Yvette Vickers, but it has been linked to a greater probability of having the kind of heart condition that did kill her.

And yet, despite its deleterious effect on health, loneliness is one of the first things ordinary Americans spend their money achieving. With money, you flee the cramped city to a house in the suburbs or, if you can afford it, a McMansion in the exurbs, inevitably spending more time in your car. Loneliness is at the American core, a by-product of a long-standing national appetite for independence: The Pilgrims who left Europe willingly abandoned the bonds and strictures of a society that could not accept their right to be different. They did not seek out loneliness, but they accepted it as the price of their autonomy. The cowboys who set off to explore a seemingly endless frontier likewise traded away personal ties in favor of pride and self-respect. The ultimate American icon is the astronaut: Who is more heroic, or more alone? The price of self-determination and self-reliance has often been loneliness. But Americans have always been willing to pay that price.

Today, the one common feature in American secular culture is its celebration of the self that breaks away from the constrictions of the family and the state, and, in its greatest expressions, from all limits entirely. The great American poem is Whitman's "Song of Myself." The great American essay is Emerson's "Self-Reliance." The great American novel is Melville's *Moby-Dick*, the tale of a man on a quest so lonely that it is incomprehensible to those around him. American culture, high and low, is about self-expression and personal authenticity. Franklin Delano Roosevelt called individualism "the great watchword of American life."

Self-invention is only half of the American story, however. The drive for isolation has always been in tension with the impulse to cluster in communities that cling and suffocate. The Pilgrims, while fomenting spiritual rebellion, also enforced ferocious cohesion. The Salem witch trials, in hindsight, read like attempts to impose solidarity—as do the McCarthy hearings. The history of the United States is like the famous parable of the porcupines in the cold, from Schopenhauer's *Studies in*

Pessimism—the ones who huddle together for warmth and shuffle away in pain, always separating and congregating.

We are now in the middle of a long period of shuffling away. In his 2000 book *Bowling Alone*, Robert D. Putnam attributed the dramatic post-war decline of social capital—the strength and value of interpersonal networks—to numerous interconnected trends in American life: suburban sprawl, television's dominance over culture, the self-absorption of the Baby Boomers, the disintegration of the traditional family. The trends he observed continued through the prosperity of the aughts, and have only become more pronounced with time: the rate of union membership declined in 2011, again; screen time rose; the Masons and the Elks continued their slide into irrelevance. We are lonely because we want to be lonely. We have made ourselves lonely.

The question of the future is this: Is Facebook part of the separating or part of the congregating; is it a huddling-together for warmth or a shuffling-away in pain?

Well before Facebook, digital technology was enabling our tendency for isolation, to an unprecedented degree. Back in the 1990s, scholars started calling the contradiction between an increased opportunity to connect and a lack of human contact the "Internet paradox." A prominent 1998 article on the phenomenon by a team of researchers at Carnegie Mellon showed that increased Internet usage was already coinciding with increased loneliness. Critics of the study pointed out that the two groups that participated in the study—high-school journalism students who were heading to university and socially active members of community-development boards—were statistically likely to become lonelier over time. Which brings us to a more fundamental question: Does the Internet make people lonely, or are lonely people more attracted to the Internet?

The question has intensified in the Facebook era. A recent study out of Australia (where close to half the population is active on Facebook), titled "Who Uses Facebook?," found a complex and sometimes confounding relationship between loneliness and social networking. Facebook users had slightly lower levels of "social loneliness"—the sense of not feeling bonded with friends—but "significantly higher levels of family loneliness"—the sense of not feeling bonded with family. It may be that Facebook encourages more contact with people outside of our household, at the expense of our family relationships—or it may be that people who have unhappy family relationships in the first place seek companionship through other means, including Facebook. The researchers also found that lonely people are inclined to spend more time on Facebook: "One of the most noteworthy findings," they wrote, "was the tendency for neurotic and lonely individuals to spend greater amounts of time on Facebook per day than non-lonely individuals." And they found that neurotics are more likely to prefer to use the wall, while extroverts tend to use chat features in addition to the wall.

Moira Burke, until recently a graduate student at the Human-Computer Institute at Carnegie Mellon, used to run a longitudinal study of 1,200 Facebook users. That study, which is ongoing, is one of the first to step outside the realm of self-selected college students and examine the effects of Facebook on a broader population, over time. She concludes that the effect of Facebook depends on what you bring to it. Just as your mother said: you get out only what you put in. If you use Facebook to communicate directly with other individuals—by using the "like" button, commenting on friends' posts, and so on—it can increase your social capital. Personalized messages, or what Burke calls "composed communication," are more satisfying than "one-click communication"—the lazy click of a like. "People who received composed communication became less lonely, while people who received one-click communication experienced no change in loneliness," Burke tells me. So, you should inform your friend in writing how charming her son looks with Harry Potter cake smeared all over his face, and how interesting her sepia-toned photograph of that tree-framed bit of skyline is, and how cool it is that she's at whatever concert she happens to be at. That's what we all want to hear. Even better than sending a private Facebook message is the semi-public conversation, the kind of back-and-forth in which you half ignore the other people who may be listening in. "People whose friends write to them semi-publicly on Facebook experience decreases in loneliness," Burke says.

On the other hand, non-personalized use of Facebook—scanning your friends' status updates and updating the world on your own activities via your wall, or what Burke calls "passive consumption" and "broadcasting"—correlates to feelings of disconnectedness. It's a lonely business, wandering the labyrinths of our friends' and pseudo-friends' projected identities, trying to figure out what part of ourselves we ought to project, who will listen, and what they will hear. According to Burke, passive consumption of Facebook also correlates to a marginal increase in depression. "If two women each talk to their friends the same amount of time, but one of them spends more time reading about friends on Facebook as well, the one reading tends to grow slightly more depressed," Burke says. Her conclusion suggests that my sometimes unhappy reactions to Facebook may be more universal than I had realized. When I scroll through page after page of my friends' descriptions of how accidentally eloquent their kids are, and how their husbands are endearingly bumbling, and how they're all about to eat a home-cooked meal prepared with fresh local organic produce bought at the farmers' market and then go for a jog and maybe check in at the office because they're so busy getting ready to hop on a plane for a week of luxury dogsledding in Lapland, I do grow slightly more miserable. A lot of other people doing the same thing feel a little bit worse, too.

Still, Burke's research does not support the assertion that Facebook creates loneliness. The people who experience loneliness on Facebook are lonely away from Facebook, too, she points out; on Facebook, as everywhere else, correlation is not causation. The popular kids are popular, and the lonely skulkers skulk alone. Perhaps it says something about me that I think Facebook is primarily a platform for lonely skulking. I mention to Burke the widely reported study, conducted by a Stanford graduate student, that showed how believing that others have strong social networks can lead to feelings of depression. What does Facebook communicate, if not the impression of social bounty? Everybody else looks so happy on Facebook, with so many friends, that our own social networks feel emptier than ever in comparison. Doesn't that *make* people feel lonely? "If people are reading about lives that are much better than theirs, two things can happen," Burke tells me. "They can feel worse about themselves, or they can feel motivated."

Burke will start working at Facebook as a data scientist this year.

Jon Cacioppo, the director of the Center for Cognitive and Social Neuroscience at the University of Chicago, is the world's leading expert on loneliness. In his landmark book, *Loneliness*, released in 2008, he revealed just how profoundly the epidemic of loneliness is affecting the basic functions of human physiology. He found higher levels of epinephrine, the stress hormone, in the morning urine of lonely people. Loneliness burrows deep: "When we drew blood from our older adults and analyzed their white cells," he writes, "we found that loneliness somehow penetrated the deepest recesses of the cell to alter the way genes were being expressed." Loneliness affects not only the brain, then, but the basic process of DNA transcription. When you are lonely, your whole body is lonely.

To Cacioppo, Internet communication allows only ersatz intimacy. "Forming connections with pets or online friends or even God is a noble attempt by an obligatorily gregarious creature to satisfy a compelling need," he writes. "But surrogates can never make up completely for the absence of the real thing." The "real thing" being actual people, in the flesh. When I speak to Cacioppo, he is refreshingly clear on what he sees as Facebook's effect on society. Yes, he allows, some research has suggested that the greater the number of Facebook friends a person has, the less lonely she is. But he argues that the impression this creates can be misleading. "For the most part," he says, "people are bringing their old friends, and feelings of loneliness or connectedness, to Facebook." The idea that a Web site could deliver a more friendly, interconnected world is bogus. The depth of one's social network outside Facebook is what determines the depth of one's social network within Facebook, not the other way around. Using social media doesn't create new social networks; it just transfers established networks from one platform to another. For the most part, Facebook doesn't destroy friendships—but it doesn't create them, either.

In one experiment, Cacioppo looked for a connection between the loneliness of subjects and the relative frequency of their interactions via Facebook, chat rooms, online games, dating sites, and face-to-face contact. The results were unequivocal. "The greater the proportion of face-to-face interactions, the less lonely you are," he says. "The greater the proportion of online interactions, the lonelier you are." Surely, I suggest to Cacioppo, this means that Facebook and the like inevitably make people lonelier. He disagrees. Facebook is merely a tool, he says, and like any tool, its effectiveness will depend on its user. "If you use Facebook to increase face-to-face contact," he says, "it increases social capital." So if social media let you organize a game of football among your friends, that's healthy. If you turn to social media instead of playing football, however, that's unhealthy.

"Facebook can be terrific, if we use it properly," Cacioppo continues. "It's like a car. You can drive it to pick up your friends. Or you can drive alone." But hasn't the car increased loneliness? If cars created the suburbs, surely they also created isolation. "That's because of how we use cars," Cacioppo replies. "How we use these technologies can lead to more integration, rather than more isolation."

The problem, then, is that we invite loneliness, even though it makes us miserable. The history of our use of technology is a history of isolation desired and achieved. When the Great Atlantic and Pacific Tea Company opened its A&P stores, giving Americans self-service access to groceries, customers stopped having relationships with their grocers. When the telephone arrived, people stopped knocking on their neighbors' doors. Social media bring this process to a much wider set of relationships. Researchers at the HP Social Computing Lab who studied the nature of people's connections on Twitter came to a depressing, if not surprising, conclusion: "Most of the links declared within Twitter were meaningless from an interaction point of view." I have to wonder: What other point of view is meaningful?

Loneliness is certainly not something that Facebook or Twitter or any of the lesser forms of social media is doing to us. We are doing it to ourselves. Casting technology as some vague, impersonal spirit of history forcing our actions is a weak excuse. We make decisions about how we use our machines, not the other way around. Every time I shop at my local grocery store, I am faced with a choice. I can buy my groceries from a human being or from a machine. I always, without exception, choose the machine. It's faster and more efficient, I tell myself, but the truth is that I prefer not having to wait with the other customers who are lined up alongside the conveyor belt: the hipster mom who disapproves of my high-carbon-footprint pineapple; the lady who tenses to the point of tears while she waits to see if the gods of the credit-card machine will accept or decline; the old man whose clumsy feebleness requires a patience that I don't possess. Much better to bypass the whole circus and just ring up the groceries myself.

Our omnipresent new technologies lure us toward increasingly superficial connections at exactly the same moment that they make avoiding the mess of human interaction easy. The beauty of Facebook, the source of its power, is that it enables us to be social while sparing us the embarrassing reality of society—the accidental revelations we make at parties, the awkward pauses, the farting and the spilled drinks and the general gaucherie of face-to-face contact. Instead, we have the lovely smoothness of a seemingly social machine. Everything's so simple: status updates, pictures, your wall.

But the price of this smooth sociability is a constant compulsion to assert one's own happiness, one's own fulfillment. Not only must we contend with the social bounty of others; we must foster the appearance of our own social bounty. Being happy all the time, pretending to be happy, actually attempting to be happy—it's exhausting. Last year a team of researchers led by Iris Mauss at the University of Denver published a study looking into "the paradoxical effects of valuing happiness." Most goals in life show a direct correlation between valuation and achievement. Studies have found, for example, that students who value good grades tend to have higher grades than those who don't value them. Happiness is an exception. The study came to a disturbing conclusion:

> Valuing happiness is not necessarily linked to greater happiness. In fact, under certain conditions, the opposite is true. Under conditions of low (but not high) life stress, the more people valued happiness, the lower were their hedonic balance, psychological well-being, and life satisfaction, and the higher their depression symptoms.

The more you try to be happy, the less happy you are. Sophocles made roughly the same point.

Facebook, of course, puts the pursuit of happiness front and center in our digital life. Its capacity to redefine our very concepts of identity and personal fulfillment is much more worrisome than the data-mining and privacy practices that have aroused anxieties about the company. Two of the most compelling critics of Facebook—neither of them a Luddite—concentrate on exactly this point. Jaron Lanier, the author of *You Are Not a Gadget*, was one of the inventors of virtual-reality technology. His view of where social media are taking us reads like dystopian science fiction: "I fear that we are beginning to design ourselves to suit digital models of us, and I worry about a leaching of empathy and humanity in that process." Lanier argues that Facebook imprisons us in the business of self-presenting, and this, to his mind, is the site's crucial and fatally unacceptable downside.

Sherry Turkle, a professor of computer culture at MIT who in 1995 published the digital-positive analysis *Life on the Screen*, is much more skeptical about the effects of online society in her 2011 book, *Alone Together*: "These days, insecure in our relationships and anxious about intimacy, we look to technology for ways to be in relationships and protect ourselves from them at the same time." The problem with digital intimacy is that it is ultimately incomplete: "The ties we form through the Internet are not, in the end, the ties that bind. But they are the ties that preoccupy," she writes. "We don't want to intrude on each other, so instead we constantly intrude on each other, but not in 'real time.'"

Lanier and Turkle are right, at least in their diagnoses. Self-presentation on Facebook is continuous, intensely mediated, and possessed of a phony nonchalance that eliminates even the potential for spontaneity. ("Look how casually I threw up these three photos from the party at which I took 300 photos!") Curating the exhibition of the self has become a 24/7 occupation. Perhaps not surprisingly, then, the Australian study "Who Uses Facebook?" found a significant correlation between Facebook use and narcissism: "Facebook users have higher levels of total narcissism, exhibitionism, and leadership than Facebook nonusers," the study's authors wrote. "In fact, it could be argued that Facebook specifically gratifies the narcissistic individual's need to engage in self-promoting and superficial behavior."

Rising narcissism isn't so much a trend as the trend behind all other trends. In preparation for the 2013 edition of its diagnostic manual, the psychiatric profession is currently struggling to update its definition of narcissistic personality disorder. Still, generally speaking, practitioners agree that narcissism manifests in patterns of fantastic grandiosity, craving for attention, and lack of empathy. In a 2008 survey, 35,000 American respondents were asked if they had ever had certain symptoms of narcissistic personality disorder. Among people older than 65, 3 percent reported symptoms. Among people in their 20s, the proportion was nearly 10 percent. Across all age groups, one in 16 Americans has experienced some symptoms of NPD. And loneliness and narcissism are intimately connected: a longitudinal study of Swedish women demonstrated a strong link between levels of narcissism in youth and levels of loneliness in old age. The connection is fundamental. Narcissism is the flip side of loneliness, and either condition is a fighting retreat from the messy reality of other people.

A considerable part of Facebook's appeal stems from its miraculous fusion of distance with intimacy, or the illusion of distance with the illusion of intimacy. Our online communities become engines of self-image, and self-image becomes the engine of community. The real danger with Facebook is not that it allows us to isolate ourselves, but that by mixing our appetite for isolation with our vanity, it threatens to alter the very nature of solitude. The new isolation is not of the kind that Americans once idealized, the lonesomeness of the proudly nonconformist, independent-minded, solitary stoic, or that of the astronaut who blasts into new worlds. Facebook's isolation is a grind. What's truly staggering about Facebook usage is not its volume—750 million photographs uploaded over a single weekend—but the constancy of the performance it demands. More than half its users—and one of every 13 people on Earth is a Facebook user—log on every day. Among 18- to 34-year-olds, nearly half check Facebook minutes after waking up, and 28 percent do so before getting out of bed. The relentlessness is what is so new, so potentially transformative. Facebook never takes a break. We never take a break. Human beings have always created elaborate acts of self-presentation. But not all the time, not every morning, before we even pour a cup of coffee. Yvette Vickers's computer was on when she died.

Nostalgia for the good old days of disconnection would not just be pointless, it would be hypocritical and ungrateful. But the very magic of the new machines, the efficiency and elegance with which they serve us, obscures what isn't being served: everything that matters. What Facebook has revealed about human nature—and this is not a minor revelation—is that a connection is not the same thing as a bond, and that instant and total connection is no salvation, no ticket to a happier, better world or a more liberated version of humanity. Solitude used to be good for self-reflection and self-reinvention. But now we are left thinking about who we are all the time, without ever really thinking about who we are. Facebook denies us a pleasure whose profundity we had underestimated: the chance to forget about ourselves for a while, the chance to disconnect.

REFLECTING AND DISCUSSING

1. How do you respond to the title of this article? Why? Reflect on your own engagement with forms of social media.

2. How—through what means and what disciplines—does Marche answer his own question? What is the effect of these approaches, and how do these various forms of evidence bolster his argument? Look specifically at the article to make your judgment.

3. "A considerable part of Facebook's appeal stems from its miraculous fusion of distance with intimacy, or the illusion of distance with the illusion of intimacy. Our online communities become engines of self-image, and self-image becomes the engine of community." Discuss this paradox of distance and intimacy and what its effects are. What are its pitfalls? What are its strengths?

CONNECTING AND WRITING

1. Research other articles that critique or celebrate social media. Find examples with a strong central argument on either side, and compare and contrast them with Marche's article. Use evidence from both to back up your own argument about the issue.

2. "Facebook arrived in the middle of a dramatic increase in the quantity and intensity of human loneliness, a rise that initially made the site's promise of greater connection seem deeply attractive. Americans are more solitary than ever before." How does Marche come to this conclusion? Examine Marche's article closely and formulate your own argument about the validity of his point of view.

Pornography

Margaret Atwood (1939–   )

In addition to her celebrated novel The Handmaid's Tale *(1985), which at the time of this writing has returned to prominence as a well-received and popular teleplay (2017), Canadian author Margaret Atwood has produced a range of novels, poems, and essays and is an activist. She has written numerous volumes of poetry—her first volume,* Double Persephone, *appeared in 1961—and several novels, including* Cat's Eye *(1988) and* The Edible Woman *(1969). Her work centers around feminist issues and futuristic satire. "Pornography" grew in part out of her research for her 1981 novel* Bodily Harm.

When I was in Finland a few years ago for an international writers' conference, I had occasion to say a few paragraphs in public on the subject of pornography. The context was a discussion of political repression, and I was suggesting the possibility of a link between the two. The immediate result was that a male journalist took several large bites out of me. Prudery and pornography are two halves of the same coin, said he, and I was clearly a prude. What could you expect from an Anglo-Canadian? Afterward, a couple of pleasant Scandinavian men asked me what I had been so worked up about. All "pornography" means, they said, is graphic depictions of whores, and what was the harm in that?

Not until then did it strike me that the male journalist and I had two entirely different things in mind. By "pornography," he meant naked bodies and sex. I, on the other hand, had recently been doing the research for my novel *Bodily Harm*, and was still in a state of shock from some of the material I had seen, including the Ontario Board of Film Censors' "outtakes." By "pornography," I meant women getting their nipples snipped off with garden shears, having meat hooks stuck into their vaginas, being disemboweled; little girls being raped; men (yes, there are some men) being smashed to a pulp and forcibly sodomized. The cutting edge of pornography, as far as I could see, was no longer simple old copulation, hanging from the chandelier or otherwise: it was death, messy, explicit and highly sadistic. I explained this to the nice Scandinavian men. "Oh, but that's just the United States," they said. "Everyone knows they're sick." In their country, they said, violent "pornography" of that kind was not permitted on television or in movies; indeed, excessive violence of any kind was not permitted. They had drawn a clear line between erotica, which earlier studies had shown did not incite men to more aggressive and brutal behavior toward women, and violence, which later studies indicated did.

Some time after that I was in Saskatchewan, where, because of the scenes in *Bodily Harm*, I found myself on an open-line radio show answering questions about "pornography." Almost no one who phoned in was in favor of it, but again they weren't talking about the same stuff I was, because they hadn't seen it. Some of them were all set to stamp out bathing suits and negligees, and, if possible, any depictions of the female body whatsoever. God, it was implied, did not approve of female bodies, and sex of any kind, including that practiced by bumble-bees, should be shoved back into the dark, where it belonged. I had more than a suspicion that *Lady Chatterley's Lover*, Margaret Laurence's *The Diviners*, and indeed most books by most serious modern authors would have ended up as confetti if left in the hands of these callers.

For me, these two experiences illustrate the two poles of the emotionally heated debate that is now thundering around this issue. They also underline the desirability and even the necessity of defining the terms. "Pornography" is now one of those catchalls, like "Marxism" and "feminism," that have become so broad they can mean almost anything, ranging from certain verses in the Bible, ads for skin lotion and sex texts for children to the contents of *Penthouse*, naughty '90s postcards and films with titles containing the word *Nazi* that show vicious scenes of torture and killing. It's easy to say that sensible people can tell the difference. Unfortunately, opinions on what constitutes a sensible person vary.

But even sensible people tend to lose their cool when they start talking about this subject. They soon stop talking and start yelling, and the name-calling begins. Those in favor of censorship (which may include groups not noticeably in agreement on other issues, such as some feminists and religious fundamentalists) accuse the others of exploiting women through the use of degrading images, contributing to the corruption of children, and adding to the general climate of violence and threat in which both women and children live in this society; or, though they may not give much of a hoot about actual women and children, they invoke moral standards and God's supposed aversion to "filth," "smut" and deviated *perversion*, which may mean ankles.

The camp in favor of total "freedom of expression" often comes out howling as loud as the Romans would have if told they could no longer have innocent fun watching the lions eat up Christians. It too may include segments of the population who are not natural bedfellows: those who proclaim their God-given right to freedom, including the freedom to tote guns, drive when drunk, drool over chicken porn and get off on videotapes of women being raped and beaten, may be waving the same anticensorship banner as responsible liberals who fear the return of Mrs. Grundy, or gay groups for whom sexual emancipation involves the concept of "sexual theatre." *Whatever turns you on* is a handy motto, as is *A man's home is his castle* (and if it includes a dungeon with beautiful maidens strung up in chains and bleeding from every pore, that's his business).

Meanwhile, theoreticians theorize and speculators speculate. Is today's pornography yet another indication of the hatred of the body, the deep mind-body split, which is supposed to pervade Western Christian society? Is it a backlash against the women's movement by men who are threatened by uppity female behavior in real life, so like to fantasize about women done up like outsize parcels, being turned into hamburger, kneeling at their feet in slavelike adoration or sucking off guns? Is it a sign of collective impotence, of a generation of men who can't relate to real women at all but have to make do with bits of celluloid and paper? Is the current flood just a result of smart marketing and aggressive promotion by the money men in what has now become a multibillion-dollar industry? If they were selling movies about men getting their testicles stuck full of knitting needles by women with swastikas on their sleeves, would they do as well, or is this penchant somehow peculiarly male? If so, why? Is pornography a power trip rather than a sex one? Some say that those ropes, chains, muzzles and other restraining devices are an argument for the immense power female sexuality still wields in the male imagination: you don't put these things on dogs unless you're afraid of them. Others, more literary, wonder about the shift from the 19th-century Magic Women or Femme Fatale image to the lollipop-licker, airhead or turkey-carcass treatment of women in porn today. The proporners don't care much about theory: they merely demand product. The antiporners don't care about it in the final analysis either: there's dirt on the street, and they want it cleaned up, now.

It seems to me that this conversation, with its *You're-a-prude/You're-a-pervert* dialectic, will never get anywhere as long as we continue to think of this material as just "entertainment." Possibly we're deluded by the packaging, the format: magazine, book, movie, theatrical presentation. We're used to thinking of these things as part of the "entertainment industry," and we're used to thinking of ourselves as free adult people who ought to be able to see any kind of "entertainment" we want to. That was what the First Choice pay-TV debate was all about. After all, it's only entertainment, right? Entertainment means fun, and only a killjoy would be antifun. What's the harm?

This is obviously the central question: *What's the harm?* If there isn't any real harm to any real people, then the antiporners can tsk-tsk and/or throw up as much as they like, but they can't rightfully expect more legal controls or sanctions. However, the no-harm position is far from being proven.

(For instance, there's a clear-cut case for banning—as the federal government has proposed—movies, photos and videos that depict children engaging in sex with adults: real children are used to make the movies, and hardly anybody thinks this is ethical. The possibilities for coercion are too great.)

To shift the viewpoint, I'd like to suggest three other models for looking at "pornography"—and here I mean the violent kind.

Those who find the idea of regulating pornographic materials repugnant because they think it's Fascist or Communist or otherwise not in accordance with the principles of an open democratic society should consider that Canada has made it illegal to disseminate material that may lead to hatred toward any group because of race or religion. I suggest that if pornography of the violent kind depicted these acts being done predominantly to Chinese, to blacks, to Catholics, it would be off the market immediately, under the present laws. Why is hate literature illegal? Because whoever made the law thought that such material might incite real people to do real awful things to other real people. The human brain is to a certain extent a computer: garbage in, garbage out. We only hear about the extreme cases (like that of American multimurderer Ted Bundy) in which pornography has contributed to the death and/or mutilation of women and/or men. Although pornography is not the only factor involved in the creation of such deviance, it certainly has upped the ante by suggesting both a variety of techniques and the social acceptability of such actions. Nobody knows yet what effect this stuff is having on the less psychotic.

Studies have shown that a large part of the market for all kinds of porn, soft and hard, is drawn from the 16-to-21-year-old population of young men. Boys used to learn about sex on the street, or (in Italy, according to Fellini movies) from friendly whores, or, in more genteel surroundings, from girls, their parents, or, once upon a time, in school, more or less. Now porn has been added, and sex education in the schools is rapidly being phased out. The buck has been passed, and boys are being taught that all women secretly like to be raped and that real men get high on scooping out women's digestive tracts.

Boys learn their concept of masculinity from other men: is this what most men want them to be learning? If word gets around that rapists are "normal" and even admirable men, will boys feel that in order to be normal, admirable and masculine they will have to be rapists? Human beings are enormously flexible, and how they turn out depends a lot on how they're educated, by the society in which they're immersed as well as by their teachers. In a society that advertises and glorifies rape or even implicitly condones it, more women get raped. It becomes socially acceptable. And at a time when men and the traditional male role have taken a lot of flak and men are confused and casting around for an acceptable way of being male (and, in some cases, not getting much comfort from women on that score), this must be at times a pleasing thought.

It would be naïve to think of violent pornography as just harmless entertainment. It's also an educational tool and a powerful propaganda device. What happens when boy educated on porn meets girl brought up on Harlequin romances? The clash of expectations can be heard around the block. She wants him to get down on his knees with a ring, he wants her to get down on all fours with a ring in her nose. Can this marriage be saved?

Pornography has certain things in common with such addictive substances as alcohol and drugs: for some, though by no means for all, it induces chemical changes in the body, which the user finds exciting and pleasurable. It also appears to attract a "hard core" of habitual users and a penumbra of those who use it occasionally but aren't dependent on it in any way. There are also significant numbers of men who aren't much interested in it, not because they're under-sexed but because real life is satisfying their needs, which may not require as many appliances as those of users.

For the "hard core," pornography may function as alcohol does for the alcoholic: tolerance develops, and a little is no longer enough. This may account for the short viewing time and fast turnover in porn theatres. Mary Brown, chairwoman of the

Ontario Board of Film Censors, estimates that for every one mainstream movie requesting entrance to Ontario, there is one porno flick. Not only the quantity consumed but the quality of explicitness must escalate, which may account for the growing violence: once the big deal was breasts, then it was genitals, then copulation, then that was no longer enough and the hard users had to have more. The ultimate kick is death, and after that, as the Marquis de Sade so boringly demonstrated, multiple death.

The existence of alcoholism has not led us to ban social drinking. On the other hand, we do have laws about drinking and driving, excessive drunkenness and other abuses of alcohol that may result in injury or death to others.

This leads us back to the key question: what's the harm? Nobody knows, but this society should find out fast, before the saturation point is reached. The Scandinavian studies that showed a connection between depictions of sexual violence and increased impulse toward it on the part of male viewers would be a starting point, but many more questions remain to be raised as well as answered. What, for instance, is the crucial difference between men who are users and men who are not? Does using affect a man's relationship with actual women, and, if so, adversely? Is there a clear line between erotica and violent pornography, or are they on an escalating continuum? Is this a "men versus women" issue, with all men secretly siding with the proporners and all women secretly siding against? (I think not; there *are* lots of men who don't think that running their true love through the Cuisinart is the best way they can think of to spend a Saturday night, and they're just as nauseated by films of someone else doing it as women are.) Is pornography merely an expression of the sexual confusion of this age or an active contributor to it?

Nobody wants to go back to the age of official repression, when even piano legs were referred to as "limbs" and had to wear pantaloons to be decent. Neither do we want to end up in George Orwell's *1984*, in which pornography is turned out by the State to keep the proles in a state of torpor, sex itself is considered dirty and the approved practise is only for reproduction. But Rome under the emperors isn't such a good model either.

If all men and women respected each other, if sex were considered joyful and life-enhancing instead of a wallow in germ-filled glop, if everyone were in love all the time, if, in other words, many people's lives were more satisfactory for them than they appear to be now, pornography might just go away on its own. But since this is obviously not happening, we as a society are going to have to make some informed and responsible decisions about how to deal with it.

REFLECTING AND DISCUSSING

1. Atwood begins this essay with a personal story. What function might this story serve? Why would Atwood choose to do this?

2. What are our cultural assumptions about pornography? How does Atwood challenge these assumptions? Is that challenge effective? Why or why not?

3. Atwood (sincerely) asks, "What's the harm?" What do you think?

CONNECTING AND WRITING

1. How does Atwood distinguish between acceptable and unacceptable forms of pornography? What various forms of classification does she provide? Do you agree or disagree with her assumptions? Be sure to support your argument with evidence from the essay or from other credible sources.

2. There are some who argue that in this essay Atwood is unfair to men. What evidence might support this reading? After closely rereading Atwood's argument, how do you think that Atwood's presumptions about gender influence the ways in which she believes men and women consume pornography differently? What do you think? Use evidence from the essay and other credible sources to support your view, whether or not you agree or disagree with Atwood.

QUESTION

Although one might clearly regard technological advancement as a boon, how does technology separate us, define us, or make us *less* than we are? Choose at least two of the pieces in this section that illustrate one of these issues and use them as evidence for your own point of view.

3 GENDER ROLES

A nother thematic issue that has been argued for a long time but is just as relevant now as in the past is gender roles. In this section, these roles are discussed through various means, such as the well-argued personal narrative, the political speech, and the political essay.

The Picture for Men: Superhero or Slacker?

Sameer Pandya (1972–   )

Sameer Pandya is a professor of Asian American studies at the University of California–Santa Barbara. He holds a Ph.D. in modern thought and literature from Stanford University and is a writer of fiction: his first collection of stories, The Blind Writer: Stories and a Novella *(2015), centers around the lives of people from India living in California. He regularly contributes to popular news outlets, including* Pacific Standard Magazine, *the* Atlantic, Salon, *and* ESPN. *This article originally appeared in the online edition of* Pacific Standard *in 2010.*

A t the end of the fourth season of the critically loved and chronically underwatched *Friday Night Lights*, the former football star Tim Riggins martyrs himself for the sake of his brother and newborn nephew. For much of the season, he and his brother Billy have been stripping down stolen cars and making the type of fast cash they cannot make legitimately. Tim wants the quick cash to fund his desire to buy a bit of sun-drenched Texas countryside, and Billy needs it for his new duties as a father.

As the season finale starts, the brothers are talking to a lawyer and working through their options after they have both been arrested and released.

Through the duration of the television hour, it becomes clear that Tim is going to take the fall so that his brother can be a present father to his new son. Their own father had run out on the brothers early in their lives. In a couple of truly emotionally stirring scenes, Tim tells his brother of his decision and then heads into the sheriff's office to turn himself in.

In the show, the character of Tim Riggins is a poster child for what Hanna Rosin has provocatively referred to, in a recent *Atlantic* cover story, as "The End of Men." Rosin argues that in our postindustrial society, women are succeeding in a way in which men cannot keep up. Women are attending and graduating from college and professional schools at a higher rate, and women are entering and ascending in the work force in greater numbers and more successfully.

And in the recession we are living through, men have been the hit hardest. "The worst-hit industries were overwhelmingly male and deeply identified with macho: construction, manufacturing, high finance."

Riggins had plenty going for him: handsome, athletically gifted, a full scholarship at a state university to play football. But in line with the self-destructive behavior the character has displayed—quick to throw punches, quiet on verbal communication— he throws much of this away. A year after the end of high school, he has abandoned college and returned home to open a mechanics shop with his brother, where business is quite slow.

In contrast, his love interest has long abandoned the small Texas town where the show takes place and moved on to her new life at Vanderbilt.

If the makers of *Friday Night Lights* and Rosin are to be believed, there is a simple message being transmitted: Men are screwed. Or to put it another way, for a large subsection of American men, their options in life have become severely limited.

The possible reasons for this are layered and complicated. But recent research points to one possible culprit: traditional forms of masculinity.

In two different studies presented Aug. 16 at the American Psychological Association meetings in San Diego, researchers examined the lives of boys.

Sharon Lamb, a distinguished professor of mental health at the University of Massachusetts–Boston along with her co-authors Lyn Mikel Brown and Mark Tappan of Colby College, found that media images, particularly of superheroes, severely limit the models of boys' behavior. Today's movie superheroes offer a basic template for superhero behavior: nonstop violence when in costume, and the exploitation of women, the flaunting of money and wielding guns when not.

In the past, Lamb argues, comic book heroes "were heroes the boys could look up to and learn from because outside of their costumes, they were real people with real problems and many vulnerabilities."

Now, boys between the ages of 4 and 18 have only two choices.

"In today's media, superheroes and slackers are the only two options boys have. Boys are told if you can't be a superhero, you can always be a slacker. Slackers are funny, but slackers are not what boys should strive to be; slackers don't like school and they shirk responsibility. We wonder if the message boys get about saving face through glorified slacking could be affecting their performance in school."

Lamb suggests teaching boys to distance themselves from these images by helping them recognize the problems with them.

Lamb's fellow researcher on the panel, Carlos Santos of Arizona State University, offers another set of questions and solutions to this larger question of masculinity. Santos examined 426 middle school boys and posed a series of sharp research questions. Are middle school boys able to resist being emotionally stoic, autonomous and physically tough—the traditional, stereotypical markers of masculinity—as they moved from the sixth to the eighth grade? What difference does ethnicity make? Do relationships with families and peers foster resistance? Does resistance affect psychological health?

His conclusions provide a certain amount of hope, given the right type of influences.

Santos found that boys who remained close to their mothers, siblings and peers did not act as tough or shut down emotionally. However, close relationships with fathers encouraged greater autonomy and detachment from friendships.

One assumes that these fathers had learned how to be men from their own fathers, thus maintaining a certain cycle of traditional masculinity. How can the cycle be broken?

"If the goal is to encourage boys to experience healthy family relationships as well as healthy relationships, clinicians and interventionists working with families may benefit from having fathers share with their sons on the importance of experiencing multiple and fulfilling relationships in their lives," Santos said.

Santos also found that boys from diverse ethnic and racial backgrounds were able to resist masculine stereotypes, thus breaking another type of stereotype about the hyper-masculinity of certain ethnic minorities.

Time is of the essence in resistance. Santos suggests that the ability to resist internalizing macho images declines as the boys grow older.

And what happens to these boys when they grow older is that they encounter Hanna Rosin announcing their end even before they have had an opportunity to begin.

Certainly, changing media images and encouraging broad-ranging relationships are both important in subverting traditional, and often socially harmful, markers of masculinity. But there is another factor that might also contribute to broadening the choices beyond gun-slinging superhero and slacker: the availability and variety of work.

Of course, making work available now and in the future is no simple task. Among the bad job and unemployment numbers that seem to come out every week, it is clear that there is a bumpy road ahead not only for men, but also for the economy as a whole.

As much as I am worried about my two young boys being bombarded by superhero-slacker images, I am even more worried about the jobs that might not be available to them when they hit adulthood.

And here the studies by Lamb and Santos come back into play. Rethinking certain masculine traits for boys—stoic, autonomous, tough—may be the key for the men they will become to survive in a postindustrial economy. Rosin writes, "The attributes that are most valuable today—social intelligence, open communication, the ability to sit still and focus—are, at a minimum, not predominantly male."

We may not be able to control the availability of jobs, but we can control how boys prepare for them.

REFLECTING AND DISCUSSING

1. "If the makers of *Friday Night Lights* and Rosin are to be believed, there is a simple message being transmitted: Men are screwed." How does the author back up this contention? Do you agree? Why or why not?
2. Pandya references several examples from popular culture, such as the TV show *Friday Night Lights*, to prove the "end of men." Think of more recent examples from television or film that either prove or disprove Pandya's points.
3. Pandya says that boys between the ages of four and eighteen have only two choices of role models. What are they? How does the article define these choices? What do you think?

CONNECTING AND WRITING

1. The author refers to a study by several mental health professionals in Boston that finds "that media images, particularly of superheroes, severely limit the models of boys' behavior. Today's movie superheroes offer a basic template for superhero behavior: nonstop violence when in costume, and the exploitation of women, the flaunting of money and wielding guns when not." Explore this superhero archetype, finding other sources that either support or refute Pandya's argument, and advance an argument of your own.
2. Look at recent advertisements, either on television, on the Internet, or in print media. What are the ways in which men are represented? Women? How do these representations either break with or conform to stereotypes, and to what effect? Be sure to be specific and argue a point of view.

Chase and Sanborn Coffee, advertisement

A popular brand of coffee through most of the twentieth century, Chase and Sanborn produced advertisements that were typical of many of its time. While a contemporary audience might find this advertisement from 1952 both amusing and disconcerting, keep in mind that such advertisements were circulated widely and set and reflected cultural expectations—just as they do today.

REFLECTING AND DISCUSSING

1. This ad was meant to be humorous and whimsical. Is it? Why or why not?

2. Are we likely to react differently to this advertisement today than viewers might have in the 1950s? Why or why not? What assumptions do you have about life and cultural norms in the 1950s?

3. "If your husband ever finds out you're not 'store testing' for fresher coffee . . ." What does this ad copy suggest about relationships, women's responsibilities, and the roles of women at the time?

CONNECTING AND WRITING

1. Compare this advertisement to a more contemporary one. How have things changed—or not? Be sure to argue your point of view with specific examples.
2. It is said that after men (and some women) returned from World War II— during which many women had entered the workforce to support the war effort—advertisements reinforced more traditional cultural norms and "family values." Look at popular visual imagery that represented women both during World War II (e.g., Rosie the Riveter) and after World War II. How do these ads exemplify cultural shifts? For what purpose were they designed?

A New England Nun

Mary E. Wilkins Freeman (1852–1930)

Mary E. Wilkins Freeman was a popular American author considered to be both a regionalist and a realist. She spent most of her life surrounded by industry workers, house carpenters, and farmers in Randolph, Massachusetts. Freeman herself experienced isolation and poverty, and her career began when she earned $50 in a literary contest. Not unlike her own life, her writing centers around impoverished heroines struggling to overcome their isolation. She became one of the first women to be elected to membership in the National Institute of Arts and Letters after winning the Howell Medal for Fiction in 1926.

It was late in the afternoon, and the light was waning. There was a difference in the look of the tree shadows out in the yard. Somewhere in the distance cows were lowing, and a little bell was tinkling; now and then a farm-wagon tilted by, and the dust flew; some blue-shirted laborers with shovels over their shoulders plodded past; little swarms of flies were dancing up and down before the peoples' faces in the soft air. There seemed to be a gentle stir arising over everything, for the mere sake of subsidence—a very premonition of rest and hush and night.

This soft diurnal commotion was over Louisa Ellis also. She had been peacefully sewing at her sitting-room window all the afternoon. Now she quilted her needle carefully into her work, which she folded precisely, and laid in a basket with her thimble and thread and scissors. Louisa Ellis could not remember that ever in her life she had mislaid one of these little feminine appurtenances, which had become, from long use and constant association, a very part of her personality.

Louisa tied a green apron round her waist, and got out a flat straw hat with a green ribbon. Then she went into the garden with a little blue crockery bowl, to pick some currants for her tea. After the currants were picked she sat on the back door-step and stemmed them, collecting the stems carefully in her apron, and afterwards throwing them into the hen-coop. She looked sharply at the grass beside the step to see if any had fallen there.

Louisa was slow and still in her movements; it took her a long time to prepare her tea; but when ready it was set forth with as much grace as if she had been a veritable guest to her own self. The little square table stood exactly in the centre of the kitchen, and was covered with a starched linen cloth whose border pattern of flowers glistened. Louisa had a damask napkin on her tea-tray, where were arranged a cut-glass tumbler full of teaspoons, a silver cream-pitcher, a china sugar-bowl, and one pink china cup and saucer. Louisa used china every day—something which none of her neighbors did. They whispered about it among themselves. Their daily tables were laid with common crockery, their sets of best china stayed in the parlor closet, and Louisa Ellis was no richer nor better bred than they. Still she would use the china. She had for her supper a glass dish full of sugared currants, a plate of little cakes, and one of little white biscuits. Also a leaf or two of lettuce, which she cut up daintily. Louisa was very fond of lettuce, which she raised to perfection in her little garden. She ate quite heartily, though, in a delicate, pecking, way; it seemed almost surprising that any considerable bulk of the food should vanish.

After tea she filled a plate with nicely baked thin corn-cakes, and carried them out into the back-yard.

"Caesar!" she called. "Caesar! Caesar!"

There was a little rush, and the clank of a chain, and a large yellow-and-white dog appeared at the door of his tiny hut, which was half hidden among the tall grasses and flowers.

Louisa patted him and gave him the corn-cakes. Then she returned to the house and washed the tea-things, polishing the china carefully. The twilight had deepened; the chorus of the frogs floated in at the open window wonderfully loud and shrill, and once in a while a long sharp drone from a tree-toad pierced it. Louisa took off her green gingham apron, disclosing a shorter one of pink and white print. She lighted her lamp, and sat down again with her sewing.

In about half an hour Joe Dagget came. She heard his heavy step on the walk, and rose and took off her pink-and- white apron. Under that was still another—white linen with a little cambric edging on the bottom; that was Louisa's company apron. She never wore it without her calico sewing apron over it unless she had a guest. She had barely folded the pink and white one with methodical haste and laid it in a table-drawer when the door opened and Joe Dagget entered.

He seemed to fill up the whole room. A little yellow canary that had been asleep in his green cage at the south window woke up and fluttered wildly, beating his little yellow wings against the wires. He always did so when Joe Dagget came into the room.

"Good-evening," said Louisa. She extended her hand with a kind of solemn cordiality.

"Good-evening, Louisa," returned the man, in a loud voice.

She placed a chair for him, and they sat facing each other, with the table between them. He sat bolt-upright, toeing out his heavy feet squarely, glancing with a good-humored uneasiness around the room. She sat gently erect, folding her slender hands in her white-linen lap.

"Been a pleasant day," remarked Dagget.

"Real pleasant," Louisa assented, softly.

"Have you been haying?" she asked, after a little while.

"Yes, I've been haying all day, down in the ten-acre lot. Pretty hot work."

"It must be."

"Yes, it's pretty hot work in the sun."

"Is your mother well to-day?"

"Yes, mother's pretty well."

"I suppose Lily Dyer's with her now?"

Dagget colored. "Yes, she's with her," he answered, slowly.

He was not very young, but there was a boyish look about his large face. Louisa was not quite as old as he, her face was fairer and smoother, but she gave people the impression of being older.

"I suppose she's a good deal of help to your mother," she said, further.

"I guess she is; I don't know how mother'd get along without her," said Dagget, with a sort of embarrassed warmth.

"She looks like a real capable girl. She's pretty-looking too," remarked Louisa.

"Yes, she is pretty fair looking."

Presently Dagget began fingering the books on the table. There was a square red autograph album, and a Young Lady's Gift-Book which had belonged to Louisa's mother. He took them up one after the other and opened them then laid them down again, the album on the Gift-Book.

Louisa kept eying them with mild uneasiness. Finally she rose and changed the position of the books, putting the album underneath. That was the way they had been arranged in the first place.

Dagget gave an awkward little laugh. "Now what difference did it make which book was on top?" said he.

Louisa looked at him with a deprecating smile. "I always keep them that way," murmured she.

"You do beat everything," said Dagget, trying to laugh again. His large face was flushed.

He remained about an hour longer, then rose to take leave. Going out, he stumbled over a rug, and trying to recover himself, hit Louisa's work-basket on the table, and knocked it on the floor.

He looked at Louisa, then at the rolling spools; he ducked himself awkwardly toward them, but she stopped him. "Never mind," said she. "I'll pick them up after you're gone."

She spoke with a mild stiffness. Either she was a little disturbed, or his nervousness affected her, and made her seem constrained in her effort to reassure him.

When Joe Dagget was outside he drew in the sweet evening air with a sigh, and felt much as an innocent and perfectly well-intentioned bear might after his exit from a china shop.

Louisa, on her part, felt much as the kind-hearted, long-suffering owner of the china shop might have done after the exit of the bear.

She tied on the pink, then the green apron, picked up all the scattered treasures and replaced them in her work-basket, and straightened the rug. Then she set the lamp on the floor, and began sharply examining the carpet. She even rubbed her fingers over it, and looked at them.

"He's tracked in a good deal of dust," she murmured. "I thought he must have."

Louisa got a dust-pan and brush, and swept Joe Dagget's track carefully.

If he could have known it, it would have increased his perplexity and uneasiness, although it would not have disturbed his loyalty in the least. He came twice a week to see Louisa Ellis, and every time, sitting there in her delicately sweet room, he felt as if surrounded by a hedge of lace. He was afraid to stir lest he should put a clumsy foot or hand through the fairy web, and he had always the consciousness that Louisa was watching fearfully lest he should.

Still the lace and Louisa commanded perforce his perfect respect and patience and loyalty. They were to be married in a month, after a singular courtship which had lasted for a matter of fifteen years. For fourteen out of the fifteen years the two had not once seen each other, and they had seldom exchanged letters. Joe had been all those years in Australia, where he had gone to make his fortune, and where he had stayed until he made it. He would have stayed fifty years if it had taken so long, and come home feeble and tottering, or never come home at all, to marry Louisa.

But the fortune had been made in the fourteen years, and he had come home now to marry the woman who had been patiently and unquestioningly waiting for him all that time.

Shortly after they were engaged he had announced to Louisa his determination to strike out into new fields, and secure a competency before they should be married. She had listened and assented with the sweet serenity which never failed her, not even when her lover set forth on that long and uncertain journey. Joe, buoyed up as he was by his sturdy determination, broke down a little at the last, but Louisa kissed him with a mild blush, and said good-by.

"It won't be for long," poor Joe had said, huskily; but it was for fourteen years.

In that length of time much had happened. Louisa's mother and brother had died, and she was all alone in the world. But greatest happening of all—a subtle happening which both were too simple to understand—Louisa's feet had turned into a path, smooth maybe under a calm, serene sky, but so straight and unswerving that it could only meet a check at her grave, and so narrow that there was no room for any one at her side.

Louisa's first emotion when Joe Dagget came home (he had not apprised her of his coming) was consternation, although she would not admit it to herself, and he never dreamed of it. Fifteen years ago she had been in love with him—at least she considered herself to be. Just at that time, gently acquiescing with and falling into the natural drift of girlhood, she had seen marriage ahead as a reasonable feature and a probable desirability of life. She had listened with calm docility to her mother's views upon the subject. Her mother was remarkable for her cool sense and sweet, even temperament. She talked wisely to her daughter when Joe Dagget presented himself, and Louisa accepted him with no hesitation. He was the first lover she had ever had.

She had been faithful to him all these years. She had never dreamed of the possibility of marrying any one else. Her life, especially for the last seven years, had been full of a pleasant peace, she had never felt discontented nor impatient over her lover's absence; still she had always looked forward to his return and their marriage as the inevitable conclusion of things. However she had fallen into a way of placing it so far in the future that it was almost equal to placing it over the boundaries of another life.

When Joe came she had been expecting him, and expecting to be married for fourteen years, but she was as much surprised and taken aback as if she had never thought of it.

Joe's consternation came later. He eyed Louisa with an instant confirmation of his old admiration. She had changed but little. She still kept her pretty manner and soft grace, and was, he considered, every whit as attractive as ever. As for himself, his stent was done; he had turned his face away from fortune-seeking and the old winds of romance whistled as loud and sweet as ever through his ears. All the song which he had been wont to hear in them was Louisa; he had for a long time a loyal belief that he heard it still, but finally it seemed to him that although the winds sang always that one song, it had another name. But for Louisa the wind had never more than murmured; now it had gone down, and everything was still. She listened for a little while with half-wistful attention then she turned quietly away and went to work on her wedding clothes.

Joe had made some extensive and quite magnificent alterations in his house. It was the old homestead; the newly-married couple would live there, for Joe could not desert his mother, who refused to leave her old home. So Louisa must leave hers. Every morning rising and going about among her neat maidenly possessions, she felt as one looking her last upon the faces of dear friends. It was true that in a measure she could take them with her, but, robbed of their old environments, they would appear in such new guises that they would almost cease to be themselves.

Then there were some peculiar features of her happy solitary life which she would probably be obliged to relinquish altogether. Sterner tasks than these graceful but half-needless ones would probably devolve upon her. There would be a large house to care for; there would be company to entertain; there would be Joe's rigorous and feeble old mother to wait upon; and it would be contrary to all thrifty village traditions for her to keep more than one servant. Louisa had a little still, and she used to occupy herself pleasantly in summer weather with distilling the sweet and aromatic essences from roses and peppermint and spear-mint. By-and-by her still must be laid away. Her store of essences was already considerable, and there would be no time for her to distil for the mere pleasure of it. Then Joe's mother would think it foolishness; she had already hinted her opinion in the matter. Louisa dearly loved to sew a linen seam, not always for use, but for the simple, mild pleasure which she took in it. She would have been loath to confess how more than once she had ripped a seam for the mere delight of sewing it together again. Sitting at her window during long sweet afternoons, drawing her needle gently through the dainty fabric, she was peace itself. But there was small chance of such foolish comfort in the future. Joe's mother, domineering, shrewd old matron that she was even in her old age, and very likely even Joe himself, with his honest masculine rudeness, would laugh and frown down all these pretty but senseless old maiden ways.

Louisa had almost the enthusiasm of an artist over the mere order and cleanliness of her solitary home. She had throbs of genuine triumph at the sight of the windowpanes which she had polished until they shone like jewels. She gloated gently over her orderly bureau-drawers, with their exquisitely folded contents redolent with lavender and sweet clover and very purity. Could she be sure of the endurance of even this? She had visions, so startling that she half repudiated them as indelicate, of coarse masculine belongings strewn about in endless litter; of dust and disorder arising necessarily from a coarse masculine presence in the midst of all this delicate harmony. Among her forebodings of disturbance, not the least was with regard to Caesar. Caesar was a veritable hermit of a dog. For the greater part of his life he had dwelt in his secluded hut, shut out from the society of his kind and all innocent canine joys. Never had Caesar since his early youth watched at a woodchuck's hole; never had he known the delights of a stray bone at a neighbor's kitchen door. And it was all on account of a sin committed when hardly out of his puppyhood. No one knew the possible depth of remorse of which this mild-visaged, altogether innocent-looking old dog might be capable—but whether or not he had encountered remorse, he had encountered a full measure of righteous retribution. Old Caesar seldom lifted up his voice in a growl or a bark; he was fat and sleepy; there were yellow rings which looked like spectacles around his dim old eyes; but there was a neighbor who bore on his hand the imprint of several of Caesar's sharp white youthful teeth, and for that he had lived at the end of a chain, all alone in a little hut, for fourteen years. The neighbor, who was choleric and smarting with the pain of his wound, had demanded either Caesar's death or complete ostracism. So Louisa's brother, to whom the dog had belonged, had built him his little kennel and tied him up. It was now fourteen years since, in a flood of youthful spirits, he had inflicted that memorable bite, and with the exception of short excursions, always at the end of the chain, under the strict guardianship of his master or Louisa, the old dog had remained a close prisoner.

It is doubtful if, with his limited ambition, he took much pride in the fact, but it is certain that he was possessed of considerable cheap fame. He was regarded by all the children in the village and by many adults as a very monster of ferocity. St. George's dragon could hardly have surpassed in evil repute Louisa Ellis's old yellow dog. Mothers cleared their children with solemn emphasis not to go too near to him, and the children listened and believed greedily, with a fascinated appetite for terror, and ran by Louisa's house stealthily, with many sidelong and backward glances at the terrible dog. If perchance he sounded a hoarse bark, there was a panic. Wayfarers chancing into Louisa's yard eyed him with respect, and inquired if the chain were stout. Caesar at large might have seemed a very ordinary dog, and excited no comment whatever chained, his reputation overshadowed him, so that he lost his own proper outlines and looked darkly vague and enormous. Joe Dagget, however, with his good-humored sense and shrewdness, saw him as he was. He strode valiantly up to him and patted him on the head, in spite of Louisa's soft clamor of warning, and even attempted to set him loose. Louisa grew so alarmed that he desisted, but kept announcing his opinion in the matter quite forcibly at intervals. "There ain't a better-natured dog in town," he would say, "and it's down-right cruel to keep him tied up there. Some day I'm going to take him out."

Louisa had very little hope that he would not, one of these days, when their interests and possessions should be more completely fused in one. She pictured to herself Caesar on the rampage through the quiet and unguarded village. She saw innocent children bleeding in his path. She was herself very fond of the old dog, because he had belonged to her dead brother, and he was always very gentle with her; still she had great faith in his ferocity. She always warned people not to go too near him. She fed him on ascetic fare of corn-mush and cakes, and never fired his dangerous temper with heating and sanguinary diet of flesh and bones. Louisa looked at the old dog munching his simple fare, and thought of her approaching marriage and trembled. Still no anticipation of disorder and confusion in lieu of sweet peace and harmony, no forebodings of Caesar on the rampage, no wild fluttering of her little yellow canary, were sufficient to turn her a hairsbreadth. Joe Dagget had been fond of her and working for her all these years. It was not for her, whatever came to pass, to prove untrue and break his heart. She put the exquisite little studies into her wedding-garments, and the time went on until it was only a week before her wedding-day. It was a Tuesday evening, and the wedding was to be a week from Wednesday.

There was a full moon that night. About nine o'clock Louisa strolled down the road a little way. There were harvest-fields on either hand, bordered by low stone walls. Luxuriant clumps of bushes grew beside the wall, and trees—wild cherry and old apple-trees—at intervals. Presently Louisa sat down on the wall and looked about her with mildly sorrowful reflectiveness. Tall shrubs of blueberry and meadow-sweet, all woven together and tangled with blackberry vines and horsebriers, shut her in on either side. She had a little clear space between them. Opposite her, on the other side of the road, was a spreading tree; the moon shone between its boughs, and the leaves twinkled like silver. The road was bespread with a beautiful shifting dapple of silver and shadow; the air was full of a mysterious sweetness. "I wonder if it's wild grapes?" murmured Louisa. She sat there some time. She was just thinking of rising, when she heard footsteps and low voices, and remained quiet. It was a lonely place, and she felt a little timid. She thought she would keep still in the shadow and let the persons, whoever they might be, pass her.

But just before they reached her the voices ceased, and the footsteps. She understood that their owners had also found seats upon the stone wall. She was wondering if she could not steal away unobserved, when the voice broke the stillness. It was Joe Dagget's. She sat still and listened.

The voice was announced by a loud sigh, which was as familiar as itself. "Well," said Dagget, "you've made up your mind, then, I suppose?"

"Yes," returned another voice; "I'm going, day after tomorrow."

"That's Lily Dyer," thought Louisa to herself. The voice embodied itself in her mind. She saw a girl tall and full-figured, with a firm, fair face, looking fairer and firmer in the moonlight, her strong yellow hair braided in a close knot. A girl full of a calm rustic strength and bloom, with a masterful way which might have beseemed a princess. Lily Dyer was a favorite with the village folk; she had just the qualities to arouse the admiration. She was good and handsome and smart. Louisa had often heard her praises sounded.

"Well," said Joe Dagget, "I ain't got a word to say."

"I don't know what you could say," returned Lily Dyer.

"Not a word to say," repeated Joe, drawing out the words heavily. Then there was a silence. "I ain't sorry," he began at last, "that that happened yesterday—that we kind of let on how we felt to each other. I guess it's just as well we knew. Of course I can't do anything any different. I'm going right on an' get married next week. I ain't going back on a woman that's waited for me fourteen years, an' break her heart."

"If you should jilt her to-morrow, I wouldn't have you," spoke up the girl, with sudden vehemence.

"Well, I ain't going to give you the chance," said he; "but I don't believe you would, either."

"You'd see I wouldn't. Honor's honor, an' right's right. An' I'd never think anything of any man that went against 'em for me or any other girl—you'd find that out, Joe Dagget."

"Well, you'll find out fast enough that I ain't going against 'em for you or any other girl," returned he. Their voices sounded almost as if they were angry with each other. Louisa was listening eagerly.

"I'm sorry you feel as if you must go away," said Joe, "but I don't know but it's best."

"Of course it's best. I hope you and I have got common-sense."

"Well, I suppose you're right." Suddenly Joe's voice got an undertone of tenderness. "Say, Lily," said he, "I'll get along well enough myself, but I can't bear to think—You don't suppose you're going to fret much over it?"

"I guess you'll find out I sha'n't fret much over a married man."

"Well, I hope you won't—I hope you won't, Lily. God knows I do. And—I hope—one of these days—you'll—come across somebody else—"

"I don't see any reason why I shouldn't." Suddenly her tone changed. She spoke in a sweet, clear voice, so loud that she could have been heard across the street. "No, Joe Dagget," said she, "I'll never marry any other man as long as I live. I've got good sense, an' I ain't going to break my heart nor make a fool of myself; but I'm never going to be married, you can be sure of that. I ain't that sort of a girl to feel this way twice."

Louisa heard an exclamation and a soft commotion behind the bushes; then Lily spoke again—the voice sounded as if she had risen. "This must be put a stop to," said she. "We've stayed here long enough. I'm going home."

Louisa sat there in a daze, listening to their retreating steps. After a while she got up and slunk softly home herself. The next day she did her housework methodically; that was as much a matter of course as breathing; but she did not sew on her wedding-clothes. She sat at her window and meditated. In the evening Joe came. Louisa Ellis had never known that she had any diplomacy in her, but when she came to look for it that night she found it, although meek of its kind, among her little feminine weapons. Even now she could hardly believe that she had heard aright, and that she would not do Joe a terrible injury should she break her troth-plight. She wanted to sound him without betraying too soon her own inclinations in the matter.

She did it successfully, and they finally came to an understanding—but it was a difficult thing, for he was as afraid of betraying himself as she.

She never mentioned Lily Dyer. She simply said that while she had no cause of complaint against him, she had lived so long in one way that she shrank from making a change.

"Well, I never shrank, Louisa," said Dagget. "I'm going to be honest enough to say that I think maybe it's better this way; but if you'd wanted to keep on, I'd have stuck to you till my dying day. I hope you know that."

"Yes, I do," said she.

That night she and Joe parted more tenderly than they had done for a long time. Standing in the door, holding each other's hands, a last great wave of regretful memory swept over them.

"Well, this ain't the way we've thought it was all going to end, is it, Louisa?" said Joe.

She shook her head. There was a little quiver on her placid face.

"You let me know if there's ever anything I can do for you," said he. "I ain't ever going to forget you, Louisa." Then he kissed her, and went down the path.

Louisa, all alone by herself that night, wept a little, she hardly knew why, but the next morning, on waking, she felt like a queen who, after fearing lest her domain be wrested away from her, sees it firmly insured in her possession. Now the tall weeds and grasses might cluster around Caesar's little hermit hut, the snow might fall on its roof year in and year out, but he never would go on a rampage through the unguarded village. Now the little canary might turn itself into a peaceful yellow ball night after night, and have no need to wake and flutter with wild terror against its bars. Louisa could sew linen seams, and distil roses, and dust and polish and fold away in lavender, as long as she listed. That afternoon she sat with her needle-work at the window, and felt fairly steeped in peace. Lily Dyer, tall and erect and blooming, went past; but she felt no qualm. If Louisa Ellis had sold her birthright she did not know it, the taste of the pottage was so delicious, and had been her sole satisfaction for so long. Serenity and placid narrowness had become to her as the birthright itself. She gazed ahead through a long reach of future days strung together like pearls in a rosary, every one like the others, and all smooth and flawless and innocent, and her heart went up in thankfulness. Outside was the fervid summer afternoon; the air was filled with the sounds of the busy harvest of men and birds and bees; there were halloos, metallic clattering, sweet calls, and long hummings. Louisa sat, prayerfully numbering her days, like an uncloistered nun.

REFLECTING AND DISCUSSING

1. The central character of this story, Louisa, has a preoccupation with her domestic responsibilities. How does Wilkins Freeman use this preoccupation to speak to larger issues regarding women?

2. Comment on the disagreement between Louisa and Joe about whether to free the dog from his chain. How might this disagreement be symbolic? What might it symbolize? For what purpose does Wilkins Freeman introduce it?

3. Wilkins Freeman writes, "Every morning rising and going among her neat, maidenly possessions, she felt as one looking her last upon the faces of dear friends.

It was true that in a measure she could take them with her, but, robbed of their old environments, they would appear in such new guises that they would almost cease to be themselves." How does this description of Louisa's possessions speak to her own perceptions of herself as she readies to leave her house for Joe's?

CONNECTING AND WRITING

1. Research women's roles at the time this story was written. Further analyze the author's implied argument about women and their choices (or lack of choices) through the lens of your findings. How does what you have found help you better understand Louisa and her reservations? Be sure to argue a point of view, comparing the evidence from your research with the evidence you find in the story.

2. Based on this story, what are your conclusions about the conventions surrounding marriage at this time? Craft an argument that compares the assumptions about marriage then with your perceptions about marriage now. What has changed? What hasn't? Consider the title: Why would the author choose to call this story "A New England Nun"? Use specific evidence from the story and any resources you find that comment on the state of marriage today.

What I've Learned from Men

Barbara Ehrenreich (1941–   )

American author and political activist Barbara Ehrenreich has been called a "veteran muckraker" and a "mythbuster by trade." Her work, which has included many articles, essays, and several books on the New York Times's *best-seller list, has been selected for the National Magazine Award, the Ford Foundation Award for Humanistic Perspectives on Contemporary issues, and the LA Times Book Award. Her most popular books include* Nickeled and Dimed: On (Not) Getting By in America *(2001);* Fear of Falling: The Inner Life of the Middle Class *(1989); and, most recently,* Living with a Wild God *(2014). The following essay was published in Ms. magazine in 1985.*

For many years I believed that women had only one thing to learn from men: how to get the attention of a waiter by some means short of kicking over the table and shrieking. Never in my life have I gotten the attention of a waiter, unless it was an off-duty waiter whose car I'd accidentally scraped in a parking lot somewhere. Men, however, can summon a maitre d' just by thinking the word "coffee," and this is a power women would be well-advised to study. What else would we possibly want to learn from them? How to interrupt someone in mid-sentence as if you were performing an act of conversational euthanasia? How to drop a pair of socks three feet from an open hamper and keep right on walking? How to make those weird guttural gargling sounds in the bathroom?

But now, at mid-life, I am willing to admit that there are some real and useful things to learn from men. Not from all men—in fact, we may have the most to learn from some of the men we like the least. This realization does not mean that my feminist principles have gone soft with age: what I think women could learn from men is how to get *tough*. After more than a decade of consciousness-raising, assertiveness training, and hand-to-hand combat in the battle of the sexes, we're still too ladylike. Let me try that again—we're just too *damn* ladylike.

Here is an example from my own experience, a story that I blush to recount. A few years ago, at an international conference held in an exotic and luxurious setting, a prestigious professor invited me to his room for what he said would be an intellectual discussion on matters of theoretical importance. So far, so good. I showed up promptly. But only minutes into the conversation—held in all-too-adjacent chairs—it emerged that he was interested in something more substantial than a meeting of minds. I was disgusted, but not enough to overcome 30-odd years of programming in ladylikeness. Every time his comments took a lecherous turn, I chattered distractingly; every time his hand found its way to my knee, I returned it as if it were something he had misplaced. This went on for an unconscionable period (as much as 20 minutes); then there was a minor scuffle, a dash for the door, and I was out—with nothing violated but my self-esteem. I, a full-grown feminist, conversant with such matters as rape crisis counseling and sexual harassment at the workplace, had behaved like a ninny—or, as I now understand it, like a lady.

The essence of ladylikeness is a persistent servility masked as "niceness." For example, we (women) tend to assume that it is our responsibility to keep everything "nice" even when the person we are with is rude, aggressive, or emotionally AWOL. (In the above example, I was so busy taking responsibility for preserving the veneer of "niceness" that I almost forgot to take responsibility for myself.) In conversations with men, we do almost all the work; sociologists have observed that in male-female social interactions it's the woman who throws out leading questions and verbal encouragements ("So how did you *feel* about that?" and so on) while the man, typically, says "Hmmmm." Wherever we go, we're perpetually smiling—the on-cue smile, like the now-outmoded curtsy, being one of our culture's little rituals of submission. We're trained to feel embarrassed if we're praised, but if we see a criticism coming at us from miles down the road, we rush to acknowledge it. And when we're feeling aggressive or angry or resentful, we just tighten up our smiles or turn them into rueful little moues. In short, we spend a great deal of time acting like wimps.

For contrast, think of the macho stars we love to watch. Think, for example, of Mel Gibson facing down punk marauders in *The Road Warrior* . . . John Travolta swaggering his way through the early scenes of *Saturday Night Fever* . . . or Marlon Brando shrugging off the local law in *The Wild One*. Would they simper their way through tight spots? Chatter aimlessly to keep the conversation going? Get all clutched up whenever they think they might—just might—have hurt someone's feelings? No, of course not, and therein, I think, lies their fascination for us.

The attraction of the "tough guy" is that he has—or at least seems to have—what most of us lack, and that is an aura of power and control. In an article, feminist psychiatrist Jean Baker Miller writes that "a woman's using self-determined power for herself is equivalent to selfishness [and] destructiveness"—an equation that makes us want to avoid even the appearance of power. Miller cites cases of women who get depressed just when they're on the verge of success—and of women who do succeed and then bury their achievement in self-deprecation. As an example, she describes one company's periodic meetings to recognize outstanding salespeople: when a woman is asked to say a few words about her achievement, she tends to say something like, "Well, I really don't know how it happened. I guess I was just lucky this time." In contrast, the men will cheerfully own up to the hard work, intelligence, and so on, to which they owe their success. By putting herself down, a woman avoids feeling brazenly powerful and potentially "selfish"; she also does the traditional lady's work of trying to make everyone else feel better ("She's not really so smart, after all, just lucky").

So we might as well get a little tougher. And a good place to start is by cutting back on small acts of deference that we've been programmed to perform since girlhood. Like unnecessary smiling. For many women—waitresses, flight attendants, receptionists—smiling is an occupational requirement, but there's no reason for anyone to go around grinning when she's not being paid for it. I'd suggest that we save our off-duty smiles for when we truly feel like sharing them, and if you're not sure what to do with your face in the meantime, study Clint Eastwood's expressions—both of them.

Along the same lines, I think women should stop taking responsibility for every human interaction we engage in. In a social encounter with a woman, the average man can go 25 minutes saying nothing more than "You don't say?" "Izzat so?" and, of course, "Hmmmm." Why should we do all the work? By taking so much responsibility for making conversations go well, we act as if we had much more at stake in the encounter than the other party—and that gives him (or her) the power advantage. Every now and then, we deserve to get more out of conversation than we put into it: I'd suggest not offering information you'd rather not share ("I'm really terrified that my sales plan won't work") and not, out of sheer politeness, soliciting information you don't really want ("Wherever did you get that lovely tie?"). There will be pauses, but they don't have to be awkward for you.

It is true that some, perhaps most, men will interpret any decrease in female deference as a deliberate act of hostility. Omit the free smiles and perky conversation-boosters and someone is bound to ask, "Well, what's come over you today?" For most of us, the first impulse is to stare at our feet and make vague references to a terminally ill aunt in Atlanta, but we should have as much right to be taciturn as the average (male) taxi driver. If you're taking a vacation from smiles and small talk and some fellow is moved to inquire about what's "bothering" you, just stare back levelly and say the international debt crisis, the arms race, or the death of God.

There are all kinds of ways to toughen up—and potentially move up—at work, and I leave the details to the purveyors of assertiveness training. But Jean Baker Miller's study underscores a fundamental principle that anyone can master on her own. We can stop acting less capable than we actually are. For example, in the matter of taking credit when credit is due, there's a key difference between saying "I was just lucky" and saying "I had a plan and it worked." If you take the credit you deserve, you're letting people know that you were confident you'd succeed all along, and that you fully intend to do so again.

Finally, we may be able to learn something from men about what to do with anger. As a general rule, women get irritated: men get mad. We make tight little smiles of ladylike exasperation; they pound on desks and roar. I wouldn't recommend emulating the full basso profundo male tantrum, but women do need ways of expressing justified anger clearly, colorfully, and, when necessary, crudely. If you're not just irritated, but *pissed off* it might help to say so.

I, for example, have rerun the scene with the prestigious professor many times in my mind. And in my mind, I play it like Bogart. I start by moving my chair over to where I can look the professor full in the face. I let him do the chattering, and when it becomes evident that he has nothing serious to say, I lean back and cross my arms, just to let him know that he's wasting my time. I do not smile, neither do I nod encouragement. Nor, of course, do I respond to his blandishments with apologetic shrugs and blushes. Then, at the first flicker of lechery, I stand up and announce coolly, "All right, I've had enough of this crap." Then I walk out—slowly, deliberately, confidently. Just like a man.

Or—now that I think of it—just like a woman.

REFLECTING AND DISCUSSING

1. Comment on this essay's title. Is Ehrenreich being ironic? (First, be sure to define irony.) How so? For what purpose?

2. "What I think women can learn from men is how to get *tough*." How might Ehrenreich define what it means to be tough? Why do her "feminist principles" seem to require that women abandon their tendency to be "ladylike"? Do you agree with Ehrenreich? Why or why not?

3. Ehrenreich uses the first person plural—"we"—in this essay. Why do you think she does this? How effective is this strategy? Is she in danger of alienating male readers? Why or why not?

CONNECTING AND WRITING

1. Perhaps you've reflected on the kind of "feminist principles" mentioned in the question above. What are those principles, and have they changed since 1985? If so, how? If not, why? Be specific.

2. Ehrenreich references then-popular movie characters, highlighting "tough guy" roles such as that played by Marlon Brando in *The Wild One*. As an audience, we seem to cheer for men who are on the verge of success, but our reactions to women in the same position aren't always the same. Are such reactions similar

to what Ehrenreich describes in 1985, or have things changed? Consider characters, both male and female, from films you have seen recently to support your argument.

An American Girl in Italy, photograph

Ruth Orkin (1921–1985)

Photographer Ruth Orkin was given a Univax camera when she was ten years old, and she started developing her own photographs when she was twelve. Her career began with photographing celebrities in her native Hollywood, but after moving to New York City in 1943, her reputation grew, and she began photographing renowned musicians such as Isaac Stern and Leonard Bernstein. Orkin was later named one of the "ten top women photographers" of 1959. (One might critique that categorization itself.) An American Girl in Italy *is considered her signature photo.*

REFLECTING AND DISCUSSING

1. Is there an implicit argument to *An American Girl in Italy*? How do you know? What about the arrangement of people in the image gives you your impression?
2. Do you think that the gender of the photo's viewers would affect their response to it? Why or why not? Should one's gender make a difference? Why?

3. Orkin took this photo as part of a project in which she included both staged and spontaneous photographs. What are the ethics involved in presenting a photographic point of view that is carefully crafted rather than spontaneous? Should whether or not a photo was staged make a difference in its reception? How has the advent of digital technologies affected our view of what we are supposed to take as "real"?

CONNECTING AND WRITING

1. What is xenophobia? Ruth Orkin captured this image as part of a project entitled "Don't Be Afraid to Travel Alone." While the photograph clearly speaks to issues of gender, one could also argue that both the title and the project itself reveal issues of xenophobia. How so? How does the photo both support and contradict the title of the project?
2. Research and find another well-known photograph that to you raises issues similar to those raised by *An American Girl in Italy*. How does each photographer capture—or contrast—these similar issues? Be sure to craft an argument that specifically responds to particular details within the photos and use those details to back up your point of view.

The Fundamental Principle of a Republic

Anna Howard Shaw (1847–1919)

At a time when women were mostly prohibited from entering college, much less medical school, Anna Howard Shaw was a suffragist, trained physician, and one of the first female ministers to be ordained by a major religious denomination (Methodism) in the United States. She became outspoken about women's rights while in medical school at Boston University and later joined the National Woman Suffrage Association, for which she worked beside Susan B. Anthony. This speech, delivered in 1915 at the City Opera House in New York, was part of the New York equal suffrage campaign. It is often recognized as one of the best-written arguments, not only in the history of women's rights, but in American history.

When I came into your hall tonight, I thought of the last time I was in your city. Twenty-one years ago I came here with Susan B. Anthony, and we came for exactly the same purpose as that for which we are here tonight. Boys have been born since that time and have become voters, and the women are still trying to persuade American men to believe in the fundamental principles of democracy, and I never quite feel as if it was a fair field to argue this question with men, because in doing it you have to assume that a man who professes to believe in a Republican form of government does not believe in a Republican form of government, for the only thing that woman's enfranchisement means at all is that a government which claims to be a Republic should be a Republic, and not an aristocracy.

The difficulty with discussing this question with those who oppose us is that they make any number of arguments but none of them have anything to do with Woman's Suffrage; they always have something to do with something else, therefore the arguments which we have to make rarely ever have anything to do with the subject, because we have to answer our opponents who always escape the subject as far as possible in order to have any sort of reason in connection with what they say.

Now one of two things is true: either a Republic is a desirable form of government, or else it is not. If it is, then we should have it, if it is not then we ought not to pretend that we have it. We ought at least be true to our ideals, and the men of New York have for the first time in their lives, the rare opportunity on the second day of next November, of making the state truly a part of the Republic. It is the greatest opportunity which has ever come to the men of the state. They have never had so serious a problem to solve before, they will never have a more serious problem to solve in any future of our nation's life, and the thing that disturbs me more than anything else in connection with it is that so few people realize what a profound problem they have to solve on November 2. It is not merely a trifling matter; it is not a little thing that does not concern the state, it is the most vital problem we could have, and any man who goes to the polls on the second day of next November without thoroughly informing himself in regard to this subject is unworthy to be a citizen of this state, and unfit to cast a ballot.

If woman's suffrage is wrong, it is a great wrong; if it is right, it is a profound and fundamental principle, and we all know, if we know what a Republic is, that it is the fundamental principle upon which a Republic must rise. Let us see where we are as a people; how we act here and what we think we are. The difficulty with the men of this country is that they are so consistent in their inconsistency that they are not aware of having been inconsistent; because their consistency has been so continuous and their inconsistency so consecutive that it has never been broken, from the beginning of our Nation's life to the present time.

If we trace our history back we will find that from the very dawn of our existence as a people, men have been imbued with a spirit and a vision more lofty than they have been able to live; they have been led by visions of the sublimest truth, both in regard to religion and in regard to government that ever inspired the souls of men from the time the Puritans left the old world to come to this country, led by the Divine ideal which is the sublimest and the supremest ideal in religious freedom which men have ever known, the theory that a man has a right to worship God according to the dictates of his own conscience, without the intervention of any other man or any other group of men. And it was this theory, this vision of the right of the human soul which led men first to the shores of this country.

Now, nobody can deny that they are sincere, honest, and earnest men. No one can deny that the Puritans were men of profound conviction, and yet these men who gave up everything in behalf of an ideal, hardly established their communities in this new country before they began to practice exactly the same sort of persecutions on other men which had been practiced upon them. They settled in their communities on the New England shores and when they formed their compacts by which they governed their local societies, they permitted no man to have a voice in the affairs unless he was a member of the church, and not a member of any church, but a member of the particular church which dominated the particular community in which he happened to be.

In Massachusetts they drove the Baptists down to Rhode Island; in Connecticut they drove the Presbyterians over to New Jersey; they burned the Quakers in Massachusetts and ducked the witches, and no colony, either Catholic or Protestant allowed a Jew to have a voice. And so a man must worship God according to the conscience of the particular community in which he was located, and yet they called that religious freedom, they were not able to live the ideal of religious liberty, and from that time to this the men of this government have been following along the same line of inconsistency, while they too have been following a vision of equal grandeur and power.

Never in the history of the world did it dawn upon the human mind as it dawned upon your ancestors, what it would mean for men to be free. They got the vision of a government in which the people would be the supreme power, and so inspired by this vision men wrote such documents as were went from the Massachusetts legislature, from the New York legislature and from the Pennsylvania group over to the Parliament of Great Britain, which rang with the profoundest measures of freedom and justice. They did not equivocate in a single word when they wrote the Declaration of Independence; no one can dream that these men had not got the sublimest ideal of democracy which had ever dawned upon the souls of men. But as soon as the war was over and our government was formed, instead of asking the question, who shall be the governing force in this great new Republic, when they brought those thirteen little territories together, they began to eliminate instead of include the men who should be the great governing forces, and they said, who shall have the voice in this great new Republic, and you would have supposed that such men as fought the Revolutionary War would have been able to answer that every man who has fought, everyone who has given up all he has and all he has been able to accumulate shall be free, it never entered their minds.

These excellent ancestors of yours had not been away from the old world long enough to realize that man is of more value than his purse, so they said every man who has an estate in the government shall have a voice; and they said what shall that estate be? And they answered that a man who had property valued at two hundred and fifty dollars will be able to cast a vote, and so they sang "The land of the free and the home of the brave." And they wrote into their Constitution, "All males who pay taxes on $250 shall cast a vote," and they called themselves a Republic, and we call ourselves a Republic, and they were not quite so much of a Republic that we should be called a Republic yet. We might call ourselves angels, but that wouldn't make us angels, you have got to be an angel before you are an angel, and you have got to be a Republic before you are a Republic. Now what did we do? Before the word "male" in the local compacts, they wrote the word "Church-members"; and they wrote in the word "taxpayer."

Then there arose a great Democrat, Thomas Jefferson, who looked down into the day when you and I are living and saw that the rapidly accumulated wealth in the hands of a few men would endanger the liberties of the people, and he knew what you and I know, that no power under heaven or among men is known in a Republic by which men can defend their liberties except by the power of the ballot, and so the Democratic party took another step in the evolution of the Republic out of a monarchy and they rubbed out the word "taxpayer" and wrote in the word "white," and then the Democrats thought the millennium had come, and they sang " The land of the free and the home of the brave" as lustily as the Republicans had sung it before them and spoke of the divine right of motherhood with the same thrill in their voices and at the same time they were selling mother's babies by the pound on the auction block—and mothers apart from their babies.

Another arose who said a man is not a good citizen because he is white, he is a good citizen because he is a man, and the Republican party took out that progressive evolutionary eraser and rubbed out the word "white" from before the word "male" and could not think of another word to put in there—they were all in, black and white, rich and poor, wise and otherwise, drunk and sober; not a man left out to be put in, and so the Republicans could not write anything before the word "male," and they had to let the little word, "male" stay alone by itself.

And God said in the beginning, "It is not good for man to stand alone." That is why we are here tonight, and that is all that woman's suffrage means; just to repeat again and again that first declaration of the Divine, "It is not good for man to stand alone," and so the women of this state are asking that the word "male" shall be stricken out of the Constitution altogether and that the Constitution stand as it ought to have stood in the beginning and as it must before this state is any part of a Republic. Every citizen possessing the necessary qualifications shall be entitled to cast one vote at every election, and have that vote counted. We are not asking as our Anti-Suffrage friends think we are, for any of the awful things that we hear will happen if we are allowed to vote; we are simply asking that that government which professes to be a Republic shall be a Republic and not pretend to be what it is not.

Now what is a Republic? Take your dictionary, encyclopedia lexicon or anything else you like and look up the definition and you will find that a Republic is a form of government in which the laws are enacted by representatives elected by the people. Now when did the people of New York ever elect their own representatives? Never in the world. The men of New York have, and I grant you that men are people, admirable people, as far as they go, but they only go half way. There is still another half of the people who have not elected representatives, and you never read a definition of a Republic in which half of the people elect representatives to govern the whole of the people. That is an aristocracy and that is just what we are. We have been many kinds of aristocracies. We have been a hierarchy of church members, then an oligarchy of sex.

There are two old theories, which are dying today. Dying hard, but dying. One of them is dying on the plains of Flanders and the Mountains of Galicia and Austria, and that is the theory of the divine right of kings. The other is dying here in the state of New York and Massachusetts and New Jersey and Pennsylvania and that is the divine right of sex. Neither of them had a foundation in reason, or justice, or common sense.

Now I want to make this proposition, and I believe every man will accept it. Of course he will if he is intelligent. Whenever a Republic prescribes the qualifications as applying equally to all the citizens of the Republic, when the Republic says in order to vote, a citizen must be twenty-one years of age, it applies to all alike, there is no discrimination against any race or sex. When the government says that a citizen must be a native-born citizen or a naturalized citizen that applies to all; we are either born or naturalized, somehow or other we are here. Whenever the government says that a citizen, in order to vote, must be a resident of a community a certain length of time, and of the state a certain length of time and of the nation a certain length of time, that applies to all equally. There is no discrimination.

We might go further and we might say that in order to vote the citizen must be able to read his ballot. We have not gone that far yet. We have been very careful of male ignorance in these United States.

I was much interested, as perhaps many of you [were], in reading the Congressional Record this last winter over the debate over the immigration bill, and when that illiteracy clause was introduced into the immigration bill, what fear there was in the souls of men for fear we would do injustice to some of the people who might want to come to our shores, and I was much interested in the language in which the President vetoed the bill, when he declared that by inserting the clause we would keep out of our shores a large body of very excellent people. I could not help wondering then how it happens that male ignorance is so much less ignorant than female ignorance. When I hear people say that if women were permitted to vote a large body of ignorant people would vote, and therefore because an ignorant woman would vote, no intelligent women should be allowed to vote, I wonder why we have made it so easy for male ignorance and so hard for female ignorance.

When I was a girl, years ago, I lived in the back woods and there the number of votes cast at each election depended entirely upon the size of the ballot box. We had what was known as the old-tissue ballots and the man who got the most tissue in was the man elected. Now the best part of our community was very much disturbed by this method, and they did not know what to do in order to get a ballot both safe and secret; but they heard that over in Australia, where the women voted, they had a ballot which was both safe and secret, so we went over there and we got the Australian ballot and we brought it here. But when we got it over we found it was not adapted to this country, because in Australia they have to be able to read their ballot. Now the question was how could we adapt it to our conditions? Someone discovered that if you should put a symbol at the head of each column, like a rooster, or an eagle, or a hand holding a hammer, that if a man has intelligence to know the difference between a rooster and an eagle he will know which political party to vote for, and when the ballot was adapted it was a very beautiful ballot, it looked like a page from *Life*.

Now almost any American could vote that ballot, or if she had not that intelligence to know the difference between an eagle and a rooster, we could take the eagle out and put in the hen. Now when we take so much pains to adapt the ballot to the male intelligence of the United States, we should be very humble when we talk about female ignorance. Now if we should take a vote and the men had to read their ballot in order to vote it, more women could vote than men. But when the government says not only that you must be twenty-one years of age, a resident of the community and native born or naturalized, those are qualifications, but when it says that an elector must be a male, that is not a qualification for citizenship; that is an insurmountable barrier between one half of the people and the other half of the citizens and their rights as citizens. No such nation can call itself a Republic. It is only an aristocracy. That barrier must be removed before the government can become a Republic, and that is exactly what we are asking right now, that the last step in the evolutionary process be taken on November 2d. and that this great state of New York shall become in fact as it is in theory, a part of a government of the people, by the people, and for the people.

Men know the inconsistencies themselves; they realize it in one way while they do not realize it in another, because you never heard a man make a political speech when he did not speak of this country as a whole as though the thing existed which does not exist and that is that the people were equally free, because you hear them declare over and over again on the Fourth of July "under God the people rule." They know it is not true, but they say it with a great hurrah, and they repeat over and over again that clause from the Declaration of Independence, "Governments derive their just powers from the consent of the governed," and they see how they can prevent half of us from giving our consent to anything, and then they give it to us on the Fourth of July in two languages, so if it is not true in one it will be in the other, "vox populi, vox Dei." "The voice of the people is the voice of God," and the orator forgets that in the people's voice there is a soprano as well as a bass.

If the voice of the people is the voice of God, how are we ever going to know what God's voice is when we are content to listen to a bass solo? Now if it is true that the voice of the people is the voice of God, we will never know what the Deity's voice in government is until the bass and soprano are mingled together, the result of which will be the divine harmony. Take any of the magnificent appeals for freedom, which men make, and rob them of their universal application and you take the very life and soul out of them.

Where is the difficulty? Just in one thing and one thing only, that men are so sentimental. We used to believe that women were the sentimental sex, but they cannot hold a tallow candle compared with the arc light of the men. Men are so sentimental in their attitude about women that they cannot reason about them. Now men are usually very fair to each other. I think the average man recognizes that he has no more right to anything at the hands of the government than has every other man. He has no right at all to anything to which every other man has not an equal right with himself. He says why have I a right to certain things in the government; why have I a right to life and liberty; why have I a right to this or this? Does he say because I am a man? Not at all, because I am human, and being human I have a right to everything which belongs to humanity, and every right which any other human being has, I have. And then he says of his neighbor, and my neighbor he also is human, therefore every right which belongs to me as a human being, belongs to him as a human being, and I have no right to anything under the government to which he is not equally entitled.

And then up comes a woman, and then they say now she's a woman; she is not quite human, but she is my wife, or my sister, or my daughter, or an aunt, or my cousin. She is not quite human; she is only related to a human, and being related to a human a human will take care of her. So we have had that care-taking human being to look after us and they have not recognized that women too are equally human with men. Now if men could forget for a minute and believe the anti-suffragists say that we want men to forget that we are related to them, they don't know men, if for a minute they could forget our relationship and remember that we are equally human with themselves, then they would say, yes, and this human being, not because she is a woman, but because she is human is entitled to every privilege and every right under the government which I, as a human being am entitled to.

The only reason men do not see as fairly in regard to women as they do in regard to each other is because they have looked upon us from an altogether different plane than what they have looked at men; that is because women have been the homemakers while men have been the so-called protectors, in the period of the world's civilization when people needed to be protected. I know that they say that men protect us now and when we ask them what they are protecting us from the only answer they can give is from themselves. I do not think that men need any very great credit for protecting us from themselves. They are not protecting us from any special thing from which we could not protect ourselves except themselves. Now this old time idea of protection was all right when the world needed this protection, but today the protection in civilization comes from within and not from without.

What are the arguments, which our good Anti-friends give us? We know that lately they have stopped to argue and call suffragists all sorts of creatures. If there is anything we believe that we do not believe, we have not heard about them, so the cry goes out of this; the cry of the infant's mind; the cry of a little child. The anti-suffragists' cries are all the cries of little children who are afraid of the unborn and are forever crying, "The goblins will catch you if you don't watch out." So that anything that has not been should not be and all that is right, when as a matter of fact if the world believed that we would be in a static condition and never move, except back like a crab. And so the cry goes on.

When suffragists are feminists, and when I ask what that is no one is able to tell me. I would give anything to know what a feminist is. They say, would you like to be a feminist? If I could find out I would, you either have to be masculine or feminine and I prefer feminine. Then they cry that we are socialists, and anarchists. Just how a human can be both at the same time, I really do not know. If I know what socialism means it means absolute government and anarchism means no government at all. So we are feminists, socialists, anarchists, and Mormons or spinsters. Now that is about the list. I have not heard the last speech. Now as a matter of fact, as a unit we are nothing, as individuals we are like all other individuals.

We have our theories, our beliefs, but as suffragists we have but one belief, but one principle, but one theory and that is the right of a human being to have a voice in the government, under which he or she lives, on that we agree, if on nothing else. Whether we agree or not on religion or politics we are concerned. A clergyman asked me the other day, "By the way, what church does your official board belong to?" I said I don't know. He said, "Don't you know what religion your official board believes?" I said, "Really it never occurred to me, but I will [missing text] them up and see, they are not elected to my board because they believe in any particular church. We had no concern either as to what we believe as religionists or as to what we believe as women in regard to theories of government, except that one fundamental theory in the right of democracy. We do not believe in this fad or the other, but whenever any question is to be settled in any community, then the people of that community shall settle that question, the women people equally with the men people.["] That is all there is to it, and yet when it comes to arguing our case they bring up all sorts of arguments, and the beauty of it is they always answer all their own arguments. They never make an argument, but they answer it. When I was asked to answer one of their debates I said, "What is the use? Divide up their literature and let them destroy themselves."

I was followed up last year by a young, married woman from New Jersey. She left her husband home for three months to tell the women that their place was at home, and that they could not leave home long enough to go to the ballot box, and she brought all her arguments out in pairs and backed them up by statistics. The anti-suffragists can gather more statistics than any other person I ever saw, and there is nothing so sweet and calm as when they say, "You cannot deny this, because here are the figures, and figures never lie." Well they don't but some liars figure.

When they start out they always begin the same. She started by proving that it was no use to give the women the ballot because if they did have it they would not use it, and she had statistics to prove it. If we would not use it then I really cannot see the harm of giving it to us, we would not hurt anybody with it and what an easy way for you men to get rid of us. No more suffrage meetings, never any nagging you again, no one could blame you for anything that went wrong with the town, if it did not run right, all you would have to say is, you have the power, why don't you go ahead and clean up.

Then the young lady, unfortunately for her first argument, proved by statistics, of which she had many, the awful results which happened where women did have the ballot; what awful laws have been brought about by women's vote; the conditions that prevail in the homes and how deeply women get interested in politics, because women are hysterical, and we cannot think of anything else, we just forget our families, cease to care for our children, cease to love our husbands and just go to the polls and vote and keep on voting for ten hours a day 365 days in the year, never let up, if we ever get to the polls once you will never get us home, so that the women will not vote at all, and they will not do anything but vote. Now these are two very strong anti-suffrage arguments and they can prove them by figures. Then they will tell you that if women are permitted to vote it will be a great expense and no use because wives will vote just as their husbands do; even if we have no husbands, that would not effect the result because we would vote just as our husbands would vote if we had one. How I wish the anti-suffragists could make the men believe that; if they could make men believe that the women would vote just as they wanted them to do you think we would ever have to make another speech or hold another meeting, we would have to vote whether we wanted to or not.

And then the very one who will tell you that women will vote just as their husbands do will tell you in five minutes that they will not vote as their husbands will and then the discord in the homes, and the divorce. Why, they have discovered that in Colorado there are more divorces than there were before women began to vote, but they have forgotten to tell you that there are four times as many people in Colorado today as there were when women began to vote, and that may have some effect, particularly as these people went from the East. Then they will tell you all the trouble that happens in the home.

A gentleman told me that in California [missing text] and when he was talking I had a wonderful thing pass through my mind, because he said that he and his wife had lived together for twenty years and never had a difference in opinion in the whole twenty years and he was afraid if women began to vote that his wife would vote differently from him and then that beautiful harmony which they had had for twenty years would be broken, and all the time he was talking I could not help wondering which was the idiot because I knew that no intelligent human beings could live together for twenty years and not have a difference of opinion.

All the time he was talking I looked at that splendid type of manhood and thought, how would a man feel being tagged up by a little woman for twenty years saying, "Me too, me too." I would not want to live in a house with a human being for twenty years who agreed with everything I said. The stagnation of a frog pond would be hilarious compared to that. What a reflection is that on men. If we should say that about men we would never hear the last of it. Now it may be that the kind of men being that the anti-suffragists live with is that kind, but they are not the kind we live with and we could not do it. Great big overgrown babies! Cannot be disputed without having a row! While we do not believe that men are saints, by any means, we do believe that the average American man is a fairly good sort of fellow.

In fact my theory of the whole matter is exactly opposite, because instead of believing that men and women will quarrel, I think just the opposite thing will happen. I think just about six weeks before election a sort of honeymoon will start and it will continue until they will think they are again hanging over the gate, all in order to get each other's votes. When men want each other's votes they do not go up and knock them down; they are very solicitous of each other, if they are thirsty or need a smoke or [missing text] well we don't worry about home. The husband and wife who are quarreling after the vote are quarreling now.

Then the other belief that the women would not vote if they had a vote and would not do anything else; and would vote just as their husbands vote, and would not vote like their husbands; that women have so many burdens that they cannot bear another burden, and that women are the leisure class.

I remember having Reverend Dr. Abbott speak before the anti-suffrage meeting in Brooklyn and he stated that if women were permitted to vote we would not have so much time for charity and philanthropy, and I would like to say, "Thank God, there will not be so much need of charity and philanthropy." The end and aim of the suffrage is not to furnish an opportunity for excellent old ladies to be charitable. There are two words that we ought to be able to get along without, and they are charity and philanthropy. They are not needed in a Republic. If we put in the word "opportunity" instead, that is what Republics stand for.

Our doctrine is not to extend the length of our bread lines or the size of our soup kitchens, what we need is for men to have the opportunity to buy their own bread and eat their own soup. We women have used up our lives and strength in fool charities, and we have made more paupers than we have ever helped by the folly of our charities and philanthropies; the unorganized methods by which we deal with the conditions of society, and instead of giving people charity we must learn to give them an opportunity to develop and make themselves capable of earning the bread; no human being has the right to live without toil; toil of some kind, and that old theory that we used to hear "The world owes a man a living" never was true and never will be true. This world does not owe anybody a living, what it does owe to every human being is the opportunity to earn a living. We have a right to the opportunity and then the right to the living thereafter. We want it. No woman, any more than a man, has the right to live an idle life in this world, we must learn to give back something for the space occupied and we must do our duty wherever duty calls, and the woman herself must decide where her duty calls, just as a man does.

Now they tell us we should not vote because we have not the time, we are so burdened that we should not have any more burdens. Then, if that is so, I think we ought to allow the women to vote instead of the men, since we pay a man anywhere from a third to a half more than we do women it would be better to use up the cheap time of the women instead of the dear time of the men. And talking about time you would think it took about a week to vote.

A dear, good friend of mine in Omaha said, "Now Miss Shaw," and she held up her child in her arms, "is not this my job." I said it certainly is, and then she said, "How can I go to the polls and vote and neglect my baby?" I said, "Has your husband a job?" and she said, "Why you know he has." I did know it; he was a banker and a very busy one. I said, "Yet your husband said he was going to leave husband [his job] and go down to the polls and vote," and she said, "Oh yes, he is so very interested in election." Then I said, "What an advantage you have over your husband, he has to leave his job and you can take your job with you and you do not need to neglect your job." Is it not strange that the only time a woman might neglect her baby is on election day, and then the dear old Antis hold up their hands and say, "You have neglected your baby." A woman can belong to a whist club and go once a week and play whist, she cannot take her baby to the whist club, and she has to keep whist herself without trying to keep a baby whist. She can go to the theatre, to church or a picnic and no one is worrying about the baby, but to vote and everyone cries out about the neglect.

You would think on Election Day that a woman grabbed up her baby and started out and just dropped it somewhere and paid no attention to it. It used to be asked when we had the question [missing text] box, "Who will take care of the babies?" I did not know what person could be got to take care of all the babies, so I thought I would go out West and find out. I went to Denver and I found that they took care of their babies just the same on election day as they did on every other day; they took their baby along with them, when they went to put a letter in a box they took their baby along and when they went to put their ballot in the box they took their baby along. If the mother had to stand in line and the baby got restless she would joggle the go-cart and when she went in to vote a neighbor would joggle the go-cart and if there was no neighbor there was the candidate and he would joggle the cart. That is one day in the year when you can get a hundred people to take care of any number of babies. I have never worried about the babies on Election Day since that time.

Then the people will tell you that women are so burdened with their duties that they can not vote, and they will tell you that women are the leisure class and the men are worked to death: but the funniest argument [was that] of the lady who followed me about in the West: Out there they were great in the temperance question, and she declared that we were not prohibition, or she declared that we were. Now in North Dakota which is one of the first prohibition states, and they are dry because they want to be dry. In that state she wanted to prove to them that if women were allowed to vote they would vote North Dakota wet and she had her figures; that women had not voted San Francisco dry, or Portland dry, or Chicago dry. Of course we had not voted on the question in Chicago, but that did not matter.

Then we went to Montana, which is wet. They have it wet there because they want it wet, so that any argument that she could bring to bear upon them to prove that we would make North Dakota wet and keep it wet would have given us the state, but that would not work, so she brought out the figures out of her pocket to prove to the men of Montana that if women were allowed to vote in Montana they would vote Montana dry. She proved that in two years in Illinois they had voted ninety-six towns dry, and that at that rate we would soon get over Montana and have it dry. Then I went to Nebraska and as soon as I reached there a reporter came and asked me the question, "How are the women going to vote on the prohibition question?" I said, "I really don't know. I know how we will vote in North Dakota, we will vote wet in North Dakota; in Montana we will vote dry, but how we will vote in Nebraska, I don't know, but I will let you know just as soon as the lady from New Jersey comes."

We will either vote as our husbands vote or we will not vote as our husbands vote. We either have time to vote or we don't have time to vote. We will either not vote at all or we will vote all the time. It reminds me of the story of the old Irish woman who had twin boys and they were so much alike that the neighbors could not tell them apart, so one of the neighbors said, "Now Mrs. Mahoney, you have two of the finest twin boys I ever saw in all my life, but how do you know them apart." "Oh," she says, "That's easy enough any one could tell them apart. When I want to know which is which I just put my finger in Patsey's mouth and if he bites it is Mikey."

Now what does it matter whether the women will vote as their husbands do or will not vote; whether they have time or have not; or whether they will vote for prohibition or not. What has that to do with the fundamental question of democracy, no one has yet discovered. Bu they cannot argue on that; they cannot argue on the fundamental basis of our existence so that they have to get off on all of these side tricks to get anything approaching an argument. So they tell you that democracy is a form of government. It is not. It was before governments were; it will prevail when governments cease to be; it is more than a form of government; it is a great spiritual force emanating from the heart of the Infinite, transforming human character until some day, some day in the distant future, man by the power of the spirit of democracy, will be able to look back into the face of the Infinite and answer, as man cannot answer today, "One is our Father, even God, and all we people are the children of one family."

And when democracy has taken possession of human lives no man will ask from him to grant to his neighbor, whether that neighbor be a man or woman; no man will then be willing to allow another man to rise to power on his shoulders, nor will he be willing to rise to power on the shoulders of another prostrate human being. But that has not yet taken possession of us, but some day we will be free, and we are getting nearer and nearer to it all the time; and never in the history of our country had the men and women of this nation a better right to approach it than they have today; never in the history of the nation did it stand out so splendidly as it stands today, and never ought we men and women to be more grateful for anything than that there presides in the White House today a man of peace.

As so our good friends go on with one thing after another and they say if women should vote they will have to sit on the jury and they ask whether we will like to see a woman sitting on a jury. I have seen some juries that ought to be sat on and I have seen some women that would be glad to sit on anything. When a woman stands up all day behind a counter, or when she stands all day doing a washing she is glad enough to sit; and when she stands for seventy-five cents she would like to sit for two dollars a day. But don't you think we need some women on juries in this country?

You read your paper and you read that one day last week or the week before or the week before a little girl went out to school and never came back; another little girl was sent on an errand and never came back; another little girl was left in charge of a little sister and her mother went out to work and when she returned the little girl was not there, and you read it over and over again, and the horror of it strikes you. You read that in these United States five thousand young girls go out and never come back, don't you think that the men and women the vampires of our country who fatten and grow rich on the ignorance and innocence of children would rather face Satan himself than a jury of mothers. I would like to see some juries of mothers. I lived in the slums of Boston for three years and I know the need of juries of mothers.

Then they tell us that if women were permitted to vote that they would take office, and you would suppose that we just took office in this country. There is a difference of getting an office in this country and in Europe. In England, a man stands for Parliament and in this country he runs for Congress, and so long as it is a question of running for office I don't think women have much chance, especially with our present hobbles. There are some women who want to hold office and I may as well own up.

I am one of them. I have been wanting to hold office for more than thirty-five years. Thirty-five years ago I lived in the slums of Boston and ever since then I have wanted to hold office. I have applied to the major to be made an officer; I wanted to be the greatest office holder in the world, I wanted the position of the man I think is to be the most envied, as far as the ability to do good is concerned, and that is a policeman. I have always wanted to be a policeman and I have applied to be appointed policeman and the very first question that was asked me was, "Could you knock a man down and take him to jail?"

That is some people's idea of the highest service that a policeman can render a community. Knock somebody down and take him to jail! My idea is not so much to arrest criminals as it is to prevent crime. That is what is needed in the police force of every community. When I lived for three years in the back alleys of Boston, I saw there that it was needed to prevent crime and from that day? This I believe there is no great public gathering of any sort whatever where we do not need women on the police force; we need them at every moving picture show, every dance house, every restaurant, every hotel, and every great store with a great bargain counter and every park and every resort where the vampires who fatten on the crimes and vices of men and women gather. We need women on the police force and we will have them there some day.

If women vote, will they go to war? They are great on having us fight. They tell you that the government rests on force, but there are a great many kinds of force in this world, and never in the history of man were the words of the Scriptures proved to the extent that they are today, that the men of the nation that lives by the sword shall die by the sword. When I was speaking in North Dakota from an automobile with a great crowd and a great number of men gathered around a man who had been sitting in front of a store whittling a stick called out to another man and asked if women get the vote will they go over to Germany and fight the Germans? I said, "Why no, why should we go over to Germany and fight Germans?" "If Germans come over here would you fight?" I said, "Why should we women fight men, but if Germany should send an army of women over here, then we would show you what we would do. We would go down and meet them and say, 'Come on, let's go up to the opera house and talk this matter over.' It might grow wearisome but it would not be death."

Would it not be better if the heads of the governments in Europe had talked things over? What might have happened to the world if a dozen men had gotten together in Europe and settled the awful controversy, which is today discriminating the nations of Europe? We women got together there last year, over in Rome, the delegates from twenty-eight different nations of women, and for two weeks we discussed problems which had like interests to us all. They were all kinds of Protestants, both kinds of Catholics, Roman, and Greek, three were Jews and Mohamedans, but we were not there to discuss our different religious beliefs, but we were there to discuss the things that were of vital importance to us all, and at the end of the two weeks, after the discussions were over we passed a great number of resolutions.

We discussed white slavery, the immigration laws, we discussed the spread of contagious and infectious diseases; we discussed various forms of education, and various forms of juvenile criminals, every question which every nation has to meet, and at the end of two weeks we passed many resolutions, but two of them were passed unanimously. One was presented by myself as Chairman on the Committee on Suffrage and on that resolution we called upon all civilizations of the world to give to women equal rights with men and there was not a dissenting vote.

The other resolution was on peace. We believed then and many of us believe today, notwithstanding all the discussion that is going on, we believe and we will continue to believe that preparedness for war is an incentive to war, and the only hope of permanent peace is the systematic and scientific disarmament of all the nations of the world, and we passed a resolution and passed it unanimously to that effect.

A few days afterward I attended a large reception given by the American ambassador, and there was an Italian diplomat there and he spoke rather superciliously and said, "You women think you have been having a very remarkable convention, and I understand that a resolution on peace was offered by the Germans, the French women seconded it, and the British presiding presented it and it was carried unanimously." We none of us dreamed what was taking place at that time, but he knew and we learned it before we arrived home, that awful, awful thing that was about to sweep over the nations of the world. The American ambassador replied to the Italian diplomat and said, "Yes Prince, it was a remarkable convention, and it is a remarkable thing that the only people who can get together internationally and discuss their various problems without acrimony and without a sword at their side are the women of the world, but we men, even when we go to the Hague to discuss peace, we go with a sword dangling at our side." It is remarkable that even at this age men cannot discuss international problems and discuss them in peace.

When I turned away from that place up in North Dakota that man in the crowd called out again, just as we were leaving, and said, "Well what does a woman know about war anyway?" I had read my paper that morning and I knew what the awful headline was, and I saw a gentleman standing in the crowd with a paper in his pocket, and I said, "Will that gentleman hold the paper up." And he held it up, and the headline read, "250,000 Men Killed Since the War Began." I said, "You ask me what a woman knows about war? No woman can read that line and comprehend the awful horror; no woman knows the significance of 250,000 dead men, but you tell me that one man lay dead and I might be able to tell you something of its awful meaning to one woman."

I would know that years before a woman whose heart beat in unison with her love and her desire for motherhood walked day by day with her face to an open grave, with courage, which no man has ever surpassed, and if she did not fill that grave, if she lived, and if there was laid in her arms a tiny little bit of helpless humanity, I would know that there went out from her soul such a cry of thankfulness as none save a mother could know. And then I would know, what men have not yet learned that women are human; that they have human hopes and human passions, aspirations and desires as men have, and I would know that that mother had laid aside all those hopes and aspirations for herself, laid them aside for her boy, and if after years had passed by she forgot her nights of sleeplessness and her days of fatiguing toil in her care of her growing boy, and when at last he became a man and she stood looking up into his eyes and beheld him, bone of her bone and flesh of her flesh, for out of her woman's life she had carved twenty beautiful years that went into the making of a man; and there he stands, the most wonderful thing in all the world; for in all the Universe of God there is nothing more sublimely wonderful than a strong limbed, clean hearted, keen brained, aggressive young man, standing as he does on the border line of life, ready to reach out and grapple with its problems.

O, how wonderful he is, and he is hers. She gave her life for him, and in an hour this country calls him out and in an hour he lies dead; that wonderful, wonderful thing lies dead; and sitting by his side, that mother looking into the dark years to come knows that when her son died her life's hope died with him, and in the face of that wretched motherhood, what man dare ask what a woman knows of war. And that is not all. Read your papers, you cannot read it because it is not printable; you cannot tell it because it is not speakable, you cannot even think it because it is not thinkable, the horrible crimes perpetrated against women by the blood drunken men of the war.

You read your paper again and the second headlines read, "It Costs Twenty Millions of Dollars a Day," for what? To buy the material to slaughter the splendid results of civilization of the centuries. Men whom it has taken centuries to build up and make into great scientific forces of brain, the flower of the manhood of the great nations of Europe, and we spend twenty millions of dollars a day to blot out all the results of civilization of hundreds and hundreds of years. And what do we do? We lay a mortgage on every unborn child for a hundred and more years to come. Mortgage his brain, his brawn, and every pulse of his heart in order to pay the debt, to buy the material to slaughter the men of our country.

And that is not all, the greatest crime of war is the crime against the unborn. Read what they are doing. They are calling out every man, every young man, and every virile man from seventeen to forty-five or fifty years old; they are calling them out. All the splendid scientific force and energy of the splendid virile manhood are being called out to be food for the cannon, and they are leaving behind the degenerate, defective imbecile, the unfit, the criminals, the diseased to be the fathers of children yet to be born. The crime of crimes of the war is the crime against the unborn children, and in the face of the fact that women are driven out of the home shall men ask if women shall fight if they are permitted to vote.

No, we women do not want the ballot in order that we may fight, but we do want the ballot in order that we may help men to keep from fighting, whether it is in the home or in the state, just as the home is not without the man, so the state is not without the woman, and you can no more build up homes without men than you can build up the state without women. We are needed everywhere where human problems are to be solved. Men and women must go through this world together from the cradle to the grave; it is God's way and the fundamental principle of a Republican form of government.

REFLECTING AND DISCUSSING

1. What is the fundamental principle of a republic in Shaw's view? How does she make her argument?

2. How does Shaw define "republic," and how does she draw on her audience's loyalty to that republic to make her argument? Is it effective? Would it still be effective today? Why or why not?

3. Shaw anticipates the objections of those who would disagree with her. How does she do this? Look carefully at the text. Is her decision to outline these objections effective as a strategy? Why or why not?

CONNECTING AND WRITING

1. Analyze the language of the speech and research other well-known speeches that use the "call-and-response" strategy. What is this strategy? Compare and contrast Shaw's speech with another, using examples from both and arguing a point of view regarding their effectiveness.

2. Research the suffragist movement in the United States and consider Shaw's speech in that context. Write an essay about the ways in which Shaw articulates the primary goals or values of the suffragist movement.

A Vindication of the Rights of Woman, excerpt

Mary Wollstonecraft (1759–1797)

An advocate for human and especially women's rights, Mary Wollstonecraft was an English writer, philosopher, and activist. Her first publication concerned the education of daughters, but Wollstonecraft went on to write about history and politics, publishing political pamphlets, novels, and reviews. She had little formal education (a situation typical for women of the time), having been taught at home by her father, Edward John Wollstonecraft. Her daughter, Mary Wollstonecraft Shelley, was very much her mother's daughter: she wrote the well-known horror story Frankenstein *(1818).*

Introduction

After considering the historic page, and viewing the living world with anxious so-licitude, the most melancholy emotions of sorrowful indignation have depressed my spirits, and I have sighed when obliged to confess, that either nature has made a great difference between man and man, or that the civilization, which has hitherto taken place in the world, has been very partial. I have turned over various books written on the subject of education, and patiently observed the conduct of parents and the management of schools; but what has been the result? a profound conviction, that the neglected education of my fellow creatures is the grand source of the misery I deplore; and that women in particular, are rendered weak and wretched by a variety of concurring causes, originating from one hasty conclusion. The conduct and manners of women, in fact, evidently prove, that their minds are not in a healthy state; for, like the flowers that are planted in too rich a soil, strength and usefulness are sacri-ficed to beauty; and the flaunting leaves, after having pleased a fastidious eye, fade, disregarded on the stalk, long before the season when they ought to have arrived at maturity. One cause of this barren blooming I attribute to a false system of education, gathered from the books written on this subject by men, who, considering females rather as women than human creatures, have been more anxious to make them al-luring mistresses than rational wives; and the understanding of the sex has been so bubbled by this specious homage, that the civilized women of the present century, with a few exceptions, are only anxious to inspire love, when they ought to cherish a nobler ambition, and by their abilities and virtues exact respect.

In a treatise, therefore, on female rights and manners, the works which have been particularly written for their improvement must not be overlooked; especially when it is asserted, in direct terms, that the minds of women are enfeebled by false refine-ment; that the books of instruction, written by men of genius, have had the same ten-dency as more frivolous productions; and that, in the true style of Mahometanism, they are only considered as females, and not as a part of the human species, when improvable reason is allowed to be the dignified distinction, which raises men above the brute creation, and puts a natural sceptre in a feeble hand.

Yet, because I am a woman, I would not lead my readers to suppose, that I mean violently to agitate the contested question respecting the equality and inferiority of the sex; but as the subject lies in my way, and I cannot pass it over without subjecting the main tendency of my reasoning to misconstruction, I shall stop a moment to deliver, in a few words, my opinion. In the government of the physical world, it is observable that the female, in general, is inferior to the male. The male pursues, the female yields—this is the law of nature; and it does not appear to be suspended or abrogated in favour of woman. This physical superiority cannot be denied—and it is a noble prerogative! But not content with this natural pre-eminence, men endeavour to sink us still lower, merely to render us alluring objects for a moment; and women, intoxicated by the adoration which men, under the influence of their senses, pay them, do not seek to obtain a durable interest in their hearts, or to become the friends of the fellow creatures who find amusement in their society.

I am aware of an obvious inference: from every quarter have I heard exclamations against masculine women; but where are they to be found? If, by this appellation, men mean to inveigh against their ardour in hunting, shooting, and gaming, I shall most cordially join in the cry; but if it be, against the imitation of manly virtues, or, more properly speaking, the attainment of those talents and virtues, the exercise of which ennobles the human character, and which raise females in the scale of animal being, when they are comprehensively termed mankind—all those who view them with a philosophical eye must, I should think, wish with me, that they may every day grow more and more masculine.

This discussion naturally divides the subject. I shall first consider women in the grand light of human creatures, who, in common with men, are placed on this earth to unfold their faculties; and afterwards I shall more particularly point out their peculiar designation.

I wish also to steer clear of an error, which many respectable writers have fallen into; for the instruction which has hitherto been addressed to women, has rather been applicable to LADIES, if the little indirect advice, that is scattered through Sandford and Merton, be excepted; but, addressing my sex in a firmer tone, I pay particular attention to those in the middle class, because they appear to be in the most natural state. Perhaps the seeds of false refinement, immorality, and vanity have ever been shed by the great. Weak, artificial beings raised above the common wants and affections of their race, in a premature unnatural manner, undermine the very foundation of virtue, and spread corruption through the whole mass of society! As a class of mankind they have the strongest claim to pity! the education of the rich tends to render them vain and helpless, and the unfolding mind is not strengthened by the practice of those duties which dignify the human character. They only live to amuse themselves, and by the same law which in nature invariably produces certain effects, they soon only afford barren amusement.

But as I purpose taking a separate view of the different ranks of society, and of the moral character of women, in each, this hint is, for the present, sufficient; and I have only alluded to the subject, because it appears to me to be the very essence of an introduction to give a cursory account of the contents of the work it introduces.

My own sex, I hope, will excuse me, if I treat them like rational creatures, instead of flattering their FASCINATING graces, and viewing them as if they were in a state of perpetual childhood, unable to stand alone. I earnestly wish to point out in what true dignity and human happiness consists—I wish to persuade women to endeavour to acquire strength, both of mind and body, and to convince them, that the soft phrases, susceptibility of heart, delicacy of sentiment, and refinement of taste, are almost synonymous with epithets of weakness, and that those beings who are only the objects of pity and that kind of love, which has been termed its sister, will soon become objects of contempt.

Dismissing then those pretty feminine phrases, which the men condescendingly use to soften our slavish dependence, and despising that weak elegancy of mind, exquisite sensibility, and sweet docility of manners, supposed to be the sexual characteristics of the weaker vessel, I wish to show that elegance is inferior to virtue, that the first object of laudable ambition is to obtain a character as a human being, regardless of the distinction of sex; and that secondary views should be brought to this simple touchstone. . . .

The Prevailing Opinion of a Sexual Character Discussed

. . . Children, I grant, should be innocent; but when the epithet is applied to men, or women, it is but a civil term for weakness. For if it be allowed that women were destined by Providence to acquire human virtues, and by the exercise of their understandings, that stability of character which is the firmest ground to rest our future hopes upon, they must be permitted to turn to the fountain of light, and not forced to shape their course by the twinkling of a mere satellite. Milton, I grant, was of a very different opinion; for he only bends to the indefeasible right of beauty, though it would be difficult to render two passages, which I now mean to contrast, consistent: but into similar inconsistencies are great men often led by their senses:—

> "To whom thus Eve with perfect beauty adorned:
> My author and disposer, what thou bidst
> Unargued I obey; so God ordains;
> God is thy law, thou mine; to know no more
> Is woman's happiest knowledge and her praise."

These are exactly the arguments that I have used to children; but I have added, "Your reason is now gaining strength, and, till it arrives at some degree of maturity, you must look up to me for advice: then you ought to THINK, and only rely on God."

Yet, in the following lines, Milton seems to coincide with me, when he makes Adam thus expostulate with his Maker:—

> "Hast thou not made me here thy substitute,
> And these inferior far beneath me set?
> Among unequals what society
> Can sort, what harmony or delight?
> Which must be mutual, in proportion due
> Given and received; but in disparity
> The one intense, the other still remiss
> Cannot well suit with either, but soon prove
> Tedious alike; of fellowship I speak
> Such as I seek fit to participate
> All rational delight."

In treating, therefore, of the manners of women, let us, disregarding sensual arguments, trace what we should endeavour to make them in order to co-operate, if the expression be not too bold, with the Supreme Being.

By individual education, I mean—for the sense of the word is not precisely defined—such an attention to a child as will slowly sharpen the senses, form the temper, regulate the passions, as they begin to ferment, and set the understanding to work before the body arrives at maturity; so that the man may only have to proceed, not to begin, the important task of learning to think and reason.

To prevent any misconstruction, I must add, that I do not believe that a private education can work the wonders which some sanguine writers have attributed to it. Men and women must be educated, in a great degree, by the opinions and manners of the society they live in. In every age there has been a stream of popular opinion that has carried all before it, and given a family character, as it were, to the century. It may then fairly be inferred, that, till society be differently constituted, much cannot be expected from education. It is, however, sufficient for my present purpose to assert, that, whatever effect circumstances have on the abilities, every being may become virtuous by the exercise of its own reason; for if but one being was created with vicious inclinations—that is, positively bad— what can save us from atheism? or if we worship a God, is not that God a devil?

Consequently, the most perfect education, in my opinion, is such an exercise of the understanding as is best calculated to strengthen the body and form the heart; or, in other words, to enable the individual to attain such habits of virtue as will render it independent. In fact, it is a farce to call any being virtuous whose virtues do not result from the exercise of its own reason. This was Rousseau's opinion respecting men: I extend it to women, and confidently assert that they have been drawn out of their sphere by false refinement, and not by an endeavour to acquire masculine qualities. Still the regal homage which they receive is so intoxicating, that, till the manners of the times are changed, and formed on more reasonable principles, it may be impossible to convince them that the illegitimate power, which they obtain by degrading themselves, is a curse, and that they must return to nature and equality, if they wish to secure the placid satisfaction that unsophisticated affections impart. But for this epoch we must wait—wait, perhaps, till kings and nobles, enlightened by reason, and, preferring the real dignity of man to childish state, throw off their gaudy hereditary trappings; and if then women do not resign the arbitrary power of beauty, they will prove that they have LESS mind than man. I may be accused of arrogance; still I must declare, what I firmly believe, that all the writers who have written on the subject of female education and manners, from Rousseau to Dr. Gregory, have contributed to render women more artificial, weaker characters, than they would otherwise have been; and, consequently, more useless members of society. I might have expressed this conviction in a lower key; but I am afraid it would have been the whine of affectation, and not the faithful expression of my feelings, of the clear result, which experience and reflection have led me to draw. When I come to that division of the subject, I shall advert to the passages that I more particularly disapprove of, in the works of the authors I have just alluded to; but it is first necessary to observe, that my objection extends to the whole purport of those books, which tend, in my opinion, to degrade one half of the human species, and render women pleasing at the expense of every solid virtue.

Though to reason on Rousseau's ground, if man did attain a degree of perfection of mind when his body arrived at maturity, it might be proper in order to make a man and his wife ONE, that she should rely entirely on his understanding; and the graceful ivy, clasping the oak that supported it, would form a whole in which strength and beauty would be equally conspicuous. But, alas! husbands, as well as their helpmates, are often only overgrown children; nay, thanks to early debauchery, scarcely men in their outward form, and if the blind lead the blind, one need not come from heaven to tell us the consequence.

Many are the causes that, in the present corrupt state of society, contribute to enslave women by cramping their understandings and sharpening their senses. One, perhaps, that silently does more mischief than all the rest, is their disregard of order.

To do every thing in an orderly manner, is a most important precept, which women, who, generally speaking, receive only a disorderly kind of education, seldom attend to with that degree of exactness that men, who from their infancy are broken into method, observe. This negligent kind of guesswork, for what other epithet can be used to point out the random exertions of a sort of instinctive common sense, never brought to the test of reason? prevents their generalizing matters of fact, so they do to-day, what they did yesterday, merely because they did it yesterday.

This contempt of the understanding in early life has more baneful consequences than is commonly supposed; for the little knowledge which women of strong minds attain, is, from various circumstances, of a more desultory kind than the knowledge of men, and it is acquired more by sheer observations on real life, than from comparing what has been individually observed with the results of experience generalized by speculation. Led by their dependent situation and domestic employments more into society, what they learn is rather by snatches; and as learning is with them, in general, only a secondary thing, they do not pursue any one branch with that persevering ardour necessary to give vigour to the faculties, and clearness to the judgment. In the present state of society, a little learning is required to support the character of a gentleman; and boys are obliged to submit to a few years of discipline. But in the education of women the cultivation of the understanding is always subordinate to the acquirement of some corporeal accomplishment; even while enervated by confinement and false notions of modesty, the body is prevented from attaining that grace and beauty which relaxed half-formed limbs never exhibit. Besides, in youth their faculties are not brought forward by emulation; and having no serious scientific study, if they have natural sagacity it is turned too soon on life and manners. They dwell on effects, and modifications, without tracing them back to causes; and complicated rules to adjust behaviour are a weak substitute for simple principles.

As a proof that education gives this appearance of weakness to females, we may instance the example of military men, who are, like them, sent into the world before their minds have been stored with knowledge or fortified by principles. The consequences are similar; soldiers acquire a little superficial knowledge, snatched from the muddy current of conversation, and, from continually mixing with society, they gain, what is termed a knowledge of the world; and this acquaintance with manners and customs has frequently been confounded with a knowledge of the human heart. But can the crude fruit of casual observation, never brought to the test of judgment, formed by comparing speculation and experience, deserve such a distinction? Soldiers, as well as women, practice the minor virtues with punctilious politeness. Where is then the sexual difference, when the education has been the same; all the difference that I can discern, arises from the superior advantage of liberty which enables the former to see more of life.

It is wandering from my present subject, perhaps, to make a political remark; but as it was produced naturally by the train of my reflections, I shall not pass it silently over.

Standing armies can never consist of resolute, robust men; they may be well disciplined machines, but they will seldom contain men under the influence of strong passions or with very vigorous faculties. And as for any depth of understanding, I will venture to affirm, that it is as rarely to be found in the army as amongst women; and the cause, I maintain, is the same. It may be further observed, that officers are also particularly attentive to their persons, fond of dancing, crowded rooms, adventures, and ridicule. Like the FAIR sex, the business of their lives is gallantry. They were taught to please, and they only live to please. Yet they do not lose their rank in the distinction of sexes, for they are still reckoned superior to women, though in what their superiority consists, beyond what I have just mentioned, it is difficult to discover.

The great misfortune is this, that they both acquire manners before morals, and a knowledge of life before they have from reflection, any acquaintance with the grand ideal outline of human nature. The consequence is natural; satisfied with common nature, they become a prey to prejudices, and taking all their opinions on credit, they blindly submit to authority. So that if they have any sense, it is a kind of instinctive glance, that catches proportions, and decides with respect to manners; but fails when arguments are to be pursued below the surface, or opinions analyzed.

May not the same remark be applied to women? Nay, the argument may be carried still further, for they are both thrown out of a useful station by the unnatural distinctions established in civilized life. Riches and hereditary honours have made cyphers of women to give consequence to the numerical figure; and idleness has produced a mixture of gallantry and despotism in society, which leads the very men who are the slaves of their mistresses, to tyrannize over their sisters, wives, and daughters. This is only keeping them in rank and file, it is true. Strengthen the female mind by enlarging it, and there will be an end to blind obedience; but, as blind obedience is ever sought for by power, tyrants and sensualists are in the right when they endeavour to keep women in the dark, because the former only want slaves, and the latter a play-thing. The sensualist, indeed, has been the most dangerous of tyrants, and women have been duped by their lovers, as princes by their ministers, whilst dreaming that they reigned over them.

I now principally allude to Rousseau, for his character of Sophia is, undoubtedly, a captivating one, though it appears to me grossly unnatural; however, it is not the superstructure, but the foundation of her character, the principles on which her education was built, that I mean to attack; nay, warmly as I admire the genius of that able writer, whose opinions I shall often have occasion to cite, indignation always takes place of admiration, and the rigid frown of insulted virtue effaces the smile of complacency, which his eloquent periods are wont to raise, when I read his voluptuous reveries. Is this the man, who, in his ardour for virtue, would banish all the soft arts of peace, and almost carry us back to Spartan discipline? Is this the man who delights to paint the useful struggles of passion, the triumphs of good dispositions, and the heroic flights which carry the glowing soul out of itself? How are these mighty sentiments lowered when he describes the pretty foot and enticing airs of his little favourite! But, for the present, I waive the subject, and, instead of severely reprehending the transient effusions of overweening sensibility, I shall only observe, that whoever has cast a benevolent eye on society, must often have been gratified by the sight of humble mutual love, not dignified by sentiment, nor strengthened by a union in intellectual pursuits. The domestic trifles of the day have afforded matter for cheerful converse, and innocent caresses have softened toils which did not require great exercise of mind, or stretch of thought: yet, has not the sight of this moderate felicity excited more tenderness than respect? An emotion similar to what we feel when children are playing, or animals sporting, whilst the contemplation of the noble struggles of suffering merit has raised admiration, and carried our thoughts to that world where sensation will give place to reason.

Women are, therefore, to be considered either as moral beings, or so weak that they must be entirely subjected to the superior faculties of men.

Let us examine this question. Rousseau declares, that a woman should never, for a moment feel herself independent, that she should be governed by fear to exercise her NATURAL cunning, and made a coquettish slave in order to render her a more alluring object of desire, a SWEETER companion to man, whenever he chooses to relax himself. He carries the arguments, which he pretends to draw from the indications of nature, still further, and insinuates that truth and fortitude, the corner stones of all human virtue, shall be cultivated with certain restrictions, because with respect to the female character, obedience is the grand lesson which ought to be impressed with unrelenting rigour.

What nonsense! When will a great man arise with sufficient strength of mind to puff away the fumes which pride and sensuality have thus spread over the subject! If women are by nature inferior to men, their virtues must be the same in quality, if not in degree, or virtue is a relative idea; consequently, their conduct should be founded on the same principles, and have the same aim.

Connected with man as daughters, wives, and mothers, their moral character may be estimated by their manner of fulfilling those simple duties; but the end, the grand end of their exertions should be to unfold their own faculties, and acquire the dignity of conscious virtue. They may try to render their road pleasant; but ought never to forget, in common with man, that life yields not the felicity which can satisfy an immortal soul. I do not mean to insinuate, that either sex should be so lost, in abstract reflections or distant views, as to forget the affections and duties that lie before them, and are, in truth, the means appointed to produce the fruit of life; on the contrary, I would warmly recommend them, even while I assert, that they afford most satisfaction when they are considered in their true subordinate light.

Probably the prevailing opinion, that woman was created for man, may have taken its rise from Moses's poetical story; yet, as very few it is presumed, who have bestowed any serious thought on the subject, ever supposed that Eve was, literally speaking, one of Adam's ribs, the deduction must be allowed to fall to the ground; or, only be so far admitted as it proves that man, from the remotest antiquity, found it convenient to exert his strength to subjugate his companion, and his invention to show that she ought to have her neck bent under the yoke; because she as well as the brute creation, was created to do his pleasure.

Let it not be concluded, that I wish to invert the order of things; I have already granted, that, from the constitution of their bodies, men seem to be designed by Providence to attain a greater degree of virtue. I speak collectively of the whole sex; but I see not the shadow of a reason to conclude that their virtues should differ in respect to their nature. In fact, how can they, if virtue has only one eternal standard? I must, therefore, if I reason consequentially, as strenuously maintain, that they have the same simple direction, as that there is a God.

It follows then, that cunning should not be opposed to wisdom, little cares to great exertions, nor insipid softness, varnished over with the name of gentleness, to that fortitude which grand views alone can inspire.

I shall be told, that woman would then lose many of her peculiar graces, and the opinion of a well known poet might be quoted to refute my unqualified assertions. For Pope has said, in the name of the whole male sex,

> "Yet ne'er so sure our passions to create,
> As when she touch'd the brink of all we hate."

In what light this sally places men and women, I shall leave to the judicious to determine; meanwhile I shall content myself with observing, that I cannot discover why, unless they are mortal, females should always be degraded by being made subservient to love or lust.

To speak disrespectfully of love is, I know, high treason against sentiment and fine feelings; but I wish to speak the simple language of truth, and rather to address the head than the heart. To endeavour to reason love out of the world, would be to out Quixote Cervantes, and equally offend against common sense; but an endeavour to restrain this tumultuous passion, and to prove that it should not be allowed to dethrone superior powers, or to usurp the sceptre which the understanding should ever coolly wield, appears less wild.

Youth is the season for love in both sexes; but in those days of thoughtless enjoyment, provision should be made for the more important years of life, when reflection takes place of sensation. But Rousseau, and most of the male writers who have followed his steps, have warmly inculcated that the whole tendency of female education ought to be directed to one point to render them pleasing.

Let me reason with the supporters of this opinion, who have any knowledge of human nature, do they imagine that marriage can eradicate the habitude of life? The woman who has only been taught to please, will soon find that her charms are oblique sun-beams, and that they cannot have much effect on her husband's heart when they are seen every day, when the summer is past and gone. Will she then have sufficient native energy to look into herself for comfort, and cultivate her dormant faculties? or, is it not more rational to expect, that she will try to please other men; and, in the emotions raised by the expectation of new conquests, endeavour to forget the mortification her love or pride has received? When the husband ceases to be a lover—and the time will inevitably come, her desire of pleasing will then grow languid, or become a spring of bitterness; and love, perhaps, the most evanescent of all passions, gives place to jealousy or vanity.

I now speak of women who are restrained by principle or prejudice; such women though they would shrink from an intrigue with real abhorrence, yet, nevertheless, wish to be convinced by the homage of gallantry, that they are cruelly neglected by their husbands; or, days and weeks are spent in dreaming of the happiness enjoyed by congenial souls, till the health is undermined and the spirits broken by discontent. How then can the great art of pleasing be such a necessary study? it is only useful to a mistress; the chaste wife, and serious mother, should only consider her power to please as the polish of her virtues, and the affection of her husband as one of the comforts that render her task less difficult, and her life happier. But, whether she be loved or neglected, her first wish should be to make herself respectable, and not rely for all her happiness on a being subject to like infirmities with herself.

The amiable Dr. Gregory fell into a similar error. I respect his heart; but entirely disapprove of his celebrated *Legacy to his Daughters*.

He advises them to cultivate a fondness for dress, because a fondness for dress, he asserts, is natural to them. I am unable to comprehend what either he or Rousseau mean, when they frequently use this indefinite term. If they told us, that in a pre-existent state the soul was fond of dress, and brought this inclination with it into a new body, I should listen to them with a half smile, as I often do when I hear a rant about innate elegance. But if he only meant to say that the exercise of the faculties will produce this fondness, I deny it. It is not natural; but arises, like false ambition in men, from a love of power.

Dr. Gregory goes much further; he actually recommends dissimulation, and advises an innocent girl to give the lie to her feelings, and not dance with spirit, when gaiety of heart would make her feet eloquent, without making her gestures immodest. In the name of truth and common sense, why should not one woman acknowledge that she can take more exercise than another? or, in other words, that she has a sound constitution; and why to damp innocent vivacity, is she darkly to be told, that men will draw conclusions which she little thinks of? Let the libertine draw what inference he pleases; but, I hope, that no sensible mother will restrain the natural frankness of youth, by instilling such indecent cautions. Out of the abundance of the heart the mouth speaketh; and a wiser than Solomon hath said, that the heart should be made clean, and not trivial ceremonies observed, which it is not very difficult to fulfill with scrupulous exactness when vice reigns in the heart.

Women ought to endeavour to purify their hearts; but can they do so when their uncultivated understandings make them entirely dependent on their senses for employment and amusement, when no noble pursuit sets them above the little vanities of the day, or enables them to curb the wild emotions that agitate a reed over which every passing breeze has power? To gain the affections of a virtuous man, is affectation necessary?

Nature has given woman a weaker frame than man; but, to ensure her husband's affections, must a wife, who, by the exercise of her mind and body, whilst she was discharging the duties of a daughter, wife, and mother, has allowed her constitution to retain its natural strength, and her nerves a healthy tone, is she, I say, to condescend, to use art, and feign a sickly delicacy, in order to secure her husband's affection? Weakness may excite tenderness, and gratify the arrogant pride of man; but the lordly caresses of a protector will not gratify a noble mind that pants for and deserves to be respected. Fondness is a poor substitute for friendship!

In a seraglio, I grant, that all these arts are necessary; the epicure must have his palate tickled, or he will sink into apathy; but have women so little ambition as to be satisfied with such a condition? Can they supinely dream life away in the lap of pleasure, or in the languor of weariness, rather than assert their claim to pursue reasonable pleasures, and render themselves conspicuous, by practising the virtues which dignify mankind? Surely she has not an immortal soul who can loiter life away, merely employed to adorn her person, that she may amuse the languid hours, and soften the cares of a fellow-creature who is willing to be enlivened by her smiles and tricks, when the serious business of life is over.

Besides, the woman who strengthens her body and exercises her mind will, by managing her family and practising various virtues, become the friend, and not the humble dependent of her husband; and if she deserves his regard by possessing such substantial qualities, she will not find it necessary to conceal her affection, nor to pretend to an unnatural coldness of constitution to excite her husband's passions. In fact, if we revert to history, we shall find that the women who have distinguished themselves have neither been the most beautiful nor the most gentle of their sex.

Nature, or to speak with strict propriety God, has made all things right; but man has sought him out many inventions to mar the work. I now allude to that part of Dr. Gregory's treatise, where he advises a wife never to let her husband know the extent of her sensibility or affection. Voluptuous precaution; and as ineffectual as absurd. Love, from its very nature, must be transitory. To seek for a secret that would render it constant, would be as wild a search as for the philosopher's stone, or the grand panacea; and the discovery would be equally useless, or rather pernicious to mankind. The most holy band of society is friendship. It has been well said, by a shrewd satirist, "that rare as true love is, true friendship is still rarer."

This is an obvious truth, and the cause not lying deep, will not elude a slight glance of inquiry.

Love, the common passion, in which chance and sensation take place of choice and reason, is in some degree, felt by the mass of mankind; for it is not necessary to speak, at present, of the emotions that rise above or sink below love. This passion, naturally increased by suspense and difficulties, draws the mind out of its accustomed state, and exalts the affections; but the security of marriage, allowing the fever of love to subside, a healthy temperature is thought insipid, only by those who have not sufficient intellect to substitute the calm tenderness of friendship, the confidence of respect, instead of blind admiration, and the sensual emotions of fondness.

This is, must be, the course of nature—friendship or indifference inevitably succeeds love. And this constitution seems perfectly to harmonize with the system of government which prevails in the moral world. Passions are spurs to action, and open the mind; but they sink into mere appetites, become a personal momentary gratification, when the object is gained, and the satisfied mind rests in enjoyment. The man who had some virtue whilst he was struggling for a crown, often becomes a voluptuous tyrant when it graces his brow; and, when the lover is not lost in the husband, the dotard a prey to childish caprices, and fond jealousies, neglects the serious duties of life, and the caresses which should excite confidence in his children are lavished on the overgrown child, his wife.

In order to fulfil the duties of life, and to be able to pursue with vigour the various employments which form the moral character, a master and mistress of a family ought not to continue to love each other with passion. I mean to say, that they ought not to indulge those emotions which disturb the order of society, and engross the thoughts that should be otherwise employed. The mind that has never been engrossed by one object wants vigour—if it can long be so, it is weak.

A mistaken education, a narrow, uncultivated mind, and many sexual prejudices, tend to make women more constant than men; but, for the present, I shall not touch on this branch of the subject. I will go still further, and advance, without dreaming of a paradox, that an unhappy marriage is often very advantageous to a family, and that the neglected wife is, in general, the best mother. And this would almost always be the consequence, if the female mind was more enlarged; for, it seems to be the common dispensation of Providence, that what we gain in present enjoyment should be deducted from the treasure of life, experience; and that when we are gathering the flowers of the day and revelling in pleasure, the solid fruit of toil and wisdom should not be caught at the same time. The way lies before us, we must turn to the right or left; and he who will pass life away in bounding from one pleasure to another, must not complain if he neither acquires wisdom nor respectability of character.

Supposing for a moment, that the soul is not immortal, and that man was only created for the present scene; I think we should have reason to complain that love, infantine fondness, ever grew insipid and palled upon the sense. Let us eat, drink, and love, for to-morrow we die, would be in fact the language of reason, the morality of life; and who but a fool would part with a reality for a fleeting shadow? But, if awed by observing the improvable powers of the mind, we disdain to confine our wishes or thoughts to such a comparatively mean field of action; that only appears grand and important as it is connected with a boundless prospect and sublime hopes; what necessity is there for falsehood in conduct, and why must the sacred majesty of truth be violated to detain a deceitful good that saps the very foundation of virtue? Why must the female mind be tainted by coquettish arts to gratify the sensualist, and prevent love from subsiding into friendship or compassionate tenderness, when there are not qualities on which friendship can be built? Let the honest heart show itself and REASON teach passion to submit to necessity; or, let the dignified pursuit of virtue and knowledge raise the mind above those emotions which rather imbitter than sweeten the cup of life, when they are not restrained within due bounds.

I do not mean to allude to the romantic passion, which is the concomitant of genius. Who can clip its wings? But that grand passion not proportioned to the puny enjoyments of life, is only true to the sentiment, and feeds on itself. The passions which have been celebrated for their durability have always been unfortunate. They have acquired strength by absence and constitutional melancholy. The fancy has hovered round a form of beauty dimly seen—but familiarity might have turned admiration into disgust; or, at least, into indifference, and allowed the imagination leisure to start fresh game. With perfect propriety, according to this view of things, does Rousseau make the mistress of his soul, Eloisa, love St. Preux, when life was fading before her; but this is no proof of the immortality of the passion.

Of the same complexion is Dr. Gregory's advice respecting delicacy of sentiment, which he advises a woman not to acquire, if she has determined to marry. This determination, however, perfectly consistent with his former advice, he calls INDELICATE, and earnestly persuades his daughters to conceal it, though it may govern their conduct: as if it were indelicate to have the common appetites of human nature.

Noble morality! and consistent with the cautious prudence of a little soul that cannot extend its views beyond the present minute division of existence. If all the faculties of woman's mind are only to be cultivated as they respect her dependence on man; if, when she obtains a husband she has arrived at her goal, and meanly proud, is satisfied with such a paltry crown, let her grovel contentedly, scarcely raised by her employments above the animal kingdom; but, if she is struggling for the prize of her high calling, let her cultivate her understanding without stopping to consider what character the husband may have whom she is destined to marry. Let her only determine, without being too anxious about present happiness, to acquire the qualities that ennoble a rational being, and a rough, inelegant husband may shock her taste without destroying her peace of mind. She will not model her soul to suit the frailties of her companion, but to bear with them: his character may be a trial, but not an impediment to virtue.

If Dr. Gregory confined his remark to romantic expectations of constant love and congenial feelings, he should have recollected, that experience will banish what advice can never make us cease to wish for, when the imagination is kept alive at the expence of reason.

I own it frequently happens, that women who have fostered a romantic unnatural delicacy of feeling, waste their lives in IMAGINING how happy they should have been with a husband who could love them with a fervid increasing affection every day, and all day. But they might as well pine married as single, and would not be a jot more unhappy with a bad husband than longing for a good one. That a proper education; or, to speak with more precision, a well stored mind, would enable a woman to support a single life with dignity, I grant; but that she should avoid cultivating her taste, lest her husband should occasionally shock it, is quitting a substance for a shadow. To say the truth, I do not know of what use is an improved taste, if the individual be not rendered more independent of the casualties of life; if new sources of enjoyment, only dependent on the solitary operations of the mind, are not opened. People of taste, married or single, without distinction, will ever be disgusted by various things that touch not less observing minds. On this conclusion the argument must not be allowed to hinge; but in the whole sum of enjoyment is taste to be denominated a blessing?

The question is, whether it procures most pain or pleasure? The answer will decide the propriety of Dr. Gregory's advice, and show how absurd and tyrannic it is thus to lay down a system of slavery; or to attempt to educate moral beings by any other rules than those deduced from pure reason, which apply to the whole species.

Gentleness of manners, forbearance, and long suffering, are such amiable god-like qualities, that in sublime poetic strains the Deity has been invested with them; and, perhaps, no representation of his goodness so strongly fastens on the human affections as those that represent him abundant in mercy and willing to pardon. Gentleness, considered in this point of view, bears on its front all the characteristics of grandeur, combined with the winning graces of condescension; but what a different aspect it assumes when it is the submissive demeanour of dependence, the support of weakness that loves, because it wants protection; and is forbearing, because it must silently endure injuries; smiling under the lash at which it dare not snarl. Abject as this picture appears, it is the portrait of an accomplished woman, according to the received opinion of female excellence, separated by specious reasoners from human excellence. Or, they (Vide Rousseau, and Swedenborg) kindly restore the rib, and make one moral being of a man and woman; not forgetting to give her all the "submissive charms."

How women are to exist in that state where there is to be neither marrying nor giving in marriage, we are not told. For though moralists have agreed, that the tenor of life seems to prove that MAN is prepared by various circumstances for a future state, they constantly concur in advising WOMAN only to provide for the present. Gentleness, docility, and a spaniel-like affection are, on this ground, consistently recommended as the cardinal virtues of the sex; and, disregarding the arbitrary economy of nature, one writer has declared that it is masculine for a woman to be melancholy. She was created to be the toy of man, his rattle, and it must jingle in his ears, whenever, dismissing reason, he chooses to be amused.

To recommend gentleness, indeed, on a broad basis is strictly philosophical. A frail being should labour to be gentle. But when forbearance confounds right and wrong, it ceases to be a virtue; and, however convenient it may be found in a companion, that companion will ever be considered as an inferior, and only inspire a vapid tenderness, which easily degenerates into contempt. Still, if advice could really make a being gentle, whose natural disposition admitted not of such a fine polish, something toward the advancement of order would be attained; but if, as might quickly be demonstrated, only affectation be produced by this indiscriminate counsel, which throws a stumbling block in the way of gradual improvement, and true melioration of temper, the sex is not much benefited by sacrificing solid virtues to the attainment of superficial graces, though for a few years they may procure the individual's regal sway.

As a philosopher, I read with indignation the plausible epithets which men use to soften their insults; and, as a moralist, I ask what is meant by such heterogeneous associations, as fair defects, amiable weaknesses, etc.? If there is but one criterion of morals, but one archetype for man, women appear to be suspended by destiny, according to the vulgar tale of Mahomet's coffin; they have neither the unerring instinct of brutes, nor are allowed to fix the eye of reason on a perfect model. They were made to be loved, and must not aim at respect, lest they should be hunted out of society as masculine.

But to view the subject in another point of view. Do passive indolent women make the best wives? Confining our discussion to the present moment of existence, let us see how such weak creatures perform their part? Do the women who, by the attainment of a few superficial accomplishments, have strengthened the prevailing prejudice, merely contribute to the happiness of their husbands? Do they display their charms merely to amuse them? And have women, who have early imbibed notions of passive obedience, sufficient character to manage a family or educate children? So far from it, that, after surveying the history of woman, I cannot help agreeing with the severest satirist, considering the sex as the weakest as well as the most oppressed half of the species. What does history disclose but marks of inferiority, and how few women have emancipated themselves from the galling yoke of sovereign man? So few, that the exceptions remind me of an ingenious conjecture respecting Newton: that he was probably a being of a superior order, accidentally caged in a human body. In the same style I have been led to imagine that the few extraordinary women who have rushed in eccentrical directions out of the orbit prescribed to their sex, were MALE spirits, confined by mistake in a female frame. But if it be not philosophical to think of sex when the soul is mentioned, the inferiority must depend on the organs; or the heavenly fire, which is to ferment the clay, is not given in equal portions.

But avoiding, as I have hitherto done, any direct comparison of the two sexes collectively, or frankly acknowledging the inferiority of woman, according to the present appearance of things, I shall only insist, that men have increased that inferiority till women are almost sunk below the standard of rational creatures. Let their faculties have room to unfold, and their virtues to gain strength, and then determine where the whole sex must stand in the intellectual scale. Yet, let it be remembered, that for a small number of distinguished women I do not ask a place.

It is difficult for us purblind mortals to say to what height human discoveries and improvements may arrive, when the gloom of despotism subsides, which makes us stumble at every step; but, when morality shall be settled on a more solid basis, then, without being gifted with a prophetic spirit, I will venture to predict, that woman will be either the friend or slave of man. We shall not, as at present, doubt whether she is a moral agent, or the link which unites man with brutes. But, should it then appear, that like the brutes they were principally created for the use of man, he will let them patiently bite the bridle, and not mock them with empty praise; or, should their rationality be proved, he will not impede their improvement merely to gratify his sensual appetites. He will not with all the graces of rhetoric, advise them to submit implicitly their understandings to the guidance of man. He will not, when he treats of the education of women, assert, that they ought never to have the free use of reason, nor would he recommend cunning and dissimulation to beings who are acquiring, in like manner as himself, the virtues of humanity.

Surely there can be but one rule of right, if morality has an eternal foundation, and whoever sacrifices virtue, strictly so called, to present convenience, or whose DUTY it is to act in such a manner, lives only for the passing day, and cannot be an accountable creature.

The poet then should have dropped his sneer when he says,

"If weak women go astray,
The stars are more in fault than they."

For that they are bound by the adamantine chain of destiny is most certain, if it be proved that they are never to exercise their own reason, never to be independent, never to rise above opinion, or to feel the dignity of a rational will that only bows to God, and often forgets that the universe contains any being but itself, and the model of perfection to which its ardent gaze is turned, to adore attributes that, softened into virtues, may be imitated in kind, though the degree overwhelms the enraptured mind.

If, I say, for I would not impress by declamation when reason offers her sober light, if they are really capable of acting like rational creatures, let them not be treated like slaves; or, like the brutes who are dependent on the reason of man, when they associate with him; but cultivate their minds, give them the salutary, sublime curb of principle, and let them attain conscious dignity by feeling themselves only dependent on God. Teach them, in common with man, to submit to necessity, instead of giving, to render them more pleasing, a sex to morals.

Further, should experience prove that they cannot attain the same degree of strength of mind, perseverance and fortitude, let their virtues be the same in kind, though they may vainly struggle for the same degree; and the superiority of man will be equally clear, if not clearer; and truth, as it is a simple principle, which admits of no modification, would be common to both. Nay, the order of society, as it is at present regulated, would not be inverted, for woman would then only have the rank that reason assigned her, and arts could not be practised to bring the balance even, much less to turn it.

These may be termed Utopian dreams. Thanks to that Being who impressed them on my soul, and gave me sufficient strength of mind to dare to exert my own reason, till becoming dependent only on him for the support of my virtue, I view with indignation, the mistaken notions that enslave my sex.

I love man as my fellow; but his sceptre real or usurped, extends not to me, unless the reason of an individual demands my homage; and even then the submission is to reason, and not to man. In fact, the conduct of an accountable being must be regulated by the operations of its own reason; or on what foundation rests the throne of God?

It appears to me necessary to dwell on these obvious truths, because females have been insulted, as it were; and while they have been stripped of the virtues that should clothe humanity, they have been decked with artificial graces, that enable them to exercise a short lived tyranny. Love, in their bosoms, taking place of every nobler passion, their sole ambition is to be fair, to raise emotion instead of inspiring respect; and this ignoble desire, like the servility in absolute monarchies, destroys all strength of character. Liberty is the mother of virtue, and if women are, by their very constitution, slaves, and not allowed to breathe the sharp invigorating air of freedom, they must ever languish like exotics, and be reckoned beautiful flaws in nature; let it also be remembered, that they are the only flaw.

As to the argument respecting the subjection in which the sex has ever been held, it retorts on man. The many have always been enthralled by the few; and, monsters who have scarcely shown any discernment of human excellence, have tyrannized over thousands of their fellow creatures. Why have men of superior endowments submitted to such degradation? For, is it not universally acknowledged that kings, viewed collectively, have ever been inferior, in abilities and virtue, to the same number of men taken from the common mass of mankind—yet, have they not, and are they not still treated with a degree of reverence, that is an insult to reason? China is not the only country where a living man has been made a God. MEN have submitted to superior strength, to enjoy with impunity the pleasure of the moment—WOMEN have only done the same, and therefore till it is proved that the courtier, who servilely resigns the birthright of a man, is not a moral agent, it cannot be demonstrated that woman is essentially inferior to man, because she has always been subjugated.

Brutal force has hitherto governed the world, and that the science of politics is in its infancy, is evident from philosophers scrupling to give the knowledge most useful to man that determinate distinction.

I shall not pursue this argument any further than to establish an obvious inference, that as sound politics diffuse liberty, mankind, including woman, will become more wise and virtuous.

REFLECTING AND DISCUSSING

1. What is "tone" in a text? Wollstonecraft's text is sprinkled with humor and some biting sarcasm. How do these contribute to the tone of the essay? What effect do they have? Be sure to provide specific examples.
2. What is Wollstonecraft's argument? How does she support it? What contemporary assumptions about women does her text reveal? Are many of the author's concerns still relevant today? How so?
3. How is the author critical of popular notions of romantic love and beauty? How does she argue that those expectations degrade women?

CONNECTING AND WRITING

1. At another point in the essay, Wollstonecraft compares women to soldiers, indicating that the only difference between them comes from the fact that soldiers are free to see more of life than women are. Explore this comparison, using examples from this excerpt from Wollstonecraft's essay, and make an argument about its effectiveness.
2. Research one of the writers mentioned by the author in her essay—for instance, Milton or Rousseau. How does Wollstonecraft use their ideas as a springboard for her own? What other evidence from their writing supports Wollstonecraft's arguments?

Cruel and Barbarous Treatment

Mary McCarthy (1912–1989)

Mary McCarthy's parents died in the influenza epidemic of 1918; consequently, she was raised by relatives in Seattle and Minneapolis. In her memoir, Memories of a Catholic Girlhood, *McCarthy examines her childhood and her "lapsed Catholicism." Her liberal views were greatly informed by her maternal grandfather, who contributed to the drafting of the United States' first Work-men's Compensation Act. Her younger brother, Kevin McCarthy, was a popular actor, and her novel, The Group, created something of a scandal with its revelations, however lightly fictional-ized, about women at Vassar College. McCarthy received two Guggenheim Fellowships and was a member of the National Institute of Arts and Letters.*

She could not bear to hurt her husband. She impressed this on the Young Man, on her confidantes, and finally on her husband himself. The thought of Telling Him actually made her heart turn over in a sudden and sickening way, she said. This was true, and yet she knew that being a potential divorcee was deeply pleasurable in somewhat the same way that being an engaged girl had been. In both cases, there was at first a subterranean courtship, whose significance it was necessary to conceal from outside observers. The concealment of the original, premarital courtship had, however, been a mere superstitious gesture, briefly sustained. It had also been, on the whole, a private secretiveness, not a partnership of silence. One put one's family and one's friends off the track because one was still afraid that the affair might not come out right, might not lead in a clean, direct line to the altar. To confess one's aspira-tions might be, in the end, to publicize one's failure. Once a solid understanding had been reached, there followed a short intermission of ritual bashfulness, in which both parties awkwardly participated, and then came the Announcement.

But with the extramarital courtship, the deception was prolonged where it had been ephemeral, necessary where it had been frivolous, conspiratorial where it had been lonely. It was, in short, serious where it had been dilettantish. That it was ac-companied by feelings of guilt, by sharp and genuine revulsions, only complicated and deepened its delights, by abrading the sensibilities, and by imposing a sense of outlawry and consequent mutual dependence upon the lovers. But what this inter-lude of deception gave her, above all, she recognized, was an opportunity, unparal-leled in her experience, for exercising feelings of superiority over others. For her husband she had, she believed, only sympathy and compunction. She got no fun, she told the Young Man, out of putting horns on her darling's head, and never for a moment, she said, did he appear to her as the comic figure of the cuckolded husband that one saw on the stage. (The Young Man assured her that his own sentiments were equally delicate, that for the wronged man he felt the most profound respect, tinged with consideration.) It was as if by the mere act of betraying her husband, she had adequately bested him; it was supererogatory for her to gloat, and, if she gloated at all, it was over her fine restraint in not-gloating, over the integrity of her moral sense, which allowed her to preserve even while engaged in sinfulness the acute realization of sin and shame. Her overt superiority feelings she reserved for her friends. Lunches, and teas, which had been time killers, matters of routine, now became perilous and dramatic adventures. The Young Man's name was a bright, highly explosive ball which she bounced casually back and forth in these feminine tete-a-tetes. She would discuss him in his status of friend of the family, speculate on what girls he might have, attack him or defend him, anatomize him, keeping her eyes clear and impersonal, her voice empty of special emphasis, her manner humorously detached. *While all the time . . . !*

Three times a week or oftener, at lunch or tea, she would let herself tremble thus on the exquisite edge of self-betrayal, involving her companions in a momentous game whose rules and whose risks only she herself knew. The Public Appearances were even more satisfactory. To meet at a friend's house by design and to register surprise, to strike just the right note of young-matronly affection at cocktail parties, to treat him formally as "my escort" at the theater during intermissions—these were triumphs of stage management, more difficult of execution, more nerve-racking than the lunches and teas, because two actors were involved. His overardent glance must be hastily deflected; his too-self-conscious reading of his lines must be entered in the debit side of her ledger of love, in anticipation of an indulgent accounting in private.

The imperfections of his performance were, indeed, pleasing to her. Not, she thought, because his impetuosities, his gaucheries, demonstrated the sincerity of his passion for her, nor because they proved him a new hand at this game of intrigue, but rather because the high finish of her own acting showed off well in comparison. "I should have gone on the stage," she could tell him gaily, "or been a diplomat's wife or an international spy," while he would admiringly agree. Actually, she doubted whether she could ever have been an actress, acknowledging that she found it more amusing and more gratifying to play herself than to interpret any character conceived by a dramatist. In these private theatricals it was her own many-faceted nature that she put on exhibit, and the audience, in this case unfortunately limited to two, could applaud both her skill of projection and intrinsic variety. Furthermore, this was a play in which the donnée was real, and the penalty for a missed cue or an inopportune entrance was, at first anyway, unthinkable.

She loved him, she knew, for being a bad actor, for his docility in accepting her tender, mock-impatient instruction. Those superiority feelings were fattening not only on the gullibility of her friends, but also on the comic flaws of her lover's character, and on the vulnerability of her lover's position. In this particular hive she was undoubtedly queen bee.

The Public Appearances were not exclusively duets. They sometimes took the form of a trio. On these occasions the studied and benevolent carefulness which she always showed for her husband's feelings served a double purpose. She would affect a conspicuous domesticity, an affectionate conjugal demonstrativeness, would sprinkle her conversation with "Darlings," and punctuate it with pats and squeezes till her husband would visibly expand and her lover plainly and painfully shrink. For the Young Man no retaliation was possible. These endearments of hers were sanctioned by law, usage, and habit; they belonged to her role of wife and could not be condemned or paralleled by a young man who was himself unmarried. They were clear provocations, but they could not be called so, and the Young Man preferred not to speak of them. *But she knew* . . . Though she was aware of the sadistic intention of these displays, she was not ashamed of them, as she was sometimes twistingly ashamed of the hurt she was preparing to inflict on her husband. Partly she felt that they were punishments which the Young Man richly deserved for the wrong he was doing her husband, and that she herself in contriving them was acting, quite fittingly, both as judge and accused. Partly, too, she believed herself justified in playing the fond wife, whatever the damage to her lover's ego, because, in a sense, she actually was a fond wife. She did have these feelings, she insisted, whether she was exploiting them or not.

Eventually, however, her reluctance to wound her husband and her solicitude for his pride were overcome by an inner conviction that her love affair must move on to its next preordained stage. The possibilities of subterranean courtship had been exhausted; it was time for the Announcement. She and the Young Man began to tell each other in a rather breathless and literary style that the Situation Was Impossible, and Things Couldn't Go On This Way Any Longer. The ostensible meaning of these flurried laments was that, under present conditions, they were not seeing enough of each other, that their hours together were too short and their periods of separation too dismal, that the whole business of deception had become morally distasteful to them. Perhaps the Young Man really believed these things; she did not. For the first time, she saw that the virtue of marriage as an institution lay in its public character. Private cohabitation, long continued, was, she concluded, a bore. Whatever the coziness of isolation, the warm delights of having a secret, a love affair finally reached the point where it needed the glare of publicity to revive the interest of its protagonists. Hence, she thought, the engagement parties, the showers, the big church weddings, the presents, the receptions. These were simply socially approved devices by which the lovers got themselves talked about. The gossip-value of a divorce and remarriage was obviously far greater than the gossip-value of a mere engagement, and she was now ready, indeed hungry, to hear What People Would Say.

The lunches, the teas, the Public Appearances were getting a little flat. It was not, in the end, enough to be a Woman With A Secret, if to one's friends one appeared to be a woman without a secret. The bliss of having a secret required, in short, the consummation of telling it, and she looked forward to the My-dear-I-had-no-idea's, the I-thought-you-and-Bill-were-so-happy-together's, the How-did-you-keep-it-so-dark's with which her intimates would greet her announcement. The audience of two no longer sufficed her; she required a larger stage. She tried it first, a little nervously, on two or three of her closest friends, swearing them to secrecy. "Bill must hear it first from me," she declared. "It would be too terrible for his pride if he found out afterwards that the whole town knew it before he did. So you mustn't tell, even later on, that I told you about this today. I felt I had to talk to someone." After these lunches she would hurry to a phone booth to give the Young Man the gist of the conversation, just as a reporter, sent to cover a fire, telephones in to the city desk. "She certainly was surprised," she could always say with a little gush of triumph. "But she thinks it's fine." But did they actually? She could not be sure. Was it possible that she sensed in these luncheon companions, her dearest friends, a certain reserve, a certain unexpressed judgment?

It was a pity, she reflected, that she was so sensitive to public opinion. "I couldn't really love a man," she murmured to herself once, "if everybody didn't think he was wonderful." Everyone seemed to like the Young Man, of course. But still . . . She was getting panicky, she thought. Surely it was only common sense that nobody is admired by everybody. And even if a man were universally despised, would there not be a kind of defiant nobility in loving him in the teeth of the whole world? There would, certainly, but it was a type of heroism that she would scarcely be called upon to practice, for the Young Man was popular, he was invited everywhere, he danced well, his manners were ingratiating, he kept up intellectually. But was he not perhaps too amiable, too accommodating? Was it for this that her friends seemed silently to criticize him?

At this time a touch of acridity entered into her relations with the Young Man. Her indulgent scoldings had an edge to them now, and it grew increasingly difficult for her to keep her make-believe impatience from becoming real. She would look for dark spots in his character and drill away at them as relentlessly as a dentist at a cavity. A compulsive didacticism possessed her: no truism of his, no cliché, no ineffectual joke could pass the rigidity of her censorship. And, hard as she tried to maintain the character of charming schoolmistress, the Young Man, she saw, was taking alarm. She suspected that, frightened and puzzled, he contemplated flight. She found herself watching him with scientific interest, speculating as to what course he would take, and she was relieved but faintly disappointed when it became clear that he ascribed her sharpness to the tension of the situation and had decided to stick it out.

The moment had come for her to tell her husband. By this single, cathartic act, she would, she believed, rid herself of the doubts and anxieties that beset her. If her husband were to impugn the Young Man's character, she could answer his accusations and at the same time discount them as arising from jealousy. From her husband, at least, she might expect the favor of an open attack to which she could respond with the prepared defense that she carried, unspoken, about with her. Further, she had an intense, childlike curiosity as to How Her Husband Would Take It, a curiosity which she disguised for decency's sake as justifiable apprehension. The confidences already imparted to her friends seemed like pale dress rehearsals of the supreme confidence she was about to make. Perhaps it was toward this moment that the whole affair had been tending, for this moment that the whole affair had been designed. This would be the ultimate testing of her husband's love, its final, rounded, quintessential expression. Never, she thought, when you live with a man do you feel the full force of his love. It is gradually rationed out to you in an impure state, compounded with all the other elements of daily existence, so that you are hardly sensible of receiving it. There is no single point at which it is concentrated; it spreads out into the past and the future until it appears as a nearly imperceptible film over the surface of your life. Only face to face with its own annihilation could it show itself wholly, and, once shown, drop into the category of completed experiences.

She was not disappointed. She told him at breakfast in a fashionable restaurant, because, she said, he would be better able to control his feelings in public. When he called at once for the check, she had a spasm of alarm lest in an access of brutality or grief he leave her there alone, conspicuous, and, as it were, unfulfilled. But they walked out of the restaurant together and through the streets, hand in hand, tears streaming, "unchecked," she whispered to herself, down their faces. Later they were in the Park, by an artificial lake, watching the ducks swim. The sun was very bright, and she felt a kind of superb pathos in the careful and irrelevant attention they gave to the pastoral scene. This was, she knew, the most profound, the most subtle, the most idyllic experience of her life. All the strings of her nature were, at last, vibrant.

She was both doer and sufferer: she inflicted pain and participated in it. And she was, at the same time, physician, for, as she was the weapon that dealt the wound, she was also the balm that could assuage it. Only she could know the hurt that engrossed him, and it was to her that he turned for the sympathy she had ready for him. Finally, though she offered him his discharge slip with one hand, with the other she beckoned him to approach. She was wooing him all over again, but wooing him to a deeper attachment than he had previously experienced, to an unconditional surrender. She was demanding his total understanding of her, his compassion, and his forgiveness. When at last he answered her repeated and agonized I-love-you's by grasping her hand more tightly and saying gently, "I know," she saw that she had won him over. She had drawn him into a truly mystical union. Their marriage was complete.

Afterwards everything was more prosaic. The Young Man had to be telephoned and summoned to a conference à trois—a conference, she said, of civilized, intelligent people. The Young Man was a little awkward, even dropped a tear or two, which embarrassed everyone else, but what after all, she thought, could you expect? He was in a difficult position; his was a thankless part. With her husband behaving so well, indeed, so gallantly, the Young Man could not fail to look a trifle inadequate. The Young Man would have preferred it, of course, if her husband had made a scene, had bullied or threatened her, so that he himself might have acted the chivalrous protector. She, however, did not hold her husband's heroic courtesy against him: in some way, it reflected credit on herself. The Young Man, apparently, was expecting to Carry Her Off, but this she would not allow. "It would be too heartless," she whispered when they were alone for a moment. "We must all go somewhere together."

So the three went out for a drink, and she watched with a sort of desperation her husband's growing abstraction, the more and more perfunctory attention he accorded the conversation she was so bravely sustaining. "He is bored," she thought. "He is going to leave." The prospect of being left alone with the Young Man seemed suddenly unendurable. If her husband were to go now, he would take with him the third dimension that had given the affair depth, and abandon her to a flat and vulgar love scene. Terrified, she wondered whether she had not already prolonged the drama beyond its natural limits, whether the confession in the restaurant and the absolution in the Park had not rounded off the artistic whole, whether the sequel of divorce and remarriage would not, in fact, constitute an anticlimax. Already she sensed that behind her husband's good manners an ironical attitude toward herself had sprung up. Was it possible that he had believed that they would return from the Park and all would continue as before? It was conceivable that her protestations of love had been misleading, and that his enormous tenderness toward her had been based, not on the idea that he was giving her up, but rather on the idea that he was taking her back—with no questions asked. If that were the case, the telephone call, the conference, and the excursion had in his eyes been a monstrous gaffe, a breach of sensibility and good taste, for which he would never forgive her. She blushed violently. Looking at him again, she thought he was watching her with an expression which declared: I have found you out: now I know what you are like. For the first time, she felt him utterly alienated.

When he left them she experienced the letdown she had feared but also a kind of relief. She told herself that it was as well that he had cut himself off from her: it made her decision simpler. There was now nothing for her to do but to push the love affair to its conclusion, whatever that might be, and this was probably what she most deeply desired. Had the poignant intimacy of the Park persisted, she might have been tempted to drop the adventure she had begun and return to her routine. But that was, looked at coldly, unthinkable. For if the adventure would seem a little flat after the scene in the Park, the resumption of her marriage would seem even flatter. If the drama of the triangle had been amputated by her confession, the curtain had been brought down with a smack on the drama of wedlock.

And, as it turned out, the drama of the triangle was not quite ended by the superficial rupture of her marriage. Though she had left her husband's apartment and been offered shelter by a confidante, it was still necessary for her to see him every day. There were clothes to be packed, and possessions to be divided, love letters to be reread and mementoes to be wept over in common. There were occasional passionate, unconsummated embraces; there were endearments and promises. And though her husband's irony remained, it was frequently vulnerable. It was not, as she had at first thought, an armor against her, but merely a sword, out of Tristan and Isolde, which lay permanently between them and enforced discretion.

They met often, also, at the houses of friends, for, as she said, "What can I do? I know it's not tactful, but we all know the same people. You can't expect me to give up my friends." These Public Appearances were heightened in interest by the fact that these audiences, unlike the earlier ones, had, as it were, purchased librettos, and were in full possession of the intricacies of the plot. She preferred, she decided, the evening parties to the cocktail parties, for there she could dance alternately with her lover and her husband to the accompaniment of subdued gasps on the part of the bystanders.

This interlude was at the same time festive and heartrending: her only dull moments were the evenings she spent alone with the Young Man. Unfortunately, the Post-Announcement period was only too plainly an interlude and its very nature demanded that it be followed by something else. She could not preserve her anomalous status indefinitely. It was not decent and, besides, people would be bored. From the point of view of one's friends, it was all very well to entertain a Triangle as a novelty; to cope with it as a permanent problem was a different matter. Once they had all three gotten drunk, and there was a scene, and, though everyone talked about it afterwards, her friends were, she thought, a little colder, a little more critical. People began to ask her when she was going to Reno. Furthermore, she noticed that her husband was getting a slight edge in popularity over the Young Man. It was natural, of course, that everyone should feel sorry for him, and be especially nice. *But yet* . . .

When she learned from her husband that he was receiving invitations from members of her own circle, invitations in which she and the Young Man were unaccountably not included, she went at once to the station and bought her ticket. Her good-by to her husband, which she had privately allocated to her last hours in town, took place prematurely, two days before she was to leave. He was rushing off to what she inwardly feared was a Gay Weekend in the country; he had only a few minutes; he wished her a pleasant trip; and he would write, of course. His highball was drained while her glass still stood half full; he sat forward nervously on his chair; and she knew herself to be acting the Ancient Mariner, but her dignity would not allow her to hurry. She hoped that he would miss his train for her, but he did not. He left her sitting in the bar, and that night the Young Man could not, as he put it, do a thing with her. There was nowhere, absolutely nowhere, she said passionately, that she wanted to go, nobody she wanted to see, nothing she wanted to do. "You need a drink," he said with the air of a diagnostician. "A drink," she answered bitterly. "I'm sick of the drinks we've been having. Gin, whisky, rum, what else is there?" He took her into a bar, and she cried, but he bought her a fancy mixed drink, something called a Ramos gin fizz, and she was a little appeased because she had never had one before. Then some friends came in, and they all had another drink together, and she felt better. "There," said the Young Man, on the way home, "don't I know what's good for you? Don't I know how to handle you?" "Yes," she answered in her most humble and feminine tones, but she knew that they had suddenly dropped into a new pattern, that they were no longer the cynosure of a social group, but merely another young couple with an evening to pass, another young couple looking desperately for entertainment, wondering whether to call on a married couple or to drop in somewhere for a drink. This time the Young Man's prescription had worked, but it was pure luck that they had chanced to meet someone they knew. A second or a third time they would scan the faces of the other drinkers in vain, would order a second drink and surreptitiously watch the door, and finally go out alone, with a quite detectable air of being unwanted.

When, a day and a half later, the Young Man came late to take her to the train, and they had to run down the platform to catch it, she found him all at once detestable. He would ride to 125th Street with her, he declared in a burst of gallantry, but she was angry all the way because she was afraid there would be trouble with the conductor. At 125th Street, he stood on the platform blowing kisses to her and shouting something that she could not hear through the glass. She made a gesture of repugnance, but, seeing him flinch, seeing him weak and charming and incompetent, she brought her hand reluctantly to her lips and blew a kiss back. The other passengers were watching, she was aware, and though their looks were doting and not derisive, she felt herself to be humiliated and somehow vulgarized. When the train began to move, and the Young Man began to run down the platform after it, still blowing kisses and shouting alternately, she got up, turned sharply away from the window and walked back to the club car. There she sat down and ordered a whisky and soda.

There were a number of men in the car, who looked up in unison as she gave her order, but, observing that they were all the middle-aged, small-business-men who "belonged" as inevitably to the club car as the white-coated porter and the leather-bound *Saturday Evening Post*, she paid them no heed. She was now suddenly overcome by a sense of depression and loss that was unprecedented for being in no way dramatic or pleasurable. In the last half hour she had seen clearly that she would never marry the Young Man, and she found herself looking into an insubstantial future with no signpost to guide her. Almost all women, she thought, when they are girls never believe that they will get married. The terror of spinsterhood hangs over them from adolescence on. Even if they are popular they think that no one really interesting will want them enough to marry them. Even if they get engaged they are afraid that something will go wrong, something will intervene. When they do get married it seems to them a sort of miracle, and, after they have been married for a time, though in retrospect the whole process looks perfectly natural and inevitable, they retain a certain unarticulated pride in the wonder they have performed. Finally, however, the terror of spinsterhood has been so thoroughly exorcised that they forget ever having been haunted by it, and it is at this stage that they contemplate divorce. "How could I have forgotten?" she said to herself and began to wonder what she would do.

She could take an apartment by herself in the Village. She would meet new people. She would entertain. But, she thought, if I have people in for cocktails, there will always come the moment when they have to leave, and I will be alone and have to pretend to have another engagement in order to save embarrassment. If I have them to dinner, it will be the same thing, but at least I will not have to pretend to have an engagement. I shall give dinners. Then, she thought, there will be the cocktail parties, and, if I go alone, I shall always stay a little too late, hoping that a young man or even a party of people will ask me to dinner. And if I fail, if no one asks me, I shall have the ignominy of walking out alone, trying to look as if I had somewhere to go. Then there will be the evenings at home with a good book when there will be no reason at all for going to bed, and I shall perhaps sit up all night. And the mornings when there will be no point in getting up, and I shall perhaps stay in bed till dinnertime. There will be the dinners in tearooms with other unmarried women, tearooms because women alone look conspicuous and forlorn in good restaurants. And then, she thought, I shall get older.

She would never, she reflected angrily, have taken this step, had she felt that she was burning her bridges behind her. She would never have left one man unless she had had another to take his place. But the Young Man, she now saw, was merely a sort of mirage which she had allowed herself to mistake for an oasis. "If the Man," she muttered, "did not exist, the Moment would create him." This was what had happened to her. She had made herself the victim of an imposture. But, she argued, with an access of cheerfulness, if this were true, if out of the need of a second, a new, husband she had conjured up the figure of one, she had possibly been impelled by unconscious forces to behave more intelligently than appearances would indicate. She was perhaps acting out in a sort of hypnotic trance a ritual whose meaning had not yet been revealed to her, a ritual which required that, first of all, the Husband be eliminated from the cast of characters. Conceivably, she was designed for the role of *femme fatale* and for such a personage considerations of safety, provisions against loneliness and old age, were not only philistine but irrelevant. She might marry a second, a third, a fourth time, or she might never marry again. But, in any case, for the thrifty bourgeois love-insurance, with its daily payments of patience, forbearance, and resignation, she was no longer eligible. She would be, she told herself delightedly, a bad risk.

She was, or soon would be, a Young Divorcee, and the term still carried glamor. Her divorce decree would be a passport conferring on her the status of citizeness of the world. She felt gratitude toward the Young Man for having unwittingly effected her transit into a new life. She looked about her at the other passengers. Later she would talk to them. They would ask, of course, where she was bound for; that was the regulation opening move of train conversations. But it was a delicate question what her reply should be. To say "Reno" straight out would be vulgar; it would smack of confidences too cheaply given. Yet to lie, to say "San Francisco" for instance, would be to cheat herself, to minimize her importance, to mislead her interlocutor into believing her an ordinary traveler with a commonplace destination. There must be some middle course which would give information without appearing to do so, which would hint at a *vie galante* yet indicate a barrier of impeccable reserve. It would probably be best, she decided, to say "West" at first, with an air of vagueness and hesitation. Then, when pressed, she might go so far as to say "Nevada." But no farther.

REFLECTING AND DISCUSSING

1. What about this fictional account might make it appropriate for a discussion of ethics and ethical concerns?
2. What are the implications of the title? What in the piece itself suggests the implications of the title?
3. Comment on the final paragraph of the story and its final lines. What are the various levels at which the notion of "cheating" operates in them?

CONNECTING AND WRITING

1. Write an essay about the ethics and self-image of the main female character, the narrator. Is she unusually free-spirited and liberated or merely selfish? Why? What about McCarthy's tone and language support your argument?
2. This story was published in 1942, during the Second World War. How did women's roles change during that war? How might those changes have influenced the perspectives revealed in the story, if in fact you believe they are connected? Research perspectives on women's "place" during this period to provide context for your point of view.

QUESTION

Choose two pieces from this section that argue a point of view about gender roles using different rhetorical strategies and genres—for example, Freeman's short story and Wollstonecraft's political essay or the Chase and Sanborn advertisement and Orkin's image. What are these pieces saying overall? How are their arguments made? Argue your own point of view about the effectiveness of these arguments, using examples from the pieces to make your points.

HIGHER GROUND

These recognizable pieces exhort us to be better and to do better. Each exemplifies a good argument that transcends time and, on occasion, denies the author's own personal conviction in favor of the greater good.

Inaugural Address, January 1961

John Fitzgerald Kennedy (1917–1963)

The thirty-fifth president of the United States and the winner of the Pulitzer Prize for Profiles in Courage, *John F. Kennedy was born into an established, wealthy Massachusetts family. A hero in World War II, Kennedy attended Harvard University before representing Massachusetts' 11th Congressional District in the U.S. House of Representatives. After this, Kennedy was elected to the U.S. Senate, and his political ascent culminated in his defeat of Richard Nixon and his election as president in 1960. Kennedy was assassinated in November of 1963.*

We observe today not a victory of party but a celebration of freedom—symbolizing an end as well as a beginning—signifying renewal as well as change. For I have sworn before you and Almighty God the same solemn oath our forebears prescribed nearly a century and three-quarters ago.

The world is very different now. For man holds in his mortal hands the power to abolish all forms of human poverty and all forms of human life. And yet the same revolutionary beliefs for which our forebears fought are still at issue around the globe—the belief that the rights of man come not from the generosity of the state but from the hand of God.

We dare not forget today that we are the heirs of that first revolution. Let the word go forth from this time and place, to friend and foe alike, that the torch has been passed to a new generation of Americans—born in this century, tempered by war, disciplined by a hard and bitter peace, proud of our ancient heritage—and unwilling to witness or permit the slow undoing of those human rights to which this nation has always been committed, and to which we are committed today at home and around the world.

Let every nation know, whether it wishes us well or ill, that we shall pay any price, bear any burden, meet any hardship, support any friend, oppose any foe to assure the survival and the success of liberty.

This much we pledge—and more.

To those old allies whose cultural and spiritual origins we share, we pledge the loyalty of faithful friends. United there is little we cannot do in a host of cooperative ventures. Divided there is little we can do—for we dare not meet a powerful challenge at odds and split asunder.

To those new states whom we welcome to the ranks of the free, we pledge our word that one form of colonial control shall not have passed away merely to be replaced by a far more iron tyranny. We shall not always expect to find them supporting our view. But we shall always hope to find them strongly supporting their own freedom—and to remember that, in the past, those who foolishly sought power by riding the back of the tiger ended up inside.

To those people in the huts and villages of half the globe struggling to break the bonds of mass misery, we pledge our best efforts to help them help themselves, for whatever period is required—not because the communists may be doing it, not because we seek their votes, but because it is right. If a free society cannot help the many who are poor, it cannot save the few who are rich.

To our sister republics south of our border, we offer a special pledge—to convert our good words into good deeds—in a new alliance for progress—to assist free men and free governments in casting off the chains of poverty. But this peaceful revolution of hope cannot become the prey of hostile powers. Let all our neighbors know that we shall join with them to oppose aggression or subversion anywhere in the Americas. And let every other power know that this Hemisphere intends to remain the master of its own house.

To that world assembly of sovereign states, the United Nations, our last best hope in an age where the instruments of war have far outpaced the instruments of peace, we renew our pledge of support—to prevent it from becoming merely a forum for invective—to strengthen its shield of the new and the weak—and to enlarge the area in which its writ may run.

Finally, to those nations who would make themselves our adversary, we offer not a pledge but a request: that both sides begin anew the quest for peace, before the dark powers of destruction unleashed by science engulf all humanity in planned or accidental self-destruction.

We dare not tempt them with weakness. For only when our arms are sufficient beyond doubt can we be certain beyond doubt that they will never be employed.

But neither can two great and powerful groups of nations take comfort from our present course—both sides overburdened by the cost of modern weapons, both rightly alarmed by the steady spread of the deadly atom, yet both racing to alter that uncertain balance of terror that stays the hand of mankind's final war.

So let us begin anew—remembering on both sides that civility is not a sign of weakness, and sincerity is always subject to proof. Let us never negotiate out of fear. But let us never fear to negotiate.

Let both sides explore what problems unite us instead of belaboring those problems which divide us.

Let both sides, for the first time, formulate serious and precise proposals for the inspection and control of arms—and bring the absolute power to destroy other nations under the absolute control of all nations.

Let both sides seek to invoke the wonders of science instead of its terrors. Together let us explore the stars, conquer the deserts, eradicate disease, tap the ocean depths and encourage the arts and commerce.

Let both sides unite to heed in all corners of the earth the command of Isaiah—to "undo the heavy burdens . . . (and) let the oppressed go free."

And if a beachhead of cooperation may push back the jungle of suspicion, let both sides join in creating a new endeavor, not a new balance of power, but a new world of law, where the strong are just and the weak secure and the peace preserved.

All this will not be finished in the first one hundred days. Nor will it be finished in the first one thousand days, nor in the life of this Administration, nor even perhaps in our lifetime on this planet. But let us begin.

In your hands, my fellow citizens, more than mine, will rest the final success or failure of our course. Since this country was founded, each generation of Americans has been summoned to give testimony to its national loyalty. The graves of young Americans who answered the call to service surround the globe.

Now the trumpet summons us again—not as a call to bear arms, though arms we need—not as a call to battle, though embattled we are—but a call to bear the burden of a long twilight struggle, year in and year out, "rejoicing in hope, patient in tribulation"—a struggle against the common enemies of man: tyranny, poverty, disease and war itself [Romans 12:12].

Can we forge against these enemies a grand and global alliance, North and South, East and West, that can assure a more fruitful life for all mankind? Will you join in that historic effort?

In the long history of the world, only a few generations have been granted the role of defending freedom in its hour of maximum danger. I do not shrink from this responsibility—I welcome it. I do not believe that any of us would exchange places with any other people or any other generation. The energy, the faith, the devotion which we bring to this endeavor will light our country and all who serve it—and the glow from that fire can truly light the world.

And so, my fellow Americans: ask not what your country can do for you—ask what you can do for your country.

My fellow citizens of the world: ask not what America will do for you, but what together we can do for the freedom of man.

Finally, whether you are citizens of America or citizens of the world, ask of us here the same high standards of strength and sacrifice which we ask of you. With a good conscience our only sure reward, with history the final judge of our deeds, let us go forth to lead the land we love, asking His blessing and His help, but knowing that here on earth God's work must truly be our own.

Language Suited to a Nation's Purpose: New York Times Review

Brooks Atkinson (1894–1984)

On the day of President Kennedy's inauguration, an album entitled *The National Purpose* appeared on this desk. Recorded by the Westinghouse Broadcasting Co., it contains eight of the articles on this subject that appeared in *Life* magazine and the *New York Times* last spring. The articles are spoken by the men who wrote them.

It is no reflection on the wisdom, concern and critical insights of the articles to go one step beyond them. Why should they have been necessary a little less than a year ago? In a vigorous era the national purpose ought to be understood by everyone. It is identical with the private purpose of decent citizens.

Apart from the preamble to the Constitution, it was stated more than a century and a half ago by George Washington. "Let us raise a standard to which the wise and the honest can repair," he said in 14 words that are simple, direct and responsible.

When the Anglo-American world passed from Churchill and Roosevelt to Attlee and Truman about 16 years ago, James Reston made a provocative observation: Churchill's and Roosevelt's mastery of the English language regenerated their world. They could define issues vividly and arouse broad interest in their solutions.

If the succeeding world seemed mediocre, it was partly because Attlee and Truman were not virtuosos with words. Since they had to preside over a world exhausted by the crises that Churchill and Roosevelt had dramatized, the comparison is not entirely fair.

But a good case could be made that the most progressive periods in American life have coincided with presidents who wrote and spoke with a fresh command of the language. Lincoln, Theodore Roosevelt, Wilson and F. D. Roosevelt kept the national spirit alive by finding trenchant words and word combinations. They turned phrases that have become part of the national idiom. For versatility in the use of words is not a social grace. It is creative.

We are now passing from an administration that had only a platitudinous feeling for words to an administration that uses words graphically. Since ex-President Eisenhower and his speech writers had mediocre literary skills, an inquiry into the national purpose by other people had a supplementary value. The national purpose was lost in slovenly syntax.

But no one will have to define the national purpose for President Kennedy. Since he is a writer and a reader as well as a student of American history, he can express the national purpose in words that get into the blood stream of the nation. He uses the language with force and precision—and not only words but phrases, and not only phrases but sentences and paragraphs that have rhythm and imagery and overtones of religion and love of our land.

When he wrote his inauguration address he was not trying to compose a literary exercise. He was expressing a considered point of view about the problems we face and the way in which he proposes to attack them. He was compressing into words the whole body of his thinking. In less than 1,500 words (one of the most concise inauguration addresses) he awoke the nation and put the rest of the world on notice. His national objective is "not a new balance of power, but a new world of law, where the strong are just and the weak secure and the peace preserved."

Only four of those 25 words have more than one syllable; none of them has more than two. But they cut through stale political rhetoric to an idea that is alive. We know that, at the very least, a vigorous mind has taken charge of our affairs.

By using words with candor, courage, and clarity, President Kennedy has quickened the life of the nation. He has described the shape and pattern of a standard to which the wise and the honest can repair if we are able to raise it.

REFLECTING AND DISCUSSING

1. What is Kennedy's central argument, and how does he make it? In what ways does Kennedy address a wide-ranging audience?

2. What is the effect of certain rhetorical strategies Kennedy uses, such as repetition and call-and-response? Why would Kennedy choose to use these strategies to make his points?

3. In the *New York Times* response to the speech, how does Atkinson position Kennedy's inaugural address alongside those of other great speakers, and why? By implication, what does Atkinson think has been the problem with previous speeches by others?

CONNECTING AND WRITING

1. The second paragraph of Kennedy's speech begins: "The world is very different now." Research the world to which Kennedy refers. What might have been his context in 1961, both at home and abroad? Select other references within the speech to the global context and analyze them. What, overall, is Kennedy trying to do with these references?

2. In Atkinson's review/response, he notes that Kennedy's inaugural address is "less than 1,500 words (one of the most concise inauguration addresses)." Nevertheless, Atkinson argues that it cuts through "stale political rhetoric to an idea that is alive." What is this idea? What ideals does Kennedy speak to in this address? Compare this speech to a more contemporary inaugural address. Does the message seem to be inspired by Kennedy's? If so, how? Which message is most effective? Why?

Letter from a Birmingham Jail

Martin Luther King, Jr. (1929–1968)

Born in Atlanta and a graduate of Morehouse College and Boston University (where he earned his Ph.D.), Dr. Martin Luther King, Jr., is perhaps the foremost representative of the civil rights movement of the 1950s and 1960s. King achieved national prominence in 1955 as the leader of a boycott against segregated buses in Montgomery, Alabama. In 1957, King and others founded the Southern Christian Leadership Conference, which emphasized the goal of achieving voting rights for African-Americans and coordinated various efforts involving nonviolent action. In 1964, King was Time *magazine's "Man of the Year" and received the Nobel Peace Prize. King was assassinated on April 4, 1968.*

While confined here in the Birmingham city jail, I came across your recent statement calling our present activities "unwise and untimely." Seldom, if ever, do I pause to answer criticism of my work and ideas. If I sought to answer all of the criticisms that cross my desk, my secretaries would be engaged in little else in the course of the day, and I would have no time for constructive work. But since I feel that you are men of genuine good will and your criticisms are sincerely set forth, I would like to answer your statement in what I hope will be patient and reasonable terms.

I think I should give the reason for my being in Birmingham, since you have been influenced by the argument of "outsiders coming in." I have the honor of serving as president of the Southern Christian Leadership Conference, an organization operating in every Southern state, with headquarters in Atlanta, Georgia. We have some eighty-five affiliate organizations all across the South, one being the Alabama Christian Movement for Human Rights. Whenever necessary and possible, we share staff, educational and financial resources with our affiliates. Several months ago our local affiliate here in Birmingham invited us to be on call to engage in a nonviolent direct-action program if such were deemed necessary. We readily consented, and when the hour came we lived up to our promises. So I am here, along with several members of my staff, because we were invited here. I am here because I have basic organizational ties here.

Beyond this, I am in Birmingham because injustice is here. Just as the eighth-century prophets left their little villages and carried their "thus saith the Lord" far beyond the boundaries of their hometowns; and just as the Apostle Paul left his little village of Tarsus and carried the gospel of Jesus Christ to practically every hamlet and city of the Greco-Roman world, I too am compelled to carry the gospel of freedom beyond my particular hometown. Like Paul, I must constantly respond to the Macedonian call for aid.

Moreover, I am cognizant of the interrelatedness of all communities and states. I cannot sit idly by in Atlanta and not be concerned about what happens in Birmingham. Injustice anywhere is a threat to justice everywhere. We are caught in an inescapable network of mutuality, tied in a single garment of destiny. Whatever affects one directly affects all indirectly. Never again can we afford to live with the narrow, provincial "outside agitator" idea. Anyone who lives inside the United States can never be considered an outsider.

You deplore the demonstrations that are presently taking place in Birmingham. But I am sorry that your statement did not express a similar concern for the conditions that brought the demonstrations into being. I am sure that each of you would want to go beyond the superficial social analyst who looks merely at effects and does not grapple with underlying causes. I would not hesitate to say that it is unfortunate that so-called demonstrations are taking place in Birmingham at this time, but I would say in more emphatic terms that it is even more unfortunate that the white power structure of this city left the Negro community with no other alternative.

In any nonviolent campaign there are four basic steps: collection of the facts to determine whether injustices are alive, negotiation, self-purification, and direct action. We have gone through all of these steps in Birmingham. There can be no gainsaying of the fact that racial injustice engulfs this community. Birmingham is probably the most thoroughly segregated city in the United States. Its ugly record of police brutality is known in every section of this country. Its unjust treatment of Negroes in the courts is a notorious reality. There have been more unsolved bombings of Negro homes and churches in Birmingham than in any other city in this nation. These are the hard, brutal, and unbelievable facts. On the basis of them, Negro leaders sought to negotiate with the city fathers. But the political leaders consistently refused to engage in good-faith negotiation.

Then came the opportunity last September to talk with some of the leaders of the economic community. In these negotiating sessions certain promises were made by the merchants, such as the promise to remove the humiliating racial signs from the stores. On the basis of these promises, Reverend Shuttlesworth and the leaders of the Alabama Christian Movement for Human Rights agreed to call a moratorium on any type of demonstration. As the weeks and months unfolded, we realized that we were the victims of a broken promise. The signs remained. As in so many experiences of the past, we were confronted with blasted hopes, and the dark shadow of a deep disappointment settled upon us. So we had no alternative except that of preparing for direct action, whereby we would present our very bodies as a means of laying our case before the conscience of the local and national community. We were not unmindful of the difficulties involved. So we decided to go through a process of self-purification. We started having workshops on nonviolence and repeatedly asked ourselves the questions, "Are you able to accept blows without retaliating?" and "Are you able to endure the ordeals of jail?" We decided to set our direct-action program around the Easter season, realizing that, with exception of Christmas, this was the largest shopping period of the year. Knowing that a strong economic withdrawal program would be the by-product of direct action, we felt that this was the best time to bring pressure on the merchants for the needed changes. Then it occurred to us that the March election was ahead, and so we speedily decided to postpone action until after election day. When we discovered that Mr. Conner was in the runoff, we decided again to postpone action so that the demonstration could not be used to cloud the issues. At this time we agreed to begin our nonviolent witness the day after the runoff.

This reveals that we did not move irresponsibly into direct action. We, too, wanted to see Mr. Conner defeated, so we went through postponement after postponement to aid in this community need. After this we felt that direct action could be delayed no longer.

You may well ask, "Why direct action, why sit-ins, marches, and so forth? Isn't negotiation a better path?" You are exactly right in your call for negotiation. Indeed, this is the purpose of direct action. Nonviolent direct action seeks to create such a crisis and establish such creative tension that a community that has consistently refused to negotiate is forced to confront the issue. It seeks so to dramatize the issue that it can no longer be ignored. I just referred to the creation of tension as a part of the work of the nonviolent resister. This may sound rather shocking. But I must confess that I am not afraid of the word "tension." I have earnestly worked and preached against violent tension, but there is a type of constructive nonviolent tension that is necessary for growth. Just as Socrates felt that it was necessary to create a tension in the mind so that individuals could rise from the bondage of myths and half-truths to the unfettered realm of creative analysis and objective appraisal, we must see the need of having nonviolent gadflies to create the kind of tension in society that will help men to rise from the dark depths of prejudice and racism to the majestic heights of understanding and brotherhood. So, the purpose of direct action is to create a situation so crisis-packed that it will inevitably open the door to negotiation. We therefore concur with you in your call for negotiation. Too long has our beloved Southland been bogged down in the tragic attempt to live in monologue rather than dialogue.

One of the basic points in your statement is that our acts are untimely. Some have asked, "Why didn't you give the new administration time to act?" The only answer that I can give to this inquiry is that the new administration must be prodded about as much as the outgoing one before it acts. We will be sadly mistaken if we feel that the election of Mr. Boutwell will bring the millennium to Birmingham. While Mr. Boutwell is much more articulate and gentle than Mr. Conner, they are both segregationists, dedicated to the task of maintaining the status quo. The hope I see in Mr. Boutwell is that he will be reasonable enough to see the futility of massive resistance to desegregation. But he will not see this without pressure from the devotees of civil rights. My friends, I must say to you that we have not made a single gain in civil rights without determined legal and nonviolent pressure. History is the long and tragic story of the fact that privileged groups seldom give up their privileges voluntarily. Individuals may see the moral light and voluntarily give up their unjust posture; but, as Reinhold Niebuhr has reminded us, groups are more immoral than individuals.

We know through painful experience that freedom is never voluntarily given by the oppressor; it must be demanded by the oppressed. Frankly, I have never yet engaged in a direct-action movement that was "well timed" according to the timetable of those who have not suffered unduly from the disease of segregation. For years now I have heard the word "wait." It rings in the ear of every Negro with a piercing familiarity. This "wait" has almost always meant "never." It has been a tranquilizing thalidomide, relieving the emotional stress for a moment, only to give birth to an ill-formed infant of frustration. We must come to see with the distinguished jurist of yesterday that "justice too long delayed is justice denied." We have waited for more than three hundred and forty years for our God-given and constitutional rights. The nations of Asia and Africa are moving with jetlike speed toward the goal of political independence, and we still creep at horse-and-buggy pace toward the gaining of a cup of coffee at a lunch counter. I guess it is easy for those who have never felt the stinging darts of segregation to say "wait." But when you have seen vicious mobs lynch your mothers and fathers at will and drown your sisters and brothers at whim; when you have seen hate-filled policemen curse, kick, brutalize, and even kill your black brothers and sisters with impunity; when you see the vast majority of your twenty million Negro brothers smothering in an airtight cage of poverty in the midst of an affluent society; when you suddenly find your tongue twisted and your speech stammering as you seek to explain to your six-year-old daughter why she cannot go to the public amusement park that has just been advertised on television, and see tears welling up in her little eyes when she is told that Funtown is closed to colored children, and see the depressing clouds of inferiority begin to form in her little mental sky, and see her begin to distort her little personality by unconsciously developing a bitterness toward white people; when you have to concoct an answer for a five-year-old son asking in agonizing pathos, "Daddy, why do white people treat colored people so mean?"; when you take a cross-country drive and find it necessary to sleep night after night in the uncomfortable corners of your automobile because no motel will accept you; when you are humiliated day in and day out by nagging signs reading "white" and "colored"; when your first name becomes "nigger" and your middle name becomes "boy" (however old you are) and your last name becomes "John," and when your wife and mother are never given the respected title "Mrs."; when you are harried by day and haunted by night by the fact that you are a Negro, living constantly at tiptoe stance, never knowing what to expect next, and plagued with inner fears and outer resentments; when you are forever fighting a degenerating sense of "nobodyness"—then you will understand why we find it difficult to wait. There comes a time when the cup of endurance runs over and men are no longer willing to be plunged into an abyss of injustice where they experience the bleakness of corroding despair. I hope, sirs, you can understand our legitimate and unavoidable impatience.

You express a great deal of anxiety over our willingness to break laws. This is certainly a legitimate concern. Since we so diligently urge people to obey the Supreme Court's decision of 1954 outlawing segregation in the public schools, it is rather strange and paradoxical to find us consciously breaking laws. One may well ask, "How can you advocate breaking some laws and obeying others?" The answer is found in the fact that there are two types of laws: there are just laws, and there are unjust laws. I would agree with St. Augustine that "An unjust law is no law at all."

Now, what is the difference between the two? How does one determine when a law is just or unjust? A just law is a man-made code that squares with the moral law, or the law of God. An unjust law is a code that is out of harmony with the moral law. To put it in the terms of St. Thomas Aquinas, an unjust law is a human law that is not rooted in eternal and natural law. Any law that uplifts human personality is just. Any law that degrades human personality is unjust. All segregation statutes are unjust because segregation distorts the soul and damages the personality. It gives the segregator a false sense of superiority and the segregated a false sense of inferiority. To use the words of Martin Buber, the great Jewish philosopher, segregation substitutes an "I–it" relationship for the "I–thou" relationship and ends up relegating persons to the status of things. So segregation is not only politically, economically, and sociologically unsound, but it is morally wrong and sinful. Paul Tillich has said that sin is separation. Isn't segregation an existential expression of man's tragic separation, an expression of his awful estrangement, his terrible sinfulness? So I can urge men to obey the 1954 decision of the Supreme Court because it is morally right, and I can urge them to disobey segregation ordinances because they are morally wrong.

Let us turn to a more concrete example of just and unjust laws. An unjust law is a code that a majority inflicts on a minority that is not binding on itself. This is difference made legal. On the other hand, a just law is a code that a majority compels a minority to follow, and that it is willing to follow itself. This is sameness made legal.

Let me give another explanation. An unjust law is a code inflicted upon a minority which that minority had no part in enacting or creating because it did not have the unhampered right to vote. Who can say that the legislature of Alabama which set up the segregation laws was democratically elected? Throughout the state of Alabama all types of conniving methods are used to prevent Negroes from becoming registered voters, and there are some counties without a single Negro registered to vote, despite the fact that the Negroes constitute a majority of the population. Can any law set up in such a state be considered democratically structured?

These are just a few examples of unjust and just laws. There are some instances when a law is just on its face and unjust in its application. For instance, I was arrested Friday on a charge of parading without a permit. Now, there is nothing wrong with an ordinance which requires a permit for a parade, but when the ordinance is used to preserve segregation and to deny citizens the First Amendment privilege of peaceful assembly and peaceful protest, then it becomes unjust.

Of course, there is nothing new about this kind of civil disobedience. It was seen sublimely in the refusal of Shadrach, Meshach, and Abednego to obey the laws of Nebuchadnezzar because a higher moral law was involved. It was practiced superbly by the early Christians, who were willing to face hungry lions and the excruciating pain of chopping blocks before submitting to certain unjust laws of the Roman Empire. To a degree, academic freedom is a reality today because Socrates practiced civil disobedience.

We can never forget that everything Hitler did in Germany was "legal" and everything the Hungarian freedom fighters did in Hungary was "illegal." It was "illegal" to aid and comfort a Jew in Hitler's Germany. But I am sure that if I had lived in Germany during that time, I would have aided and comforted my Jewish brothers even though it was illegal. If I lived in a Communist country today where certain principles dear to the Christian faith are suppressed, I believe I would openly advocate disobeying these anti-religious laws.

I must make two honest confessions to you, my Christian and Jewish brothers. First, I must confess that over the last few years I have been gravely disappointed with the white moderate. I have almost reached the regrettable conclusion that the Negro's great stumbling block in the stride toward freedom is not the White Citizens Councillor or the Ku Klux Klanner but the white moderate who is more devoted to order than to justice; who prefers a negative peace which is the absence of tension to a positive peace which is the presence of justice; who constantly says, "I agree with you in the goal you seek, but I can't agree with your methods of direct action"; who paternalistically feels that he can set the timetable for another man's freedom; who lives by the myth of time; and who constantly advises the Negro to wait until a "more convenient season." Shallow understanding from people of good will is more frustrating than absolute misunderstanding from people of ill will. Lukewarm acceptance is much more bewildering than outright rejection.

In your statement you asserted that our actions, even though peaceful, must be condemned because they precipitate violence. But can this assertion be logically made? Isn't this like condemning the robbed man because his possession of money precipitated the evil act of robbery? Isn't this like condemning Socrates because his unswerving commitment to truth and his philosophical delvings precipitated the misguided popular mind to make him drink the hemlock? Isn't this like condemning Jesus because His unique God-consciousness and never-ceasing devotion to His will precipitated the evil act of crucifixion? We must come to see, as federal courts have consistently affirmed, that it is immoral to urge an individual to withdraw his efforts to gain his basic constitutional rights because the quest precipitates violence. Society must protect the robbed and punish the robber.

I had also hoped that the white moderate would reject the myth of time. I received a letter this morning from a white brother in Texas which said, "All Christians know that the colored people will receive equal rights eventually, but is it possible that you are in too great of a religious hurry? It has taken Christianity almost 2,000 years to accomplish what it has. The teachings of Christ take time to come to earth." All that is said here grows out of a tragic misconception of time. It is the strangely irrational notion that there is something in the very flow of time that will inevitably cure all ills. Actually, time is neutral. It can be used either destructively or constructively. I am coming to feel that the people of ill will have used time much more effectively than the people of good will. We will have to repent in this generation not merely for the vitriolic words and actions of the bad people but for the appalling silence of the good people. We must come to see that human progress never rolls in on wheels of inevitability. It comes through the tireless efforts and persistent work of men willing to be coworkers with God, and without this hard work time itself becomes an ally of the forces of social stagnation.

You spoke of our activity in Birmingham as extreme. At first I was rather disappointed that fellow clergymen would see my nonviolent efforts as those of an extremist. I started thinking about the fact that I stand in the middle of two opposing forces in the Negro community. One is a force of complacency made up of Negroes who, as a result of long years of oppression, have been so completely drained of self-respect and a sense of "somebodyness" that they have adjusted to segregation, and, on the other hand, of a few Negroes in the middle class who, because of a degree of academic and economic security and because at points they profit by segregation, have unconsciously become insensitive to the problems of the masses. The other force is one of bitterness and hatred and comes perilously close to advocating violence. It is expressed in the various black nationalist groups that are springing up over the nation, the largest and best known being Elijah Muhammad's Muslim movement. This movement is nourished by the contemporary frustration over the continued existence of racial discrimination. It is made up of people who have lost faith in America, who have absolutely repudiated Christianity, and who have concluded that the white man is an incurable devil. I have tried to stand between these two forces, saying that we need not follow the do-nothingism of the complacent or the hatred and despair of the black nationalist. There is a more excellent way, of love and nonviolent protest. I'm grateful to God that, through the Negro church, the dimension of nonviolence entered our struggle. If this philosophy had not emerged, I am convinced that by now many streets of the South would be flowing with floods of blood. And I am further convinced that if our white brothers dismiss as "rabble-rousers" and "outside agitators" those of us who are working through the channels of nonviolent direct action and refuse to support our nonviolent efforts, millions of Negroes, out of frustration and despair, will seek solace and security in black nationalist ideologies, a development that will lead inevitably to a frightening racial nightmare.

Oppressed people cannot remain oppressed forever. The urge for freedom will eventually come. This is what has happened to the American Negro. Something within has reminded him of his birthright of freedom; something without has reminded him that he can gain it. Consciously and unconsciously, he has been swept in by what the Germans call the Zeitgeist, and with his black brothers of Africa and his brown and yellow brothers of Asia, South America, and the Caribbean, he is moving with a sense of cosmic urgency toward the promised land of racial justice. Recognizing this vital urge that has engulfed the Negro community, one should readily understand public demonstrations. The Negro has many pent-up resentments and latent frustrations. He has to get them out. So let him march sometime; let him have his prayer pilgrimages to the city hall; understand why he must have sit-ins and freedom rides. If his repressed emotions do not come out in these nonviolent ways, they will come out in ominous expressions of violence. This is not a threat; it is a fact of history. So I have not said to my people, "Get rid of your discontent." But I have tried to say that this normal and healthy discontent can be channeled through the creative outlet of nonviolent direct action. Now this approach is being dismissed as extremist. I must admit that I was initially disappointed in being so categorized.

But as I continued to think about the matter, I gradually gained a bit of satisfaction from being considered an extremist. Was not Jesus an extremist in love?—"Love your enemies, bless them that curse you, pray for them that despitefully use you." Was not Amos an extremist for justice?—"Let justice roll down like waters and righteousness like a mighty stream." Was not Paul an extremist for the gospel of Jesus Christ?—"I bear in my body the marks of the Lord Jesus." Was not Martin Luther an extremist?—"Here I stand; I can do no other so help me God." Was not John Bunyan an extremist?—"I will stay in jail to the end of my days before I make a mockery of my conscience." Was not Abraham Lincoln an extremist?—"This nation cannot survive half slave and half free." Was not Thomas Jefferson an extremist?— "We hold these truths to be self-evident, that all men are created equal." So the question is not whether we will be extremist, but what kind of extremists we will be. Will we be extremists for hate, or will we be extremists for love? Will we be extremists for the preservation of injustice, or will we be extremists for the cause of justice?

I had hoped that the white moderate would see this. Maybe I was too optimistic. Maybe I expected too much. I guess I should have realized that few members of a race that has oppressed another race can understand or appreciate the deep groans and passionate yearnings of those that have been oppressed, and still fewer have the vision to see that injustice must be rooted out by strong, persistent, and determined action. I am thankful, however, that some of our white brothers have grasped the meaning of this social revolution and committed themselves to it. They are still all too small in quantity, but they are big in quality. Some, like Ralph McGill, Lillian Smith, Harry Golden, and James Dabbs, have written about our struggle in eloquent, prophetic, and understanding terms. Others have marched with us down nameless streets of the South. They sat in with us at lunch counters and rode in with us on the freedom rides. They have languished in filthy roach-infested jails, suffering the abuse and brutality of angry policemen who see them as "dirty nigger lovers." They, unlike many of their moderate brothers, have recognized the urgency of the moment and sensed the need for powerful "action" antidotes to combat the disease of segregation.

Let me rush on to mention my other disappointment. I have been disappointed with the white church and its leadership. Of course, there are some notable exceptions. I am not unmindful of the fact that each of you has taken some significant stands on this issue. I commend you, Reverend Stallings, for your Christian stand this past Sunday in welcoming Negroes to your Baptist Church worship service on a nonsegregated basis. I commend the Catholic leaders of this state for integrating Springhill College several years ago.

But despite these notable exceptions, I must honestly reiterate that I have been disappointed with the church. I do not say that as one of those negative critics who can always find something wrong with the church. I say it as a minister of the gospel who loves the church, who was nurtured in its bosom, who has been sustained by its Spiritual blessings, and who will remain true to it as long as the cord of life shall lengthen.

I had the strange feeling when I was suddenly catapulted into the leadership of the bus protest in Montgomery several years ago that we would have the support of the white church. I felt that the white ministers, priests, and rabbis of the South would be some of our strongest allies. Instead, some few have been outright opponents, refusing to understand the freedom movement and misrepresenting its leaders; all too many others have been more cautious than courageous and have remained silent behind the anesthetizing security of stained-glass windows.

In spite of my shattered dreams of the past, I came to Birmingham with the hope that the white religious leadership of this community would see the justice of our cause and with deep moral concern serve as the channel through which our just grievances could get to the power structure. I had hoped that each of you would understand. But again I have been disappointed.

I have heard numerous religious leaders of the South call upon their worshipers to comply with a desegregation decision because it is the law, but I have longed to hear white ministers say, follow this decree because integration is morally right and the Negro is your brother. In the midst of blatant injustices inflicted upon the

Negro, I have watched white churches stand on the sidelines and merely mouth pious irrelevancies and sanctimonious trivialities. In the midst of a mighty struggle to rid our nation of racial and economic injustice, I have heard so many ministers say, "Those are social issues which the gospel has nothing to do with," and I have watched so many churches commit themselves to a completely otherworldly religion which made a strange distinction between bodies and souls, the sacred and the secular.

There was a time when the church was very powerful. It was during that period that the early Christians rejoiced when they were deemed worthy to suffer for what they believed. In those days the church was not merely a thermometer that recorded the ideas and principles of popular opinion; it was the thermostat that transformed the mores of society. Wherever the early Christians entered a town the power structure got disturbed and immediately sought to convict them for being "disturbers of the peace" and "outside agitators." But they went on with the conviction that they were "a colony of heaven" and had to obey God rather than man. They were small in number but big in commitment. They were too God-intoxicated to be "astronomically intimidated." They brought an end to such ancient evils as infanticide and gladiatorial contest.

Things are different now. The contemporary church is so often a weak, ineffectual voice with an uncertain sound. It is so often the arch supporter of the status quo. Far from being disturbed by the presence of the church, the power structure of the average community is consoled by the church's often vocal sanction of things as they are.

But the judgment of God is upon the church as never before. If the church of today does not recapture the sacrificial spirit of the early church, it will lose its authentic ring, forfeit the loyalty of millions, and be dismissed as an irrelevant social club with no meaning for the twentieth century. I meet young people every day whose disappointment with the church has risen to outright disgust.

I hope the church as a whole will meet the challenge of this decisive hour. But even if the church does not come to the aid of justice, I have no despair about the future. I have no fear about the outcome of our struggle in Birmingham, even if our motives are presently misunderstood. We will reach the goal of freedom in Birmingham and all over the nation, because the goal of America is freedom. Abused and scorned though we may be, our destiny is tied up with the destiny of America. Before the Pilgrims landed at Plymouth, we were here. Before the pen of Jefferson scratched across the pages of history the majestic word of the Declaration of Independence, we were here. For more than two centuries our foreparents labored here without wages; they made cotton king; and they built the homes of their masters in the midst of brutal injustice and shameful humiliation—and yet out of a bottomless vitality our people continue to thrive and develop. If the inexpressible cruelties of slavery could not stop us, the opposition we now face will surely fail. We will win our freedom because the sacred heritage of our nation and the eternal will of God are embodied in our echoing demands.

I must close now. But before closing I am impelled to mention one other point in your statement that troubled me profoundly. You warmly commended the

Birmingham police force for keeping "order" and "preventing violence." I don't believe you would have so warmly commended the police force if you had seen its angry violent dogs literally biting six unarmed, nonviolent Negroes. I don't believe you would so quickly commend the policemen if you would observe their ugly and inhuman treatment of Negroes here in the city jail; if you would watch them push and curse old Negro women and young Negro girls; if you would see them slap and kick old Negro men and young boys, if you would observe them, as they did on two occasions, refusing to give us food because we wanted to sing our grace together. I'm sorry that I can't join you in your praise for the police department.

It is true that they have been rather disciplined in their public handling of the demonstrators. In this sense they have been publicly "nonviolent." But for what purpose? To preserve the evil system of segregation. Over the last few years I have consistently preached that nonviolence demands that the means we use must be as pure as the ends we seek. So I have tried to make it clear that it is wrong to use immoral means to attain moral ends. But now I must affirm that it is just as wrong, or even more, to use moral means to preserve immoral ends.

I wish you had commended the Negro demonstrators of Birmingham for their sublime courage, their willingness to suffer, and their amazing discipline in the midst of the most inhuman provocation. One day the South will recognize its real heroes. They will be the James Merediths, courageously and with a majestic sense of purpose facing jeering and hostile mobs and the agonizing loneliness that characterizes the life of the pioneer. They will be old, oppressed, battered Negro women, symbolized in a seventy-two-year-old woman of Montgomery, Alabama, who rose up with a sense of dignity and with her people decided not to ride the segregated buses, and responded to one who inquired about her tiredness with ungrammatical profundity, "My feets is tired, but my soul is rested." They will be young high school and college students, young ministers of the gospel and a host of their elders courageously and nonviolently sitting in at lunch counters and will-ingly going to jail for conscience's sake. One day the South will know that when these disinherited children of God sat down at lunch counters they were in reality standing up for the best in the American dream and the most sacred values in our Judeo-Christian heritage.

Never before have I written a letter this long—or should I say a book? I'm afraid that it is much too long to take your precious time. I can assure you that it would have been much shorter if I had been writing from a comfortable desk, but what else is there to do when you are alone for days in the dull monotony of a narrow jail cell other than write long letters, think strange thoughts, and pray long prayers?

If I have said anything in this letter that is an understatement of the truth and is indicative of an unreasonable impatience, I beg you to forgive me. If I have said anything in this letter that is an overstatement of the truth and is indicative of my having a patience that makes me patient with anything less than brotherhood, I beg God to forgive me.

Yours for the cause of Peace and Brotherhood,
MARTIN LUTHER KING, JR.

REFLECTING AND DISCUSSING

1. This essay is widely regarded as one of the best-written and best-argued perspectives of the twentieth century. What about it do you notice? How does King make his argument, and why does he choose to write a letter (rather than, say, a newspaper column) to make it?
2. Toward the middle of the letter, King says, "I must make two honest confessions to you . . ." Why does King wait until this point in the letter to address the clergy? What aspects of the letter might have changed had he begun with that statement? How so?
3. Analyze King's choice of language. What, for instance, does King mean when he says that in the South, people "live in monologue rather than dialogue"?

CONNECTING AND WRITING

1. "Letter from a Birmingham Jail" was written in 1963 in response to a statement published in a local newspaper entitled "A Call for Unity" in which eight white Alabama clergymen rallied against King. Find "A Call for Unity" and analyze the points to which King responds and the effect of his argument in the context of what inspired his letter.
2. Consider King's call to action alongside more contemporary examples of political leaders' explicit directives to people to engage in constructive political activism. How do they compare? How do they differ? Argue a specific point of view, using King's letter and the other information you find as examples.

The Four Freedoms

Franklin Delano Roosevelt (1882–1945)

Franklin Delano Roosevelt is considered by many to be among the very greatest of U.S. presidents. Born in upstate New York, he attended Columbia University Law School but dropped out before graduation when he passed the New York bar examination. He first entered the political arena in 1911, when he became a state senator in New York, and soon rose in popularity as one of the nation's preeminent Democrats. Roosevelt went on to become assistant secretary of the Navy in 1913 and in 1920 was chosen as the vice presidential candidate to running mate James M. Cox of Ohio. Wheelchair bound due to polio, Roosevelt was indispensable in shepherding the country through the Great Depression and World War II. What follows is his State of the Union address delivered four years before his death—Roosevelt was the only and last president to be elected to four terms—a speech marked by his characteristic thoughtfulness and eloquence.

M r. President, Mr. Speaker, members of the 77th Congress:
I address you, the members of this new Congress, at a moment unprecedented in the history of the union. I use the word "unprecedented" because at no previous time has American security been as seriously threatened from without as it is today.

Since the permanent formation of our government under the Constitution in 1789, most of the periods of crisis in our history have related to our domestic affairs. And, fortunately, only one of these—the four-year war between the States—ever threatened our national unity. Today, thank God, 130,000,000 Americans in 48 States have forgotten points of the compass in our national unity.

It is true that prior to 1914 the United States often has been disturbed by events in other continents. We have even engaged in two wars with European nations and in a number of undeclared wars in the West Indies, in the Mediterranean and in the Pacific, for the maintenance of American rights and for the principles of peaceful commerce. But in no case had a serious threat been raised against our national safety or our continued independence.

What I seek to convey is the historic truth that the United States as a nation has at all times maintained opposition—clear, definite opposition—to any attempt to lock us in behind an ancient Chinese wall while the procession of civilization went past. Today, thinking of our children and of their children, we oppose enforced isolation for ourselves or for any other part of the Americas.

That determination of ours, extending over all these years, was proved, for example, in the early days during the quarter century of wars following the French Revolution. While the Napoleonic struggles did threaten interests of the United States because of the French foothold in the West Indies and in Louisiana, and while we engaged in the War of 1812 to vindicate our right to peaceful trade, it is nevertheless clear that neither France nor Great Britain nor any other nation was aiming at domination of the whole world.

And in like fashion, from 1815 to 1914—ninety-nine years—no single war in Europe or in Asia constituted a real threat against our future or against the future of any other American nation.

Except in the Maximilian interlude in Mexico, no foreign power sought to establish itself in this hemisphere. And the strength of the British fleet in the Atlantic has been a friendly strength; it is still a friendly strength.

Even when the World War broke out in 1914, it seemed to contain only small threat of danger to our own American future. But as time went on, as we remember, the American people began to visualize what the downfall of democratic nations might mean to our own democracy.

We need not overemphasize imperfections in the peace of Versailles. We need not harp on failure of the democracies to deal with problems of world reconstruction. We should remember that the peace of 1919 was far less unjust than the kind of pacification which began even before Munich, and which is being carried on under the new order of tyranny that seeks to spread over every continent today. The American people have unalterably set their faces against that tyranny.

I suppose that every realist knows that the democratic way of life is at this moment being directly assailed in every part of the world—assailed either by arms or by secret spreading of poisonous propaganda by those who seek to destroy unity and promote discord in nations that are still at peace. During 16 long months this assault has blotted out the whole pattern of democratic life in an appalling number of independent nations, great and small. And the assailants are still on the march, threatening other nations, great and small.

Therefore, as your President, performing my constitutional duty to "give to the Congress information of the state of the union," I find it unhappily necessary to report that the future and the safety of our country and of our democracy are overwhelmingly involved in events far beyond our borders.

Armed defense of democratic existence is now being gallantly waged in four continents. If that defense fails, all the population and all the resources of Europe and Asia, and Africa and Austral-Asia will be dominated by conquerors. And let us remember that the total of those populations in those four continents, the total of those populations and their resources greatly exceed the sum total of the population and the resources of the whole of the Western Hemisphere—yes, many times over.

In times like these it is immature—and, incidentally, untrue—for anybody to brag that an unprepared America, single-handed and with one hand tied behind its back, can hold off the whole world.

No realistic American can expect from a dictator's peace international generosity, or return of true independence, or world disarmament, or freedom of expression, or freedom of religion—or even good business. Such a peace would bring no security for us or for our neighbors. Those who would give up essential liberty to purchase a little temporary safety deserve neither liberty nor safety.

As a nation we may take pride in the fact that we are soft-hearted; but we cannot afford to be soft-headed. We must always be wary of those who with sounding brass and a tinkling cymbal preach the "ism" of appeasement. We must especially beware of that small group of selfish men who would clip the wings of the American eagle in order to feather their own nests.

I have recently pointed out how quickly the tempo of modern warfare could bring into our very midst the physical attack which we must eventually expect if the dictator nations win this war.

There is much loose talk of our immunity from immediate and direct invasion from across the seas. Obviously, as long as the British Navy retains its power, no such danger exists. Even if there were no British Navy, it is not probable that any enemy would be stupid enough to attack us by landing troops in the United States from across thousands of miles of ocean, until it had acquired strategic bases from which to operate.

But we learn much from the lessons of the past years in Europe—particularly the lesson of Norway, whose essential seaports were captured by treachery and surprise built up over a series of years. The first phase of the invasion of this hemisphere would not be the landing of regular troops. The necessary strategic points would be occupied by secret agents and by their dupes—and great numbers of them are already here and in Latin America. As long as the aggressor nations maintain the offensive they, not we, will choose the time and the place and the method of their attack.

And that is why the future of all the American Republics is today in serious danger. That is why this annual message to the Congress is unique in our history. That is why every member of the executive branch of the government and every member of the Congress face great responsibility, great accountability. The need of the moment is that our actions and our policy should be devoted primarily—almost exclusively—to meeting this foreign peril. For all our domestic problems are now a part of the great emergency.

Just as our national policy in internal affairs has been based upon a decent re-spect for the rights and the dignity of all our fellow men within our gates, so our national policy in foreign affairs has been based on a decent respect for the rights and the dignity of all nations, large and small. And the justice of morality must and will win in the end.

Our national policy is this:

First, by an impressive expression of the public will and without regard to partisanship, we are committed to all-inclusive national defense.

Secondly, by an impressive expression of the public will and without regard to partisanship, we are committed to full support of all those resolute people everywhere who are resisting aggression and are thereby keeping war away from our hemisphere. By this support we express our determination that the democratic cause shall prevail, and we strengthen the defense and the security of our own nation.

Third, by an impressive expression of the public will and without regard to partisanship, we are committed to the proposition that principles of morality and considerations for our own security will never permit us to acquiesce in a peace dic-tated by aggressors and sponsored by appeasers. We know that enduring peace cannot be bought at the cost of other people's freedom.

In the recent national election there was no substantial difference between the two great parties in respect to that national policy. No issue was fought out on this line before the American electorate. And today it is abundantly evident that American citizens everywhere are demanding and supporting speedy and complete action in recognition of obvious danger.

Therefore, the immediate need is a swift and driving increase in our armament production. Leaders of industry and labor have responded to our summons. Goals of speed have been set. In some cases these goals are being reached ahead of time. In some cases we are on schedule; in other cases there are slight but not serious delays. And in some cases—and, I am sorry to say, very important cases—we are all concerned by the slowness of the accomplishment of our plans.

The Army and Navy, however, have made substantial progress during the past year. Actual experience is improving and speeding up our methods of production with every passing day. And today's best is not good enough for tomorrow.

I am not satisfied with the progress thus far made. The men in charge of the program represent the best in training, in ability, and in patriotism. They are not satisfied with the progress thus far made. None of us will be satisfied until the job is done.

No matter whether the original goal was set too high or too low, our objective is quicker and better results.

To give you two illustrations:

We are behind schedule in turning out finished airplanes. We are working day and night to solve the innumerable problems and to catch up.

We are ahead of schedule in building warships, but we are working to get even further ahead of that schedule.

To change a whole nation from a basis of peacetime production of implements of peace to a basis of wartime production of implements of war is no small task. And the greatest difficulty comes at the beginning of the program, when new tools, new plant facilities, new assembly lines, new shipways must first be constructed before the actual material begins to flow steadily and speedily from them.

The Congress of course, must rightly keep itself informed at all times of the progress of the program. However, there is certain information, as the Congress itself will readily recognize, which, in the interests of our own security and those of the nations that we are supporting, must of needs be kept in confidence.

New circumstances are constantly begetting new needs for our safety. I shall ask this Congress for greatly increased new appropriations and authorizations to carry on what we have begun.

I also ask this Congress for authority and for funds sufficient to manufacture additional munitions and war supplies of many kinds, to be turned over to those nations which are now in actual war with aggressor nations. Our most useful and im-mediate role is to act as an arsenal for them as well as for ourselves. They do not need manpower, but they do need billions of dollars' worth of the weapons of defense.

The time is near when they will not be able to pay for them all in ready cash. We cannot, and we will not, tell them that they must surrender merely because of present inability to pay for the weapons which we know they must have.

I do not recommend that we make them a loan of dollars with which to pay for these weapons—a loan to be repaid in dollars. I recommend that we make it possible for those nations to continue to obtain war materials in the United States, fitting their orders into our own program. And nearly all of their material would, if the time ever came, be useful in our own defense.

Taking counsel of expert military and naval authorities, considering what is best for our own security, we are free to decide how much should be kept here and how much should be sent abroad to our friends who, by their determined and heroic resistance, are giving us time in which to make ready our own defense.

For what we send abroad we shall be repaid, repaid within a reasonable time following the close of hostilities, repaid in similar materials, or at our option in other goods of many kinds which they can produce and which we need.

Let us say to the democracies: "We Americans are vitally concerned in your defense of freedom. We are putting forth our energies, our resources, and our organizing powers to give you the strength to regain and maintain a free world. We shall send you in ever-increasing numbers, ships, planes, tanks, guns. That is our purpose and our pledge."

In fulfillment of this purpose we will not be intimidated by the threats of dictators that they will regard as a breach of international law or as an act of war our aid to the democracies which dare to resist their aggression. Such aid—such aid is not an act of war, even if a dictator should unilaterally proclaim it so to be.

And when the dictators—if the dictators—are ready to make war upon us, they will not wait for an act of war on our part.

They did not wait for Norway or Belgium or the Netherlands to commit an act of war. Their only interest is in a new one-way international law, which lacks mutuality in its observance and therefore becomes an instrument of oppression. The happiness of future generations of Americans may well depend on how effective and how immediate we can make our aid felt. No one can tell the exact character of the emergency situations that we may be called upon to meet. The nation's hands must not be tied when the nation's life is in danger.

Yes, and we must prepare, all of us prepare, to make the sacrifices that the emergency—almost as serious as war itself—demands. Whatever stands in the way of speed and efficiency in defense, in defense preparations of any kind, must give way to the national need.

A free nation has the right to expect full cooperation from all groups. A free nation has the right to look to the leaders of business, of labor, and of agriculture to take the lead in stimulating effort, not among other groups but within their own group.

The best way of dealing with the few slackers or trouble-makers in our midst is, first, to shame them by patriotic example, and if that fails, to use the sovereignty of government to save government.

As men do not live by bread alone, they do not fight by armaments alone. Those who man our defenses and those behind them who build our defenses must have the stamina and the courage which come from unshakable belief in the manner of life which they are defending. The mighty action that we are calling for cannot be based on a disregard of all the things worth fighting for.

The nation takes great satisfaction and much strength from the things which have been done to make its people conscious of their individual stake in the preservation of democratic life in America. Those things have toughened the fiber of our people, have renewed their faith and strengthened their devotion to the institutions we make ready to protect.

Certainly this is no time for any of us to stop thinking about the social and economic problems which are the root cause of the social revolution which is today a supreme factor in the world. For there is nothing mysterious about the foundations of a healthy and strong democracy.

The basic things expected by our people of their political and economic systems are simple. They are:

> Equality of opportunity for youth and for others.
> Jobs for those who can work.
> Security for those who need it.
> The ending of special privilege for the few.
> The preservation of civil liberties for all.
> The enjoyment—the enjoyment of the fruits of scientific progress in a wider and constantly rising standard of living.

These are the simple, the basic things that must never be lost sight of in the turmoil and unbelievable complexity of our modern world. The inner and abiding strength of our economic and political systems is dependent upon the degree to which they fulfill these expectations.

Many subjects connected with our social economy call for immediate improvement. As examples:

We should bring more citizens under the coverage of old-age pensions and unemployment insurance.

We should widen the opportunities for adequate medical care.

We should plan a better system by which persons deserving or needing gainful employment may obtain it.

I have called for personal sacrifice, and I am assured of the willingness of almost all Americans to respond to that call. A part of the sacrifice means the payment of more money in taxes. In my budget message I will recommend that a greater portion of this great defense program be paid for from taxation than we are paying for today. No person should try, or be allowed to get rich out of the program, and the principle of tax payments in accordance with ability to pay should be constantly before our eyes to guide our legislation.

If the Congress maintains these principles the voters, putting patriotism ahead pocketbooks, will give you their applause.

In the future days, which we seek to make secure, we look forward to a world founded upon four essential human freedoms.

The first is freedom of *speech* and expression—everywhere in the world.

The second is freedom of every person to *worship* God in his own way—everywhere in the world.

The third is freedom from *want*, which, translated into world terms, means economic understandings which will secure to every nation a healthy peacetime life for its inhabitants—everywhere in the world.

The fourth is freedom from *fear*, which, translated into world terms, means a world-wide reduction of armaments to such a point and in such a thorough fashion that no nation will be in a position to commit an act of physical aggression against any neighbor—anywhere in the world.

That is no vision of a distant millennium. It is a definite basis for a kind of world attainable in our own time and generation. That kind of world is the very antithesis of the so-called "new order" of tyranny which the dictators seek to create with the crash of a bomb.

To that new order we oppose the greater conception—the moral order. A good society is able to face schemes of world domination and foreign revolutions alike without fear.

Since the beginning of our American history we have been engaged in change, in a perpetual, peaceful revolution, a revolution which goes on steadily, quietly, adjusting itself to changing conditions without the concentration camp or the quicklime in the ditch. The world order which we seek is the cooperation of free countries, working together in a friendly, civilized society.

This nation has placed its destiny in the hands and heads and hearts of its millions of free men and women, and its faith in freedom under the guidance of God. Freedom means the supremacy of human rights everywhere. Our support goes to those who struggle to gain those rights and keep them. Our strength is our unity of purpose.

To that high concept there can be no end save victory.

REFLECTING AND DISCUSSING

1. What are the four freedoms as defined by Roosevelt? Discuss.
2. This speech was delivered to Congress eleven months before the United States declared war on Japan and entered World War II. Read about our entry into World War II and discuss how this context adds urgency to the speech, which was heard on the radio by the American public.
3. Roosevelt introduces the notion of "freedom from fear." How does this differ from current political uses of "fear" as a way to motivate the public? How is the concept of "fear" used by Roosevelt—and how is it used now? What effects has each usage had?

CONNECTING AND WRITING

1. Following up on the context of this State of the Union address, research responses to and the effects of Roosevelt's speech. What were his contemporaries' different perspectives on the speech? Argue your own point of view regarding these responses, and use examples from credible resources to support your arguments.
2. Using this speech as an example, how might we characterize Roosevelt's America? What values and ideals does the speech aim to protect—and evoke in each citizen? Using a more contemporary State of the Union address, compare Roosevelt's vision of America during a time of crisis with another president's vision during a different, if similarly charged, time. Look at both language and historical contexts to craft your arguments and to support your points.

In Defense of White Racist Speech—*Pappas v. Giuliani*

Sonia Sotomayor (1954–   )

Sonia Sotomayor is the first Hispanic and third woman to serve on the U.S. Supreme Court. Born in the Bronx to Puerto Rican parents, she attended New York City public schools and graduated first in her high school class. Sotomayor attended Princeton University, where she graduated summa cum laude, followed by Yale Law School. In 1991, President George H. W. Bush nominated her to the U.S. District Court for the Southern District of New York, where she gained fame as the judge who "saved major league baseball." In 1997, President Bill Clinton nominated her to the U.S. Court of Appeals for the Second Circuit; in May 2009, President Barack Obama nominated her to the Supreme Court, and in August of that year she was confirmed.

The judgment of the district court is affirmed.

I agree with Judge Leval's thoughtful explanation of why the City's decision to fire Appellant did not run afoul of the Pickering doctrine. I write separately, however, because I do not think we need to reach Pickering. I agree with the district court that Appellant was engaged in purely private speech.

Whether an employee's speech addresses a matter of public concern must be determined by the "content, form, and context of a given statement, as revealed by the whole record." *Connick v. Myers*, 461 U.S. 138, 147–48, 103 S.Ct. 1684, 75 L.Ed.2d 708 (1983). To fall within the realm of "public concern," an employee's speech must satisfy two criteria. It must relate to a matter of political, social or other concern to the community. And the employee must speak "as a citizen upon matters of public concern," not simply "as an employee upon matters only of personal interest." *Id.* at 147, 103 S.Ct. 1684. Context as well as content matters.

The vile speech for which Appellant was disciplined touched on matters of paramount political and social concern in this country. See, e.g., *Connick*, 461 U.S. at 148 n. 8, 103 S.Ct. 1684 (noting that the right to protest racial discrimination is of public concern); *Jeffries v. Harleston*, 21 F.3d 1238, 1242 (2d Cir.), vacated on other grounds, 513 U.S. 996, 115 S.Ct. 502, 130 L.Ed.2d 411 (1994) (finding that professor's anti-semitic speech at a festival was public speech). From that proposition, the other members of the panel conclude that it qualifies as public concern speech. But that is not the law. "[S]peaking up on a topic that may be deemed one of public importance does not automatically mean the employee's statements address a matter of public concern as that term is employed in *Connick*." *Kokkinis v. Ivkovich*, 185 F.3d 840, 844 (7th Cir.1999). For example, courts in this Circuit and elsewhere have held that complaints of race or gender discrimination—an issue of overwhelming social importance—are not "public concern" speech if they relate only to a personal employment grievance. *Saulpaugh v. Monroe Cmty. Hosp.*, 4 F.3d 134, 143 (2d Cir.1993) (finding that employee's complaints of sex discrimination did not implicate matters of public concern because they "were motivated by and dealt with her individual employment situation"); *Walker v. New York City Transit Auth.*, No. 99 CIV. 2227(DC), 2001 WL 1098022, at *12 (S.D.N.Y. Sept.19, 2001) (rejecting the argument that all complaints relating to race or gender discrimination implicate matters of public concern); *Nonnenmann v. City of New York*, 174 F.Supp.2d 121, 135–36 (S.D.N.Y.2001) (finding that police officer's testimony on behalf of a female, black co-worker in discrimination case was not a matter of public concern); *de Silva v. New York City Transit Auth.*, No. CV 96-2758 (RJD), 1999 WL 1288683, at *17 (E.D.N.Y. Nov. 17, 1999) (citations omitted) ("an EEOC complaint based on race and sex discrimination is not a matter of public concern, and therefore, is not protected speech under the First Amendment"). See also *Morgan v. Ford*, 6 F.3d 750, 754–55 (11th Cir.1993) (holding that female employee's complaints of sex harassment were designed to improve her own working conditions, rather than to raise issues of public concern).

Connick itself made the point that not all speech on matters of public significance is "public concern" speech. 461 U.S. at 147–48, 103 S.Ct. 1684. The assistant district attorney who was dismissed in that case circulated a survey containing questions about the functioning of the District Attorney's Office that addressed issues of undoubted public importance. Nonetheless, the Supreme Court concluded that the assistant's speech, viewed in its context (she was gathering ammunition for a new round of controversy with her supervisors), did not touch on matters of public concern, but only the employee's personal interest. The *Connick* court looked behind pretextual "public concern" rationale proffered by the disciplined employee in order to discern whether her conduct, taken as a whole, was actually meant to address matters of public concern, or was simply a vehicle for furthering her private interests. *Id.*

So, here, must we. As this Court recently recognized, "the court should focus on the motive of the speaker and attempt to determine whether the speech was calculated to redress personal grievances or whether it had a broader public purpose." *Lewis v. Cowen*, 165 F.3d 154, 163–64 (2d Cir.1999) (citing *Curtis v. Oklahoma City Pub. Sch. Bd. of Educ.*, 147 F.3d 1200, 1212 (10th Cir.1998)). The procedure endorsed in *Lewis* is the procedure that Judge Buchwald followed below—reaching, in my opinion, a correct result—and is the procedure we should follow on this appeal.

Nothing in *Locurto v. Safir*, 264 F.3d 154 (2d Cir.2001), suggests that *Lewis* is no longer good law, or that the context prong of the *Connick* analysis drops out when the speech concerns race relations. In *Locurto*, the police officer and fire fighters were fired for appearing in blackface at a Labor Day parade, on a float that, however tasteless, commented on the effect of integration on the future racial composition of the neighborhood (a phenomenon known as "tipping")—an issue that has been the subject of litigation in this Court.[1] The civic context of the officers' speech on this hot-button topic made its public concern nature so obvious that no one seriously contested it, and this Court proceeded accordingly. *Locurto*, 264 F.3d at 166. Because the "public concern" issue was not litigated in *Locurto*, that case does not help us resolve this one, where the issue is being litigated, and on radically different facts.

The proposition that Pappas engaged in hateful and inflammatory speech to advance a purely private interest can hardly be disputed. Pappas sent several hundred mailings containing this poisonous material anonymously to not-for-profit organizations of all sorts, including a police benevolent society (an error that led to his downfall). The only sin these organizations committed was to ask Pappas for money, and he sent them racist and anti-semitic literature to express his pique at receiving unsolicited mail. While Appellant initially suggested that his mailings were simply a "hobby" with no purpose, *Pappas v. Giuliani*, 118 F.Supp.2d 433, 445 (S.D.N.Y.2000) (citing Tr. of March 24, 1998 interview at 16), he admitted at his disciplinary hearing that the mailings were a form of "protest" against "being shaken down for money by the so-called charitable organizations." *Id.* (citing Trial Tr. at 108–10). Pappas explained that he hoped the mailings would stop the organizations from soliciting him. *Id.* That is a matter of personal interest if ever there was one.

Pappas argues that his membership in certain White Supremacist organizations transforms speech furthering his private interests into public concern speech. But as the district court correctly noted, Pappas' choice of forum is relevant to any assessment of such a claim. *Connick*, 461 U.S. at 148, 103 S.Ct. 1684; *Kurtz v. Vickrey*, 855 F.2d 723, 729 (11th Cir.1988) ("profession of public concern loses force when it is considered that he took no affirmative steps to inform the public at large about the problems with which he was so gravely concerned"); *Terrell v. Univ. of Texas Sys. Police*, 792 F.2d 1360, 1362–63 (5th Cir.1986) (emphasizing the pertinence of failure to make any effort to communicate contents of notebooks to the public in determining whether notebooks contained protected speech). While it is true that speech need not be made in a public forum to qualify as "public concern" speech, *Givhan v. Western Line Consol. Sch. Dist.*, 439 U.S. 410, 414–15, 99 S.Ct. 693, 58 L.Ed.2d 619 (1979), *Givhan* does not make either the non-public nature of speech or the identity of the audience to which it is directed irrelevant to a private interest/public concern analysis. If it did, all speech by public employees touching on controversial issues, regardless of context, would automatically be speech of "public concern." As we acknowledged in *Lewis*, that is not the case.

Here, Pappas made no effort to forward his "protests" to parties who might profit from knowing about the public's dissatisfaction over unsolicited direct mail fundraising (such as the Better Business Bureau, charitable oversight agencies, IRS, the media, or the public at large). *Pappas*, 118 F.Supp.2d at 445. This belies his effort to cloak his private interest in the garb of "public concern" speech.

The record admits of but one interpretation: Pappas engaged in vile and offensive activity with the sole goal of getting his name excised from direct mail solicitation lists. He so stated when it mattered most—at his disciplinary hearing—and we should take him at his word. His own mouth condemneth him. Because removing his name from mailing lists is a purely personal concern, Pappas was engaged in purely personal speech, even though the words he spoke touched on matters of public importance. I would thus affirm for the reasons stated by the district court in Part B(1) of its opinion.

Today the Court enters uncharted territory in our First Amendment jurisprudence. The Court holds that the government does not violate the First Amendment when it fires a police department employee for racially inflammatory speech—where the speech consists of mailings in which the employee did not identify himself, let alone connect himself to the police department; where the speech occurred away from the office and on the employee's own time; where the employee's position involved no policymaking authority or public contact; where there is virtually no evidence of workplace disruption resulting directly from the speech; and where it ultimately required the investigatory resources of two police departments to bring the speech to the attention of the community. Precedent requires us to consider these factors as we apply the Pickering balancing test, and each counsels against granting summary judgment in favor of the police department employer. To be sure, I find the speech in this case patently offensive, hateful, and insulting. The Court should not, however, gloss over three decades of jurisprudence and the centrality of First Amendment freedoms in our lives because it is confronted with speech it does not like and because a government employer fears a potential public response that it alone precipitated.

I. Public Concern

As a threshold matter, the majority is correct to assume that the materials at issue in this case constitute speech on a matter of public concern. Issues of race relations are "inherently of public concern." *Connick v. Myers*, 461 U.S. 138, 148 n. 8, 103 S.Ct. 1684, 75 L.Ed.2d 708 (1983); see also *Perry v. McGinnis*, 209 F.3d 597, 608 (6th Cir.2000)

("In *Connick* the Supreme Court clearly established that racial discrimination is inherently a matter of public concern"). And while we are more comfortable when the speech we are protecting involves protestations against racial discrimination, it is not our role to approve or disapprove of the viewpoint advanced.

In *Jeffries v. Harleston*, 21 F.3d 1238, 1242 (2d Cir.), vacated on other grounds, 513 U.S. 996, 115 S.Ct. 502, 130 L.Ed.2d 411 (1994), we were confronted with racial remarks that were "hateful," "repugnant," and clearly inflammatory. The public employee in *Jeffries* had asserted, among other things, that "'rich Jews' had financed the slave trade" and that Jews had conspired with Mafia figures in Hollywood for the "'destruction of black people.'" *Id.* at 1242. We found that the comments "unquestionably involved public issues" and were entitled to First Amendment protection. *Id.* at 1245. Pappas's statements in this case about "how the Jews control the TV networks and why they should be in the hands of the American public and not the Jews" are similarly public in nature. As we recognized in *Jeffries*, "First Amendment protection does not hinge on the palatability of the presentation; it extends to all speech on public matters, no matter how vulgar or misguided." 21 F.3d at 1245–46.[2] While the forum in which Pappas expressed his views was less public than in *Jeffries*—which involved a speech at a festival—that fact does not deprive Pappas's speech of constitutional protection. The Supreme Court addressed this precise issue in *Givhan v. Western Line Consolidated School District*, squarely rejecting the notion "that a public employee forfeits his protection against governmental abridgment of freedom of speech if he decides to express his views privately rather than publicly." 439 U.S. 410, 414, 99 S.Ct. 693, 58 L.Ed.2d 619 (1979). None of the cases cited by Judge McMahon's concurrence are to the contrary, as they involved employees speaking about issues concerning their own employment.[3] This case involves the categorically different scenario of an employee speaking on issues of race relations entirely unrelated to his job.

II. Pickering Balancing Test

Proceeding to the Pickering balancing test, the majority finds that the NYPD's interest in fulfilling its mission outweighs Pappas's First Amendment rights under the circumstances of this case. I disagree. I of course do not dispute the majority's premise that a public employee's free speech interest is often subordinated to the effective functioning of a government employer. I also agree that it is appropriate to consider the agency's mission in relation to the nature of the speech, and I appreciate the enormous importance of race relations to the operation of the NYPD. These facts alone, however, do not support the constitutionality of the NYPD's termination of Pappas. The well-established caselaw of the Supreme Court and this Court requires a more searching inquiry.

A court must consider not only the agency's mission in relation to the nature of the speech, but also the employee's responsibilities in relation to that mission. We are not free to disregard this part of the analysis. The Supreme Court has instructed that "in weighing the State's interest in discharging an employee based on any claim that the content of a statement made by the employee somehow undermines the mission of the public employer, some attention must be paid to the responsibilities of the employee within the agency." *Rankin v. McPherson*, 483

U.S. 378, 390, 107 S.Ct. 2891, 97 L.Ed.2d 315 (1987) (emphasis added); see also
McEvoy v. Spencer, 124 F.3d 92, 102–03 (2d Cir.1997) (emphasizing this aspect of
Rankin). As this Court has explained, "the more the employee's job requires confi-
dentiality, policymaking, or public contact, the greater the state's interest in firing
her for expression that offends her employer." *McEvoy*, 124 F.3d at 103 (quotation
marks omitted) (citing *Caruso v. DeLuca*, 81 F.3d 666, 670 n. 3 (7th Cir.1996)); *Hall
v. Ford*, 856 F.2d 255, 261–64 (D.C.Cir.1988). The importance of these factors, we
have explained, "should not be surprising." *Id*. "Common sense tells us that the
expressive activities of a highly placed supervisory, confidential, policymaking, or
advisory employee will be more disruptive to the operation of the workplace than
similar activity by a low level employee with little authority or discretion." *Id*. (citing
Bates v. Hunt, 3 F.3d 374, 378 (11th Cir.1993); *Kinsey v. Salado Indep. Sch. Dist.*, 950
F.2d 988, 994 (5th Cir.1992)).

We apply this factor in the law enforcement context by asking whether Pappas
held some high-level, "supervisory," "confidential," or "policymaking" role within
the police department. If, for example, the Police Commissioner or one of his depu-
ties engaged in racist speech, the mission of the NYPD could be seriously undermined and the city's interest in dismissing him would be compelling. We must also
ask whether Pappas's role with the NYPD involved "public contact." A police officer
walking the beat, while not exercising broad policymaking authority, is often the
representative with whom the public interacts. It is not difficult to see how such an
officer who expresses racist views in certain situations could damage the efficient
operation of the NYPD. This goes to the heart of the majority's reasoning. The majority explains that, in a city like New York, it is the perceived bias among the police
department's rank and file that causes the most problems. *Ante*, at 149. The truth
of this assertion is undeniable, but varies greatly depending on which police employees are involved. This is why the Supreme Court and this Court scrutinize the
individual employee's responsibilities with such care. In *Rankin*, the Supreme Court
applied this analysis to the law enforcement context and found that "where an employee serves no confidential, policymaking, or public contact role, the danger to the
agency's successful functioning from that employee's private speech is minimal."
Rankin, 483 U.S. at 390–91, 107 S.Ct. 2891. Examples mentioned by the Court of
police employees whose speech would likely implicate this "minimal" governmental
interest included "computer operator, electrician, [and] file clerk." *Id*. at 391, 107 S.Ct.
2891. Turning to the instant case, it is clear that Pappas's position with the NYPD
involved neither the policymaking authority of an executive official nor the public
contact of a street cop. He was an internal "computer operator" working for the
Management Information Systems Division. *Pappas v. Giuliani*, 118 F.Supp.2d 433,
435 (S.D.N.Y.2000). While this fact is "not conclusive," our precedents deem it a
"very significant" weight on the scales in Pappas's favor as we conduct the Pickering
balancing test. *McEvoy*, 124 F.3d at 103.

The majority further explains that for a police officer to disseminate racist materials tends to promote the view that New York police officers are racists. According to the Court, "[t]he capacity of such statements to damage the effectiveness
of the police department in the community is immense." *Ante*, at 147. Here again,

the majority's observation has an element of undeniable truth but requires refinement. At some level of abstraction or aggregation, the potential for racist statements to damage the NYPD may indeed be "immense." But that is not how the fact-specific Pickering test is applied. The question is how potentially damaging is this speech—that is, these leaflets sent by this employee under these particular circumstances. We have stated unambiguously that, in conducting the balancing test, "a court must consider whether the statement sought to be protected 'impairs discipline by superiors or harmony among co-workers, has a detrimental impact on close working relationships or impedes the performance of the speaker's duties or interferes with the regular operation of the enterprise.'" *Lewis v. Cowen*, 165 F.3d 154, 162 (2d Cir.1999) (quoting *Rankin*, 483 U.S. at 388, 107 S.Ct. 2891, and citing *Connick*, 461 U.S. at 151–52, 103 S.Ct. 1684) (emphasis added). To conduct this analysis, we look at the "'manner, time, and place' in which the speech occurs." *Id.* (citing *Connick*, 461 U.S. at 152, 103 S.Ct. 1684). In this case, Pappas engaged in the speech anonymously, on his own time, and through mailings sent from his home. I address these factors in turn.

It is significant that Pappas did not purport to speak for the NYPD. We recently explained that the central reason why "[public employees'] free speech claims are subject to the Pickering balancing test" is "the state's significant interest in regulating the expressive conduct of its employees while they are acting on behalf of the state." *Knight v. Conn. Dep't of Pub. Health*, 275 F.3d 156, 167 (2d Cir.2001). This fact alone does not deprive the government of its legitimate interest in the matter, but its interest is higher with respect to "employees who purport to speak for the government." *Moore v. City of Wynnewood*, 57 F.3d 924, 933 (10th Cir.1995). The significance of this factor depends upon the presence of another factor, already discussed, regarding the responsibilities of the employee. For example, the fact that the Police Commissioner did not purport to represent the NYPD when making a racist statement would mean little. Where, as here, the employee has no such authority or public contact, this aspect is significant. Moreover, the facts of this case are particularly compelling in this regard: Not only did Pappas fail to connect himself to the NYPD, his mailings were entirely anonymous, making it considerably less likely that the effect of the speech on the NYPD's operations would be "immense."

It is also significant that the speech occurred away from the office on the employee's own time. In *Connick*, the speech at issue was a workplace questionnaire that "touched upon matters of public concern in only a most limited sense" and would be "most accurately characterized as an employee grievance concerning internal office policy." *Connick*, 461 U.S. at 154, 103 S.Ct. 1684. Finding the First Amendment concerns virtually non-existent and the countervailing interests compelling, the Supreme Court ruled in the government's favor. *Id.* Notwithstanding the relatively minimal free speech interests at stake, the Court nonetheless cautioned that "[e]mployee speech which transpires entirely on the employee's own time, and in non-work areas of the office, bring different factors into the Pickering calculus, and might lead to a different conclusion." *Id.* at 153 n. 13, 103 S.Ct. 1684. We adopted this dictum in *Lewis*. 165 F.3d at 162 (stating that "the Pickering balance is more likely to favor the government when an employee directly confronts his supervisor with objectionable language than when an employee engages in equivalent speech on his own time and not in front of co-workers") (citing *Connick*, 461 U.S. at 152–53 & n. 13, 103 S.Ct. 1684). The fact that speech takes place in private and away from the workplace favors the employee on both sides of the balancing test: First, it reduces the likelihood of disruption. See *Lewis*, 165 F.3d at 162. Second, it enhances the free speech interests at stake because the employee is speaking in his capacity "as the member of the general public he seeks to be." *Pickering v. Board of Educ.*, 391 U.S. 563, 574, 88 S.Ct. 1731, 20 L.Ed.2d 811 (1968). In the instant case, Pappas's speech was as far removed from the workplace as possible. He acted as a private citizen, off-duty, anonymously sending mailings from his own home on matters of public concern unrelated to his job as a computer operator for the NYPD. Moreover, the speech in this case implicates matters of public concern far more than did the employee questionnaire in *Connick*, see supra Part I, tipping the scales further in Pappas's favor. See *Lewis*, 165 F.3d at 162 ("The more the employee's speech touches on matters of significant public concern, the greater the level of disruption to the government that must be shown") (citations omitted).

The majority nonetheless maintains that Pappas "deliberately sought to publicize his views," and that "[a]lthough Pappas tried to conceal his identity as speaker, he took the risk that the effort would fail." *Ante*, at 148. Ultimately, the governmental interest that the majority seeks to protect in this case is publicity. The majority's core concern seems to be that, even though Pappas was a low-level employee with no public contact who was speaking privately and anonymously, the possibility remained that the news would get "out into the world" that the NYPD was employing a racist. I agree this is a significant issue, and I do not take it lightly. This Court has made clear that negative publicity affecting the community's faith in government can be a significant factor in the Pickering balancing test. See *Lewis*, 165 F.3d at 164–65. And as the majority points out, news of Pappas's speech did in fact reach the local media. This issue, however, requires closer scrutiny.

This case differs from others we have confronted in a critical respect. In the typical public employee speech case where negative publicity is at issue, the government has reacted to speech—which others have publicized—in an effort to diffuse some potential disruption. In this case, whatever disruption occurred was the result of the police department's decision to publicize the results of its investigation, which revealed the source of the anonymous mailings. It was, apparently, the NYPD itself that disclosed this information to the media and the public. Thus, it is not empty rhetoric when Pappas argues that he was terminated because of his opinions. *Ante*, at 147–48. The majority's decision allows a government employer to launch an investigation, ferret out an employee's views anonymously expressed away from the workplace and unrelated to the employee's job, bring the speech to the attention of the media and the community, hold a public disciplinary hearing, and then terminate the employee because, at that point, the government "reasonably believed that the speech would potentially disrupt the government's activities." *Heil v. Santoro*, 147 F.3d 103, 109 (2d Cir.1998). This is a perversion of our "reasonable belief" standard, and does not give due respect to the First Amendment interests at stake.

Conclusion

I recognize that the Pickering test affords substantial deference to government employers, particularly in the law enforcement context. The NYPD's concerns about race relations in the community are especially poignant. But there are limits. "At some point, such concerns are so removed from the effective functioning of the public employer that they cannot prevail over the free speech rights of the public employee." *Rankin*, 483 U.S. at 391, 107 S.Ct. 2891. The question is on what side of the line does this case fall. By finding that there is no issue of material fact for trial, the majority lays down too broad a rule regarding the government's ability to disqualify an individual from public employment based on the expression of an unpopular viewpoint. While I agree with the majority that no one factor in the Pickering test deserves "talismanic or determinative significance," a full application of this multi-factor test to the unique circumstances of this case indicates that summary judgment was inappropriate. I respectfully dissent.

Notes

1. *United States v. Starrett City Assoc.*, 840 F.2d 1096 (2d Cir.1988).
2. More recently, this Court strongly implied that racial speech, even more purely inflammatory than the speech in *Jeffries* or the instant case, is of "public concern." In *Locurto v. Safir*, 264 F.3d 154 (2d Cir.2001), members of the New York City Police Department and Fire Department were fired after participating in the presentation of a racist, deeply offensive float at a Labor Day parade in Broad Channel, Queens. The float, entitled "Black to the Future," ridiculed African Americans while referring to the future effects of racial integration in their community. The offensive aspects included the participants' wearing blackface, eating watermelon, and worse. See *id.* at 159. This Court proceeded with its analysis on the assumption that the speech was of public concern, noting that the defendant employers "do not strenuously dispute" that the activity "constituted First Amendment speech on a matter of public concern." *Id.* at 166.
3. Moreover, Judge McMahon's reliance on *Kurtz v. Vickrey*, 855 F.2d 723 (11th Cir.1988), for the proposition that public concern value is diminished where an employee "took no affirmative steps to inform the public at large about[ ] the problems with which he was so gravely concerned" is misplaced. Judge McMahon neglects to mention that the *Kurtz* court strongly cautioned against placing dispositive weight on this factor because "such a focus overlooks the Court's holding in *Givhan* that a public employee's freedom of speech is not sacrificed merely because the employee 'arranges to communicate privately with his employer rather than to spread his views before the public.'" *Id.* at 727 (quoting *Givhan*, 439 U.S. at 415–16, 99 S.Ct. 693). Furthermore, the *Kurtz* court found this factor important only with respect to matters that were distinctly employment-related, such as the handling of salary issues at the university where the plaintiff was employed. See *id.* at 728–29. With respect to matters of more public interest, such as the closing of a branch of the university, the court found that the speech was of public concern and therefore protected—notwithstanding the private context of the communication. See *id.* at 729–30.

REFLECTING AND DISCUSSING

1. This is the actual court opinion written by Justice Sotomayor, and consequently, there is much "legalese" and what might seem to be jargon. As a general reader, how does the language affect your understanding of the case and her decision?

2. Sotomayor outlines her reasons for deciding in favor of free speech in an otherwise reprehensible situation. What reasons does she provide? What is your response? What are the consequences if speech is suppressed, even if we don't like what is being said?

3. What does Sotomayor assume her audience understands? How do you know? What are the precedents and contextual knowledge she assumes her audience is aware of?

CONNECTING AND WRITING

1. Research the facts of the original case. What transpired? Why would this case be especially problematic? Research an opinion of a credible person who disagrees with her. How does this person make his or her argument? Which argument do you find most effective, and why? Use specific examples to back up your points.

2. Do some research on the First Amendment. Is there another case in which a justice has decided in favor of free speech even when the speech itself was, as Sotomayor writes here, "patently offensive, hateful, and insulting"? Compare and contrast the two cases and decisions, arguing your own point of view on both.

Shooting an Elephant

George Orwell (1903–1950)

Born in England, George Orwell was the pseudonym of Eric Arthur Blair. Orwell is still celebrated for his numerous novels, biographical works, and essays, especially his frightening and satirical political novels, Animal Farm *(1948) and* 1984 *(1949). Orwell fought in the Spanish Civil War after living in poverty as a writer in London and Paris. His most significant works are concerned with the sociopolitical conditions of his time and the issue of human freedom. This essay was inspired by his time living in Burma (Myanmar), during which he served with the Indian Imperial Police.*

In Moulmein, in lower Burma, I was hated by large numbers of people—the only time in my life that I have been important enough for this to happen to me. I was sub-divisional police officer of the town, and in an aimless, petty kind of way anti-European feeling was very bitter. No one had the guts to raise a riot, but if a European woman went through the bazaars alone somebody would probably spit betel juice over her dress. As a police officer I was an obvious target and was baited whenever it seemed safe to do so. When a nimble Burman tripped me up on the football field and the referee (another Burman) looked the other way, the crowd yelled with hideous laughter. This happened more than once. In the end the sneering yellow faces of young men that met me everywhere, the insults hooted after me when I was at a safe distance, got badly on my nerves. The young Buddhist priests were the worst of all. There were several thousands of them in the town and none of them seemed to have anything to do except stand on street corners and jeer at Europeans.

All this was perplexing and upsetting. For at that time I had already made up my mind that imperialism was an evil thing and the sooner I chucked up my job and got out of it the better. Theoretically—and secretly, of course—I was all for the Burmese and all against their oppressors, the British. As for the job I was doing, I hated it more bitterly than I can perhaps make clear. In a job like that you see the dirty work of Empire at close quarters. The wretched prisoners huddling in the stinking cages of the lock-ups, the grey, cowed faces of the long-term convicts, the scarred buttocks of the men who had been flogged with bamboos—all these oppressed me with an intolerable sense of guilt. But I could get nothing into perspective. I was young and ill-educated and I had had to think out my problems in the utter silence that is imposed on every Englishman in the East. I did not even know that the British Empire is dying, still less did I know that it is a great deal better than the younger empires that are going to supplant it. All I knew was that I was stuck between my hatred of the empire I served and my rage against the evil-spirited little beasts who tried to make my job impossible. With one part of my mind I thought of the British Raj as an unbreakable tyranny, as something clamped down, in *saecula saeculorum*, upon the will of prostrate peoples; with another part I thought that the greatest joy in the world would be to drive a bayonet into a Buddhist priest's guts. Feelings like these are the normal byproducts of imperialism; ask any Anglo-Indian official, if you can catch him off duty.

One day something happened which in a roundabout way was enlightening. It was a tiny incident in itself, but it gave me a better glimpse than I had had before of the real nature of imperialism—the real motives for which despotic governments act. Early one morning the sub-inspector at a police station the other end of the town rang me up on the phone and said that an elephant was ravaging the bazaar. Would I please come and do something about it? I did not know what I could do, but I wanted to see what was happening and I got on to a pony and started out. I took my rifle, an old .44 Winchester and much too small to kill an elephant, but I thought the noise might be useful *in terrorem*. Various Burmans stopped me on the way and told me about the elephant's doings. It was not, of course, a wild elephant, but a tame one which had gone "must." It had been chained up, as tame elephants always are when their attack of "must" is due, but on the previous night it had broken its chain and escaped. Its mahout, the only person who could manage it when it was in that state, had set out in pursuit, but had taken the wrong direction and was now twelve hours' journey away, and in the morning the elephant had suddenly reappeared in the town. The Burmese population had no weapons and were quite helpless against it. It had already destroyed somebody's bamboo hut, killed a cow and raided some fruit-stalls and devoured the stock; also it had met the municipal rubbish van and, when the driver jumped out and took to his heels, had turned the van over and in-flicted violences upon it.

The Burmese sub-inspector and some Indian constables were waiting for me in the quarter where the elephant had been seen. It was a very poor quarter, a labyrinth of squalid bamboo huts, thatched with palmleaf, winding all over a steep hillside. I remember that it was a cloudy, stuffy morning at the beginning of the rains. We began questioning the people as to where the elephant had gone and, as usual, failed to get any definite information. That is invariably the case in the East; a story always sounds clear enough at a distance, but the nearer you get to the scene of events the vaguer it becomes. Some of the people said that the elephant had gone in one direc-tion, some said that he had gone in another, some professed not even to have heard of any elephant. I had almost made up my mind that the whole story was a pack of lies, when we heard yells a little distance away. There was a loud, scandalized cry of "Go away, child! Go away this instant!" and an old woman with a switch in her hand came round the corner of a hut, violently shooing away a crowd of naked children. Some more women followed, clicking their tongues and exclaiming; evidently there was something that the children ought not to have seen. I rounded the hut and saw a man's dead body sprawling in the mud. He was an Indian, a black Dravidian coolie, almost naked, and he could not have been dead many minutes. The people said that the elephant had come suddenly upon him round the corner of the hut, caught him with its trunk, put its foot on his back and ground him into the earth. This was the rainy season and the ground was soft, and his face had scored a trench a foot deep and a couple of yards long. He was lying on his belly with arms crucified and head sharply twisted to one side. His face was coated with mud, the eyes wide open, the teeth bared and grinning with an expression of unendurable agony. (Never tell me, by the way, that the dead look peaceful. Most of the corpses I have seen looked devilish.) The friction of the great beast's foot had stripped the skin from his back as neatly as one skins a rabbit. As soon as I saw the dead man I sent an orderly to a friend's house nearby to borrow an elephant rifle. I had already sent back the pony, not wanting it to go mad with fright and throw me if it smelt the elephant.

The orderly came back in a few minutes with a rifle and five cartridges, and meanwhile some Burmans had arrived and told us that the elephant was in the paddy fields below, only a few hundred yards away. As I started forward practically the whole population of the quarter flocked out of the houses and followed me. They had seen the rifle and were all shouting excitedly that I was going to shoot the elephant. They had not shown much interest in the elephant when he was merely ravaging their homes, but it was different now that he was going to be shot. It was a bit of fun to them, as it would be to an English crowd; besides they wanted the meat. It made me vaguely uneasy. I had no intention of shooting the elephant—I had merely sent for the rifle to defend myself if necessary—and it is always unnerv-ing to have a crowd following you. I marched down the hill, looking and feeling a fool, with the rifle over my shoulder and an ever-growing army of people jostling at my heels. At the bottom, when you get away from the huts, there was a metalled road and beyond that a miry waste of paddy fields a thousand yards across, not yet ploughed but soggy from the first rains and dotted with coarse grass. The elephant was standing eight yards from the road, his left side towards us. He took not the slightest notice of the crowd's approach. He was tearing up bunches of grass, beating them against his knees to clean them and stuffing them into his mouth.

I had halted on the road. As soon as I saw the elephant I knew with perfect certainty that I ought not to shoot him. It is a serious matter to shoot a working elephant—it is comparable to destroying a huge and costly piece of machinery—and obviously one ought not to do it if it can possibly be avoided. And at that distance, peacefully eating, the elephant looked no more dangerous than a cow. I thought then and I think now that his attack of "must" was already passing off; in which case he would merely wander harmlessly about until the mahout came back and caught him. Moreover, I did not in the least want to shoot him. I decided that I would watch him for a little while to make sure that he did not turn savage again, and then go home.

But at that moment I glanced round at the crowd that had followed me. It was an immense crowd, two thousand at the least and growing every minute. It blocked the road for a long distance on either side. I looked at the sea of yellow faces above the garish clothes—faces all happy and excited over this bit of fun, all certain that the elephant was going to be shot. They were watching me as they would watch a conjurer about to perform a trick. They did not like me, but with the magical rifle in my hands I was momentarily worth watching. And suddenly I realized that I should have to shoot the elephant after all. The people expected it of me and I had got to do it; I could feel their two thousand wills pressing me forward, irresistibly. And it was at this moment, as I stood there with the rifle in my hands, that I first grasped the hollowness, the futility of the white man's dominion in the East. Here was I, the white man with his gun, standing in front of the unarmed native crowd—seemingly the leading actor of the piece; but in reality I was only an absurd puppet pushed to and fro by the will of those yellow faces behind. I perceived in this moment that when the white man turns tyrant it is his own freedom that he destroys. He becomes a sort of hollow, posing dummy, the conventionalized figure of a sahib. For it is the condition of his rule that he shall spend his life in trying to impress the "natives," and so in every crisis he has got to do what the "natives" expect of him. He wears a mask, and his face grows to fit it. I had got to shoot the elephant. I had committed myself to doing it when I sent for the rifle. A sahib has got to act like a sahib; he has got to appear resolute, to know his own mind and do definite things. To come all that way, rifle in hand, with two thousand people marching at my heels, and then to trail feebly away, having done nothing—no, that was impossible. The crowd would laugh at me. And my whole life, every white man's life in the East, was one long struggle not to be laughed at.

But I did not want to shoot the elephant. I watched him beating his bunch of grass against his knees, with that preoccupied grandmotherly air that elephants have. It seemed to me that it would be murder to shoot him. At that age I was not squeamish about killing animals, but I had never shot an elephant and never wanted to. (Somehow it always seems worse to kill a large animal.) Besides, there was the beast's owner to be considered. Alive, the elephant was worth at least a hundred pounds; dead, he would only be worth the value of his tusks, five pounds, possibly. But I had got to act quickly. I turned to some experienced-looking Burmans who had been there when we arrived, and asked them how the elephant had been behaving.

They all said the same thing: he took no notice of you if you left him alone, but he might charge if you went too close to him.

It was perfectly clear to me what I ought to do. I ought to walk up to within, say, twenty-five yards of the elephant and test his behavior. If he charged, I could shoot; if he took no notice of me, it would be safe to leave him until the mahout came back. But also I knew that I was going to do no such thing. I was a poor shot with a rifle and the ground was soft mud into which one would sink at every step. If the elephant charged and I missed him, I should have about as much chance as a toad under a steam-roller. But even then I was not thinking particularly of my own skin, only of the watchful yellow faces behind. For at that moment, with the crowd watching me, I was not afraid in the ordinary sense, as I would have been if I had been alone. A white man mustn't be frightened in front of "natives"; and so, in general, he isn't frightened. The sole thought in my mind was that if anything went wrong those two thousand Burmans would see me pursued, caught, trampled on and reduced to a grinning corpse like that Indian up the hill. And if that happened it was quite probable that some of them would laugh. That would never do.

There was only one alternative. I shoved the cartridges into the magazine and lay down on the road to get a better aim. The crowd grew very still, and a deep, low, happy sigh, as of people who see the theatre curtain go up at last, breathed from innumerable throats. They were going to have their bit of fun after all. The rifle was a beautiful German thing with cross-hair sights. I did not then know that in shooting an elephant one would shoot to cut an imaginary bar running from ear-hole to ear-hole. I ought, therefore, as the elephant was sideways on, to have aimed straight at his ear-hole, actually I aimed several inches in front of this, thinking the brain would be further forward.

When I pulled the trigger I did not hear the bang or feel the kick—one never does when a shot goes home—but I heard the devilish roar of glee that went up from the crowd. In that instant, in too short a time, one would have thought, even for the bullet to get there, a mysterious, terrible change had come over the elephant. He neither stirred nor fell, but every line of his body had altered. He looked suddenly stricken, shrunken, immensely old, as though the frightful impact of the bullet had paralysed him without knocking him down. At last, after what seemed a long time—it might have been five seconds, I dare say—he sagged flabbily to his knees. His mouth slobbered. An enormous senility seemed to have settled upon him. One could have imagined him thousands of years old. I fired again into the same spot. At the second shot he did not collapse but climbed with desperate slowness to his feet and stood weakly upright, with legs sagging and head drooping. I fired a third time. That was the shot that did for him. You could see the agony of it jolt his whole body and knock the last remnant of strength from his legs. But in falling he seemed for a moment to rise, for as his hind legs collapsed beneath him he seemed to tower upward like a huge rock toppling, his trunk reaching skyward like a tree. He trumpeted, for the first and only time. And then down he came, his belly towards me, with a crash that seemed to shake the ground even where I lay.

I got up. The Burmans were already racing past me across the mud. It was obvious that the elephant would never rise again, but he was not dead. He was breathing very rhythmically with long rattling gasps, his great mound of a side painfully rising and falling. His mouth was wide open—I could see far down into caverns of pale pink throat.

I waited a long time for him to die, but his breathing did not weaken. Finally I fired my two remaining shots into the spot where I thought his heart must be. The thick blood welled out of him like red velvet, but still he did not die. His body did not even jerk when the shots hit him, the tortured breathing continued without a pause. He was dying, very slowly and in great agony, but in some world remote from me where not even a bullet could damage him further. I felt that I had got to put an end to that dreadful noise. It seemed dreadful to see the great beast lying there, powerless to move and yet powerless to die, and not even to be able to finish him. I sent back for my small rifle and poured shot after shot into his heart and down his throat. They seemed to make no impression. The tortured gasps continued as steadily as the ticking of a clock.

In the end I could not stand it any longer and went away. I heard later that it took him half an hour to die. Burmans were bringing dahs and baskets even before I left, and I was told they had stripped his body almost to the bones by the afternoon.

Afterwards, of course, there were endless discussions about the shooting of the elephant. The owner was furious, but he was only an Indian and could do nothing. Besides, legally I had done the right thing, for a mad elephant has to be killed, like a mad dog, if its owner fails to control it. Among the Europeans opinion was divided. The older men said I was right, the younger men said it was a damn shame to shoot an elephant for killing a coolie, because an elephant was worth more than any damn Coringhee coolie. And afterwards I was very glad that the coolie had been killed; it put me legally in the right and it gave me a sufficient pretext for shooting the elephant. I often wondered whether any of the others grasped that I had done it solely to avoid looking a fool.

REFLECTING AND DISCUSSING

1. This essay reveals through specific, personal events "the real nature of imperialism." How does Orwell accomplish this? Consider the essay's organization, use of language, and details.

2. What might a Burmese perspective on this event be? Why might it be different from Orwell's?

3. Quite often, even in contemporary times, you will hear the word "Orwellian" used to describe invasions of privacy and other potential disruptions of personal space. What, in your life, could be described as "Orwellian"? How does one circumvent these issues, if one can?

CONNECTING AND WRITING

1. Research the concept of imperialism, looking specifically at British imperialism in Burma. On what assumptions is imperialism based? How does this context shape your view of Orwell's narrative? Use specific examples to back up your central argument.

2. As we said earlier, this essay reveals "the real nature of imperialism." How does it also reveal the pressures of personal decision-making? Using examples from the text, argue a point of view about how Orwell's essay fares in this regard.

The Tyranny of the Majority

Lani Guinier (1950–   )

Civil rights theorist and writer Lani Guinier is the Bennett Boskey Professor of Law at Harvard Law School and the first woman of color appointed to a tenured professorship at that institution. Guinier's work as an attorney on civil rights led then-president Bill Clinton in 1993 to nominate her for the position of assistant attorney general. Because of dissent from conservatives, Clinton was forced to withdraw the nomination. Guinier has published five books, including The Tyranny of the Meritocracy: Democratizing Higher Education in a Democracy *(2015) and* The Tyranny of the Majority: Fundamental Fairness in Representative Democracy *(1994), from which this excerpt comes.*

I have always wanted to be a civil rights lawyer. This lifelong ambition is based on a deep-seated commitment to democratic fair play—to playing by the rules as long as the rules are fair. When the rules seem unfair, I have worked to change them, not subvert them. When I was eight years old, I was a Brownie. I was especially proud of my uniform, which represented a commitment to good citizenship and good deeds. But one day, when my Brownie group staged a hat-making contest, I realized that uniforms are only as honorable as the people who wear them. The contest was rigged. The winner was assisted by her milliner mother, who actually made the winning entry in full view of all the participants. At the time, I was too young to be able to change the rules, but I was old enough to resign, which I promptly did.

To me, fair play means that the rules encourage everyone to play. They should reward those who win, but they must be acceptable to those who lose. The central theme of my academic writing is that not all rules lead to elemental fair play. Some even commonplace rules work against it.

The professional milliner competing with amateur Brownies stands as an example of rules that are patently rigged or patently subverted. Yet, sometimes, even when rules are perfectly fair in form, they serve in practice to exclude particular groups from meaningful participation. When they do not encourage everyone to play, or when, over the long haul, they do not make the losers feel as good about the outcomes as the winners, they can seem as unfair as the milliner who makes the winning hat for her daughter.

Sometimes, too, we construct rules that force us to be divided into winners and losers when we might have otherwise joined together. This idea was cogently expressed by my son, Nikolas, when he was four years old, far exceeding the thoughtfulness of his mother when she was an eight-year-old Brownie. While I was writing one of my law journal articles, Nikolas and I had a conversation about voting prompted by a *Sesame Street Magazine* exercise. The magazine pictured six children: four children had raised their hands because they wanted to play tag; two had their hands down because they wanted to play hide-and-seek. The magazine asked its readers to count the number of children whose hands were raised and then decide what game the children would play.

Nikolas quite realistically replied, "They will play both. First they will play tag. Then they will play hide-and-seek." Despite the magazine's "rules," he was right. To children, it is natural to take turns. The winner may get to play first or more often, but even the "loser" gets something. His was a positive-sum solution that many adult rulemakers ignore.

The traditional answer to the magazine's problem would have been a zero-sum solution: "The children—all the children—will play tag, and only tag." As a zero-sum solution, everything is seen in terms of "I win; you lose." The conventional answer relies on winner-take-all majority rule, in which the tag players, as the majority, win the right to decide for all the children what game to play. The hide-and-seek preference becomes irrelevant. The numerically more powerful majority choice simply subsumes minority preferences.

In the conventional case, the majority that rules gains all the power and the minority that loses gets none. For example, two years ago Brother Rice High School in Chicago held two senior proms. It was not planned that way. The prom committee at Brother Rice, a boys' Catholic high school, expected just one prom when it hired a disc jockey, picked a rock band, and selected music for the prom by consulting student preferences. Each senior was asked to list his three favorite songs, and the band would play the songs that appeared most frequently on the lists.

Seems attractively democratic. But Brother Rice is predominantly white, and the prom committee was all white. That's how they got two proms. The black seniors at Brother Rice felt so shut out by the "democratic process" that they organized their own prom. As one black student put it: "For every vote we had, there were eight votes for what they wanted. . . . [W]ith us being in the minority we're always outvoted. It's as if we don't count."

Some embittered white seniors saw things differently. They complained that the black students should have gone along with the majority: "The majority makes a decision. That's the way it works."

In a way, both groups were right. From the white students' perspective, this was ordinary decisionmaking. To the black students, majority rule sent the message: "we don't count" is the "way it works" for minorities. In a racially divided society, majority rule may be perceived as majority tyranny.

That is a large claim, and I do not rest my case for it solely on the actions of the prom committee in one Chicago high school. To expand the range of the argument, I first consider the ideal of majority rule itself, particularly as reflected in the writings of James Madison and other founding members of our Republic. These early democrats explored the relationship between majority rule and democracy. James Madison warned, "If a majority be united by a common interest, the rights of the minority will be insecure." The tyranny of the majority, according to Madison, requires safeguards to protect "one part of the society against the injustice of the other part."

For Madison, majority tyranny represented the great danger to our early constitutional democracy. Although the American revolution was fought against the tyranny of the British monarch, it soon became clear that there was another tyranny to be avoided. The accumulations of all powers in the same hands, Madison warned, "whether of one, a few, or many, and whether hereditary, self-appointed, or elective, may justly be pronounced the very definition of tyranny."

As another columnist suggested in papers published in Philadelphia, "We have been so long habituated to a jealousy of tyranny from monarchy and aristocracy, that we have yet to learn the dangers of it from democracy." Despotism had to be opposed "whether it came from Kings, Lords or the people."

The debate about majority tyranny reflected Madison's concern that the majority may not represent the whole. In a homogeneous society, the interest of the majority would likely be that of the minority also. But in a heterogeneous community, the majority may not represent all competing interests. The majority is likely to be self-interested and ignorant or indifferent to the concerns of the minority. In such case, Madison observed, the assumption that the majority represents the minority is "altogether fictitious."

Yet even a self-interested majority can govern fairly if it cooperates with the minority. One reason for such cooperation is that the self-interested majority values the principle of reciprocity. The self-interested majority worries that the minority may attract defectors from the majority and become the next governing majority. The Golden Rule principle of reciprocity functions to check the tendency of a self-interested majority to act tyrannically.

So the argument for the majority principle connects it with the value of reciprocity: You cooperate when you lose in part because members of the current majority will cooperate when they lose. The conventional case for the fairness of majority rule is that it is not really the rule of a fixed group—The Majority—on all issues; instead it is the rule of shifting majorities, as the losers at one time or on one issue join with others and become part of the governing coalition at another time or on another issue. The result will be a fair system of mutually beneficial cooperation. I call a majority that rules but does not dominate a Madisonian Majority.

The problem of majority tyranny arises, however, when the self-interested majority does not need to worry about defections. When the majority is fixed and permanent, there are no checks on its ability to be overbearing. A majority that does not worry about defectors is a majority with total power.

In such a case, Madison's concern about majority tyranny arises. In a heterogeneous community, any faction with total power might subject "the minority to the caprice and arbitrary decisions of the majority, who instead of consulting the interest of the whole community collectively, attend sometimes to partial and local advantages."

"What remedy can be found in a republican Government, where the majority must ultimately decide," argued Madison, but to ensure "that no one common interest or passion will be likely to unite a majority of the whole number in an unjust pursuit." The answer was to disaggregate the majority to ensure checks and balances or fluid, rotating interests. The minority needed protection against an overbearing majority, so that "a common sentiment is less likely to be felt, and the requisite concert less likely to be formed, by a majority of the whole."

Political struggles would not be simply a contest between rulers and people; the political struggles would be among the people themselves. The work of government was not to transcend different interests but to reconcile them. In an ideal democracy, the people would rule, but the minorities would also be protected against the power of majorities. Again, where the rules of decisionmaking protect the minority, the Madisonian Majority rules without dominating.

But if a group is unfairly treated, for example, when it forms a racial minority, *and* if the problems of unfairness are not cured by conventional assumptions about majority rule, then what is to be done? The answer is that we may need an *alternative* to winner-take-all majoritarianism. In this book, a collection of my law review articles, I describe the alternative, which, with Nikolas's help, I now call the "principle of taking turns." In a racially divided society, this principle does better than simple majority rule if it accommodates the values of self-government, fairness, deliberation, compromise, and consensus that lie at the heart of the democratic ideal.

In my legal writing, I follow the caveat of James Madison and other early American democrats. I explore decisionmaking rules that might work in a multi-racial society to ensure that majority rule does not become majority tyranny. I pursue voting systems that might disaggregate The Majority so that it does not exercise power unfairly or tyrannically. I aspire to a more cooperative political style of decisionmaking to enable all of the students at Brother Rice to feel comfortable attending the same prom. In looking to create Madisonian Majorities, I pursue a positive-sum, taking-turns solution.

Structuring decisionmaking to allow the minority "a turn" may be necessary to restore the reciprocity ideal when a fixed majority refuses to cooperate with the minority. If the fixed majority loses its incentive to follow the Golden Rule principle of shifting majorities, the minority never gets to take a turn. Giving the minority a turn does not mean the minority gets to rule; what it does mean is that the minority gets to influence decisionmaking and the majority rules more legitimately.

Instead of automatically rewarding the preferences of the monolithic majority, a taking-turns approach anticipates that the majority rules, but is not overbearing. Because those with 51 percent of the votes are not assured 100 percent of the power, the majority cooperates with, or at least does not tyrannize, the minority.

The sports analogy of "I win; you lose" competition within a political hierarchy makes sense when only one team can win; Nikolas's intuition that it is often possible to take turns suggests an alternative approach. Take family decisionmaking, for example. It utilizes a taking-turns approach. When parents sit around the kitchen table deciding on a vacation destination or activities for a rainy day, often they do not simply rely on a show of hands, especially if that means that the older children always prevail or if affinity groups among the children (those who prefer movies to video games, or those who prefer baseball to playing cards) never get to play their activity of choice. Instead of allowing the majority simply to rule, the parents may propose that everyone takes turns, going to the movies one night and playing video games the next. Or as Nikolas proposes, they might do both on a given night.

Taking turns attempts to build consensus while recognizing political or social differences, and it encourages everyone to play. The taking-turns approach gives those with the most support more turns, but it also legitimates the outcome from each individual's perspective, including those whose views are shared only by a minority.

In the end, I do not believe that democracy should encourage rule by the powerful—even a powerful majority. Instead, the idea of democracy promises a fair discussion among self-defined equals about how to achieve our common aspirations. To redeem that promise, we need to put the idea of taking turns and disaggregating the majority at the center of our conception of representation. Particularly as we move into the twenty-first century as a more highly diversified citizenry, it is essential that we consider the ways in which voting and representational systems succeed or fail at encouraging Madisonian Majorities.

To use Nikolas's terminology, "it is no fair" if a fixed, tyrannical majority excludes or alienates the minority. It is no fair if a fixed, tyrannical majority monopolizes all the power all the time. It is no fair if we engage in the periodic ritual of elections, but only the permanent majority gets to choose who is elected. Where we have tyranny by The Majority, we do not have genuine democracy.

REFLECTING AND DISCUSSING

1. What is Guinier arguing in this excerpt? How persuasive is she? Why?
2. Why does Guinier alternate personal stories with her own theoretical argument? How does this strategy enhance her overall argument, if it does?
3. In what ways can you assume, by her prose style and language choices, that Guinier has a legal background? How do these choices on her part support or strengthen her argument?

CONNECTING AND WRITING

1. Guinier writes, "We construct rules that force us to be divided into winners and losers when we might have otherwise joined together." Research examples from the political climate of the early 1990s to support Guinier's contention and compare them with current events. Does Guinier's contention still hold? Why or why not? Be sure to back up your argument with specific examples.
2. How would you argue that both the majority and the minority in a given situation can sometimes be right? Use examples from Guinier's text as well as ones that you research on your own.
3. Guinier's book concludes as follows: "In the end, I do not believe that Democracy should include rule by the powerful—even a powerful majority." Research political theories in twentieth-century America and then draw connections and/or contrasts between Guinier's thinking on this point and that of another legal thinker. Form a central argument on this issue that you support with Guinier's work as well as that of the other writer.

QUESTION

Looking carefully at the two presidential addresses (those of Kennedy and Roosevelt), analyze the rhetorical strategies and language of each. Why does each president argue as he does? What do the speeches have in common? How are they different? How does each argue for a purpose? Offer your own argument about these speeches' commonalities and differences and use the texts to support your argument.

5 ETHICS

Regardless of topic or particular issue, the pieces in this section address the notion of ethics and ethical behavior. Not unlike "Higher Ground," the essays and articles evoke our sense of who we are, what we believe, how we behave, and why.

People Like Us

David Brooks (1961–   )

Born in Toronto and raised in New York City, David Brooks is a popular conservative-leaning columnist for the New York Times *and a contributor to PBS's* News Hour, *on which he weekly appears with journalist Mark Shields and host Judy Woodruff. His books include* Bobos in Paradise: The New Upper Class and How They Got There *(2000),* The Social Animal *(2011), and* The Road to Character *(2015). This essay first appeared in the* Atlantic *in 2000.*

Maybe it's time to admit the obvious. We don't really care about diversity all that much in America, even though we talk about it a great deal. Maybe somewhere in this country there is a truly diverse neighborhood in which a black Pentecostal minister lives next to a white anti-globalization activist, who lives next to an Asian short-order cook, who lives next to a professional golfer, who lives next to a postmodern-literature professor and a cardiovascular surgeon. But I have never been to or heard of that neighborhood. Instead, what I have seen all around the country is people making strenuous efforts to group themselves with people who are basically like themselves.

Human beings are capable of drawing amazingly subtle social distinctions and then shaping their lives around them. In the Washington, D.C., area Democratic lawyers tend to live in suburban Maryland, and Republican lawyers tend to live in suburban Virginia. If you asked a Democratic lawyer to move from her $750,000 house in Bethesda, Maryland, to a $750,000 house in Great Falls, Virginia, she'd look at you as if you had just asked her to buy a pickup truck with a gun rack and to shove chewing tobacco in her kid's mouth. In Manhattan the owner of a $3 million SoHo loft would feel out of place moving into a $3 million Fifth Avenue apartment. A West Hollywood interior decorator would feel dislocated if you asked him to move to Orange County. In Georgia a barista from Athens would probably not fit in serving coffee in Americus.

It is a common complaint that every place is starting to look the same. But in the information age, the late writer James Chapin once told me, every place becomes more like itself. People are less often tied down to factories and mills, and they can search for places to live on the basis of cultural affinity. Once they find a town in which people share their values, they flock there, and reinforce whatever was distinctive about the town in the first place. Once Boulder, Colorado, became known as congenial to politically progressive mountain bikers, half the politically progressive mountain bikers in the country (it seems) moved there; they made the place so culturally pure that it has become practically a parody of itself.

But people love it. Make no mistake—we are increasing our happiness by segmenting off so rigorously. We are finding places where we are comfortable and where we feel we can flourish. But the choices we make toward that end lead to the very opposite of diversity. The United States might be a diverse nation when considered as a whole, but block by block and institution by institution it is a relatively homogeneous nation.

When we use the word "diversity" today we usually mean racial integration. But even here our good intentions seem to have run into the brick wall of human nature. Over the past generation reformers have tried heroically, and in many cases successfully, to end housing discrimination. But recent patterns aren't encouraging: according to an analysis of the 2000 census data, the 1990s saw only a slight increase in the racial integration of neighborhoods in the United States. The number of middle-class and upper-middle-class African-American families is rising, but for whatever reasons—racism, psychological comfort—these families tend to congregate in predominantly black neighborhoods.

In fact, evidence suggests that some neighborhoods become more segregated over time. New suburbs in Arizona and Nevada, for example, start out reasonably well integrated. These neighborhoods don't yet have reputations, so people choose their houses for other, mostly economic reasons. But as neighborhoods age, they develop personalities (that's where the Asians live, and that's where the Hispanics live), and segmentation occurs. It could be that in a few years the new suburbs in the Southwest will be nearly as segregated as the established ones in the Northeast and the Midwest.

Even though race and ethnicity run deep in American society, we should in theory be able to find areas that are at least culturally diverse. But here, too, people show few signs of being truly interested in building diverse communities. If you run a retail company and you're thinking of opening new stores, you can choose among dozens of consulting firms that are quite effective at locating your potential customers. They can do this because people with similar tastes and preferences tend to congregate by ZIP code.

The most famous of these precision marketing firms is Claritas, which breaks down the U.S. population into sixty-two psycho-demographic clusters, based on such factors as how much money people make, what they like to read and watch, and what products they have bought in the past. For example, the "suburban sprawl" cluster is composed of young families making about $41,000 a year and living in fast-growing places such as Burnsville, Minnesota, and Bensalem, Pennsylvania. These people are almost twice as likely as other Americans to have three-way calling. They are two and a half times as likely to buy Light n' Lively Kid Yogurt. Members of the "towns & gowns" cluster are recent college graduates in places such as Berkeley, California, and Gainesville, Florida. They are big consumers of DoveBars and *Saturday Night Live*. They tend to drive small foreign cars and to read *Rolling Stone* and *Scientific American*.

Looking through the market research, one can sometimes be amazed by how efficiently people cluster—and by how predictable we all are. If you wanted to sell imported wine, obviously you would have to find places where rich people live. But did you know that the sixteen counties with the greatest proportion of imported-wine drinkers are all in the same three metropolitan areas (New York, San Francisco, and Washington, D.C.)? If you tried to open a motor-home dealership in Montgomery County, Pennsylvania, you'd probably go broke, because people in this ring of the Philadelphia suburbs think RVs are kind of uncool. But if you traveled just a short way north, to Monroe County, Pennsylvania, you would find yourself in the fifth motor-home-friendliest county in America.

Geography is not the only way we find ourselves divided from people unlike us. Some of us watch Fox News, while others listen to NPR. Some like David Letterman, and others—typically in less urban neighborhoods—like Jay Leno. Some go to charismatic churches; some go to mainstream churches. Americans tend more and more often to marry people with education levels similar to their own, and to befriend people with backgrounds similar to their own.

My favorite illustration of this latter pattern comes from the first, noncontroversial chapter of *The Bell Curve*. Think of your twelve closest friends, Richard J. Herrnstein and Charles Murray write. If you had chosen them randomly from the American population, the odds that half of your twelve closest friends would be college graduates would be six in a thousand. The odds that half of the twelve would have advanced degrees would be less than one in a million. Have any of your twelve closest friends graduated from Harvard, Stanford, Yale, Princeton, Caltech, MIT, Duke, Dartmouth, Cornell, Columbia, Chicago, or Brown? If you chose your friends randomly from the American population, the odds against your having four or more friends from those schools would be more than a billion to one.

Many of us live in absurdly unlikely groupings, because we have organized our lives that way.

It's striking that the institutions that talk the most about diversity often practice it the least. For example, no group of people sings the diversity anthem more frequently and fervently than administrators at just such elite universities. But elite universities are amazingly undiverse in their values, politics, and mores. Professors in particular are drawn from a rather narrow segment of the population. If faculties reflected the general population, 32 percent of professors would be registered

Democrats and 31 percent would be registered Republicans. Forty percent would be evangelical Christians. But a recent study of several universities by the conservative Center for the Study of Popular Culture and the American Enterprise Institute found that roughly 90 percent of those professors in the arts and sciences who had registered with a political party had registered Democratic. Fifty-seven professors at Brown were found on the voter-registration rolls. Of those, fifty-four were Democrats. Of the forty-two professors in the English, history, sociology, and political-science departments, all were Democrats. The results at Harvard, Penn State, Maryland, and the University of California at Santa Barbara were similar to the results at Brown.

What we are looking at here is human nature. People want to be around others who are roughly like themselves. That's called community. It probably would be psychologically difficult for most Brown professors to share an office with someone who was pro-life, a member of the National Rifle Association, or an evangelical Christian. It's likely that hiring committees would subtly—even unconsciously—screen out any such people they encountered. Republicans and evangelical Christians have sensed that they are not welcome at places like Brown, so they don't even consider working there. In fact, any registered Republican who contemplates a career in academia these days is both a hero and a fool. So, in a semi-self-selective pattern, brainy people with generally liberal social mores flow to academia, and brainy people with generally conservative mores flow elsewhere.

The dream of diversity is like the dream of equality. Both are based on ideals we celebrate even as we undermine them daily. (How many times have you seen someone renounce a high-paying job or pull his child from an elite college on the grounds that these things are bad for equality?) On the one hand, the situation is appalling. It is appalling that Americans know so little about one another. It is appalling that many of us are so narrow-minded that we can't tolerate a few people with ideas significantly different from our own. It's appalling that evangelical Christians are practically absent from entire professions, such as academia, the media, and filmmaking. It's appalling that people should be content to cut themselves off from everyone unlike themselves.

The segmentation of society means that often we don't even have arguments across the political divide. Within their little validating communities, liberals and conservatives circulate half-truths about the supposed awfulness of the other side. These distortions are believed because it feels good to believe them.

On the other hand, there are limits to how diverse any community can or should be. I've come to think that it is not useful to try to hammer diversity into every neighborhood and institution in the United States. Sure, Augusta National should probably admit women, and university sociology departments should probably hire a conservative or two. It would be nice if all neighborhoods had a good mixture of ethnicities. But human nature being what it is, most places and institutions are going to remain culturally homogeneous.

It's probably better to think about diverse lives, not diverse institutions. Human beings, if they are to live well, will have to move through a series of institutions and environments, which may be individually homogeneous but, taken together, will offer diverse experiences. It might also be a good idea to make national service a rite of passage for young people in this country: it would take them out of their narrow neighborhood segment and thrust them in with people unlike themselves. Finally, it's probably important for adults to get out of their own familiar circles. If you live in a coastal, socially liberal neighborhood, maybe you should take out a subscription to the *Door*, the evangelical humor magazine; or maybe you should visit Branson, Missouri. Maybe you should stop in at a megachurch. Sure, it would be superficial familiarity, but it beats the iron curtains that now separate the nation's various cultural zones.

Look around at your daily life. Are you really in touch with the broad diversity of American life? Do you care?

REFLECTING AND DISCUSSING

1. Brooks writes, "We don't really care about diversity all that much in America, even though we talk about it a great deal." In what ways is this an effective way for Brooks to begin his argument, and how does it challenge (or not) what readers might assume about our country before reading his essay? How does it challenge your own assumptions—or not? Why?

2. The essay ends with two questions: "Are you really in touch with the broad diversity of American life? Do you care?" How might you answer those questions?

3. This essay was published in 2000. Are Brooks's arguments still relevant today? Why or why not?

CONNECTING AND WRITING

1. Brooks argues "In fact, any registered Republican who contemplates a career in academia these days is both a hero and a fool." This conversation is perhaps even more relevant now than it was in 2000 (when it was also relevant). What role, if any, does partisanship play within academia? Using additional credible resources, argue for or against Brooks's assertion.

2. Throughout the essay, Brooks uses "we." As a reader, do you feel included in this "we," or is this technique unconvincing? Why? Use specific examples from the essay—and aspects of your own experience—to back up your argument.

The Guest

Albert Camus (1913–1960)

Considered one of the most significant writers of the twentieth century, Albert Camus was born in Algeria, and his experiences there had a formative impact on his work. In his youth, Camus was active in social reform efforts and was connected to the Communist Party. During the Second World War, he joined the resistance to the Nazis and edited an underground newspaper entitled Combat. *His novels, essays, theater plays, and short stories grapple with the themes of the absurd, rebellion and love. "The Guest" is a short story that was published in 1957 and is part of the collection entitled* Exile and the Kingdom.

The schoolmaster was watching the two men climb toward him. One was on horse-
back, the other on foot. They had not yet tackled the abrupt rise leading to the
schoolhouse built on the hillside. They were toiling onward, making slow progress
in the snow, among the stones, on the vast expanse of the high, deserted plateau.
From time to time the horse stumbled. Without hearing anything yet, he could see the
breath issuing from the horse's nostrils. One of the men, at least, knew the region.
They were following the trail although it had disappeared days ago under a layer of
dirty white snow. The schoolmaster calculated that it would take them half an hour to
get onto the hill. It was cold; he went back into the school to get a sweater.

He crossed the empty, frigid classroom. On the blackboard the four rivers of
France, drawn with four different coloured chalks, had been flowing toward their
estuaries for the past three days. Snow had suddenly fallen in mid-October after
eight months of drought without the transition of rain, and the twenty pupils, more
or less, who lived in the villages scattered over the plateau had stopped coming. With
fair weather they would return. Daru now heated only the single room that was his
lodging, adjoining the classroom and giving also onto the plateau to the east. Like
the class windows, his window looked to the south too. On that side the school was
a few kilometres from the point where the plateau began to slope toward the south.
In clear weather could be seen the purple mass of the mountain range where the gap
opened onto the desert.

Somewhat warmed, Daru returned to the window from which he had first seen
the two men. They were no longer visible. Hence they must have tackled the rise. The
sky was not so dark, for the snow had stopped falling during the night. The morning
had opened with a dirty light which had scarcely become brighter as the ceiling of
clouds lifted. At two in the afternoon it seemed as if the day were merely beginning.
But still this was better than those three days when the thick snow was falling amidst
unbroken darkness with little gusts of wind that rattled the double door of the classroom. Then Daru had spent long hours in his room, leaving it only to go to the shed
and feed the chickens or get some coal. Fortunately the delivery truck from Tadjid,
the nearest village to the north, had brought his supplies two days before the bliz-
zard. It would return in forty-eight hours.

Besides, he had enough to resist a siege, for the little room was cluttered with
bags of wheat that the administration left as a stock to distribute to those of his
pupils whose families had suffered from the drought. Actually they had all been victims because they were all poor. Every day Daru would distribute a ration to the
children. They had missed it, he knew, during these bad days. Possibly one of the
fathers would come this afternoon and he could supply them with grain. It was just a
matter of carrying them over to the next harvest. Now shiploads of wheat were arriving from France and the worst was over. But it would be hard to forget that poverty,
that army of ragged ghosts wandering in the sunlight, the plateaus burned to a cinder
month after month, the earth shrivelled up little by little, literally scorched, every
stone bursting into dust under one's foot. The sheep had died then by thousands and
even a few men, here and there, sometimes without anyone's knowing

In contrast with such poverty, he who lived almost like a monk in his remote
schoolhouse, nonetheless satisfied with the little he had and with the rough life, had

felt like a lord with his whitewashed walls, his narrow couch, his unpainted shelves, his well, and his weekly provision of water and food. And suddenly this snow, without warning, without the foretaste of rain. This is the way the region was, cruel to live in, even without men—who didn't help matters either. But Daru had been born here. Everywhere else, he felt exiled.

He stepped out onto the terrace in front of the schoolhouse. The two men were now halfway up the slope. He recognized the horseman as Balducci, the old gendarme he had known for a long time. Balducci was holding on the end of a rope an Arab who was walking behind him with hands bound and head lowered. The gendarme waved a greeting to which Daru did not reply, lost as he was in contemplation of the Arab dressed in a faded blue jellaba, his feet in sandals but covered with socks of heavy raw wool, his head surmounted by a narrow, short *chèche*. They were approaching. Balducci was holding back his horse in order not to hurt the Arab, and the group was advancing slowly.

Within earshot, Balducci shouted: "One hour to do the three kilometres from El Ameur!" Daru did not answer. Short and square in his thick sweater he watched them climb. Not once had the Arab raised his head. "Hello," said Daru when they got up onto the terrace. "Come in and warm up." Balducci painfully got down from his horse without letting go the rope. From under his bristling moustache he smiled at the schoolmaster. His little dark eyes, deep-set under a tanned forehead, and his mouth surrounded with wrinkles made him look attentive and studious. Daru took the bridle, led the horse to the shed, and came back to the two men, who were now waiting for him in the school. He led them into his room. "I am going to heat up the classroom," he said. "We'll be more comfortable there." When he entered the room again, Balducci was on the couch. He had undone the rope tying him to the Arab, who had squashed near the stove. His hands still bound, the *chèche* pushed back on his head, he was looking toward the window. At first Daru noticed only his huge lips, fat, smooth, almost Negroid; yet his nose was straight, his eyes were dark and full of fever. The *chèche* revealed an obstinate forehead and, under the weathered skin now rather discoloured by the cold, the whole face had a restless and rebellious look that struck Daru when the Arab, turning his face toward him, looked him straight in the eyes. "Go into the other room," said the schoolmaster, "and I'll make you some mint tea." "Thanks," Balducci said. "What a chore! How I long for retirement." And addressing his prisoner in Arabic: "Come on, you." The Arab got up and, slowly, holding his bound wrists in front of him, went into the classroom.

With the tea, Daru brought a chair. But Balducci was already enthroned on the nearest pupil's desk and the Arab had squatted against the teacher's platform facing the stove, which stood between the desk and the window. When he held out the glass of tea to the prisoner, Daru hesitated at the sight of his bound hands. "He might perhaps be untied." "Sure," said Balducci. "That was for the trip." He started to get to his feet. But Daru, setting the glass on the floor, had knelt beside the Arab. Without saying anything, the Arab watched him with his feverish eyes. Once his hands were free, he rubbed his swollen wrists against each other, took the glass of tea, and sucked up the burning liquid in swift little sips.

"Good," said Daru. "And where are you headed?"

Balducci withdrew his moustache from the tea. "Here, Son."

"Odd pupils! And you're spending the night?"

"No. I'm going back to El Ameur. And you will deliver this fellow to Tinguit. He is expected at police headquarters."

Balducci was looking at Daru with a friendly little smile.

"What's this story?" asked the schoolmaster. "Are you pulling my leg?"

"No, son. Those are the orders."

"The orders? I'm not . . ." Daru hesitated, not wanting to hurt the old Corsican. "I mean, that's not my job."

"What! What's the meaning of that? In wartime people do all kinds of jobs."

"Then I'll wait for the declaration of war!"

Balducci nodded.

"O.K. But the orders exist and they concern you too. Things are brewing, it appears. There is talk of a forthcoming revolt. We are mobilized, in a way."

Daru still had his obstinate look.

"Listen, Son," Balducci said. "I like you and you must understand. There's only a dozen of us at El Ameur to patrol throughout the whole territory of a small department and I must get back in a hurry. I was told to hand this guy over to you and return without delay. He couldn't be kept there. His village was beginning to stir; they wanted to take him back. You must take him to Tinguit tomorrow before the day is over. Twenty kilometres shouldn't faze a husky fellow like you. After that, all will be over. You'll come back to your pupils and your comfortable life."

Behind the wall the horse could be heard snorting and pawing the earth. Daru was looking out the window. Decidedly, the weather was clearing and the light was increasing over the snowy plateau. When all the snow had melted, the sun would take over again and once more would burn the fields of stone. For days, still, the unchanging sky would shed its dry light on the solitary expanse where nothing had any connection with man.

"After all," he said, turning around toward Balducci, "what did he do?" And, before the gendarme had opened his mouth, he asked: "Does he speak French?"

"No, not a word. We had been looking for him for a month, but they were hiding him. He killed his cousin."

"Is he against us?"

"I don't think so. But you can never be sure."

"Why did he kill?"

"A family squabble, I think. One owed the other grain, it seems. It's not all clear. In short, he killed his cousin with a billhook. You know, like a sheep, *kreeck*!"

Balducci made the gesture of drawing a blade across his throat and the Arab, his attention attracted, watched him with a sort of anxiety. Daru felt a sudden wrath against the man, against all men with their rotten spite, their tireless hates, their blood lust.

But the kettle was singing on the stove. He served Balducci more tea, hesitated, then served the Arab again, who, a second time, drank avidly. His raised arms made the jellaba fall open and the schoolmaster saw his thin, muscular chest.

"Thanks, kid," Balducci said. "And now, I'm off."

He got up and went toward the Arab, taking a small rope from his pocket.

"What are you doing?" Daru asked dryly. Balducci, disconcerted, showed him the rope.

"Don't bother."

The old gendarme hesitated. "It's up to you. Of course, you are armed?"

"I have my shotgun."

"Where?"

"In the trunk."

"You ought to have it near your bed."

"Why? I have nothing to fear."

"You're crazy, son. If there's an uprising, no one is safe, we're all in the same boat."

"I'll defend myself. I'll have time to see them coming."

Balducci began to laugh, then suddenly the moustache covered the white teeth.

"You'll have time? O.K. That's just what I was saying. You have always been a little cracked. That's why I like you, my son was like that."

At the same time he took out his revolver and put it on the desk.

"Keep it; I don't need two weapons from here to El Ameur."

The revolver shone against the black paint of the table. When the gendarme turned toward him, the schoolmaster caught the smell of leather and horseflesh.

"Listen, Balducci," Daru said suddenly, "every bit of this disgusts me, and first of all your fellow here. But I won't hand him over. Fight, yes, if I have to. But not that."

The old gendarme stood in front of him and looked at him severely.

"You're being a fool," he said slowly. "I don't like it either. You don't get used to putting a rope on a man even after years of it, and you're even ashamed, yes, ashamed. But you can't let them have their way."

"I won't hand him over," Daru said again.

"It's an order, son, and I repeat it."

"That's right. Repeat to them what I've said to you: I won't hand him over."

Balducci made a visible effort to reflect. He looked at the Arab and at Daru. At last he decided.

"No, I won't tell them anything. If you want to drop us, go ahead. I'll not denounce you. I have an order to deliver the prisoner and I'm doing so. And now you'll just sign this paper for me."

"There's no need. I'll not deny that you left him with me."

"Don't be mean with me. I know you'll tell the truth. You're from hereabouts and you are a man. But you must sign, that's the rule."

Daru opened his drawer, took out a little square bottle of purple ink, the red wooden penholder with the "sergeant-major" pen he used for making models of penmanship, and signed. The gendarme carefully folded the paper and put it into his wallet. Then he moved toward the door.

"I'll see you off," Daru said.

"No," said Balducci. "There's no use being polite. You insulted me."

He looked at the Arab, motionless in the same spot, sniffed peevishly, and turned away toward the door. "Good-by, son," he said. The door shut behind him. Balducci appeared suddenly outside the window and then disappeared. His footsteps were muffled by the snow. The horse stirred on the other side of the wall and several chickens fluttered in fright. A moment later Balducci reappeared outside the window leading the horse by the bridle. He walked toward the little rise without turning around and disappeared from sight with the horse following him. A big stone could be heard bouncing down. Daru walked back toward the prisoner, who, without stirring, never took his eyes off him. "Wait," the schoolmaster said in Arabic and went toward the bedroom. As he was going through the door, he had a second thought, went to the desk, took the revolver, and stuck it in his pocket. Then, without looking back, he went into his room.

For some time he lay on his couch watching the sky gradually close over, listening to the silence. It was this silence that had seemed painful to him during the first days here, after the war. He had requested a post in the little town at the base of the foothills separating the upper plateaus from the desert. There, rocky walls, green and black to the north, pink and lavender to the south, marked the frontier of eternal summer. He had been named to a post farther north, on the plateau itself. In the beginning, the solitude and the silence had been hard for him on these wastelands peopled only by stones. Occasionally, furrows suggested cultivation, but they had been dug to uncover a certain kind of stone good for building. The only plowing here was to harvest rocks. Elsewhere a thin layer of soil accumulated in the hollows would be scraped out to enrich paltry village gardens. This is the way it was: bare rock covered three quarters of the region. Towns sprang up, flourished, then disappeared; men came by, loved one another or fought bitterly, then died. No one in this desert, neither he nor his guest, mattered. And yet, outside this desert neither of them, Daru knew, could have really lived.

When he got up, no noise came from the classroom. He was amazed at the unmixed joy he derived from the mere thought that the Arab might have fled and that he would be alone with no decision to make. But the prisoner was there. He had merely stretched out between the stove and the desk. With eyes open, he was staring at the ceiling. In that position, his thick lips were particularly noticeable, giving him a pouting look. "Come," said Daru. The Arab got up and followed him. In the bedroom, the schoolmaster pointed to a chair near the table under the window. The Arab sat down without taking his eyes off Daru.

"Are you hungry?"

"Yes," the prisoner said.

Daru set the table for two. He took flour and oil, shaped a cake in a frying-pan, and lighted the little stove that functioned on bottled gas. While the cake was cooking, he went out to the shed to get cheese, eggs, dates and condensed milk. When the cake was done he set it on the window sill to cool, heated some condensed milk diluted with water, and beat up the eggs into an omelette. In one of his motions he knocked against the revolver stuck in his right pocket. He set the bowl down, went into the classroom and put the revolver in his desk drawer. When he came back to the room night was falling. He put on the light and served the Arab. "Eat," he said. The Arab took a piece of the cake, lifted it eagerly to his mouth, and stopped short.

"And you?" he asked.

"After you. I'll eat too."

The thick lips opened slightly. The Arab hesitated, then bit into the cake determinedly. The meal over, the Arab looked at the schoolmaster.

"Are you the judge?"

"No, I'm simply keeping you until tomorrow."

"Why do you eat with me?"

"I'm hungry."

The Arab fell silent. Daru got up and went out. He brought back a folding bed from the shed, set it up between the table and the stove, perpendicular to his own bed. From a large suitcase which, upright in a corner, served as a shelf for papers, he took two blankets and arranged them on the camp bed. Then he stopped, felt useless, and sat down on his bed. There was nothing more to do or to get ready. He had to look at this man. He looked at him, therefore, trying to imagine his face bursting with rage. He couldn't do so. He could see nothing but the dark yet shining eyes and the animal mouth.

"Why did you kill him?" he asked in a voice whose hostile tone surprised him.

The Arab looked away.

"He ran away. I ran after him." He raised his eyes to Daru again and they were full of a sort of woeful interrogation. "Now what will they do to me?"

"Are you afraid?" He stiffened, turning his eyes away.

"Are you sorry?"

The Arab stared at him open-mouthed. Obviously he did not understand. Daru's annoyance was growing. At the same time he felt awkward and self-conscious with his big body wedged between the two beds.

"Lie down there," he said impatiently. "That's your bed."

The Arab didn't move. He called to Daru:

"Tell me!"

The schoolmaster looked at him.

"Is the gendarme coming back tomorrow?"

"I don't know."

"Are you coming with us?"

"I don't know. Why?"

The prisoner got up and stretched out on top of the blankets, his feet toward the window. The light from the electric bulb shone straight into his eyes and he closed them at once.

"Why?" Daru repeated, standing beside the bed.

The Arab opened his eyes under the blinding light and looked at him, trying not to blink.

"Come with us," he said.

In the middle of the night, Daru was still not asleep. He had gone to bed after undressing completely; he generally slept naked. But when he suddenly realized that he had nothing on, he hesitated. He felt vulnerable and the temptation came to him to put his clothes back on. Then he shrugged his shoulders; after all, he wasn't a child and, if need be, he could break his adversary in two. From his bed he could observe him, lying on his back, still motionless with his eyes closed under the harsh light.

When Daru turned out the light, the darkness seemed to coagulate all of a sudden. Little by little, the night came back to life in the window where the starless sky was stirring gently. The schoolmaster soon made out the body lying at his feet. The Arab still did not move, but his eyes seemed open. A light wind was prowling around the schoolhouse. Perhaps it would drive away the clouds and the sun would reappear.

During the night the wind increased. The hens fluttered a little and then were silent. The Arab turned over on his side with his back to Daru, who thought he heard him moan. Then he listened for his guest's breathing, become heavier and more regular. He listened to that breath so close to him and mused without being able to go to sleep. In this room where he had been sleeping alone for a year, this presence bothered him. But it bothered him also by imposing on him a sort of brotherhood he knew well but refused to accept in the present circumstances. Men who share the same rooms, soldiers or prisoners, develop a strange alliance as if, having cast off their armour with their clothing, they fraternized every evening, over and above their differences, in the ancient community of dream and fatigue. But Daru shook himself; he didn't like such musings, and it was essential to sleep.

A little later, however, when the Arab stirred slightly, the schoolmaster was still not asleep. When the prisoner made a second move, he stiffened, on the alert. The Arab was lifting himself slowly on his arms with almost the motion of a sleepwalker. Seated upright in bed, he waited motionless without turning his head toward Daru, as if he were listening attentively. Daru did not stir; it had just occurred to him that the revolver was still in the drawer of his desk. It was better to act at once. Yet he continued to observe the prisoner, who, with the same slithery motion, put his feet on the ground, waited again, then began to stand up slowly. Daru was about to call out to him when the Arab began to walk, in a quite natural but extraordinarily silent way. He was heading toward the door at the end of the room that opened into the shed. He lifted the latch with precaution and went out, pushing the door behind him but without shutting it. Daru had not stirred. "He is running away," he merely thought. "Good riddance!" Yet he listened attentively. The hens were not fluttering; the guest must be on the plateau. A faint sound of water reached him, and he didn't know what it was until the Arab again stood framed in the doorway, closed the door carefully, and came back to bed without a sound. Then Daru turned his back on him and fell asleep. Still later he seemed, from the depths of his sleep, to hear furtive steps around the schoolhouse. "I'm dreaming! I'm dreaming!" he repeated to himself. And he went on sleeping.

When he awoke, the sky was clear; the loose window let in a cold, pure air. The Arab was asleep, hunched up under the blankets now, his mouth open, utterly relaxed. But when Daru shook him, he started dreadfully, staring at Daru with wild eyes as if he had never seen him and such a frightened expression that the schoolmaster stepped back. "Don't be afraid. It's me. You must eat." The Arab nodded his head and said yes. Calm had returned to his face, but his expression was vacant and listless.

The coffee was ready. They drank it seated together on the folding bed as they munched their pieces of the cake. Then Daru led the Arab under the shed and showed him the faucet where he washed. He went back into the room, folded the blankets and the bed, made his own bed and put the room in order. Then he went through the classroom and out onto the terrace. The sun was already rising in the blue sky; a soft, bright light was bathing the deserted plateau. On the ridge the snow was melting in spots. The stones were about to reappear. Crouched on the edge of the plateau, the schoolmaster looked at the deserted expanse. He thought of Balducci. He had hurt him, for he had sent him off in a way as if he didn't want to be associated with him. He could still hear the gendarme's farewell and, without knowing why, he felt strangely empty and vulnerable. At that moment, from the other side of the school-house, the prisoner coughed. Daru listened to him almost despite himself and then furious, threw a pebble that whistled through the air before sinking into the snow. That man's stupid crime revolted him, but to hand him over was contrary to honour. Merely thinking of it made him smart with humiliation. And he cursed at one and the same time his own people who had sent him this Arab and the Arab too who had dared to kill and not managed to get away. Daru got up, walked in a circle on the ter-race, waited motionless, and then went back into the schoolhouse.

The Arab, leaning over the cement floor of the shed, was washing his teeth with two fingers. Daru looked at him and said: "Come." He went back into the room ahead of the prisoner. He slipped a hunting-jacket on over his sweater and put on walking-shoes. Standing, he waited until the Arab had put on his *chèche* and sandals. They went into the classroom and the schoolmaster pointed to the exit, saying: "Go ahead." The fellow didn't budge. "I'm coming," said Daru. The Arab went out. Daru went back into the room and made a package of pieces of rusk, dates, and sugar. In the classroom, before going out, he hesitated a second in front of his desk, then crossed the threshold and locked the door. "That's the way," he said. He started toward the east, followed by the prisoner. But, a short distance from the school-house, he thought he heard a slight sound behind them. He retraced his steps and examined the surroundings of the house; there was no one there. The Arab watched him without seeming to understand. "Come on," said Daru.

They walked for an hour and rested beside a sharp peak of limestone. The snow was melting faster and faster and the sun was drinking up the puddles at once, rapidly cleaning the plateau, which gradually dried and vibrated like the air itself. When they resumed walking, the ground rang under their feet. From time to time a bird rent the space in front of them with a joyful cry. Daru breathed in deeply the fresh morning light. He felt a sort of rapture before the vast familiar expanse, now almost entirely yellow under its dome of blue sky. They walked an hour more, descending toward the south. They reached a level height made up of crumbly rocks. From there on, the pla-teau sloped down, eastward, toward a low plain where there were a few spindly trees and, to the south, toward outcroppings of rock that gave the landscape a chaotic look.

Daru surveyed the two directions. There was nothing but the sky on the horizon. Not a man could be seen. He turned toward the Arab, who was looking at him blankly. Daru held out the package to him. "Take it," he said. "There are dates, bread, and sugar. You can hold out for two days. Here are a thousand francs too." The Arab took the package and the money but kept his full hands at chest level as if he didn't know what to do with what was being given him. "Now look," the schoolmaster said as he pointed in the direction of the east, "there's the way to Tinguit. You have a two-hour walk. At Tinguit you'll find the administration and the police. They are expecting you." The Arab looked toward the east, still holding the package and the money against his chest.

Daru took his elbow and turned him rather roughly toward the south. At the foot of the height on which they stood could be seen a faint path. "That's the trail across the plateau. In a day's walk from here you'll find pasturelands and the first nomads. They'll take you in and shelter you according to their law." The Arab had now turned toward Daru and a sort of panic was visible in his expression. "Listen," he said. Daru shook his head: "No, be quiet. Now I'm leaving you." He turned his back on him, took two long steps in the direction of the school, looking hesitantly at the motionless Arab and started off again. For a few minutes he heard nothing but his own step resounding on the cold ground and did not turn his head. A moment later however he turned around. The Arab was still there on the edge of the hill, his arms hanging now, and he was looking at the schoolmaster. Daru felt something rise in his throat. But he swore with impatience, waved vaguely, and started off again. He had already gone some distance when he again stopped and looked. There was no longer anyone on the hill.

Daru hesitated. The sun was now rather high in the sky and was beginning to beat down on his head. The schoolmaster retraced his steps at first somewhat uncertainly then with decision. When he reached the little hill he was bathed in sweat. He climbed it as fast as he could and stopped. Out of breath at the top. The rock-fields to the south stood out sharply against the blue sky but on the plain to the east a steamy heat was already rising. And in that slight haze Daru with heavy heart made out the Arab walking slowly on the road to prison.

A little later, standing before the window of the classroom, the schoolmaster was watching the clear light bathing the whole surface of the plateau, but he hardly saw it. Behind him on the blackboard among the winding French rivers sprawled the clumsily chalked-up words he had just read. "You handed over our brother. You will pay for this." Daru looked at the sky, the plateau and beyond the invisible lands stretching all the way to the sea. In this vast landscape he had loved so much, he was alone.

REFLECTING AND DISCUSSING

1. As one of the few pieces of fiction in this volume, "The Guest" uses literature to address very real questions about humanity. What are these questions? What in the story reveals them to you, and how?

2. Discuss Daru's dilemma. What is it? How does his decision represent the primary conflict within the story? Use specific examples from the story to back up your points.

3. What is the definition of irony? What are the values demonstrated by the character's choices, and what are the ironies of those choices?

CONNECTING AND WRITING

1. While this story is a work of fiction, in awarding Camus the Nobel Prize for Literature in 1957, the prize committee commented that his work "illuminates the problem of the human conscience of our time." How is this demonstrated in "The Guest"? Research some of the conflicts to which Camus might have been

responding when he wrote this story during the 1950s and consider its implied argument within those contexts.

2. The original title of the story in French is "L'Hôte," which can mean both "host" and "guest." What is the significance of this title, particularly at the end of this story, and how does it speak to the relationship between the characters? Be sure to provide evidence from the story to back up your points.

Doin' Time with a New Ticker

Steve Lopez (1953–   )

The son of Spanish and Italian immigrants to the United States, Steve Lopez is a columnist known for his eclectic topics and his "pull-no-punches" style. He has written for Time, Life, Entertainment Weekly, *and* Sports Illustrated, *and has won a Society of Professional Journalists award for his story about Philadelphia murderer Ira Einhorn. Lopez has also published several works of fiction, including* Third and Indiana *(2010),* The Sunday Macaroni Club *(1997),* The Soloist *(2008), and* In the Clear *(2002). The following piece was published in the* Los Angeles Times, *for which Lopez is a columnist.*

When my parents got dumped by their medical insurance company and found that a new plan was going to cost at least twice as much, they asked my two cents' worth. My dad has a heart condition, so I told him they ought to lay out some cash and get the best plan available.

Now I realize it was bad advice. I should have told them to get a couple of Saturday night specials and start knocking off convenience stores.

A California convict, serving time for a 1996 robbery in Los Angeles, got a heart transplant on Jan. 3 at Stanford Medical Center. A story by the *Times'* Mitchell Landsberg reported that the bill will come to as much as $1 million. But the patient didn't have Blue Cross, so you and I will be covering the tab.

Now I'm not someone who will argue that prisoners surrender all rights the moment the door slams shut. People often tell me they're appalled that inmates have televisions or ball fields, and I can't get worked up about it. I've been on the inside of enough prisons to know there are no holidays there. What appalls me is that a huge percentage of the prison population is doing time for simple drug addiction, essentially, while deep-pocketed execs from the likes of Enron and Arthur Andersen pillage and plunder and still walk the streets.

But getting back to the crooks who are actually behind bars, the question is whether they should get taken care of when they're sick, even if treatment is complicated and expensive. And the answer is yes. They're still citizens, and more important, they're human beings. The law doesn't offer a choice in the matter, anyway.

But should it be the best care available when you and I are the ones paying? Do we really want to make that kind of top-shelf investment in the future of somebody who lives on a cell block?

My dad worked his entire life, has not been in jail that I know of, and pays a growing chunk of his fixed income on health care. The only time he's been to Stanford is to see a football game. He's been having a rough time lately because his doctors, forced by insurance company bean counters to practice cut-rate, assembly-line medicine, failed to treat him for a condition that was diagnosed two years ago. A convict, meanwhile, is being fussed over at one of the finest hospitals in the world, and my dad is paying for it.

According to Landsberg's story, the average heart transplant costs $209,000, plus $15,000 a year for follow-up treatment. That being the case, it's not clear to me why this guy got the Cadillac of heart transplants. Did state prison officials shop around at all? Have they heard of priceline.com? Did it have to be Stanford?

When I first heard about it, I wondered how this con managed to get to the top of the waiting list. You don't just show up at the hospital, have them zip you open, and go home with a new heart. You've got to get your name on a list and wait your turn, and for some people, that turn doesn't come in time. A lot of factors are taken into account, such as the location of the donor heart, the location of the recipient, the degree of illness, and other compatibility factors.

On the day this 31-year-old, two-time felon hit the jackpot, there were 4,119 people in this country waiting for a new heart that might save their lives. You have to wonder if a law-abiding, tax-paying citizen drew one last breath while Jailhouse Joe was getting a second wind.

A person's moral standing ought to be irrelevant, a bioethicist argued in Landsberg's story. "Should merit be considered a criteria?" she asked skeptically. "Should organs go to people who are 'good,' who have lived good lives?"

Let me put it this way:

Yes.

When it comes to organ transplants, we're already playing God to a certain degree, extending life beyond its natural course. I'm not saying a prison inmate should never receive a life-saving medical procedure. But when a fresh donor heart is on ice and the choice is between a two-time loser or someone who doesn't wear a jumpsuit every day, I don't have a problem giving extra points to the latter.

Before his transplant, the inmate had applied for a so-called compassionate release because of his condition. He might still get one, because even though he's got a new pump, he may be classified as terminally ill. Taking up a life of crime could be the smartest thing this guy ever did.

I've got to talk to my parents.

REFLECTING AND DISCUSSING

1. What is Lopez's central argument? In what ways does he craft his argument?
2. How does the emotional and sarcastic appeal of Lopez's story about his parents contribute to the article's argument? Is this an effective rhetorical strategy? Why or why not? Point to evidence from the article itself to support your claim.
3. How does Lopez juxtapose his concerns about inmates with the story of his parents? In what ways is this dichotomy potentially unfair to the inmates? Are they less deserving of care than Lopez's parents? Why or why not?

CONNECTING AND WRITING

1. Lopez quotes a bioethicist as asking, "Should organs go to people who are 'good,' who have lived good lives?" Find articles that take different positions on this issue and compare and contrast these positions. Then take a position yourself and use evidence from these pieces to back up your contentions.

2. Research issues regarding health care and health insurance in light of this article. What are some of the major issues that confront us in these areas? How do these issues reflect not only ethical concerns but also our values as a society?

Lifeboat Ethics: The Case Against Helping the Poor

Garrett Hardin (1915–2003)

Garrett Hardin was a prominent ecologist and philosopher who received a Ph.D. in biology from Stanford University in 1941. It has been said that Hardin was especially skilled at addressing issues that others would rather avoid. He wrote numerous books grappling with a variety of controversial subjects, such as eugenics, abortion, and human overpopulation. Hardin is also known for developing "Hardin's First Law of Human Ecology," which argues as follows: "We can never do merely one thing. Any intrusion into nature has numerous effects, many of which are unpredictable." The following essay was published in 1974.

Environmentalists use the metaphor of the earth as a "spaceship" in trying to persuade countries, industries and people to stop wasting and polluting our natural resources. Since we all share life on this planet, they argue, no single person or institution has the right to destroy, waste, or use more than a fair share of its resources.

But does everyone on earth have an equal right to an equal share of its resources? The spaceship metaphor can be dangerous when used by misguided idealists to justify suicidal policies for sharing our resources through uncontrolled immigration and foreign aid. In their enthusiastic but unrealistic generosity, they confuse the ethics of a spaceship with those of a lifeboat.

A true spaceship would have to be under the control of a captain, since no ship could possibly survive if its course were determined by committee. Spaceship Earth certainly has no captain; the United Nations is merely a toothless tiger, with little power to enforce any policy upon its bickering members.

If we divide the world crudely into rich nations and poor nations, two thirds of them are desperately poor, and only one third comparatively rich, with the United States the wealthiest of all. Metaphorically each rich nation can be seen as a lifeboat full of comparatively rich people. In the ocean outside each lifeboat swim the poor of the world, who would like to get in, or at least to share some of the wealth. What should the lifeboat passengers do?

First, we must recognize the limited capacity of any lifeboat. For example, a nation's land has a limited capacity to support a population and as the current energy crisis has shown us, in some ways we have already exceeded the carrying capacity of our land.

Adrift in a Moral Sea

So here we sit, say 50 people in our lifeboat. To be generous, let us assume it has room for 10 more, making a total capacity of 60. Suppose the 50 of us in the lifeboat see 100 others swimming in the water outside, begging for admission to our boat or for handouts. We have several options: we may be tempted to try to live by the Christian ideal of being "our brother's keeper," or by the Marxist ideal of "to each according to his needs." Since the needs of all in the water are the same, and since they can all be seen as "our brothers," we could take them all into our boat, making a total of 150 in a boat designed for 60. The boat swamps, everyone drowns. Complete justice, complete catastrophe.

Since the boat has an unused excess capacity of 10 more passengers, we could admit just 10 more to it. But which 10 do we let in? How do we choose? Do we pick the best 10, "first come, first served"? And what do we say to the 90 we exclude? If we do let an extra 10 into our lifeboat, we will have lost our "safety factor," an engineering principle of critical importance. For example, if we don't leave room for excess capacity as a safety factor in our country's agriculture, a new plant disease or a bad change in the weather could have disastrous consequences.

Suppose we decide to preserve our small safety factor and admit no more to the lifeboat. Our survival is then possible although we shall have to be constantly on guard against boarding parties.

While this last solution clearly offers the only means of our survival, it is morally abhorrent to many people. Some say they feel guilty about their good luck. My reply is simple: "Get out and yield your place to others." This may solve the problem of the guilt-ridden person's conscience, but it does not change the ethics of the lifeboat. The needy person to whom the guilt-ridden person yields his place will not himself feel guilty about his good luck. If he did, he would not climb aboard. The net result of conscience-stricken people giving up their unjustly held seats is the elimination of that sort of conscience from the lifeboat.

This is the basic metaphor within which we must work out our solutions. Let us now enrich the image, step by step, with substantive additions from the real world, a world that must solve real and pressing problems of overpopulation and hunger.

The harsh ethics of the lifeboat become even harsher when we consider the reproductive differences between the rich nations and the poor nations. The people inside the lifeboats are doubling in numbers every 87 years; those swimming around outside are doubling, on the average, every 35 years, more than twice as fast as the rich. And since the world's resources are dwindling, the difference in prosperity between the rich and the poor can only increase.

As of 1973, the U.S. had a population of 210 million people, who were increasing by 0.8 percent per year. Outside our lifeboat, let us imagine another 210 million people (say the combined populations of Colombia, Ecuador, Venezuela, Morocco, Pakistan, Thailand and the Philippines) who are increasing at a rate of 3.3 percent per year. Put differently, the doubling time for this aggregate population is 21 years, compared to 87 years for the U.S.

The harsh ethics of the lifeboat become harsher when we consider the reproductive differences between rich and poor.

Multiplying the Rich and the Poor

Now suppose the U.S. agreed to pool its resources with those seven countries, with everyone receiving an equal share. Initially the ratio of Americans to non-Americans in this model would be one-to-one. But consider what the ratio would be after 87 years, by which time the Americans would have doubled to a population of 420 million. By then, doubling every 21 years, the other group would have swollen to 3.54 billion. Each American would have to share the available resources with more than eight people.

But, one could argue, this discussion assumes that current population trends will continue, and they may not. Quite so. Most likely the rate of population increase will decline much faster in the U.S. than it will in the other countries, and there does not seem to be much we can do about it. In sharing with "each according to his needs," we must recognize that needs are determined by population size, which is determined by the rate of reproduction, which at present is regarded as a sovereign right of every nation, poor or not. This being so, the philanthropic load created by the sharing ethic of the spaceship can only increase.

The Tragedy of the Commons

The fundamental error of spaceship ethics, and the sharing it requires, is that it leads to what I call "the tragedy of the commons." Under a system of private property, the men who own property recognize their responsibility to care for it, for if they don't they will eventually suffer. A farmer, for instance, will allow no more cattle in a pasture than its carrying capacity justifies. If he overloads it, erosion sets in, weeds take over, and he loses the use of the pasture.

If a pasture becomes a commons open to all, the right of each to use it may not be matched by a corresponding responsibility to protect it. Asking everyone to use it with discretion will hardly do, for the considerate herdsman who refrains from overloading the commons suffers more than a selfish one who says his needs are greater. If everyone would restrain himself, all would be well; but it takes only one less than everyone to ruin a system of voluntary restraint. In a crowded world of less than perfect human beings, mutual ruin is inevitable if there are no controls. This is the tragedy of the commons.

One of the major tasks of education today should be the creation of such an acute awareness of the dangers of the commons that people will recognize its many varieties. For example, the air and water have become polluted because they are treated as commons. Further growth in the population or per-capita conversion of natural resources into pollutants will only make the problem worse. The same holds true for the fish of the oceans. Fishing fleets have nearly disappeared in many parts of the world, technological improvements in the art of fishing are hastening the day of complete ruin. Only the replacement of the system of the commons with a responsible system of control will save the land, air, water and oceanic fisheries.

The World Food Bank

In recent years there has been a push to create a new commons called a World Food Bank, an international depository of food reserves to which nations would contribute according to their abilities and from which they would draw according to their needs. This humanitarian proposal has received support from many liberal international groups, and from such prominent citizens as Margaret Mead, U.N. Secretary General Kurt Waldheim, and Senators Edward Kennedy and George McGovern.

A world food bank appeals powerfully to our humanitarian impulses. But before we rush ahead with such a plan, let us recognize where the greatest political push comes from, lest we be disillusioned later. Our experience with the "Food for Peace program," or Public Law 480, gives us the answer. This program moved billions of dollars worth of U.S. surplus grain to food-short, population-long countries during the past two decades. But when P.L. 480 first became law, a headline in the business magazine *Forbes* revealed the real power behind it: "Feeding the World's Hungry Millions: How It Will Mean Billions for U.S. Business."

And indeed it did. In the years 1960 to 1970, U.S. taxpayers spent a total of $7.9 billion on the Food for Peace program. Between 1948 and 1970, they also paid an additional $50 billion for other economic-aid programs, some of which went for food and food-producing machinery and technology. Though all U.S. taxpayers were forced to contribute to the cost of P.L. 480 certain special interest groups gained handsomely under the program. Farmers did not have to contribute the grain; the Government or rather the taxpayers, bought it from them at full market prices. The increased demand raised prices of farm products generally. The manufacturers of farm machinery, fertilizers and pesticides benefited by the farmers' extra efforts to grow more food. Grain elevators profited from storing the surplus until it could be shipped. Railroads made money hauling it to ports, and shipping lines profited from carrying it overseas. The implementation of P.L. 480 required the creation of a vast Government bureaucracy, which then acquired its own vested interest in continuing the program regardless of its merits.

Extracting Dollars

Those who proposed and defended the Food for Peace program in public rarely mentioned its importance to any of these special interests. The public emphasis was always on its humanitarian effects. The combination of silent selfish interests and highly vocal humanitarian apologists made a powerful and successful lobby for extracting money from taxpayers. We can expect the same lobby to push now for the creation of a World Food Bank.

However great the potential benefit to selfish interests, it should not be a decisive argument against a truly humanitarian program. We must ask if such a program would actually do more good than harm, not only momentarily but also in the long run. Those who propose the food bank usually refer to a current "emergency" or "crisis" in terms of world food supply. But what is an emergency? Although they may be infrequent and sudden, everyone knows that emergencies will occur from time to time. A well-run family, company, organization or country prepares for the likelihood of accidents and emergencies. It expects them, it budgets for them, it saves for them.

Learning the Hard Way

What happens if some organizations or countries budget for accidents and others do not? If each country is solely responsible for its own well-being, poorly managed ones will suffer. But they can learn from experience. They may mend their ways, and learn to budget for infrequent but certain emergencies. For example, the weather varies from year to year, and periodic crop failures are certain. A wise and competent government saves out of the production of the good years in anticipation of bad years to come. Joseph taught this policy to Pharaoh in Egypt more than 2,000 years ago. Yet the great majority of the governments in the world today do not follow such a policy. They lack either the wisdom or the competence, or both. Should those nations that do manage to put something aside be forced to come to the rescue each time an emergency occurs among the poor nations?

"But it isn't their fault!" Some kind-hearted liberals argue. "How can we blame the poor people who are caught in an emergency? Why must they suffer for the sins of their governments?" The concept of blame is simply not relevant here. The real question is, what are the operational consequences of establishing a world food bank? If it is open to every country every time a need develops, slovenly rulers will not be motivated to take Joseph's advice. Someone will always come to their aid. Some countries will deposit food in the world food bank, and others will withdraw it. There will be almost no overlap. As a result of such solutions to food shortage emergencies, the poor countries will not learn to mend their ways, and will suffer progressively greater emergencies as their populations grow.

Population Control the Crude Way

On the average poor countries undergo a 2.5 percent increase in population each year; rich countries, about 0.8 percent. Only rich countries have anything in the way of food reserves set aside, and even they do not have as much as they should. Poor countries have none. If poor countries received no food from the outside, the rate of their population growth would be periodically checked by crop failures and famines. But if they can always draw on a world food bank in time of need, their population can continue to grow unchecked, and so will their "need" for aid. In the short run, a world food bank may diminish that need, but in the long run it actually increases the need without limit.

Without some system of worldwide food sharing, the proportion of people in the rich and poor nations might eventually stabilize. The overpopulated poor countries would decrease in numbers, while the rich countries that had room for more people would increase. But with a well-meaning system of sharing, such as a world food bank, the growth differential between the rich and the poor countries will not only persist, it will increase. Because of the higher rate of population growth in the poor countries of the world, 88 percent of today's children are born poor, and only

12 percent rich. Year by year the ratio becomes worse, as the fast-reproducing poor outnumber the slow-reproducing rich.

A world food bank is thus a commons in disguise. People will have more motivation to draw from it than to add to any common store. The less provident and less able will multiply at the expense of the abler and more provident, bringing eventual ruin upon all who share in the commons. Besides, any system of "sharing" that amounts to foreign aid from the rich nations to the poor nations will carry the taint of charity, which will contribute little to the world peace so devoutly desired by those who support the idea of a world food bank.

As past U.S. foreign-aid programs have amply and depressingly demonstrated, international charity frequently inspires mistrust and antagonism rather than gratitude on the part of the recipient nation. . . .

Chinese Fish and Miracle Rice

The modern approach to foreign aid stresses the export of technology and advice, rather than money and food. As an ancient Chinese proverb goes: "Give a man a fish and he will eat for a day; teach him how to fish and he will eat for the rest of his days." Acting on this advice, the Rockefeller and Ford Foundations have financed a number of programs for improving agriculture in the hungry nations. Known as the "Green Revolution," these programs have led to the development of "miracle rice" and "miracle wheat," new strains that offer bigger harvests and greater resistance to crop damage. Norman Borlaug, the Nobel Prize winning agronomist who, supported by the Rockefeller Foundation, developed "miracle wheat," is one of the most prominent advocates of a world food bank.

Whether or not the Green Revolution can increase food production as much as its champions claim is a debatable but possibly irrelevant point. Those who support this well-intended humanitarian effort should first consider some of the fundamentals of human ecology. Ironically, one man who did was the late Alan Gregg, a vice president of the Rockefeller Foundation. Two decades ago he expressed strong doubts about the wisdom of such attempts to increase food production. He likened the growth and spread of humanity over the surface of the earth to the spread of cancer in the human body, remarking that "cancerous growths demand food; but, as far as I know, they have never been cured by getting it."

Overloading the Environment

Every human born constitutes a draft on all aspects of the environment: food, air, water, forests, beaches, wildlife, scenery and solitude. Food can, perhaps, be significantly increased to meet a growing demand. But what about clean beaches, unspoiled forests, and solitude? If we satisfy a growing population's need for food, we necessarily decrease its per capita supply of the other resources needed by men.

India, for example, now has a population of 600 million, which increases by 15 million each year. This population already puts a huge load on a relatively impoverished environment. The country's forests are now only a small fraction of what they were three centuries ago and floods and erosion continually destroy the insufficient farmland that remains. Every one of the 15 million new lives added to India's population puts an additional burden on the environment, and increases the economic and social costs of crowding. However humanitarian our intent, every Indian life saved through medical or nutritional assistance from abroad diminishes the quality of life for those who remain, and for subsequent generations. If rich countries make it possible, through foreign aid, for 600 million Indians to swell to 1.2 billion in a mere 28 years, as their current growth rate threatens, will future generations of Indians thank us for hastening the destruction of their environment? Will our good intentions be sufficient excuse for the consequences of our actions?

My final example of a commons in action is one for which the public has the least desire for rational discussion—immigration. Anyone who publicly questions the wisdom of current U.S. immigration policy is promptly charged with bigotry, prejudice, ethnocentrism, chauvinism, isolationism or selfishness. Rather than encounter such accusations, one would rather talk about other matters leaving immigration policy to wallow in the crosscurrents of special interests that take no account of the good of the whole, or the interests of posterity.

Perhaps we still feel guilty about things we said in the past. Two generations ago the popular press frequently referred to Dagos, Wops, Polacks, Chinks and Krauts in articles about how America was being "overrun" by foreigners of supposedly inferior genetic stock. . . . But because the implied inferiority of foreigners was used then as justification for keeping them out, people now assume that restrictive policies could only be based on such misguided notions. There are other grounds.

A Nation of Immigrants

Just consider the numbers involved. Our Government acknowledges a net inflow of 400,000 immigrants a year. While we have no hard data on the extent of illegal entries, educated guesses put the figure at about 600,000 a year. Since the natural increase (excess of births over deaths) of the resident population now runs about 1.7 million per year, the yearly gain from immigration amounts to at least 19 percent of the total annual increase, and may be as much as 37 percent if we include the estimate for illegal immigrants. Considering the growing use of birth-control devices, the potential effect of education campaigns by such organizations as Planned Parenthood Federation of America and Zero Population Growth, and the influence of inflation and the housing shortage, the fertility rate of American women may decline so much that immigration could account for all the yearly increase in population. Should we not at least ask if that is what we want?

For the sake of those who worry about whether the "quality" of the average immigrant compares favorably with the quality of the average resident, let us assume that immigrants and native-born citizens are of exactly equal quality, however one defines that term. We will focus here only on quantity; and since our conclusions will depend on nothing else, all charges of bigotry and chauvinism become irrelevant.

Immigration vs. Food Supply

World food banks move food to the people, hastening the exhaustion of the environment of the poor countries. Unrestricted immigration, on the other hand, moves people to the food, thus speeding up the destruction of the environment of the rich countries. We can easily understand why poor people should want to make this latter transfer, but why should rich hosts encourage it?

As in the case of foreign-aid programs, immigration receives support from self-ish interests and humanitarian impulses. The primary selfish interest in unimpeded immigration is the desire of employers for cheap labor, particularly in industries and trades that offer degrading work. In the past, one wave of foreigners after another was brought into the U.S. to work at wretched jobs for wretched wages. In recent years the Cubans, Puerto Ricans and Mexicans have had this dubious honor. The interests of the employers of cheap labor mesh well with the guilty silence of the country's liberal intelligentsia. White Anglo-Saxon Protestants are particularly reluc-tant to call for a closing of the doors to immigration for fear of being called bigots.

But not all countries have such reluctant leadership. Most educated Hawaiians, for example, are keenly aware of the limits of their environment, particularly in terms of population growth. There is only so much room on the islands, and the island-ers know it. To Hawaiians, immigrants from the other 49 states present as great a threat as those from other nations. At a recent meeting of Hawaiian government officials in Honolulu, I had the ironic delight of hearing a speaker who like most of his audience was of Japanese ancestry, ask how the country might practically and constitutionally close its doors to further immigration. One member of the audience countered: "How can we shut the doors now? We have many friends and relatives in Japan that we'd like to bring here some day so that they can enjoy Hawaii too." The Japanese-American speaker smiled sympathetically and answered: "Yes, but we have children now, and someday we'll have grandchildren too. We can bring more people here from Japan only by giving away some of the land that we hope to pass on to our grandchildren some day. What right do we have to do that?"

At this point, I can hear U.S. liberals asking: "How can you justify slamming the door once you're inside? You say that immigrants should be kept out. But aren't we all immigrants, or the descendants of immigrants? If we insist on staying, must we not admit all others?" Our craving for intellectual order leads us to seek and prefer sym-metrical rules and morals: a single rule for me and everybody else; the same rule yes-terday, today and tomorrow. Justice, we feel, should not change with time and place.

We Americans of non-Indian ancestry can look upon ourselves as the descen-dants of thieves who are guilty morally, if not legally, of stealing this land from its Indian owners. Should we then give back the land to the now living American descen-dants of those Indians? However morally or logically sound this proposal may be, I, for one, am unwilling to live by it and I know no one else who is. Besides, the logical consequence would be absurd. Suppose that, intoxicated with a sense of pure justice, we should decide to turn our land over to the Indians. Since all our other wealth has also been derived from the land, wouldn't we be morally obliged to give that back to the Indians too?

Pure Justice vs. Reality

Clearly, the concept of pure justice produces an infinite regression to absurdity. Centu-ries ago, wise men invented statutes of limitations to justify the rejection of such pure justice, in the interest of preventing continual disorder. The law zealously defends property rights, but only relatively recent property rights. Drawing a line after an arbitrary time has elapsed may be unjust, but the alternatives are worse.

We are all the descendants of thieves, and the world's resources are inequitably distributed. But we must begin the journey to tomorrow from the point where we are today. We cannot remake the past. We cannot safely divide the wealth equitably among all peoples so long as people reproduce at different rates. To do so would guarantee that our grandchildren and everyone else's grandchildren, would have only a ruined world to inhabit.

To be generous with one's own possessions is quite different from being generous with those of posterity. We should call this point to the attention of those who from a commendable love of justice and equality, would institute a system of the commons, either in the form of a world food bank, or of unrestricted immigration. We must convince them if we wish to save at least some parts of the world from environmental ruin.

Without a true world government to control reproduction and the use of available resources, the sharing ethic of the spaceship is impossible. For the foreseeable future, our survival demands that we govern our actions by the ethics of a lifeboat, harsh though they may be. Posterity will be satisfied with nothing less.

REFLECTING AND DISCUSSING

1. What are "lifeboat ethics," according to Hardin? Discuss this philosophical dilemma as it is posed in the first pages of the essay.
2. Hardin engages in some fairly blatant name-calling—against U.S. liberals, for instance—that makes his political stance clear. What effect does this have on his credibility, and in your view, is this an ethical form of argument? Why or why not?
3. How is Hardin's stance an overtly controversial one, revealed even as early as the subtitle to the essay? What effect does this rather startling title have? For what purpose do you think Hardin made this choice?

CONNECTING AND WRITING

1. Looking at current articles regarding world hunger and ethical approaches to solving that problem, determine if, in your opinion, Hardin's argument has been supported or refuted since it was made. Support your viewpoint with examples from your reading.
2. The essay begins, "Environmentalists use the metaphor of the Earth as a 'spaceship' in trying to persuade countries, industries and people to stop wasting and polluting our natural resources." Hardin later argues that the spaceship metaphor can be dangerous. Do you agree or disagree with the use of this central metaphor? Is it useful? Dangerous? Why? Write an essay that argues a particular position, using evidence from both Hardin and other sources you find.
3. Hardin touches on the subject of open borders in this 1974 essay. Compare and contrast Hardin's viewpoint with contemporary debates on this issue. Your argument should point to the differences among these views, not necessarily your own opinion.

The Cost of Public Humiliation

Joseph Telushkin (1948–   )

Well-known rabbi, lecturer, and author, Joseph Telushkin was ordained by the Yeshiva Institute of New York. Telushkin has written over a dozen books, including Jewish Literacy *(1991);* Jewish Humor *(1992); and* Words That Hurt, Words That Heal *(1998). Owing to his writings' appeal to a wide audience, United Nations High Commissioner for Refugees Antonio Guterres invited Telushkin to speak before the Commission in Geneva in 2013. Several of Telushkin's books have been adapted for television and have enjoyed great popularity—especially* The Practice *(on television from 1997 to 2004).*

Some eighteen hundred years ago in Israel, Rabbi Judah the Prince, the leading scholar of his age, was delivering an important lecture when suddenly he found himself in a very aggravating circumstance: A member of the audience who had eaten a large amount of garlic was emitting such an unpleasant odor that the rabbi found it difficult to concentrate. Rabbi Judah abruptly stopped speaking and called out: "Whoever ate the garlic, leave!"

Almost immediately Rabbi Hiyya, a scholar only slightly less prominent than the speaker, rose from his seat and started toward the back. Many other listeners, mortified by Rabbi Hiyya's public embarrassment, followed him out, and the lecture was canceled.

The next morning, Rabbi Judah's son confronted Rabbi Hiyya, and criticized him for spoiling his father's lecture.

"God forbid that I would ever trouble your father," Rabbi Hiyya responded.

"How can you deny what you did?" the son answered. "Wasn't it you who stood up when my father demanded that the one who had eaten the garlic leave?"

"I stood up only to avoid the public humiliation of the person whose breath was bothering your father. Since I already have a certain status among the rabbis, I was willing to accept the embarrassment of being publicly singled out like that. Imagine, though, if the person who had eaten the garlic was a rabbi of lesser stature than me, or worse, a student. That person would have been deeply humiliated, and likely would have become an object of mockery."[1]

So far we have been examining the cost of harsh words spoken in anger or criticism. But what of the occasional cruelties to which we are all prone? In the preceding example, Rabbi Hiyya was concerned with more than just guarding the unfortunate garlic eater's dignity. He also wished to prevent Rabbi Judah from violating one of Judaism's most serious ethical offenses: humiliating a fellow human being.

"Whoever shames his neighbor in public," the Talmud teaches, "it is as if he shed his blood." The analogy is deemed apt, because a shamed person's skin blanches as the blood drains from his face.

---

1 The Babylonian Talmud, *Sanhedrin* 11a, recounts this incident. I have greatly expanded on Rabbi Hiyya's terse explanation for his behavior, putting into his mouth statements that are only suggested in the text and commentaries.

Abhorrence at the thought of publicly shaming others, however, does not seem to preoccupy a large number of contemporary journalists, prominent figures, and opinion makers, or, for that matter, ordinary citizens.

In 1959 a prominent businessman donated half a million dollars to a university in Saint Louis, Missouri. The *St. Louis Post-Dispatch* assigned reporters to write a feature about him. The reporters soon discovered that the man had served three prison terms, totaling almost ten years, for forgery, larceny, and issuing fraudulent checks. In the thirty-five years since he had left prison, his record had been spotless; in fact, the FBI had cleared him for defense-related work. More significantly, there was no reason to believe that any of his current money, including the half-million dollars he had donated to the university, had been earned illegally.

Nonetheless, the reporters headlined the article, which initially was supposed to be complimentary: [SO-AND-SO] . . . MAIN UNIVERSAL MATCH OWNER, IS EX-CONVICT. The man's wife and son, both of whom did not know of his earlier criminal record, denounced the piece as "vicious," to which Raymond L. Crowley, the paper's managing editor, responded: "I think the stories simply speak for themselves."

The Talmud's moral standard differs markedly from Crowley's. "If a person is a penitent," it teaches, "it is forbidden to say to him, 'Remember your early deeds.'" Needless to say, it's even more cruel to spread embarrassing reports about the person to *others* when his or her subsequent behavior has been exemplary.

The *St. Louis Post-Dispatch* article was harmful to far more people than just this man and his family; it sent a very demoralizing message to everyone who has tried to undo past misdeeds. It told them that no matter how hard they try, through hard work, charitable contributions, or anything that constitutes "doing good," they will forever be linked to the worst acts of their lives; they can never win back their good name. Wouldn't this alone make a person feel that there is little point in changing his ways?

The irony of the message communicated by the *St. Louis Post-Dispatch* "exposé" is profound. Years earlier, criminal courts had justifiably punished the man for doing evil. Now, the newspaper was punishing him for doing good.

This case is unusual. As a rule, reporters and newspapers rarely go out of their way to humiliate someone against whom they have no grudge. More commonly, journalists, like many of us, are apt to shame only those at whom they already are angry.

The desire to humiliate adversaries is particularly common in politics. When South Carolinian Tom Turnipseed ran for Congress in 1980, his Republican rival unearthed and publicized evidence that Turnipseed once had suffered an episode of depression for which he had received electric shock treatment. When Turnipseed responded with an anguished attack on his opponent's campaign ethics, Lee Atwater (who later became famous as the director of George Bush's 1988 presidential campaign, but was then directing the Republican campaign in South Carolina) responded that he had no intention of answering charges made by a person "hooked up to jumper cables."

What a grotesque violation of privacy and the dictum against publicly humiliating another! Atwater put into the voters' heads a vicious, graphic image that potentially poisoned not only their perceptions of Turnipseed, but of everyone who has had electric shock therapy.

Is it any wonder that some ten years later, when Atwater himself was stricken with an inoperable brain tumor, and found himself attached to unpleasant hospital machinery, that he was moved to write Turnipseed a letter asking forgiveness?

In contemporary America, one of the most prestigious and highly paid professions, the law, commonly encourages its practitioners to humiliate those who oppose them in court. Particularly among criminal defense lawyers, *humiliating* an opposing witness is sometimes regarded as a singularly effective way to discredit testimony. Seymour Wishman, a successful and well-known criminal defense attorney, recalls a difficult defense he had to mount for a client accused of raping and sodomizing a nurse.

Although Wishman had no reason to assume the nurse had fabricated the allegation, he was ecstatic upon learning that the examining police physician had neglected to mention in his medical report whether there was any physical evidence that force had been used against the nurse. This omission freed him to pursue a particularly aggressive cross-examination of the woman, one filled with reputation-damaging and humiliating questions:

WISHMAN: Isn't it a fact that after you met the defendant at a bar, you asked him if he wanted to have a good time?
WITNESS: No! That's a lie!
WISHMAN: Isn't it true that you took him and his three friends back to your apartment and had that good time?
WITNESS: No!
WISHMAN: And, after you had that good time, didn't you ask for money?
WITNESS: No such way!
WISHMAN: Isn't it a fact that the only reason you made a complaint was because you were furious for not getting paid?
WITNESS: No! No! That's a lie!
WISHMAN: You claim to have been raped and sodomized. As a nurse, you surely have an idea of the effect of such an assault on a woman's body. Are you aware, Mrs. Lewis, that the police doctors found no evidence of force or trauma?
WITNESS: I don't know what the doctors found.

After the trial ended, Wishman was proud when the presiding judge congratulated him for dealing with the woman "brilliantly." He felt considerably less proud half a year later when he accidentally encountered the nurse at her workplace. As soon as she recognized Wishman, she started screaming: "That's the son-of-a-bitch that did it to me!"

Of course, she was referring not to the alleged rape and sodomy, but to the verbal "rape" to which the lawyer had subjected her. According to Wishman, this encounter left him shaken and feeling somewhat guilty.

What *is* amazing is the lawyer's surprise at his own reaction. Why shouldn't he have felt guilty? It's difficult to imagine a greater cruelty toward, and humiliation of, a woman than to suggest that she was a prostitute who had made a false allegation of rape because she hadn't been paid.

Atwater's and Wishman's very sincere regrets bring to mind a striking image in the epilogue to George Bernard Shaw's play *Saint Joan*. The scene is set some twenty-five years after Joan of Arc has been convicted of heresy and burned at the stake. When a group of people gather to discuss her impact on their lives, one man says that he feels fortunate to have been present at her execution, because having seen how dreadful it was to burn a person, he subsequently became much kinder. "Must then a Christ perish in torment in every age," another character asks, "for the sake of those who have no imagination?"

Is it just some journalists, politicians, and lawyers who lack the empathy to understand how wrong it is to humiliate others? Apparently many of us share in this failing, because the shaming of individuals occurs thousands of times each day. The settings in which this emotional pain is inflicted may be less public, but the damage done can be just as devastating:

Take the case of Joanne, a woman I know in her mid-thirties, who is a middle manager at a large corporation. Her job ideally requires her to make public addresses and briefings, but for years her professional advancement has been stunted because of her inordinate fear of public speaking.

To Joanne and her many friends, her extreme nervousness has never made sense. Since she has considerable professional expertise, and is very articulate about her work in one-on-one settings, there exists no *logical* reason for her to freeze up every time she is called to make an address in public.

In desperation Joanne consulted a psychologist, who hypnotized her. After inducing a deep state of relaxation, the psychologist instructed her to focus on any recollections or associations involving discomfort around public speaking. Joanne began to regress, and was soon vividly reliving a series of episodes that had occurred when she was seven years old. At that time, her parents had recently moved from Chile to Brazil. Although Joanne quickly acquired an adequate grasp of Portuguese, she still made many grammatical mistakes. Unfortunately, her second-grade teacher delighted in summoning Joanne to the blackboard at the front of the classroom and questioning her on material the class had been studying. On several occasions when she answered correctly but made grammatical mistakes, the teacher would ridicule her. After a few such episodes, Joanne chose not to answer at all. "Why do you stand there like a dummy?" the teacher would ask her. "Do you expect the answer to drop down to you from God in heaven?"

Twenty-five years later, this highly accomplished adult still finds herself paralyzed when called upon to speak in front of an audience. The school-teacher's gratification of a sadistic impulse has left Joanne with a lifelong emotional scar. To this day, she continues to go to great (and, from a career standpoint, self-destructive) lengths to avoid situations where she again might be humiliated.

Roberta, another woman I know, recalls a recurring and humiliating trauma from her teenage years. As a young child, she had been her mother's favorite. But when she became an adolescent and gained twenty pounds, her mother's expressions of love turned to withering verbal attacks.

Once, when her aunt was visiting, Roberta brought some food to the kitchen table. As she walked away, her mother said to her aunt in a loud voice: "Do you see how big her ass is, how fat she's become? Doesn't it look disgusting?" The mother repeated this sentiment many times, always in the presence of others.

During her high school years, Roberta would wait until every other student had left the room when a class ended; she did not want people to see her from the rear. Although she's now over fifty, and her mother has long been dead, her miserable physical self-image remains perhaps the largest part of the legacy her mother bequeathed her.

When You've Humiliated Another Person

The great Jewish writer Rabbi Milton Steinberg once said, "When I was young, I admired clever people. Now that I am older, I admire kind people." Steinberg understood that it's a greater accomplishment to be kind than to be brilliant.

Harry Truman might not have been the greatest intellectual ever to occupy the office of president. But in addition to his penetrating common sense, Truman possessed kind instincts, epitomized by the extraordinary care he took not to humiliate others.

In 1962, some ten years after he left the White House, Truman lectured before a group of university students in Los Angeles. During the question-and-answer period, a student asked him: "What do you think of our local yokel?" referring to California Governor Pat Brown.

Mr. Truman bristled and told the boy he should be ashamed of himself for speaking of the governor in so disrespectful a manner. He continued scolding the boy a while longer; by the time he finished, the student was close to tears.

What marks this story off as different from every other account until now is what happened next: "When the question period was over," writes Merle Miller, author of an oral biography of the president, "Mr. Truman went to the boy and said that he hoped he would understand that what he had said had to do with the principle involved and that he meant nothing personal. The boy said that he did understand, and the two shook hands. Afterward Mr. Truman went to see the dean to ask him to send reports from time to time on the boy's progress in school. The dean said he would. . . . I asked Mr. Truman if he had ever heard from the boy himself, and he said, 'He's written me two or three times, and I've written him back. He's doing very well.'"[2]

Compare Truman's behavior with that of Winston Churchill, arguably the greatest statesman of this century and a man of penetrating mind and wit. In an adulatory compilation of Churchill's greatest quotes and quips, James Hume writes of an incident during the 1930s in which a teenager annoyed and heckled Churchill during a speech. The second time the young man spoke up, Churchill replied: "I

---

2 President Truman's concern about not inflicting gratuitous hurt is confirmed in an anecdote related by Tip O'Neill, the late speaker of the House: "I met [President Truman] with a group of us freshmen when I came to Congress in 1953, and the conversation turned to Mamie Eisenhower [wife of the newly elected Republican president]. Truman said that he had no use for Ike. 'But leave his family alone,' the President continued, his voice rising. 'If I ever hear that one of you attacked the wife or a family member of the President of the United States, I'll personally go into your district and campaign against you'" (Tip O'Neill with Gary Hymel, *All Politics Is Local* [New York: Times Books, 1994], p. 35).

admire a manly man, and I rejoice in a womanly woman—but I cannot abide a boily boy. Come back in a few years when your cause is as free from spots as your complexion [will then be]." The boy's arguments might well have deserved to be attacked, but if this story is true, why did Churchill have to mock the fact that he had pimples?[3]

While there is little question that the British leader was a greater statesman and intellectual than Truman, it was Truman who had the awareness and sensitivity to realize—not ten years later or even one year later but immediately—that the public scolding he had given the boy, *even if justified*, could subject him to ridicule and contempt. Imagine how different Joanne's life would have been if the teacher who had mocked her had realized right away the unfairness and evil of what she was doing, and desisted and apologized.

Other observers of Truman have noted that being attentive to others' feelings was very important to him. In 1964, when newsman Eric Sevareid interviewed him about his presidential experiences, Truman commented: "What you don't understand is the power of a President to hurt."

Sevareid was struck by this remark. "An American President has the power to build, to set fateful events in motion, to destroy an enemy civilization. . . . But the power of a President to hurt the feelings of another human being—this, I think, had scarcely occurred to me, and still less had it occurred to me that a President in office would have the time and need to be aware of this particular power among so many others. Mr. Truman went on to observe that a word, a harsh glance, a peremptory motion by a President of the United States, could so injure another man's pride that it would remain a scar on his emotional system all his life."

If an American president, constantly besieged with personal, administrative, and political demands, can find the time to reflect on whether his words unintentionally shame another, doesn't it behoove all of us to do the same?

Guidelines for Ensuring that we Don't Humiliate Others

What was it about Harry Truman that caused him to be so conscious of the damage words can cause? It wasn't an exceedingly mild disposition, for the many Truman biographies indicate that he was an impassioned man who frequently lost his temper. But even when he expressed anger, what stopped him from humiliating others, or caused him immediately to set out to repair the damage if he feared he had done so, was his conscious internalization of the observation he made to Sevareid: "What you don't understand is the power of a President to hurt."

Change "the power of a President" to "the power of words," and you realize that we all have the ability to shame others.

If you reflect for a few moments, you'll realize how many people you can wound verbally (and perhaps already have): your spouse, parents, other relatives, friends, and/or people who work for you.

---

3   There is reason to suspect that as Churchill grew older, he became far more sensitive to the power of cruel words to hurt.

The first step in ensuring that we don't abuse this power is to be aware that we have it; otherwise, we'll feel no need to guard our tongues.

While it is important to recognize the power of words to hurt, such recognition alone is certainly not sufficient to stop us from using words destructively. No doubt many readers have nodded as they have read each episode in this chapter, mentally acknowledging the great evil of shaming others. However, unless you make such an acknowledgment *again and again*, you will probably forget it, particularly during moments of anger.

A popular British story tells of a very prominent politician who one night had imbibed too much liquor, and stumbled into a heavy-set female member of Parliament from the opposition party. Annoyed, the woman said to him, "You are drunk, and what's more, you are disgustingly drunk." To which the British parliamentarian responded: "And might I say, you are ugly, and what's more, disgustingly ugly. But tomorrow, I shall be sober."

If you, like the politician in question, have a quick temper and pride yourself on having a sharp wit, it is important that you *reflect again and again on the moral evil of shaming another person.*

For Lee Atwater it was only when he was lying on his deathbed that it became obvious to him how cruel it was to have mocked one of the most painful episodes in another man's life. I am sure that had Atwater been taught throughout his life *again and again*, as I believe all of us must be taught *again and again*, that humiliating another person is as evil as going up to someone in the street and punching him in the face, he wouldn't have done so in the first place.

Similarly, if my friend Roberta's mother, who jeered at her for being overweight, had reminded herself repeatedly how hurtful her words could be—so much so that, *forty years later*, her daughter still looks contemptuously at herself in the mirror—would she not have learned to curb her tongue? I suspect she would have, for Roberta is certain that her mother loved her, since she expressed many warm feelings toward her daughter on other occasions. Yet because Roberta's mother never learned to reflect on her potentially destructive power of words, she didn't feel the need to restrain her tongue when angry. She went through life like a reckless child playing with a loaded gun, and never understood that words are like bullets, and the damage they wreak often cannot be undone.

An ancient Jewish teaching observes: "It would be better for a person not to have been born at all than to experience these seven things: the death of his children in his lifetime, economic dependence upon others, an unnatural death, forgetting his learning, suffering, slavery, and publicly shaming his fellow man."

The first six items on this list represent some of the most horrific fates imaginable. Anyone who knows someone who has buried a child realizes that no parent ever fully recovers from such pain. Similarly, the prospect of becoming totally dependent on others, or even worse becoming another's slave, is horrifying. As for "forgetting his learning," we have all heard of people committing suicide after being diagnosed with Alzheimer's disease. Although most people won't take so drastic a step, I suspect most of us would prefer to die than to go through life with severe brain damage.

It's striking that the Rabbis included "and publicly shaming his fellow man" on the listing of terrible occurrences. Note that they did not say "being *publicly shamed*," but "*publicly shaming* his fellow man." To the Rabbis, becoming the kind of malevolent human being who humiliates others is as appalling a fate as losing a child—or one's mind.

Why? Every monotheistic faith believes that our mental capacities are God-given and that human beings were brought into this world to do good. If it's wrong to squander the gifts bestowed by God, how much worse it is to turn them to such an evil purpose as deliberately hurting another!

Finally, remember that *it is when you are most upset that you need to consider your words most carefully*. Admittedly, thinking about the consequences of what you say before you say it is particularly difficult at such a time. Rabbi Judah the Prince was so bothered by the smell of garlic that he didn't reflect on the shame his words might inflict on the person who had eaten it. Winston Churchill was so annoyed by the young man's irritating behavior that he only wished to find a "put-down" that would make others laugh at the boy's unappealing physical traits. But while Rabbi Judah and Churchill were justified in being annoyed at the provocative behavior directed toward them, the "punishment" inflicted by their sharp words far outweighed the victims' "crimes."

Jewish law asks us to take care not to humiliate others even in far-fetched cases: "If someone was hanged in a person's family, don't say to him, 'Hang up this fish for me,'" lest you trigger that distressful memory or remind others who are present of the shameful event. If we are supposed to be morally vigilant even in such a remote case, how much more careful should we be not to publicly mock someone's bad breath, acne, or ugliness.

If you have humiliated another person, of course you should apologize to him or her. But the far more moral thing to do is to exercise restraint *before* you inflict shame, for the greatest remorse and the best will in the world never can erase your words. You can do everything possible to try to minimize their impact, but unfortunately, that is all you can do.

REFLECTING AND DISCUSSING

1. Telushkin takes a strong moral stand in this essay. How does he reveal his point of view? How does he make his argument?

2. Comment on the range of examples that the author uses to back up his overall argument. What purpose do these examples serve? Which are most effective, from your point of view? Why?

3. Think about contemporary examples of "public humiliation." What might be added to Telushkin's examples—and arguments—if this essay were to be revised today? How is Telushkin's overall point still relevant? Why?

CONNECTING AND WRITING

1. Telushkin writes at length about the importance of leaders having a moral compass and an awareness of the impact their words might have on other people, using Harry Truman and Winston Churchill as primary examples. Truman, he notes, "might not have been the greatest intellectual ever to occupy the office of president. But in addition to his penetrating common sense, Truman possessed kind instincts,

epitomized by the extraordinary care he took not to humiliate others." Select a more current figure and analyze him or her from Telushkin's perspective.

2. Social media can be said to have taken public humiliation and made it both public and private at the same time. Analyze and discuss one such aspect of social media, using research (and credible sources) to back up your points.

University of Arizona Class of 1898–1899, banned photograph

This photograph provides evidence of the ways in which cultural norms, expectations, and mores change over time. The questions below provide additional context for our interest in this photograph—and the controversies it generated in its time.

REFLECTING AND DISCUSSING

1. What do you notice when you look at this photograph? What is notable?

2. According to information at the Special Collections department of the University of Arizona Library, then-President Millard Mayhew Parker "denied [the] publication or even the sale of the picture to members of the student body, because he was offended at the inappropriate behavior of two couples." The picture would not be made public for fifty-two years because of these concerns. What about this photo might have been shocking? How do you respond to it? How have things changed since it was taken?

3. While it might seem laughable to think that this photo was ever shocking, comment on contemporary images in the media. When it comes to shock value—and inappropriate behavior, for that matter—has the pendulum swung too far in the other direction? How so? How not?

CONNECTING AND WRITING

1. Research the on-again, off-again controversy surrounding the banning of photographs or books and the ethical and legal issues that such censorship brings into play. Argue the pitfalls of or valid reasons for restricting or barring controversial images or books from public view.
2. Many of these issues also relate to perceptions regarding pornography. Consider the controversial pieces written after Hugh Hefner, founder of *Playboy*, died. Select two of the op-ed pieces that appeared soon after his death and compare and contrast them, arguing your own point of view with examples from these articles.

The Birthmark

Nathaniel Hawthorne (1804–1864)

Nathaniel Hawthorne was born in Salem, Massachusetts, a descendant of a venerable Puritan family. A prolific writer of short stories, he is often credited with inventing the form and was part of a robust literary and philosophical movement in New England that included writers and philosophers such as Ralph Waldo Emerson and Henry Thoreau. Hawthorne's best writings explore the dark recesses of the American character and often express ambivalence toward women and sexuality. This is especially true of his best-known work, The Scarlet Letter.

In the latter part of the last century there lived a man of science, an eminent proficient in every branch of natural philosophy, who not long before our story opens had made experience of a spiritual affinity more attractive than any chemical one. He had left his laboratory to the care of an assistant, cleared his fine countenance from the furnace smoke, washed the stain of acids from his fingers, and persuaded a beautiful woman to become his wife. In those days when the comparatively recent discovery of electricity and other kindred mysteries of Nature seemed to open paths into the region of miracle, it was not unusual for the love of science to rival the love of woman in its depth and absorbing energy. The higher intellect, the imagination, the spirit, and even the heart might all find their congenial aliment in pursuits which, as some of their ardent votaries believed, would ascend from one step of powerful intelligence to another, until the philosopher should lay his hand on the secret of creative force and perhaps make new worlds for himself. We know not whether Aylmer possessed this degree of faith in man's ultimate control over Nature. He had devoted himself, however, too unreservedly to scientific studies ever to be weaned from them by any second passion. His love for his young wife might prove the stronger of the two; but it could only be by intertwining itself with his love of science, and uniting the strength of the latter to his own.

Such a union accordingly took place, and was attended with truly remarkable consequences and a deeply impressive moral. One day, very soon after their marriage, Aylmer sat gazing at his wife with a trouble in his countenance that grew stronger until he spoke.

"Georgiana," said he, "has it never occurred to you that the mark upon your cheek might be removed?"

"No, indeed," said she, smiling; but perceiving the seriousness of his manner, she blushed deeply. "To tell you the truth it has been so often called a charm that I was simple enough to imagine it might be so."

"Ah, upon another face perhaps it might," replied her husband; "but never on yours. No, dearest Georgiana, you came so nearly perfect from the hand of Nature that this slightest possible defect, which we hesitate whether to term a defect or a beauty, shocks me, as being the visible mark of earthly imperfection."

"Shocks you, my husband!" cried Georgiana, deeply hurt; at first reddening with momentary anger, but then bursting into tears. "Then why did you take me from my mother's side? You cannot love what shocks you!"

To explain this conversation it must be mentioned that in the centre of Georgiana's left cheek there was a singular mark, deeply interwoven, as it were, with the texture and substance of her face. In the usual state of her complexion—a healthy though delicate bloom—the mark wore a tint of deeper crimson, which imperfectly defined its shape amid the surrounding rosiness. When she blushed it gradually became more indistinct, and finally vanished amid the triumphant rush of blood that bathed the whole cheek with its brilliant glow. But if any shifting motion caused her to turn pale there was the mark again, a crimson stain upon the snow, in what Aylmer sometimes deemed an almost fearful distinctness. Its shape bore not a little similarity to the human hand, though of the smallest pygmy size. Georgiana's lovers were wont to say that some fairy at her birth hour had laid her tiny hand upon the infant's cheek, and left this impress there in token of the magic endowments that were to give her such sway over all hearts. Many a desperate swain would have risked life for the privilege of pressing his lips to the mysterious hand. It must not be concealed, however, that the impression wrought by this fairy sign manual varied exceedingly, according to the difference of temperament in the beholders. Some fastidious persons—but they were exclusively of her own sex—affirmed that the bloody hand, as they chose to call it, quite destroyed the effect of Georgiana's beauty, and rendered her countenance even hideous. But it would be as reasonable to say that one of those small blue stains which sometimes occur in the purest statuary marble would convert the Eve of Powers to a monster. Masculine observers, if the birthmark did not heighten their admiration, contented themselves with wishing it away, that the world might possess one living specimen of ideal loveliness without the semblance of a flaw. After his marriage,—for he thought little or nothing of the matter before,—Aylmer discovered that this was the case with himself.

Had she been less beautiful,—if Envy's self could have found aught else to sneer at,—he might have felt his affection heightened by the prettiness of this mimic hand, now vaguely portrayed, now lost, now stealing forth again and glimmering to and fro with every pulse of emotion that throbbed within her heart; but seeing her otherwise so perfect, he found this one defect grow more and more intolerable with every moment of their united lives. It was the fatal flaw of humanity which Nature, in one shape or another, stamps ineffaceably on all her productions, either to imply that they are temporary and finite, or that their perfection must be wrought by toil and pain. The crimson hand expressed the ineludible grip in which mortality clutches the highest and purest of earthly mould, degrading them into kindred with the lowest, and even with the very brutes, like whom their visible frames return to dust. In this manner, selecting it as the symbol of his wife's liability to sin, sorrow, decay, and death, Aylmer's sombre imagination was not long in rendering the birthmark a frightful object, causing him more trouble and horror than ever Georgiana's beauty, whether of soul or sense, had given him delight.

At all the seasons which should have been their happiest, he invariably and without intending it, nay, in spite of a purpose to the contrary, reverted to this one disastrous topic. Trifling as it at first appeared, it so connected itself with innumerable trains of thought and modes of feeling that it became the central point of all. With the morning twilight Aylmer opened his eyes upon his wife's face and recognized the symbol of imperfection; and when they sat together at the evening hearth his eyes wandered stealthily to her cheek, and beheld, flickering with the blaze of the wood fire, the spectral hand that wrote mortality where he would fain have worshipped. Georgiana soon learned to shudder at his gaze. It needed but a glance with the peculiar expression that his face often wore to change the roses of her cheek into a death-like paleness, amid which the crimson hand was brought strongly out, like a bas-relief of ruby on the whitest marble.

Late one night when the lights were growing dim, so as hardly to betray the stain on the poor wife's cheek, she herself, for the first time, voluntarily took up the subject.

"Do you remember, my dear Aylmer," said she, with a feeble attempt at a smile, "have you any recollection of a dream last night about this odious hand?"

"None! none whatever!" replied Aylmer, starting; but then he added, in a dry, cold tone, affected for the sake of concealing the real depth of his emotion, "I might well dream of it; for before I fell asleep it had taken a pretty firm hold of my fancy."

"And you did dream of it?" continued Georgiana, hastily; for she dreaded lest a gush of tears should interrupt what she had to say. "A terrible dream! I wonder that you can forget it. Is it possible to forget this one expression?—'It is in her heart now; we must have it out!' Reflect, my husband; for by all means I would have you recall that dream."

The mind is in a sad state when Sleep, the all-involving, cannot confine her spectres within the dim region of her sway, but suffers them to break forth, affrighting this actual life with secrets that perchance belong to a deeper one. Aylmer now remembered his dream. He had fancied himself with his servant Aminadab, attempting an operation for the removal of the birthmark; but the deeper went the knife, the deeper sank the hand, until at length its tiny grasp appeared to have caught hold of

Georgiana's heart; whence, however, her husband was inexorably resolved to cut or wrench it away.

When the dream had shaped itself perfectly in his memory, Aylmer sat in his wife's presence with a guilty feeling. Truth often finds its way to the mind close muffled in robes of sleep, and then speaks with uncompromising directness of matters in regard to which we practise an unconscious self-deception during our waking moments. Until now he had not been aware of the tyrannizing influence acquired by one idea over his mind, and of the lengths which he might find in his heart to go for the sake of giving himself peace.

"Aylmer," resumed Georgiana, solemnly, "I know not what may be the cost to both of us to rid me of this fatal birthmark. Perhaps its removal may cause cureless deformity; or it may be the stain goes as deep as life itself. Again: do we know that there is a possibility, on any terms, of unclasping the firm grip of this little hand which was laid upon me before I came into the world?"

"Dearest Georgiana, I have spent much thought upon the subject," hastily interrupted Aylmer. "I am convinced of the perfect practicability of its removal."

"If there be the remotest possibility of it," continued Georgiana, "let the attempt be made at whatever risk. Danger is nothing to me; for life, while this hateful mark makes me the object of your horror and disgust,—life is a burden which I would fling down with joy. Either remove this dreadful hand, or take my wretched life! You have deep science. All the world bears witness of it. You have achieved great wonders. Cannot you remove this little, little mark, which I cover with the tips of two small fingers? Is this beyond your power, for the sake of your own peace, and to save your poor wife from madness?"

"Noblest, dearest, tenderest wife," cried Aylmer, rapturously, "doubt not my power. I have already given this matter the deepest thought—thought which might almost have enlightened me to create a being less perfect than yourself. Georgiana, you have led me deeper than ever into the heart of science. I feel myself fully competent to render this dear cheek as faultless as its fellow; and then, most beloved, what will be my triumph when I shall have corrected what Nature left imperfect in her fairest work! Even Pygmalion, when his sculptured woman assumed life, felt not greater ecstasy than mine will be."

"It is resolved, then," said Georgiana, faintly smiling. "And, Aylmer, spare me not, though you should find the birthmark take refuge in my heart at last."

Her husband tenderly kissed her cheek—her right cheek—not that which bore the impress of the crimson hand.

The next day Aylmer apprised his wife of a plan that he had formed whereby he might have opportunity for the intense thought and constant watchfulness which the proposed operation would require; while Georgiana, likewise, would enjoy the perfect repose essential to its success. They were to seclude themselves in the extensive apartments occupied by Aylmer as a laboratory, and where, during his toilsome youth, he had made discoveries in the elemental powers of Nature that had roused the admiration of all the learned societies in Europe. Seated calmly in this laboratory, the pale philosopher had investigated the secrets of the highest cloud region and of the profoundest mines; he had satisfied himself of the causes that kindled and kept alive the fires of the volcano; and had explained the mystery of fountains, and how it is that they gush forth, some so bright and pure, and others with such rich medicinal virtues, from the dark bosom of the earth. Here, too, at an earlier period, he had studied the wonders of the human frame, and attempted to fathom the very process by which Nature assimilates all her precious influences from earth and air, and from the spiritual world, to create and foster man, her masterpiece. The latter pursuit, however, Aylmer had long laid aside in unwilling recognition of the truth—against which all seekers sooner or later stumble—that our great creative Mother, while she amuses us with apparently working in the broadest sunshine, is yet severely careful to keep her own secrets, and, in spite of her pretended openness, shows us nothing but results. She permits us, indeed, to mar, but seldom to mend, and, like a jealous patentee, on no account to make. Now, however, Aylmer resumed these half-forgotten investigations; not, of course, with such hopes or wishes as first suggested them; but because they involved much physiological truth and lay in the path of his proposed scheme for the treatment of Georgiana.

As he led her over the threshold of the laboratory, Georgiana was cold and tremulous. Aylmer looked cheerfully into her face, with intent to reassure her, but was so startled with the intense glow of the birthmark upon the whiteness of her cheek that he could not restrain a strong convulsive shudder. His wife fainted.

"Aminadab! Aminadab!" shouted Aylmer, stamping violently on the floor.

Forthwith there issued from an inner apartment a man of low stature, but bulky frame, with shaggy hair hanging about his visage, which was grimed with the vapors of the furnace. This personage had been Aylmer's underworker during his whole scientific career, and was admirably fitted for that office by his great mechanical readiness, and the skill with which, while incapable of comprehending a single principle, he executed all the details of his master's experiments. With his vast strength, his shaggy hair, his smoky aspect, and the indescribable earthiness that incrusted him, he seemed to represent man's physical nature; while Aylmer's slender figure, and pale, intellectual face, were no less apt a type of the spiritual element.

"Throw open the door of the boudoir, Aminadab," said Aylmer, "and burn a pastil."

"Yes, master," answered Aminadab, looking intently at the lifeless form of Georgiana; and then he muttered to himself, "If she were my wife, I'd never part with that birthmark."

When Georgiana recovered consciousness she found herself breathing an atmosphere of penetrating fragrance, the gentle potency of which had recalled her from her deathlike faintness. The scene around her looked like enchantment. Aylmer had converted those smoky, dingy, sombre rooms, where he had spent his brightest years in recondite pursuits, into a series of beautiful apartments not unfit to be the secluded abode of a lovely woman. The walls were hung with gorgeous curtains, which imparted the combination of grandeur and grace that no other species of adornment can achieve; and as they fell from the ceiling to the floor, their rich and ponderous folds, concealing all angles and straight lines, appeared to shut in the scene from infinite space. For aught Georgiana knew, it might be a pavilion among the clouds. And Aylmer, excluding the sunshine, which would have interfered with his chemical processes, had supplied its place with perfumed lamps, emitting flames of various hue, but all uniting in a soft, impurpled radiance. He now knelt by his wife's side, watching her earnestly, but without alarm; for he was confident in his science, and felt that he could draw a magic circle round her within which no evil might intrude.

"Where am I? Ah, I remember," said Georgiana, faintly; and she placed her hand over her cheek to hide the terrible mark from her husband's eyes.

"Fear not, dearest!" exclaimed he. "Do not shrink from me! Believe me, Georgiana, I even rejoice in this single imperfection, since it will be such a rapture to remove it."

"Oh, spare me!" sadly replied his wife. "Pray do not look at it again. I never can forget that convulsive shudder."

In order to soothe Georgiana, and, as it were, to release her mind from the burden of actual things, Aylmer now put in practice some of the light and play-ful secrets which science had taught him among its profounder lore. Airy figures, absolutely bodiless ideas, and forms of unsubstantial beauty came and danced before her, imprinting their momentary footsteps on beams of light. Though she had some indistinct idea of the method of these optical phenomena, still the illu-sion was almost perfect enough to warrant the belief that her husband possessed sway over the spiritual world. Then again, when she felt a wish to look forth from her seclusion, immediately, as if her thoughts were answered, the procession of external existence flitted across a screen. The scenery and the figures of actual life were perfectly represented, but with that bewitching, yet indescribable difference which always makes a picture, an image, or a shadow so much more attractive than the original. When wearied of this, Aylmer bade her cast her eyes upon a vessel containing a quantity of earth. She did so, with little interest at first; but was soon startled to perceive the germ of a plant shooting upward from the soil. Then came the slender stalk; the leaves gradually unfolded themselves; and amid them was a perfect and lovely flower.

"It is magical!" cried Georgiana. "I dare not touch it."

"Nay, pluck it," answered Aylmer,—"pluck it, and inhale its brief perfume while you may. The flower will wither in a few moments and leave nothing save its brown seed vessels; but thence may be perpetuated a race as ephemeral as itself."

But Georgiana had no sooner touched the flower than the whole plant suffered a blight, its leaves turning coal-black as if by the agency of fire.

"There was too powerful a stimulus," said Aylmer, thoughtfully.

To make up for this abortive experiment, he proposed to take her portrait by a sci-entific process of his own invention. It was to be effected by rays of light striking upon a polished plate of metal. Georgiana assented; but, on looking at the result, was af-frighted to find the features of the portrait blurred and indefinable; while the minute figure of a hand appeared where the cheek should have been. Aylmer snatched the metallic plate and threw it into a jar of corrosive acid.

Soon, however, he forgot these mortifying failures. In the intervals of study and chemical experiment he came to her flushed and exhausted, but seemed invigorated by her presence, and spoke in glowing language of the resources of his art. He gave a history of the long dynasty of the alchemists, who spent so many ages in quest of the universal solvent by which the golden principle might be elicited from all things vile and base. Aylmer appeared to believe that, by the plainest scientific logic, it was altogether within the limits of possibility to discover this long-sought medium; "but," he added, "a philosopher who should go deep enough to acquire the power would attain too lofty a wisdom to stoop to the exercise of it." Not less singular were his opinions in regard to the elixir vitae. He more than intimated that it was at his option to concoct a liquid that should prolong life for years, perhaps interminably; but that it would produce a discord in Nature which all the world, and chiefly the quaffer of the immortal nostrum, would find cause to curse.

"Aylmer, are you in earnest?" asked Georgiana, looking at him with amazement and fear. "It is terrible to possess such power, or even to dream of possessing it."

"Oh, do not tremble, my love," said her husband. "I would not wrong either you or myself by working such inharmonious effects upon our lives; but I would have you consider how trifling, in comparison, is the skill requisite to remove this little hand."

At the mention of the birthmark, Georgiana, as usual, shrank as if a redhot iron had touched her cheek.

Again Aylmer applied himself to his labors. She could hear his voice in the distant furnace room giving directions to Aminadab, whose harsh, uncouth, misshapen tones were audible in response, more like the grunt or growl of a brute than human speech. After hours of absence, Aylmer reappeared and proposed that she should now examine his cabinet of chemical products and natural treasures of the earth. Among the former he showed her a small vial, in which, he remarked, was contained a gentle yet most powerful fragrance, capable of impregnating all the breezes that blow across a kingdom. They were of inestimable value, the contents of that little vial; and, as he said so, he threw some of the perfume into the air and filled the room with piercing and invigorating delight.

"And what is this?" asked Georgiana, pointing to a small crystal globe containing a gold-colored liquid. "It is so beautiful to the eye that I could imagine it the elixir of life."

"In one sense it is," replied Aylmer; "or, rather, the elixir of immortality. It is the most precious poison that ever was concocted in this world. By its aid I could apportion the lifetime of any mortal at whom you might point your finger. The strength of the dose would determine whether he were to linger out years, or drop dead in the midst of a breath. No king on his guarded throne could keep his life if I, in my private station, should deem that the welfare of millions justified me in depriving him of it."

"Why do you keep such a terrific drug?" inquired Georgiana in horror.

"Do not mistrust me, dearest," said her husband, smiling; "its virtuous potency is yet greater than its harmful one. But see! here is a powerful cosmetic. With a few drops of this in a vase of water, freckles may be washed away as easily as the hands are cleansed. A stronger infusion would take the blood out of the cheek, and leave the rosiest beauty a pale ghost."

"Is it with this lotion that you intend to bathe my cheek?" asked Georgiana, anxiously.

"Oh, no," hastily replied her husband; "this is merely superficial. Your case demands a remedy that shall go deeper."

In his interviews with Georgiana, Aylmer generally made minute inquiries as to her sensations and whether the confinement of the rooms and the temperature of the atmosphere agreed with her. These questions had such a particular drift that Georgiana began to conjecture that she was already subjected to certain physical influences, either breathed in with the fragrant air or taken with her food. She fancied likewise, but it might be altogether fancy, that there was a stirring up of her system—a strange, indefinite sensation creeping through her veins, and tingling, half painfully, half pleasurably, at her heart. Still, whenever she dared to look into the mirror, there she beheld herself pale as a white rose and with the crimson birthmark stamped upon her cheek. Not even Aylmer now hated it so much as she.

To dispel the tedium of the hours which her husband found it necessary to devote to the processes of combination and analysis, Georgiana turned over the volumes of his scientific library. In many dark old tomes she met with chapters full of romance and poetry. They were the works of philosophers of the middle ages, such as Albertus Magnus, Cornelius Agrippa, Paracelsus, and the famous friar who created the prophetic Brazen Head. All these antique naturalists stood in advance of their centuries, yet were imbued with some of their credulity, and therefore were believed, and perhaps imagined themselves to have acquired from the investigation of Nature a power above Nature, and from physics a sway over the spiritual world. Hardly less curious and imaginative were the early volumes of the Transactions of the Royal Society, in which the members, knowing little of the limits of natural possibility, were continually recording wonders or proposing methods whereby wonders might be wrought.

But to Georgiana the most engrossing volume was a large folio from her husband's own hand, in which he had recorded every experiment of his scientific career, its original aim, the methods adopted for its development, and its final success or failure, with the circumstances to which either event was attributable. The book, in truth, was both the history and emblem of his ardent, ambitious, imaginative, yet practical and laborious life. He handled physical details as if there were nothing beyond them; yet spiritualized them all, and redeemed himself from materialism by his strong and eager aspiration towards the infinite. In his grasp the veriest clod of earth assumed a soul. Georgiana, as she read, reverenced Aylmer and loved him more profoundly than ever, but with a less entire dependence on his judgment than heretofore. Much as he had accomplished, she could not but observe that his most splendid successes were almost invariably failures, if compared with the ideal at which he aimed. His brightest diamonds were the merest pebbles, and felt to be so by himself, in comparison with the inestimable gems which lay hidden beyond his reach. The volume, rich with achievements that had won renown for its author, was yet as melancholy a record as ever mortal hand had penned. It was the sad confession and continual exemplification of the shortcomings of the composite man, the spirit burdened with clay and working in matter, and of the despair that assails the higher nature at finding itself so miserably thwarted by the earthly part. Perhaps every man of genius in whatever sphere might recognize the image of his own experience in Aylmer's journal.

So deeply did these reflections affect Georgiana that she laid her face upon the open volume and burst into tears. In this situation she was found by her husband.

"It is dangerous to read in a sorcerer's books," said he with a smile, though his countenance was uneasy and displeased. "Georgiana, there are pages in that volume which I can scarcely glance over and keep my senses. Take heed lest it prove as detrimental to you."

"It has made me worship you more than ever," said she.

"Ah, wait for this one success," rejoined he, "then worship me if you will. I shall deem myself hardly unworthy of it. But come, I have sought you for the luxury of your voice. Sing to me, dearest."

So she poured out the liquid music of her voice to quench the thirst of his spirit. He then took his leave with a boyish exuberance of gayety, assuring her that her seclusion would endure but a little longer, and that the result was already certain. Scarcely had he departed when Georgiana felt irresistibly impelled to follow him. She had forgotten to inform Aylmer of a symptom which for two or three hours past had begun to excite her attention. It was a sensation in the fatal birthmark, not painful, but which induced a restlessness throughout her system. Hastening after her husband, she intruded for the first time into the laboratory.

The first thing that struck her eye was the furnace, that hot and feverish worker, with the intense glow of its fire, which by the quantities of soot clustered above it seemed to have been burning for ages. There was a distilling apparatus in full operation. Around the room were retorts, tubes, cylinders, crucibles, and other apparatus of chemical research. An electrical machine stood ready for immediate use. The atmosphere felt oppressively close, and was tainted with gaseous odors which had been tormented forth by the processes of science. The severe and homely simplicity of the apartment, with its naked walls and brick pavement, looked strange, accustomed as Georgiana had become to the fantastic elegance of her boudoir. But what chiefly, indeed almost solely, drew her attention, was the aspect of Aylmer himself.

He was pale as death, anxious and absorbed, and hung over the furnace as if it depended upon his utmost watchfulness whether the liquid which it was distilling should be the draught of immortal happiness or misery. How different from the sanguine and joyous mien that he had assumed for Georgiana's encouragement!

"Carefully now, Aminadab; carefully, thou human machine; carefully, thou man of clay!" muttered Aylmer, more to himself than his assistant. "Now, if there be a thought too much or too little, it is all over."

"Ho! ho!" mumbled Aminadab. "Look, master! look!"

Aylmer raised his eyes hastily, and at first reddened, then grew paler than ever, on beholding Georgiana. He rushed towards her and seized her arm with a grip that left the print of his fingers upon it.

"Why do you come hither? Have you no trust in your husband?" cried he, impetuously. "Would you throw the blight of that fatal birthmark over my labors? It is not well done. Go, prying woman, go!"

"Nay, Aylmer," said Georgiana with the firmness of which she possessed no stinted endowment, "it is not you that have a right to complain. You mistrust your wife; you have concealed the anxiety with which you watch the development of this experiment. Think not so unworthily of me, my husband. Tell me all the risk we run, and fear not that I shall shrink; for my share in it is far less than your own."

"No, no, Georgiana!" said Aylmer, impatiently; "it must not be."

"I submit," replied she calmly. "And, Aylmer, I shall quaff whatever draught you bring me; but it will be on the same principle that would induce me to take a dose of poison if offered by your hand."

"My noble wife," said Aylmer, deeply moved, "I knew not the height and depth of your nature until now. Nothing shall be concealed. Know, then, that this crimson hand, superficial as it seems, has clutched its grasp into your being with a strength of which I had no previous conception. I have already administered agents powerful enough to do aught except to change your entire physical system. Only one thing remains to be tried. If that fail us we are ruined."

"Why did you hesitate to tell me this?" asked she.

"Because, Georgiana," said Aylmer, in a low voice, "there is danger."

"Danger? There is but one danger—that this horrible stigma shall be left upon my cheek!" cried Georgiana. "Remove it, remove it, whatever be the cost, or we shall both go mad!"

"Heaven knows your words are too true," said Aylmer, sadly. "And now, dearest, return to your boudoir. In a little while all will be tested."

He conducted her back and took leave of her with a solemn tenderness which spoke far more than his words how much was now at stake. After his departure Georgiana became rapt in musings. She considered the character of Aylmer, and did it completer justice than at any previous moment. Her heart exulted, while it trembled, at his honorable love—so pure and lofty that it would accept nothing less than perfection nor miserably make itself contented with an earthlier nature than he had dreamed of. She felt how much more precious was such a sentiment than that meaner kind which would have borne with the imperfection for her sake, and have been guilty of treason to holy love by degrading its perfect idea to the level of the actual; and with her whole spirit she prayed that, for a single moment, she might satisfy his highest and deepest conception. Longer than one moment she well knew it could not be; for his spirit was ever on the march, ever ascending, and each instant required something that was beyond the scope of the instant before.

The sound of her husband's footsteps aroused her. He bore a crystal goblet containing a liquor colorless as water, but bright enough to be the draught of immortality. Aylmer was pale; but it seemed rather the consequence of a highly-wrought state of mind and tension of spirit than of fear or doubt.

"The concoction of the draught has been perfect," said he, in answer to Georgiana's look. "Unless all my science have deceived me, it cannot fail."

"Save on your account, my dearest Aylmer," observed his wife, "I might wish to put off this birthmark of mortality by relinquishing mortality itself in preference to any other mode. Life is but a sad possession to those who have attained precisely the degree of moral advancement at which I stand. Were I weaker and blinder it might be happiness. Were I stronger, it might be endured hopefully. But, being what I find myself, methinks I am of all mortals the most fit to die."

"You are fit for heaven without tasting death!" replied her husband. "But why do we speak of dying? The draught cannot fail. Behold its effect upon this plant."

On the window seat there stood a geranium diseased with yellow blotches, which had overspread all its leaves. Aylmer poured a small quantity of the liquid upon the soil in which it grew. In a little time, when the roots of the plant had taken up the moisture, the unsightly blotches began to be extinguished in a living verdure.

"There needed no proof," said Georgiana, quietly. "Give me the goblet. I joyfully stake all upon your word."

"Drink, then, thou lofty creature!" exclaimed Aylmer, with fervid admiration. "There is no taint of imperfection on thy spirit. Thy sensible frame, too, shall soon be all perfect."

She quaffed the liquid and returned the goblet to his hand.

"It is grateful," said she with a placid smile. "Methinks it is like water from a heavenly fountain; for it contains I know not what of unobtrusive fragrance and deliciousness. It allays a feverish thirst that had parched me for many days. Now, dearest, let me sleep. My earthly senses are closing over my spirit like the leaves around the heart of a rose at sunset."

She spoke the last words with a gentle reluctance, as if it required almost more energy than she could command to pronounce the faint and lingering syllables. Scarcely had they loitered through her lips ere she was lost in slumber. Aylmer sat by her side, watching her aspect with the emotions proper to a man the whole value of whose existence was involved in the process now to be tested. Mingled with this mood, however, was the philosophic investigation characteristic of the man of science. Not the minutest symptom escaped him. A heightened flush of the cheek, a slight irregularity of breath, a quiver of the eyelid, a hardly perceptible tremor through the frame,—such were the details which, as the moments passed, he wrote down in his folio volume. Intense thought had set its stamp upon every previous page of that volume, but the thoughts of years were all concentrated upon the last.

While thus employed, he failed not to gaze often at the fatal hand, and not without a shudder. Yet once, by a strange and unaccountable impulse he pressed it with his lips. His spirit recoiled, however, in the very act, and Georgiana, out of the midst of her deep sleep, moved uneasily and murmured as if in remonstrance. Again Aylmer resumed his watch. Nor was it without avail. The crimson hand, which at first had been strongly visible upon the marble paleness of Georgiana's cheek, now grew more faintly outlined. She remained not less pale than ever; but the birthmark with every breath that came and went, lost somewhat of its former distinctness. Its presence had been awful; its departure was more awful still. Watch the stain of the rainbow fading out the sky, and you will know how that mysterious symbol passed away.

"By Heaven! it is well-nigh gone!" said Aylmer to himself, in almost irrepressible ecstasy. "I can scarcely trace it now. Success! success! And now it is like the faintest rose color. The lightest flush of blood across her cheek would overcome it. But she is so pale!"

He drew aside the window curtain and suffered the light of natural day to fall into the room and rest upon her cheek. At the same time he heard a gross, hoarse chuckle, which he had long known as his servant Aminadab's expression of delight.

"Ah, clod! ah, earthly mass!" cried Aylmer, laughing in a sort of frenzy, "you have served me well! Matter and spirit—earth and heaven—have both done their part in this! Laugh, thing of the senses! You have earned the right to laugh."

These exclamations broke Georgiana's sleep. She slowly unclosed her eyes and gazed into the mirror which her husband had arranged for that purpose. A faint smile flitted over her lips when she recognized how barely perceptible was now that crimson hand which had once blazed forth with such disastrous brilliancy as to scare away all their happiness. But then her eyes sought Aylmer's face with a trouble and anxiety that he could by no means account for.

"My poor Aylmer!" murmured she.

"Poor? Nay, richest, happiest, most favored!" exclaimed he. "My peerless bride, it is successful! You are perfect!"

"My poor Aylmer," she repeated, with a more than human tenderness, "you have aimed loftily; you have done nobly. Do not repent that with so high and pure a feeling, you have rejected the best the earth could offer. Aylmer, dearest Aylmer, I am dying!"

Alas! it was too true! The fatal hand had grappled with the mystery of life, and was the bond by which an angelic spirit kept itself in union with a mortal frame. As the last crimson tint of the birthmark—that sole token of human imperfection—faded from her cheek, the parting breath of the now perfect woman passed into the atmosphere, and her soul, lingering a moment near her husband, took its heavenward flight. Then a hoarse, chuckling laugh was heard again! Thus ever does the gross fatality of earth exult in its invariable triumph over the immortal essence which, in this dim sphere of half development, demands the completeness of a higher state. Yet, had Aylmer reached a profounder wisdom, he need not thus have flung away the happiness which would have woven his mortal life of the selfsame texture with the celestial. The momentary circumstance was too strong for him; he failed to look beyond the shadowy scope of time, and, living once for all in eternity, to find the perfect future in the present.

REFLECTING AND DISCUSSING

1. Many have commented on the moral ambiguity of this tale. Do you think the question of morality here is at all ambiguous? Why or why not?

2. What does Hawthorne's portrait of Georgiana say about prevailing attitudes toward women at the time at which this was written? Is Hawthorne critiquing these attitudes? Why or why not? How do you know?

3. Comment on the character of Aylmer. What are his motivations? What do you think of them? Do you have any indication of what Hawthorne thinks of them? Be specific in your response, pointing to evidence in the story.

CONNECTING AND WRITING

1. Based on this story, what seem to be Hawthorne's attitudes toward science and scientists? What evidence from the story tells you this? Analyze the language used by the narrator and the characters to support your point of view.

2. Does this story contrast with or fit general attitudes about science at the time it was written? Research other writers and thinkers from the early nineteenth century to come to a conclusion, using specific examples to back it up.

QUESTION

Use two or more selections (poem, stories, or essays) from this section to argue in favor of or against sacrificing oneself or one's country for the greater good. Or, if you prefer, articulate the position of each author and explore how their ideas of ethics compare.

PROPOSITIONS

This eclectic group of pieces—images, essays, advertisements, and so on—make serious, humorous, or satiric propositions to the reader.

The Recliner of Turin, photograph

Jay Boersma (1947–   )

Jay Boersma is a photographer, digital artist, and former Web designer whose work deals with both the surreal and the absurd and captures striking images of architecture and decay. A graduate of Columbia College Chicago and the Rhode Island School of Design, Boersma has produced work that has appeared in numerous galleries and is part of several permanent collections, including that of the Art Institute of Chicago. The following image, The Recliner of Turin, *was made in 1989 using film and traditional darkroom methods.*

REFLECTING AND DISCUSSING

1. What religious artifact is the photograph satirizing? What is the overall effect of superimposing it on a recliner in a department store? What do you think is the artist's intention?
2. How can photographs and other images make arguments? What is the argument of this particular photograph, and how do you know?
3. Discuss religious satire. In your view, are there limits to what should be considered a permissible subject for satire?

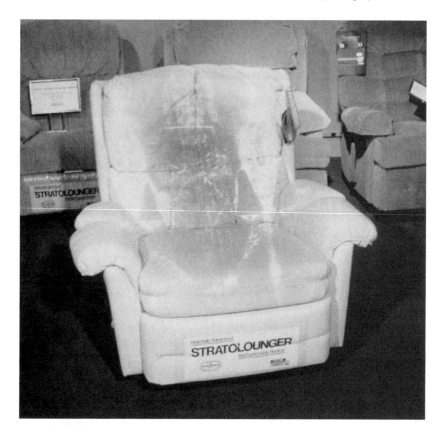

CONNECTING AND WRITING

1. This image was created using traditional darkroom methods for the purpose of satire before the digital world made such work much easier. Consider the piece—an obvious, deliberate satire of religion—and compare it with another example of satire, whether photographic or textual, of your choosing. What are the similarities and differences between the two? How do you know you are encountering a satiric work?

2. Has the advent of computer technology exacerbated an existing problem—that of image manipulation? Setting apart for now this particular image, which is clearly intended as satire, how does the manipulation of a photograph create problematic notions of truth, especially in the digital era? Research digital images that intentionally challenge fact and create an argument about the ethical implications of a digital world where the manipulation of images isn't often explicit.

A Modest Proposal

Jonathan Swift (1667–1745)

Considered among the greatest writers of clear and direct prose in the English language, Jonathan Swift was born in Dublin, Ireland, to English parents. Swift devoted a good deal of his life to politics and religion, serving as dean of St. Patrick's Cathedral in Dublin, but he is remembered less for his religious interest and more for his writing, especially his satire. In a letter to poet Alexander Pope, Swift declared that although he could love individuals, he "hated that animal called man." Clearly, Swift's propensity toward satire is the practical manifestation of those sentiments. The response to "A Modest Proposal" was somewhat predictable: it delighted some, but horrified others, who assumed that Swift was, indeed, serious.

It is a melancholy object to those, who walk through this great town, or travel in the country, when they see the streets, the roads and cabin doors crowded with beggars of the female sex, followed by three, four, or six children, all in rags, and importuning every passenger for an alms. These mothers instead of being able to work for their honest livelihood, are forced to employ all their time in strolling to beg sustenance for their helpless infants who, as they grow up, either turn thieves for want of work, or leave their dear native country, to fight for the Pretender in Spain, or sell themselves to the Barbados.

I think it is agreed by all parties, that this prodigious number of children in the arms, or on the backs, or at the heels of their mothers, and frequently of their fathers, is in the present deplorable state of the kingdom, a very great additional grievance; and therefore whoever could find out a fair, cheap and easy method of making these children sound and useful members of the common-wealth, would deserve so well of the public, as to have his statue set up for a preserver of the nation.

But my intention is very far from being confined to provide only for the children of professed beggars: it is of a much greater extent, and shall take in the whole number of infants at a certain age, who are born of parents in effect as little able to support them, as those who demand our charity in the streets.

As to my own part, having turned my thoughts for many years, upon this important subject, and maturely weighed the several schemes of our projectors, I have always found them grossly mistaken in their computation. It is true, a child just dropped from its dam, may be supported by her milk, for a solar year, with little other nourishment: at most not above the value of two shillings, which the mother may certainly get, or the value in scraps, by her lawful occupation of begging; and it is exactly at one year old that I propose to provide for them in such a manner, as, instead of being a charge upon their parents, or the parish, or wanting food and raiment for the rest of their lives, they shall, on the contrary, contribute to the feeding, and partly to the clothing of many thousands.

There is likewise another great advantage in my scheme, that it will prevent those voluntary abortions, and that horrid practice of women murdering their bastard children, alas! too frequent among us, sacrificing the poor innocent babes, I doubt, more to avoid the expense than the shame, which would move tears and pity in the most savage and inhuman breast.

The number of souls in this kingdom being usually reckoned one million and a half, of these I calculate there may be about two hundred thousand couple whose wives are breeders; from which number I subtract thirty thousand couple, who are able to maintain their own children, (although I apprehend there cannot be so many, under the present distresses of the kingdom) but this being granted, there will remain an hundred and seventy thousand breeders. I again subtract fifty thousand, for those women who miscarry, or whose children die by accident or disease within the year. There only remain an hundred and twenty thousand children of poor parents annually born. The question therefore is, How this number shall be reared, and provided for? which, as I have already said, under the present situation of affairs, is utterly impossible by all the methods hitherto proposed. For we can neither employ them in handicraft or agriculture; they neither build houses, (I mean in the country) nor cultivate land: they can very seldom pick up a livelihood by stealing till they arrive at six years old; except where they are of towardly parts, although I confess they learn the rudiments much earlier; during which time they can however be properly looked upon only as probationers: As I have been informed by a principal gentleman in the county of Cavan, who protested to me, that he never knew above one or two instances under the age of six, even in a part of the kingdom so renowned for the quickest proficiency in that art.

I am assured by our merchants, that a boy or a girl before twelve years old, is no saleable commodity, and even when they come to this age, they will not yield above three pounds, or three pounds and half a crown at most, on the exchange; which cannot turn to account either to the parents or kingdom, the charge of nutriments and rags having been at least four times that value.

I shall now therefore humbly propose my own thoughts, which I hope will not be liable to the least objection.

I have been assured by a very knowing American of my acquaintance in London, that a young healthy child well nursed, is, at a year old, a most delicious nourishing and wholesome food, whether stewed, roasted, baked, or boiled; and I make no doubt that it will equally serve in a fricassee, or a ragout.

I do therefore humbly offer it to public consideration, that of the hundred and twenty thousand children, already computed, twenty thousand may be reserved for breed, whereof only one fourth part to be males; which is more than we allow to sheep, black cattle, or swine, and my reason is, that these children are seldom the fruits of marriage, a circumstance not much regarded by our savages, therefore, one male will be sufficient to serve four females. That the remaining hundred thousand may, at a year old, be offered in sale to the persons of quality and fortune, through the kingdom, always advising the mother to let them suck plentifully in the last month, so as to render them plump, and fat for a good table. A child will make two dishes at an entertainment for friends, and when the family dines alone, the fore or hind quarter will make a reasonable dish, and seasoned with a little pepper or salt, will be very good boiled on the fourth day, especially in winter.

I have reckoned upon a medium, that a child just born will weigh 12 pounds, and in a solar year, if tolerably nursed, will increase to 28 pounds.

I grant this food will be somewhat dear, and therefore very proper for landlords, who, as they have already devoured most of the parents, seem to have the best title to the children.

Infant's flesh will be in season throughout the year, but more plentiful in March, and a little before and after; for we are told by a grave author, an eminent French physician, that fish being a prolific diet, there are more children born in Roman Catholic countries about nine months after Lent, the markets will be more glutted than usual, because the number of Popish infants, is at least three to one in this kingdom, and therefore it will have one other collateral advantage, by lessening the number of Papists among us.

I have already computed the charge of nursing a beggar's child (in which list I reckon all cottagers, laborers, and four-fifths of the farmers) to be about two shillings per annum, rags included; and I believe no gentleman would repine to give ten shillings for the carcass of a good fat child, which, as I have said, will make four dishes of excellent nutritive meat, when he hath only some particular friend, or his own family to dine with him. Thus the squire will learn to be a good landlord, and grow popular among his tenants, the mother will have eight shillings neat profit, and be fit for work till she produces another child.

Those who are more thrifty (as I must confess the times require) may flea the carcass; the skin of which, artificially dressed, will make admirable gloves for ladies, and summer boots for fine gentlemen.

As to our City of Dublin, shambles may be appointed for this purpose, in the most convenient parts of it, and butchers we may be assured will not be wanting; although I rather recommend buying the children alive, and dressing them hot from the knife, as we do roasting pigs.

A very worthy person, a true lover of his country, and whose virtues I highly esteem, was lately pleased, in discoursing on this matter, to offer a refinement upon my scheme. He said, that many gentlemen of this kingdom, having of late destroyed their deer, he conceived that the want of venison might be well supplied by the bodies of young lads and maidens, not exceeding fourteen years of age, nor under twelve; so great a number of both sexes in every country being now ready to starve for want of work and service: And these to be disposed of by their parents if alive, or otherwise by their nearest relations. But with due deference to so excellent a friend, and so deserving a patriot, I cannot be altogether in his sentiments; for as to the males, my American acquaintance assured me from frequent experience, that their flesh was generally tough and lean, like that of our school-boys, by continual exercise, and their taste disagreeable, and to fatten them would not answer the charge. Then as to the females, it would, I think, with humble submission, be a loss to the public, because they soon would become breeders themselves: And besides, it is not improbable that some scrupulous people might be apt to censure such a practice, (although indeed very unjustly) as a little bordering upon cruelty, which, I confess, hath always been with me the strongest objection against any project, how well soever intended.

But in order to justify my friend, he confessed that this expedient was put into his head by the famous Psalmanazar[,] a native of the island Formosa, who came from thence to London, above twenty years ago, and in conversation told my friend, that in his country, when any young person happened to be put to death, the executioner sold the carcass to persons of quality, as a prime dainty; and that, in his time, the body of a plump girl of fifteen, who was crucified for an attempt to poison the Emperor, was sold to his imperial majesty's prime minister of state, and other great mandarins of the court in joints from the gibbet, at four hundred crowns. Neither indeed can I deny, that if the same use were made of several plump young girls in this town, who without one single groat to their fortunes, cannot stir abroad without a chair, and appear at a play-house and assemblies in foreign fineries which they never will pay for; the kingdom would not be the worse.

Some persons of a desponding spirit are in great concern about that vast number of poor people, who are aged, diseased, or maimed; and I have been desired to employ my thoughts what course may be taken, to ease the nation of so grievous an encumbrance. But I am not in the least pain upon that matter, because it is very well known, that they are every day dying, and rotting, by cold and famine, and filth, and vermin, as fast as can be reasonably expected. And as to the young laborers, they are now in almost as hopeful a condition. They cannot get work, and consequently pine away from want of nourishment, to a degree, that if at any time they are accidentally hired to common labor, they have not strength to perform it, and thus the country and themselves are happily delivered from the evils to come.

I have too long digressed, and therefore shall return to my subject. I think the advantages by the proposal which I have made are obvious and many, as well as of the highest importance.

For first, as I have already observed, it would greatly lessen the number of Papists, with whom we are yearly over-run, being the principal breeders of the nation, as well as our most dangerous enemies, and who stay at home on purpose with a design to deliver the kingdom to the Pretender, hoping to take their advantage by the absence of so many good Protestants, who have chosen rather to leave their country, than stay at home and pay tithes against their conscience to an episcopal curate.

Secondly, The poorer tenants will have something valuable of their own, which by law may be made liable to a distress, and help to pay their landlord's rent, their corn and cattle being already seized, and money a thing unknown.

Thirdly, Whereas the maintenance of an hundred thousand children, from two years old, and upwards, cannot be computed at less than ten shillings a piece per annum, the nation's stock will be thereby increased fifty thousand pounds per annum, besides the profit of a new dish, introduced to the tables of all gentlemen of fortune in the kingdom, who have any refinement in taste. And the money will circulate among ourselves, the goods being entirely of our own growth and manufacture.

Fourthly, The constant breeders, besides the gain of eight shillings sterling per annum by the sale of their children, will be rid of the charge of maintaining them after the first year.

Fifthly, This food would likewise bring great custom to taverns, where the vintners will certainly be so prudent as to procure the best receipts for dressing it to perfection; and consequently have their houses frequented by all the fine gentlemen, who justly value themselves upon their knowledge in good eating; and a skillful cook, who understands how to oblige his guests, will contrive to make it as expensive as they please.

Sixthly, This would be a great inducement to marriage, which all wise nations have either encouraged by rewards, or enforced by laws and penalties. It would increase the care and tenderness of mothers towards their children, when they were sure of a settlement for life to the poor babes, provided in some sort by the public, to their annual profit instead of expense. We should soon see an honest emulation among the married women, which of them could bring the fattest child to the market. Men would become as fond of their wives, during the time of their pregnancy, as they are now of their mares in foal, their cows in calf, or sow when they are ready to farrow; nor offer to beat or kick them (as is too frequent a practice) for fear of a miscarriage.

Many other advantages might be enumerated. For instance, the addition of some thousand carcasses in our exportation of barreled beef: the propagation of swine's flesh, and improvement in the art of making good bacon, so much wanted among us by the great destruction of pigs, too frequent at our tables; which are no way comparable in taste or magnificence to a well grown, fat yearly child, which roasted whole will make a considerable figure at a Lord Mayor's feast, or any other public entertainment. But this, and many others, I omit, being studious of brevity.

Supposing that one thousand families in this city, would be constant customers for infants flesh, besides others who might have it at merry meetings, particularly at weddings and christenings, I compute that Dublin would take off annually about twenty thousand carcasses; and the rest of the kingdom (where probably they will be sold somewhat cheaper) the remaining eighty thousand.

I can think of no one objection, that will possibly be raised against this proposal, unless it should be urged, that the number of people will be thereby much lessened in the kingdom. This I freely own, and 'twas indeed one principal design in offering it to the world. I desire the reader will observe, that I calculate my remedy for this one individual Kingdom of Ireland, and for no other that ever was, is, or, I think, ever can be upon Earth. Therefore let no man talk to me of other expedients: Of taxing our absentees at five shillings a pound: Of using neither cloths, nor household furniture, except what is of our own growth and manufacture: Of utterly rejecting the materials and instruments that promote foreign luxury: Of curing the expensiveness of pride, vanity, idleness, and gaming in our women: Of introducing a vein of parsimony, prudence and temperance: Of learning to love our country, wherein we differ even from Laplanders, and the inhabitants of Topinamboo: Of quitting our animosities and factions, nor acting any longer like the Jews, who were murdering one another at the very moment their city was taken: Of being a little cautious not to sell our country and consciences for nothing: Of teaching landlords to have at least one degree of mercy towards their tenants. Lastly, of putting a spirit of honesty, industry, and skill into our shop-keepers, who, if a resolution could now be taken to buy only our native goods, would immediately unite to cheat and exact upon us in the price, the measure, and the goodness, nor could ever yet be brought to make one fair proposal of just dealing, though often and earnestly invited to it.

Therefore I repeat, let no man talk to me of these and the like expedients, 'till he hath at least some glimpse of hope, that there will ever be some hearty and sincere attempt to put them into practice.

But, as to myself, having been wearied out for many years with offering vain, idle, visionary thoughts, and at length utterly despairing of success, I fortunately fell upon this proposal, which, as it is wholly new, so it hath something solid and real, of no expense and little trouble, full in our own power, and whereby we can incur no danger in disobliging England. For this kind of commodity will not bear exportation, and flesh being of too tender a consistence, to admit a long continuance in salt, although perhaps I could name a country, which would be glad to eat up our whole nation without it.

After all, I am not so violently bent upon my own opinion, as to reject any offer, proposed by wise men, which shall be found equally innocent, cheap, easy, and effectual. But before something of that kind shall be advanced in contradiction to my scheme, and offering a better, I desire the author or authors will be pleased maturely to consider two points. First, as things now stand, how they will be able to find food and raiment for a hundred thousand useless mouths and backs. And secondly, There being a round million of creatures in humane figure throughout this kingdom, whose whole subsistence put into a common stock, would leave them in debt 2,000,000 pounds sterling, adding those who are beggars by profession, to the bulk of farmers, cottagers and laborers, with their wives and children, who are beggars in effect; I desire those politicians who dislike my overture, and may perhaps be so bold to attempt an answer, that they will first ask the parents of these mortals, whether they would not at this day think it a great happiness to have been sold for food at a year old, in the manner I prescribe, and thereby have avoided such a perpetual scene of misfortunes, as they have since gone through, by the oppression of landlords, the impossibility of paying rent without money or trade, the want of common sustenance, with neither house nor cloths to cover them from the inclemencies of the weather, and the most inevitable prospect of entailing the like, or greater miseries, upon their breed for ever.

I profess, in the sincerity of my heart, that I have not the least personal interest in endeavoring to promote this necessary work, having no other motive than the public good of my country, by advancing our trade, providing for infants, relieving the poor, and giving some pleasure to the rich. I have no children, by which I can propose to get a single penny; the youngest being nine years old, and my wife past child-bearing.

REFLECTING AND DISCUSSING

1. As we have asked elsewhere in this book, what is satire? What is irony? What is the difference between the two? Think of contemporary examples of satiric commentary—late night TV shows, for instance—to illustrate these concepts.

2. The full title of this essay is "A Modest Proposal for Preventing the Children of Poor People from Being a Burthen to Their Parents or Country, and for Making Them Beneficial to the Publick." How is the work's satirical nature introduced in the title, and how must the title have been received in 1729, when the essay was

published? Be sure to confirm your understanding of satire; at what point do you begin to realize that Swift is not completely serious?

3. Analyze and comment on the speaker's various solutions for addressing the problem of the Irish poor.

CONNECTING AND WRITING

1. Research the historical context of this essay to better understand what motivated Swift to write it. It is said that satire works only when it suggests a bit of truth. What are the truths that are revealed in Swift's essay despite its satire, based on your research?

2. Is there a distinction between the way the speaker sees himself and how the reader sees him? Consider language and tone and explain your point of view using examples from the text.

U.S. Government to Discontinue Long-Term, Low-Yield Investment in Nation's Youth

The Onion

The Onion, a news satire publication founded in 1996, respects no boundaries in its choice of subject matter. Its stories cover both fictional and real events, and they often respond to current issues related to governmental policy. Even its own "biography" on The Onion *website is satirical. The following story appeared in 2003.*

WASHINGTON, DC—In an effort to streamline federal financial holdings and spur growth, Treasury Secretary John Snow announced Monday that the federal government will discontinue its long-term, low-yield investment in the nation's youth.

"For generations, we've viewed spending on our nation's young people as an investment in the future," Snow said. "Unfortunately, investments of this type take a minimum of 18 years to mature, and even then, there's no guarantee of a profit. It's just not good business."

Snow compared funneling money into public schools, youth programs, and child health-care clinics to letting the nation's money languish in a low-interest savings account.

"This is taxpayer money we're talking about," Snow said. "We can't keep pouring it into slow-growth ventures, speculating on a minuscule payout some time in the future."

"Federal expenditures are recouped when a child grows up and becomes a productive, taxpaying member of society," Snow said. "But we don't see a sizable return on our investment unless a child invents something profitable, or cures a costly disease, like cancer. The wisdom of making such long-range, long-shot investments is questionable at best, especially when you consider inflation. America would do better to invest in profitable business ventures. It's just that simple."

In the first quarter of 2004, the U.S. will scale back such youth-market investments as Head Start, a federal preschool program for the poor, and D.A.R.E., a drug-use prevention program for minors. Snow said such programs focus on preparing tomorrow's leaders at the expense of turning a profit today. The extensive federal public-education system will also experience major cutbacks.

"With the economy showing signs of recovery, now is the time to cut away the dead wood," Snow said. "As the stock market turns around, we have a real opportunity to make some money. But that's only if we shift the nation's funds into high-yield, short-term investments."

Snow said he plans to support the private sector with corporate subsidies, and to invest overseas.

"This nation needs something really big to turn it around, something like the '90s tech bubble," Snow said. "We need a winning business model, something that after-school art workshops and inner-city basketball programs simply do not offer."

Federal Reserve Chairman Alan Greenspan expressed cautious support for the divestments.

"Investments in our nation's young people have never yielded very impressive gains," Greenspan said. "On the other hand, as the market improves, disinflation is a major concern for future quarters. The education system is a huge employer in this country, and consumer spending could be affected."

Jack Carpenter, a financial consultant for Deloitte Touche Tohmatsu, said he is excited by the prospects for the nation's financial future.

"In such tough markets, the federal government should be putting its money in fliers, but instead, it's wasting it all on crawlers," Carpenter said. "Right now, we should focus on high-growth industries. Professional and technical services, finance

and insurance, and information management are hot right now. Inner-city community youth programs—not so much."

Carpenter noted that not all investments in America's youth are low-yield, pointing to several youth-targeted efforts in the private sector that have generated immense returns.

"Coca-Cola and Microsoft," Carpenter said. "Both organizations have done very
well in the youth market. Coke markets their beverages largely to children and young
adults, showing steady gains. And Microsoft, maker of the X-Box, has increased profits and beat earnings expectations in each of the past eight quarters. The federal
government has a lot to learn from these businesses."

In spite of an outcry from teachers and union leaders, Snow insisted that the
divestment will be a boon for all Americans.

"Taking a student through high school costs the federal government nearly
$100,000 in taxpayer money," Snow said. "If that figure upsets you, then think about
the times that we invest in a child and then he pulls out of the program before he
matures."

Secretary of Education Rod Paige, whose post has historically been strongly
committed to investment in youth and the bridges from one century to the next,
surprised many when he came out in favor of the controversial plan. Paige said data
collected over the past five years shows that there is reason to divest our stake in the
nation's youth.

"Look at our recent graduates," Paige said. "So many recipients of years of federal
investments are laying around in a state of unemployment. It's just not reasonable to
continue to invest billions of dollars in such risky ventures."

Paige was quick to add that the new investment strategy doesn't involve dismantling
the public school system, just restructuring it.

"The proposed plan actually includes *increased* investments in vouchers for
private schools," Paige said. "Through the years, we've seen consistent returns from
blue-chip schools."

In addition, Paige said Republican leaders are investing record levels of federal
money in support of President Bush's No Child Left Behind program, which calls for
expanded testing, higher-quality teachers, and greater achievement among students,
particularly those in poor districts.

"Testing is exactly the sort of research the government should do before making
spending decisions," Paige said. "How else will we know which individuals are sound
investments and which are likely to waste our time and money?"

REFLECTING AND DISCUSSING

1. What is satire? What is *The Onion* satirizing here? To what effect?
2. The article features an image of then-President George W. Bush visiting a group of
   school children. The satirical caption reads, "President Bush explains the nation's
   new investment strategy at an inner city school in Baltimore." How do the caption
   and the photo support the satire of the article? What is absurd about it? What
   effect do this image and its caption have on readers?

3. Discuss the tone and the language of the article. How does it walk a line between humor and seriousness? What is serious about this piece, despite its attempt to generate laughter?

CONNECTING AND WRITING

1. This article was likely a response to No Child Left Behind, a federal government initiative that has been generally discredited. Research the original law and critiques of it. Why did this initiative fail? Be sure to back up your point of view with evidence from your research.
2. Write an essay in which you argue the ethics of political satire. What are the responsibilities of the satirist? Do publications like *The Onion* have an ethical responsibility to the public? Do some research to find experts to help you argue your point of view.

Civil Disobedience

Henry David Thoreau (1817–1862)

Among the best-known American essayists, poets, and thinkers of the nineteenth century, Henry David Thoreau is especially noted for Walden *(first published in 1854) and for his part in the Transcendental movement. Thoreau was a social rebel who influenced later leaders such as Mahatma Gandhi and Martin Luther King, Jr. "Civil Disobedience" is Thoreau's most famous essay, prompted by a night he spent in a Concord, Massachusetts, jail for nonpayment of taxes—a political protest against the use of taxes to support slavery.*

I heartily accept the motto, "That government is best which governs least"; and I should like to see it acted up to more rapidly and systematically. Carried out, it finally amounts to this, which also I believe—"That government is best which governs not at all"; and when men are prepared for it, that will be the kind of government which they will have. Government is at best but an expedient; but most governments are usually, and all governments are sometimes, inexpedient. The objections which have been brought against a standing army, and they are many and weighty, and deserve to prevail, may also at last be brought against a standing government. The standing army is only an arm of the standing government. The government itself, which is only the mode which the people have chosen to execute their will, is equally liable to be abused and perverted before the people can act through it. Witness the present Mexican war, the work of comparatively a few individuals using the standing government as their tool; for, in the outset, the people would not have consented to this measure.

This American government—what is it but a tradition, though a recent one, endeavoring to transmit itself unimpaired to posterity, but each instant losing some of its integrity? It has not the vitality and force of a single living man; for a single man can bend it to his will. It is a sort of wooden gun to the people themselves. But it is not the less necessary for this; for the people must have some complicated machinery or other, and hear its din, to satisfy that idea of government which they have. Governments show thus how successfully men can be imposed on, even impose on themselves, for their own advantage. It is excellent, we must all allow. Yet this government never of itself furthered any enterprise, but by the alacrity with which it got out of its way. It does not keep the country free. It does not settle the West. It does not educate. The character inherent in the American people has done all that has been accomplished; and it would have done somewhat more, if the government had not sometimes got in its way. For government is an expedient by which men would fain succeed in letting one another alone; and, as has been said, when it is most expedient, the governed are most let alone by it. Trade and commerce, if they were not made of india-rubber, would never manage to bounce over the obstacles which legislators are continually putting in their way; and, if one were to judge these men wholly by the effects of their actions and not partly by their intentions, they would deserve to be classed and punished with those mischievous persons who put obstructions on the railroads.

But, to speak practically and as a citizen, unlike those who call themselves no-government men, I ask for, not at once no government, but at once a better government. Let every man make known what kind of government would command his respect, and that will be one step toward obtaining it.

After all, the practical reason why, when the power is once in the hands of the people, a majority are permitted, and for a long period continue, to rule is not because they are most likely to be in the right, nor because this seems fairest to the minority, but because they are physically the strongest. But a government in which the majority rule in all cases cannot be based on justice, even as far as men understand it. Can there not be a government in which majorities do not virtually decide right and wrong, but conscience?—in which majorities decide only those questions to which the rule of expediency is applicable? Must the citizen ever for a moment, or in the least degree, resign his conscience to the legislation? Why has every man a conscience, then? I think that we should be men first, and subjects afterward. It is not desirable to cultivate a respect for the law, so much as for the right. The only obligation which I have a right to assume is to do at any time what I think right. It is truly enough said that a corporation has no conscience; but a corporation of conscientious men is a corporation with a conscience. Law never made men a whit more just; and, by means of their respect for it, even the well-disposed are daily made the agents of injustice. A common and natural result of an undue respect for law is, that you may see a file of soldiers, colonel, captain, corporal, privates, powder-monkeys, and all, marching in admirable order over hill and dale to the wars, against their wills, ay, against their common sense and consciences, which makes it very steep marching indeed, and produces a palpitation of the heart. They have no doubt that it is a damnable business in which they are concerned; they are all peaceably inclined. Now, what are they? Men at all? or small movable forts and magazines, at the service of some unscrupulous man in power? Visit the Navy-Yard, and behold a marine, such a man as an American government can make, or such as it can make a man with its black arts—a mere shadow and reminiscence of humanity, a man laid out alive and standing, and already, as one may say, buried under arms with funeral accompaniments, though it may be,

"Not a drum was heard, not a funeral note,
As his corse to the rampart we hurried;
Not a soldier discharged his farewell shot
O'er the grave where our hero we buried."

The mass of men serve the state thus, not as men mainly, but as machines, with their bodies. They are the standing army, and the militia, jailers, constables, posse comitatus, etc. In most cases there is no free exercise whatever of the judgment or of the moral sense; but they put themselves on a level with wood and earth and stones; and wooden men can perhaps be manufactured that will serve the purpose as well. Such command no more respect than men of straw or a lump of dirt. They have the same sort of worth only as horses and dogs. Yet such as these even are commonly esteemed good citizens. Others—as most legislators, politicians, lawyers, ministers, and office-holders—serve the state chiefly with their heads; and, as they rarely make any moral distinctions, they are as likely to serve the devil, without intending it, as God. A very few—as heroes, patriots, martyrs, reformers in the great sense, and men—serve the state with their consciences also, and so necessarily resist it for the most part; and they are commonly treated as enemies by it. A wise man will only be useful as a man, and will not submit to be "clay," and "stop a hole to keep the wind away," but leave that office to his dust at least:

"I am too high-born to be propertied,
To be a secondary at control,
Or useful serving-man and instrument
To any sovereign state throughout the world."

He who gives himself entirely to his fellow-men appears to them useless and selfish; but he who gives himself partially to them is pronounced a benefactor and philanthropist.

How does it become a man to behave toward this American government today? I answer, that he cannot without disgrace be associated with it. I cannot for an instant recognize that political organization as my government which is the slave's government also.

All men recognize the right of revolution; that is, the right to refuse allegiance to, and to resist, the government, when its tyranny or its inefficiency are great and unendurable. But almost all say that such is not the case now. But such was the case, they think, in the Revolution of '75. If one were to tell me that this was a bad government because it taxed certain foreign commodities brought to its ports, it is most probable that I should not make an ado about it, for I can do without them. All machines have their friction; and possibly this does enough good to counterbalance the evil. At any rate, it is a great evil to make a stir about it. But when the friction comes to have its machine, and oppression and robbery are organized, I say, let us not have such a machine any longer. In other words, when a sixth of the population of a nation which has undertaken to be the refuge of liberty are slaves, and a whole country is unjustly overrun and conquered by a foreign army, and subjected to military law, I think that it is not too soon for honest men to rebel and revolutionize. What makes this duty the more urgent is the fact that the country so overrun is not our own, but ours is the invading army.

Paley, a common authority with many on moral questions, in his chapter on the "Duty of Submission to Civil Government," resolves all civil obligation into expediency; and he proceeds to say that "so long as the interest of the whole society requires it, that is, so long as the established government cannot be resisted or changed without public inconveniency, it is the will of God . . . that the established government be obeyed—and no longer. This principle being admitted, the justice of every particular case of resistance is reduced to a computation of the quantity of the danger and grievance on the one side, and of the probability and expense of redressing it on the other." Of this, he says, every man shall judge for himself. But Paley appears never to have contemplated those cases to which the rule of expediency does not apply, in which a people, as well as an individual, must do justice, cost what it may. If I have unjustly wrested a plank from a drowning man, I must restore it to him though I drown myself. This, according to Paley, would be inconvenient. But he that would save his life, in such a case, shall lose it. This people must cease to hold slaves, and to make war on Mexico, though it cost them their existence as a people.

In their practice, nations agree with Paley; but does any one think that Massachusetts does exactly what is right at the present crisis?

> "A drab of state, a cloth-o'-silver slut,
> To have her train borne up, and her soul trail in the dirt."

Practically speaking, the opponents to a reform in Massachusetts are not a hundred thousand politicians at the South, but a hundred thousand merchants and farmers here, who are more interested in commerce and agriculture than they are in humanity, and are not prepared to do justice to the slave and to Mexico, cost what it may. I quarrel not with far-off foes, but with those who, near at home, cooperate with, and do the bidding of those far away, and without whom the latter would be harmless. We are accustomed to say, that the mass of men are unprepared; but improvement is slow, because the few are not materially wiser or better than the many. It is not so important that many should be as good as you, as that there be some absolute goodness somewhere; for that will leaven the whole lump. There are thousands who are in opinion opposed to slavery and to the war, who yet in effect do nothing to put an end to them; who, esteeming themselves children of Washington and Franklin, sit down with their hands in their pockets, and say that they know not what to do, and do nothing; who even postpone the question of freedom to the question of free trade, and quietly read the prices-current along with the latest advices from Mexico, after dinner, and, it may be, fall asleep over them both. What is the price current of an honest man and patriot today? They hesitate, and they regret, and sometimes they petition; but they do nothing in earnest and with effect. They will wait, well disposed, for others to remedy the evil, that they may no longer have it to regret. At most, they give only a cheap vote, and a feeble countenance and God-speed, to the right, as it goes by them. There are nine hundred and ninety-nine patrons of virtue to one virtuous man. But it is easier to deal with the real possessor of a thing than with the temporary guardian of it.

All voting is a sort of gaming, like checkers or backgammon, with a slight moral tinge to it, a playing with right and wrong, with moral questions; and betting naturally accompanies it. The character of the voters is not staked. I cast my vote, perchance, as I think right; but I am not vitally concerned that that right should prevail. I am willing to leave it to the majority. Its obligation, therefore, never exceeds that of expediency. Even voting for the right is doing nothing for it. It is only expressing to men feebly your desire that it should prevail. A wise man will not leave the right to the mercy of chance, nor wish it to prevail through the power of the majority. There is but little virtue in the action of masses of men. When the majority shall at length vote for the abolition of slavery, it will be because they are indifferent to slavery, or because there is but little slavery left to be abolished by their vote. They will then be the only slaves. Only his vote can hasten the abolition of slavery who asserts his own freedom by his vote.

I hear of a convention to be held at Baltimore, or elsewhere, for the selection of a candidate for the Presidency, made up chiefly of editors, and men who are politicians by profession; but I think, what is it to any independent, intelligent, and respectable man what decision they may come to? Shall we not have the advantage of his wisdom and honesty, nevertheless? Can we not count upon some independent votes? Are there not many individuals in the country who do not attend conventions? But no: I find that the respectable man, so called, has immediately drifted from his position, and despairs of his country, when his country has more reason to despair of him. He forthwith adopts one of the candidates thus selected as the only available one, thus proving that he is himself available for any purposes of the demagogue. His vote is of no more worth than that of any unprincipled foreigner or hireling native, who may have been bought. O for a man who is a man, and, as my neighbor says, has a bone in his back which you cannot pass your hand through! Our statistics are at fault: the population has been returned too large. How many men are there to a square thousand miles in this country? Hardly one. Does not America offer any inducement for men to settle here? The American has dwindled into an Odd Fellow-one who may be known by the development of his organ of gregariousness, and a manifest lack of intellect and cheerful self-reliance; whose first and chief concern, on coming into the world, is to see that the almshouses are in good repair; and, before yet he has lawfully donned the virile garb, to collect a fund for the support of the widows and orphans that may be; who, in short, ventures to live only by the aid of the Mutual Insurance company, which has promised to bury him decently.

It is not a man's duty, as a matter of course, to devote himself to the eradication of any, even the most enormous, wrong; he may still properly have other concerns to engage him; but it is his duty, at least, to wash his hands of it, and, if he gives it no thought longer, not to give it practically his support. If I devote myself to other pursuits and contemplations, I must first see, at least, that I do not pursue them sitting upon another man's shoulders. I must get off him first, that he may pursue his contemplations too. See what gross inconsistency is tolerated. I have heard some of my townsmen say, "I should like to have them order me out to help put down an insurrection of the slaves, or to march to Mexico;—see if I would go"; and yet these very men have each, directly by their allegiance, and so indirectly, at least, by their money, furnished a substitute. The soldier is applauded who refuses to serve in an unjust war by those who do not refuse to sustain the unjust government which makes the war; is applauded by those whose own act and authority he disregards and sets at naught; as if the state were penitent to that degree that it differed one to scourge it while it sinned, but not to that degree that it left off sinning for a moment. Thus, under the name of Order and Civil Government, we are all made at last to pay homage to and support our own meanness. After the first blush of sin comes its indifference; and from immoral it becomes, as it were, unmoral, and not quite unnecessary to that life which we have made.

The broadest and most prevalent error requires the most disinterested virtue to sustain it. The slight reproach to which the virtue of patriotism is commonly liable, the noble are most likely to incur. Those who, while they disapprove of the character and measures of a government, yield to it their allegiance and support are undoubtedly its most conscientious supporters, and so frequently the most serious obstacles to reform. Some are petitioning the State to dissolve the Union, to disregard the requisitions of the President. Why do they not dissolve it themselves—the union between themselves and the State—and refuse to pay their quota into its treasury? Do not they stand in the same relation to the State that the State does to the Union? And have not the same reasons prevented the State from resisting the Union which have prevented them from resisting the State?

How can a man be satisfied to entertain an opinion merely, and enjoy it? Is there any enjoyment in it, if his opinion is that he is aggrieved? If you are cheated out of a single dollar by your neighbor, you do not rest satisfied with knowing that you are cheated, or with saying that you are cheated, or even with petitioning him to pay you your due; but you take effectual steps at once to obtain the full amount, and see that you are never cheated again. Action from principle, the perception and the performance of right, changes things and relations; it is essentially revolutionary, and does not consist wholly with anything which was. It not only divides States and churches, it divides families; ay, it divides the individual, separating the diabolical in him from the divine.

Unjust laws exist: shall we be content to obey them, or shall we endeavor to amend them, and obey them until we have succeeded, or shall we transgress them at once? Men generally, under such a government as this, think that they ought to wait until they have persuaded the majority to alter them. They think that, if they should resist, the remedy would be worse than the evil. But it is the fault of the government itself that the remedy is worse than the evil. It makes it worse. Why is it not more apt to anticipate and provide for reform? Why does it not cherish its wise minority? Why does it cry and resist before it is hurt? Why does it not encourage its citizens to be on the alert to point out its faults, and do better than it would have them? Why does it always crucify Christ, and excommunicate Copernicus and Luther, and pronounce Washington and Franklin rebels?

One would think that a deliberate and practical denial of its authority was the only offence never contemplated by government; else, why has it not assigned its definite, its suitable and proportionate, penalty? If a man who has no property refuses but once to earn nine shillings for the State, he is put in prison for a period unlimited by any law that I know, and determined only by the discretion of those who placed him there; but if he should steal ninety times nine shillings from the State, he is soon permitted to go at large again.

If the injustice is part of the necessary friction of the machine of government, let it go, let it go: perchance it will wear smooth—certainly the machine will wear out. If the injustice has a spring, or a pulley, or a rope, or a crank, exclusively for itself, then perhaps you may consider whether the remedy will not be worse than the evil; but if it is of such a nature that it requires you to be the agent of injustice to another, then, I say, break the law. Let your life be a counter-friction to stop the machine. What I have to do is to see, at any rate, that I do not lend myself to the wrong which I condemn.

As for adopting the ways which the State has provided for remedying the evil, I know not of such ways. They take too much time, and a man's life will be gone. I have other affairs to attend to. I came into this world, not chiefly to make this a good place to live in, but to live in it, be it good or bad. A man has not everything to do, but something; and because he cannot do everything, it is not necessary that he should do something wrong. It is not my business to be petitioning the Governor or the Legislature any more than it is theirs to petition me; and if they should not bear my petition, what should I do then? But in this case the State has provided no way: its very Constitution is the evil. This may seem to be harsh and stubborn and unconciliatory; but it is to treat with the utmost kindness and consideration the only spirit that can appreciate or deserves it. So is an change for the better, like birth and death, which convulse the body.

I do not hesitate to say, that those who call themselves Abolitionists should at once effectually withdraw their support, both in person and property, from the government of Massachusetts, and not wait till they constitute a majority of one, before they suffer the right to prevail through them. I think that it is enough if they have God on their side, without waiting for that other one. Moreover, any man more right than his neighbors constitutes a majority of one already.

I meet this American government, or its representative, the State government, directly, and face to face, once a year—no more—in the person of its tax-gatherer; this is the only mode in which a man situated as I am necessarily meets it; and it then says distinctly, Recognize me; and the simplest, the most effectual, and, in the present posture of affairs, the indispensablest mode of treating with it on this head, of expressing your little satisfaction with and love for it, is to deny it then. My civil neighbor, the tax-gatherer, is the very man I have to deal with—for it is, after all, with men and not with parchment that I quarrel—and he has voluntarily chosen to be an agent of the government. How shall he ever know well what he is and does as an officer of the government, or as a man, until he is obliged to consider whether he shall treat me, his neighbor, for whom he has respect, as a neighbor and well-disposed man, or as a maniac and disturber of the peace, and see if he can get over this obstruction to his neighborliness without a ruder and more impetuous thought or speech corresponding with his action. I know this well, that if one thousand, if one hundred, if ten men whom I could name—if ten honest men only—ay, if one HONEST man, in this State of Massachusetts, ceasing to hold slaves, were actually to withdraw from this copartnership, and be locked up in the county jail therefor, it would be the abolition of slavery in America. For it matters not how small the beginning may seem to be: what is once well done is done forever. But we love better to talk about it: that we say is our mission. Reform keeps many scores of newspapers in its service, but not one man. If my esteemed neighbor, the State's ambassador, who will devote his days to the settlement of the question of human rights in the Council Chamber, instead of being threatened with the prisons of Carolina, were to sit down the prisoner of Massachusetts, that State which is so anxious to foist the sin of slavery upon her sister—though at present she can discover only an act of inhospitality to be the ground of a quarrel with her—the Legislature would not wholly waive the subject the following winter.

Under a government which imprisons any unjustly, the true place for a just man is also a prison. The proper place today, the only place which Massachusetts has provided for her freer and less desponding spirits, is in her prisons, to be put out and locked out of the State by her own act, as they have already put themselves out by their principles. It is there that the fugitive slave, and the Mexican prisoner on parole, and the Indian come to plead the wrongs of his race should find them; on that separate, but more free and honorable, ground, where the State places those who are not with her, but against her—the only house in a slave State in which a free man can abide with honor. If any think that their influence would be lost there, and their voices no longer afflict the ear of the State, that they would not be as an enemy within its walls, they do not know by how much truth is stronger than error, nor how much more eloquently and effectively he can combat injustice who has experienced a little in his own person. Cast your whole vote, not a strip of paper merely, but your whole influence. A minority is powerless while it conforms to the majority; it is not even a minority then; but it is irresistible when it clogs by its whole weight. If the alternative is to keep all just men in prison, or give up war and slavery, the State will not hesitate which to choose. If a thousand men were not to pay their tax-bills this year, that would not be a violent and bloody measure, as it would be to pay them, and enable the State to commit violence and shed innocent blood. This is, in fact, the definition of a peaceable revolution, if any such is possible. If the tax-gatherer, or any other public officer, asks me, as one has done, "But what shall I do?" my answer is, "If you really wish to do anything, resign your office." When the subject has refused allegiance, and the officer has resigned his office, then the revolution is accomplished. But even suppose blood should flow. Is there not a sort of blood shed when the conscience is wounded? Through this wound a man's real manhood and immortality flow out, and he bleeds to an everlasting death. I see this blood flowing now.

I have contemplated the imprisonment of the offender, rather than the seizure of his goods—though both will serve the same purpose—because they who assert the purest right, and consequently are most dangerous to a corrupt State, commonly have not spent much time in accumulating property. To such the State renders comparatively small service, and a slight tax is wont to appear exorbitant, particularly if they are obliged to earn it by special labor with their hands. If there were one who lived wholly without the use of money, the State itself would hesitate to demand it of him. But the rich man—not to make any invidious comparison—is always sold to the institution which makes him rich. Absolutely speaking, the more money, the less virtue; for money comes between a man and his objects, and obtains them for him; and it was certainly no great virtue to obtain it. It puts to rest many questions which he would otherwise be taxed to answer; while the only new question which it puts is the hard but superfluous one, how to spend it. Thus his moral ground is taken from under his feet. The opportunities of living are diminished in proportion as what are called the "means" are increased. The best thing a man can do for his culture when he is rich is to endeavor to carry out those schemes which he entertained when he was poor. Christ answered the Herodians according to their condition. "Show me the tribute-money," said he;—and one took a penny out of his pocket;—if you use money which has the image of Caesar on it, and which he has made current and valuable, that is, if you are men of the State, and gladly enjoy the advantages of Caesar's government, then pay him back some of his own when he demands it. "Render therefore to Caesar that which is Caesar's, and to God those things which are God's"—leaving them no wiser than before as to which was which; for they did not wish to know.

When I converse with the freest of my neighbors, I perceive that, whatever they may say about the magnitude and seriousness of the question, and their regard for the public tranquillity, the long and the short of the matter is, that they cannot spare the protection of the existing government, and they dread the consequences to their property and families of disobedience to it. For my own part, I should not like to think that I ever rely on the protection of the State. But, if I deny the authority of the State when it presents its tax-bill, it will soon take and waste all my property, and so harass me and my children without end. This is hard. This makes it impossible for a man to live honestly, and at the same time comfortably, in outward respects. It will not be worth the while to accumulate property; that would be sure to go again. You must hire or squat somewhere, and raise but a small crop, and eat that soon. You must live within yourself, and depend upon yourself always tucked up and ready for a start, and not have many affairs. A man may grow rich in Turkey even, if he will be in all respects a good subject of the Turkish government. Confucius said: "If a state is governed by the principles of reason, poverty and misery are subjects of shame; if a state is not governed by the principles of reason, riches and honors are the subjects of shame." No: until I want the protection of Massachusetts to be extended to me in some distant Southern port, where my liberty is endangered, or until I am bent solely on building up an estate at home by peaceful enterprise, I can afford to refuse allegiance to Massachusetts, and her right to my property and life. It costs me less in every sense to incur the penalty of disobedience to the State than it would to obey. I should feel as if I were worth less in that case.

Some years ago, the State met me in behalf of the Church, and commanded me to pay a certain sum toward the support of a clergyman whose preaching my father attended, but never I myself. "Pay," it said, "or be locked up in the jail." I declined to pay. But, unfortunately, another man saw fit to pay it. I did not see why the schoolmaster should be taxed to support the priest, and not the priest the schoolmaster; for I was not the State's schoolmaster, but I supported myself by voluntary subscription. I did not see why the lyceum should not present its tax-bill, and have the State to back its demand, as well as the Church. However, at the request of the selectmen, I condescended to make some such statement as this in writing:—"Know all men by these presents, that I, Henry Thoreau, do not wish to be regarded as a member of any incorporated society which I have not joined." This I gave to the town clerk; and he has it. The State, having thus learned that I did not wish to be regarded as a member of that church, has never made a like demand on me since; though it said that it must adhere to its original presumption that time. If I had known how to name them, I should then have signed off in detail from all the societies which I never signed on to; but I did not know where to find a complete list.

I have paid no poll-tax for six years. I was put into a jail once on this account, for one night; and, as I stood considering the walls of solid stone, two or three feet thick, the door of wood and iron, a foot thick, and the iron grating which strained the light, I could not help being struck with the foolishness of that institution which treated me as if I were mere flesh and blood and bones, to be locked up. I wondered that it should have concluded at length that this was the best use it could put me to, and had never thought to avail itself of my services in some way. I saw that, if there was a wall of stone between me and my townsmen, there was a still more difficult one to climb or break through before they could get to be as free as I was. I did not for a moment feel confined, and the walls seemed a great waste of stone and mortar. I felt as if I alone of all my townsmen had paid my tax. They plainly did not know how to treat me, but behaved like persons who are underbred. In every threat and in every compliment there was a blunder; for they thought that my chief desire was to stand the other side of that stone wall. I could not but smile to see how industriously they locked the door on my meditations, which followed them out again without let or hindrance, and they were really all that was dangerous. As they could not reach me, they had resolved to punish my body; just as boys, if they cannot come at some person against whom they have a spite, will abuse his dog. I saw that the State was half-witted, that it was timid as a lone woman with her silver spoons, and that it did not know its friends from its foes, and I lost all my remaining respect for it, and pitied it.

Thus the State never intentionally confronts a man's sense, intellectual or moral, but only his body, his senses. It is not armed with superior wit or honesty, but with superior physical strength. I was not born to be forced. I will breathe after my own fashion. Let us see who is the strongest. What force has a multitude? They only can force me who obey a higher law than I. They force me to become like themselves. I do not hear of men being forced to have this way or that by masses of men. What sort of life were that to live? When I meet a government which says to me, "Your money or your life," why should I be in haste to give it my money? It may be in a great strait, and not know what to do: I cannot help that. It must help itself; do as I do. It is not worth the while to snivel about it. I am not responsible for the successful working of the machinery of society. I am not the son of the engineer. I perceive that, when an acorn and a chestnut fall side by side, the one does not remain inert to make way for the other, but both obey their own laws, and spring and grow and flourish as best they can, till one, perchance, overshadows and destroys the other. If a plant cannot live according to its nature, it dies; and so a man.

The night in prison was novel and interesting enough. The prisoners in their shirt-sleeves were enjoying a chat and the evening air in the doorway, when I entered. But the jailer said, "Come, boys, it is time to lock up"; and so they dispersed, and I heard the sound of their steps returning into the hollow apartments. My room-mate was introduced to me by the jailer as "a first-rate fellow and a clever man." When the door was locked, he showed me where to hang my hat, and how he managed matters there. The rooms were whitewashed once a month; and this one, at least, was the whitest, most simply furnished, and probably the neatest apartment in the town. He naturally wanted to know where I came from, and what brought me there; and, when I had told him, I asked him in my turn how he came there, presuming him to be an honest man, of course; and, as the world goes, I believe he was. "Why," said he, "they accuse me of burning a barn; but I never did it." As near as I could discover, he had probably gone to bed in a barn when drunk, and smoked his pipe there; and so a barn was burnt. He had the reputation of being a clever man, had been there some three months waiting for his trial to come on, and would have to wait as much longer; but he was quite domesticated and contented, since he got his board for nothing, and thought that he was well treated.

He occupied one window, and I the other; and I saw that if one stayed there long, his principal business would be to look out the window. I had soon read all the tracts that were left there, and examined where former prisoners had broken out, and where a grate had been sawed off, and heard the history of the various occupants of that room; for I found that even here there was a history and a gossip which never circulated beyond the walls of the jail. Probably this is the only house in the town where verses are composed, which are afterward printed in a circular form, but not published. I was shown quite a long list of verses which were composed by some young men who had been detected in an attempt to escape, who avenged themselves by singing them.

I pumped my fellow-prisoner as dry as I could, for fear I should never see him again; but at length he showed me which was my bed, and left me to blow out the lamp.

It was like travelling into a far country, such as I had never expected to behold, to lie there for one night. It seemed to me that I never had heard the town clock strike before, nor the evening sounds of the village; for we slept with the windows open, which were inside the grating. It was to see my native village in the light of the Middle Ages, and our Concord was turned into a Rhine stream, and visions of knights and castles passed before me. They were the voices of old burghers that I heard in the streets. I was an involuntary spectator and auditor of whatever was done and said in the kitchen of the adjacent village inn—a wholly new and rare experience to me. It was a closer view of my native town. I was fairly inside of it. I never had seen its institutions before. This is one of its peculiar institutions; for it is a shire town. I began to comprehend what its inhabitants were about.

In the morning, our breakfasts were put through the hole in the door, in small oblong-square tin pans, made to fit, and holding a pint of chocolate, with brown bread, and an iron spoon. When they called for the vessels again, I was green enough to return what bread I had left; but my comrade seized it, and said that I should lay that up for lunch or dinner. Soon after he was let out to work at haying in a neighboring field, whither he went every day, and would not be back till noon; so he bade me good-day, saying that he doubted if he should see me again.

When I came out of prison—for some one interfered, and paid that tax—I did not perceive that great changes had taken place on the common, such as he observed who went in a youth and emerged a tottering and gray-headed man; and yet a change had to my eyes come over the scene—the town, and State, and country—greater than any that mere time could effect. I saw yet more distinctly the State in which I lived. I saw to what extent the people among whom I lived could be trusted as good neighbors and friends; that their friendship was for summer weather only; that they did not greatly propose to do right; that they were a distinct race from me by their prejudices and superstitions, as the Chinamen and Malays are; that in their sacrifices to humanity they ran no risks, not even to their property; that after all they were not so noble but they treated the thief as he had treated them, and hoped, by a certain outward observance and a few prayers, and by walking in a particular straight though useless path from time to time, to save their souls. This may be to judge my neighbors harshly; for I believe that many of them are not aware that they have such an institution as the jail in their village.

It was formerly the custom in our village, when a poor debtor came out of jail, for his acquaintances to salute him, looking through their fingers, which were crossed to represent the grating of a jail window, "How do ye do?" My neighbors did not thus salute me, but first looked at me, and then at one another, as if I had returned from a long journey. I was put into jail as I was going to the shoemaker's to get a shoe which was mended. When I was let out the next morning, I proceeded to finish my errand, and, having put on my mended shoe, joined a huckleberry party, who were impatient to put themselves under my conduct; and in half an hour—for the horse was soon tackled—was in the midst of a huckleberry field, on one of our highest hills, two miles off, and then the State was nowhere to be seen.

This is the whole history of "My Prisons."

I have never declined paying the highway tax, because I am as desirous of being a good neighbor as I am of being a bad subject; and as for supporting schools, I am doing my part to educate my fellow-countrymen now. It is for no particular item in the tax-bill that I refuse to pay it. I simply wish to refuse allegiance to the State, to withdraw and stand aloof from it effectually. I do not care to trace the course of my dollar, if I could, till it buys a man or a musket to shoot one with—the dollar is innocent—but I am concerned to trace the effects of my allegiance. In fact, I quietly declare war with the State, after my fashion, though I will still make what use and get what advantage of her I can, as is usual in such cases.

If others pay the tax which is demanded of me, from a sympathy with the State, they do but what they have already done in their own case, or rather they abet injustice to a greater extent than the State requires. If they pay the tax from a mistaken interest in the individual taxed, to save his property, or prevent his going to jail, it is because they have not considered wisely how far they let their private feelings interfere with the public good.

This, then, is my position at present. But one cannot be too much on his guard in such a case, lest his action be biased by obstinacy or an undue regard for the opinions of men. Let him see that he does only what belongs to himself and to the hour.

I think sometimes, Why, this people mean well, they are only ignorant; they would do better if they knew how: why give your neighbors this pain to treat you as they are not inclined to? But I think again, This is no reason why I should do as they do, or permit others to suffer much greater pain of a different kind. Again, I sometimes say to myself, When many millions of men, without heat, without ill will, without personal feeling of any kind, demand of you a few shillings only, without the possibility, such is their constitution, of retracting or altering their present demand, and without the possibility, on your side, of appeal to any other millions, why expose yourself to this overwhelming brute force? You do not resist cold and hunger, the winds and the waves, thus obstinately; you quietly submit to a thousand similar necessities. You do not put your head into the fire. But just in proportion as I regard this as not wholly a brute force, but partly a human force, and consider that I have relations to those millions as to so many millions of men, and not of mere brute or inanimate things, I see that appeal is possible, first and instantaneously, from them to the Maker of them, and, secondly, from them to themselves. But if I put my head deliberately into the fire, there is no appeal to fire or to the Maker of fire, and I have only myself to blame. If I could convince myself that I have any right to be satisfied with men as they are, and to treat them accordingly, and not according, in some respects, to my requisitions and expectations of what they and I ought to be, then, like a good Mussulman and fatalist, I should endeavor to be satisfied with things as they are, and say it is the will of God. And, above all, there is this difference between resisting this and a purely brute or natural force, that I can resist this with some effect; but I cannot expect, like Orpheus, to change the nature of the rocks and trees and beasts.

I do not wish to quarrel with any man or nation. I do not wish to split hairs, to make fine distinctions, or set myself up as better than my neighbors. I seek rather, I may say, even an excuse for conforming to the laws of the land. I am but too ready to conform to them. Indeed, I have reason to suspect myself on this head; and each year, as the tax-gatherer comes round, I find myself disposed to review the acts and position of the general and State governments, and the spirit of the people, to discover a pretext for conformity.

> "We must affect our country as our parents,
> And if at any time we alienate
> Our love or industry from doing it honor,
> We must respect effects and teach the soul
> Matter of conscience and religion,
> And not desire of rule or benefit."

I believe that the State will soon be able to take all my work of this sort out of my hands, and then I shall be no better a patriot than my fellow-countrymen. Seen from a lower point of view, the Constitution, with all its faults, is very good; the law and the courts are very respectable; even this State and this American government are, in many respects, very admirable, and rare things, to be thankful for, such as a great many have described them; but seen from a point of view a little higher, they are what I have described them; seen from a higher still, and the highest, who shall say what they are, or that they are worth looking at or thinking of at all?

However, the government does not concern me much, and I shall bestow the fewest possible thoughts on it. It is not many moments that I live under a government, even in this world. If a man is thought-free, fancy-free, imagination-free, that which is not never for a long time appearing to be to him, unwise rulers or reformers cannot fatally interrupt him.

I know that most men think differently from myself; but those whose lives are by profession devoted to the study of these or kindred subjects content me as little as any. Statesmen and legislators, standing so completely within the institution, never distinctly and nakedly behold it. They speak of moving society, but have no resting-place without it. They may be men of a certain experience and discrimination, and have no doubt invented ingenious and even useful systems, for which we sincerely thank them; but all their wit and usefulness lie within certain not very wide limits. They are wont to forget that the world is not governed by policy and expediency. Webster never goes behind government, and so cannot speak with authority about it. His words are wisdom to those legislators who contemplate no essential reform in the existing government; but for thinkers, and those who legislate for all time, he never once glances at the subject. I know of those whose serene and wise speculations on this theme would soon reveal the limits of his mind's range and hospitality. Yet, compared with the cheap professions of most reformers, and the still cheaper wisdom and eloquence of politicians in general, his are almost the only sensible and valuable words, and we thank Heaven for him. Comparatively, he is always strong, original, and, above all, practical. Still, his quality is not wisdom, but prudence. The lawyer's truth is not Truth, but consistency or a consistent expediency. Truth is always in harmony with herself, and is not concerned chiefly to reveal the justice that may consist with wrong-doing. He well deserves to be called, as he has been called, the Defender of the Constitution. There are really no blows to be given by him but defensive ones. He is not a leader, but a follower. His leaders are the men of '87—"I have never made an effort," he says, "and never propose to make an effort; I have never countenanced an effort, and never mean to countenance an effort, to disturb the arrangement as originally made, by which the various States came into the Union." Still thinking of the sanction which the Constitution gives to slavery, he says, "Because it was a part of the original compact—let it stand." Notwithstanding his special acuteness and ability, he is unable to take a fact out of its merely political relations, and behold it as it lies absolutely to be disposed of by the intellect—what, for instance, it behooves a man to do here in America today with regard to slavery—but ventures, or is driven, to make some such desperate answer as the following, while professing to speak absolutely, and as a private man—from which what new and singular code of social duties might be inferred? "The manner," says he, "in which the governments of those States where slavery exists are to regulate it is for their own consideration, under their responsibility to their constituents, to the general laws of propriety, humanity, and justice, and to God. Associations formed elsewhere, springing from a feeling of humanity, or any other cause, have nothing whatever to do with it. They have never received any encouragement from me, and they never will."

They who know of no purer sources of truth, who have traced up its stream no higher, stand, and wisely stand, by the Bible and the Constitution, and drink at it there with reverence and humility; but they who behold where it comes trickling into this lake or that pool, gird up their loins once more, and continue their pilgrimage toward its fountain-head.

No man with a genius for legislation has appeared in America. They are rare in the history of the world. There are orators, politicians, and eloquent men, by the thousand; but the speaker has not yet opened his mouth to speak who is capable of settling the much-vexed questions of the day. We love eloquence for its own sake, and not for any truth which it may utter, or any heroism it may inspire. Our legislators have not yet learned the comparative value of free trade and of freedom, of union, and of rectitude, to a nation. They have no genius or talent for comparatively humble questions of taxation and finance, commerce and manufactures and agriculture. If we were left solely to the wordy wit of legislators in Congress for our guidance, uncorrected by the seasonable experience and the effectual complaints of the people, America would not long retain her rank among the nations. For eighteen hundred years, though perchance I have no right to say it, the New Testament has been written; yet where is the legislator who has wisdom and practical talent enough to avail himself of the light which it sheds on the science of legislation?

The authority of government, even such as I am willing to submit to—for I will cheerfully obey those who know and can do better than I, and in many things even those who neither know nor can do so well—is still an impure one: to be strictly just, it must have the sanction and consent of the governed. It can have no pure right over my person and property but what I concede to it. The progress from an absolute to a limited monarchy, from a limited monarchy to a democracy, is a progress toward a true respect for the individual. Even the Chinese philosopher was wise enough to regard the individual as the basis of the empire. Is a democracy, such as we know it, the last improvement possible in government? Is it not possible to take a step further towards recognizing and organizing the rights of man? There will never be a really free and enlightened State until the State comes to recognize the individual as a higher and independent power, from which all its own power and authority are derived, and treats him accordingly. I please myself with imagining a State at least which can afford to be just to all men, and to treat the individual with respect as a neighbor; which even would not think it inconsistent with its own repose if a few were to live aloof from it, not meddling with it, nor embraced by it, who fulfilled all the duties of neighbors and fellow-men. A State which bore this kind of fruit, and suffered it to drop off as fast as it ripened, would prepare the way for a still more perfect and glorious State, which also I have imagined, but not yet anywhere seen.

REFLECTING AND DISCUSSING

1. What is good governance, according to Thoreau? What is good citizenship?

2. In your own words, what does it mean to be "civilly disobedient"? Are there contemporary examples of civil disobedience? What effect have these instances had?

3. From Thoreau's perspective, who matters most—the citizenry, the individual, or the government? Do you agree? Why or why not? What in the text supports his (or your) observations?

CONNECTING AND WRITING

1. When, if ever, is civil disobedience appropriate or morally necessary? Use Thoreau's arguments—and research other sources—to support your point of view.
2. Do some reading about Transcendentalism and the Transcendentalists. What are the core beliefs of this movement? What might we learn today from the movement and its adherents?

Lungs, advertisement

World Wildlife Fund

The mission of the World Wildlife Fund (WWF) is "to conserve nature and reduce the most pressing threats to the diversity of life on earth." The organization's work focuses on such areas as climate change, wildlife conservation, and forest and water preservation. This advertisement, which was published in April 2008, was developed by WWF France.

REFLECTING AND DISCUSSING

1. What is being depicted in this image? How do you know?
2. What are both the implicit and the explicit arguments being made by this image? Are they effective?
3. Define metaphor. How might this image be metaphorical? Why? Is it effective? Why or why not?

CONNECTING AND WRITING

1. Research other print advertisements by the World Wildlife Fund. Select one or two. Are their themes similar? Different? How so? Compare and contrast them, formulating an argument backed up with specific examples.
2. Research the environmental and/or health problem to which you think the ad is responding. What is the call to action? Use other resources to further analyze the motivations behind this advertisement.

Disinformocracy

Howard Rheingold (1947–   )

Howard Rheingold has written science fiction and books on science and technology. He is often praised for translating complex ideas into simple language. Early on, he tackled the serious implications of newer technologies in works such as Tools for Thought: The People and Ideas Behind the Next Computer Revolution *(1985). He is a visiting professor in Stanford University's Department of Communication, in which he teaches digital journalism, virtual communities, and social media. Rheingold has published numerous books, including* The Virtual Community: Homesteading on the Electronic Frontier *(2000),* Smart Mobs: The Next Social Revolution *(2003), and* Net Smart: *How to Thrive Online (2014). The following piece is taken from* The Virtual Community, *a volume with a title similar to that of his 2000 book but published in 1994.*

Virtual communities could help citizens revitalize democracy, or they could be luring us into an attractively packaged substitute for democratic discourse. A few true believers in electronic democracy have had their say. It's time to hear from the other side. We owe it to ourselves and future generations to look closely at what the enthusiasts fail to tell us, and to listen attentively to what the skeptics fear. . . .

Three different kinds of social criticisms of technology are relevant to claims of CMC [computer-mediated communications] as a means of enhancing democracy. One school of criticism emerges from the longer-term history of communications media, and focuses on the way electronic communications media already have pre-empted public discussions by turning more and more of the content of the media into advertisements for various commodities—a process these critics call commodification. Even the political process, according to this school of critics, has been turned into a commodity. The formal name for this criticism is "the commodification of the public sphere." The public sphere is what these social critics claim we used to have as citizens of a democracy, but have lost to the tide of commodization. The public sphere is also the focus of the hopes of online activists, who see CMC as a way of revitalizing the open and wide-spread discussions among citizens that feed the roots of democratic societies.

The second school of criticism focuses on the fact that high-bandwidth interactive networks could be used in conjunction with other technologies as a means of surveillance, control, and disinformation as well as a conduit for useful information.

This direct assault on personal liberty is compounded by a more diffuse erosion of old social values due to the capabilities of new technologies; the most problematic example is the way traditional notions of privacy are challenged on several fronts by the ease of collecting and disseminating detailed information about individuals via cyberspace technologies. When people use the convenience of electronic communication or transaction, we leave invisible digital trails; now that technologies for tracking those trails are maturing, there is cause to worry. The spreading use of computer matching to piece together the digital trails we all leave in cyberspace is one indication of privacy problems to come.

Along with all the person-to-person communications exchanged on the world's telecommunications networks are vast flows of other kinds of personal information—credit information, transaction processing, health information. Most people take it for granted that no one can search through all the electronic transactions that move through the world's networks in order to pin down an individual for marketing—or political—motives. Remember the "knowbots" that would act as personal servants, swimming in the info-tides, fishing for information to suit your interests? What if people could turn loose knowbots to collect all the information digitally linked to you? What if the Net and cheap, powerful computers give that power not only to governments and large corporations but to everyone?

Every time we travel or shop or communicate, citizens of the credit-card society contribute to streams of information that travel between point of purchase, remote credit bureaus, municipal and federal information systems, crime information databases, central transaction databases. And all these other forms of cyberspace infraction take place via the same packet-switched, high-bandwidth network technology—those packets can contain transactions as well as video clips and text files. When these streams of information begin to connect together, the unscrupulous or would-be tyrants can use the Net to catch citizens in a more ominous kind of net.

The same channels of communication that enable citizens around the world to communicate with one another also allow government and private interests to gather information about them. This school of criticism is known as Panoptic in reference to the perfect prison proposed in the eighteenth century by Jeremy Bentham—a theoretical model that happens to fit the real capabilities of today's technologies.

Another category of critical claim deserves mention, despite the rather bizarre and incredible imagery used by its most well known spokesmen—the hyper-realist school. These critics believe that information technologies have already changed what used to pass for reality into a slicked-up electronic simulation. Twenty years before the United States elected a Hollywood actor as president, the first hyper-realists pointed out how politics had become a movie, a spectacle that raised the old Roman tactic of bread and circuses to the level of mass hypnotism. We live in a hyper-reality that was carefully constructed to mimic the real world and extract money from the pockets of consumers: the forests around the Matterhorn might be dying, but the Disneyland version continues to rake in the dollars. The television programs, movie stars, and theme parks work together to create global industry devoted to maintaining a web of illusion that grows more lifelike as more people buy into it and as technologies grow more powerful.

Many other social scientists have intellectual suspicions of the hyper-realist critiques, because so many are abstract and theoretical, based on little or no direct knowledge of technology itself. Nevertheless, this perspective does capture something about the way the effects of communications technologies have changed our modes of thought. One good reason for paying attention to the claims of the hyper-realists is that the society they predicted decades ago bears a disturbingly closer resemblance to real life than do the forecasts of the rosier-visioned technological utopians. While McLuhan's image of the global village has taken on a certain irony in light of what has happened since his predictions of the 1960s, "the society of the spectacle"—another prediction from the 1960s, based on the advent of electronic media—offered a far less rosy and, as events have proved, more realistic portrayal of the way information technologies have changed social customs.

The Selling of Democracy: Commodification and the Public Sphere

There is an intimate connection between informal conversations, the kind that take place in communities and virtual communities, in the coffee shops and computer conferences, and the ability of large social groups to govern themselves without monarchs or dictators. This social-political connection shares a metaphor with the idea of cyberspace, for it takes place in a kind of virtual space that has come to be known by specialists as the public sphere.

Here is what the preeminent contemporary writer about the public sphere, social critic and philosopher Jurgen Habermas, had to say about the meaning of this abstraction:

> By "public sphere," we mean first of all a domain of our social life in which such a thing as public opinion can be formed. Access to the public sphere is open in principle to all citizens. A portion of the public sphere is constituted in every conversation in which private persons come together to form a public. They are then acting neither as business or professional people conducting their private affairs, nor as legal consocates subject to the legal regulations of a state bureaucracy and obligated to obedience. Citizens act as a public when they deal with matters of general interest without being subject to coercion; thus with the guarantee that they may assemble and unite freely, and express and publicize their opinions freely.

In this definition, Habermas formalized what people in free societies mean when we say "The public wouldn't stand for that" or "It depends on public opinion." And he drew attention to the intimate connection between this web of free, informal, personal communications and the foundations of democratic society. People can govern themselves only if they communicate widely, freely, and in groups—publicly. The First Amendment of the U.S. Constitution's Bill of Rights protects citizens from government interference in their communications—the rights of speech, press, and assembly are communication rights. Without those rights, there is no public sphere. Ask any citizen of Prague, Budapest, or Moscow.

Because the public sphere depends on free communication and discussion of ideas, as soon as your political entity grows larger than the number of citizens you can fit into a modest town hall, this vital marketplace for political ideas can be power-fully influenced by changes in communications technology. According to Habermas,

> When the public is large, this kind of communication requires certain means of
> dissemination and influence; today, newspapers and periodicals, radio and tele-
> vision are the media of the public sphere. . . . The term "public opinion" refers
> to the functions of criticism and control or organized state authority that the
> public exercises informally, as well as formally during periodic elections. Regula-
> tions concerning the publicness (or publicity [Publizitat] in its original meaning)
> of state-related activities, as, for instance, the public accessibility required of
> legal proceedings, are also connected with this function of public opinion. To
> the public sphere as a sphere mediating between state and society, a sphere in
> which the public is the vehicle of publicness—the publicness that once had to
> win out against the secret politics of monarchs and that since then has permit-
> ted democratic control of state activity.

Ask anybody in China about the right to talk freely among friends and neighbors, to own a printing press, to call a meeting to protest government policy, or to run a BBS [bulletin-board systems]. But brute totalitarian seizure of communications technology is not the only way that political powers can neutralize the ability of citizens to talk freely. It is also possible to alter the nature of discourse by inventing a kind of paid fake discourse. If a few people have control of what goes into the daily reporting of the news, and those people are in the business of selling advertising, all kinds of things become possible for those who can afford to pay.

Habermas had this to say about the corrupting influence of ersatz public opinion:

> Whereas at one time publicness was intended to subject persons or things to
> the public use of reason and to make political decisions subject to revision before
> the tribunal of public opinion, today it has often enough already been enlisted
> in the aid of the secret policies of interest groups; in the form of "publicity" it
> now acquires public prestige for persons or things and renders them capable
> of acclamation in a climate of nonpublic opinion. The term "public relations"
> itself indicates how a public sphere that formerly emerged from the structure of
> society must now be produced circumstantially on a case-by-case basis.

The idea that public opinion can be manufactured and the fact that electronic spectacles can capture the attention of a majority of the citizenry damaged the foundations of democracy. According to Habermas,

> It is no accident that these concepts of the public sphere and public opinion
> were not formed until the eighteenth century. They derive their specific meaning
> from a concrete historical situation. It was then that one learned to distinguish
> between opinion and public opinion. . . . Public opinion, in terms of its very idea,
> can be formed only if a public that engages in rational discussion exists. Public
> discussions that are institutionally protected and that take, with critical intent,
> the exercise of political authority as their theme have not existed since time
> immemorial.

The public sphere and democracy were born at the same time, from the same sources. Now that the public sphere, cut off from its roots, seems to be dying, democracy is in danger, too.

The concept of the public sphere as discussed by Habermas and others includes several requirements for authenticity that people who live in democratic societies would recognize: open access, voluntary participation, participation outside institutional roles, the generation of public opinion through assemblies of citizens who engage in rational argument, the freedom to express opinions, and the freedom to discuss matters of the state and criticize the way state power is organized. Acts of speech and publication that specifically discuss the state are perhaps the most important kind protected by the First Amendment of the U.S. Constitution and similar civil guarantees elsewhere in the world. Former Soviets and Eastern Europeans who regained it after decades of censorship offer testimony that the most important freedom of speech is the freedom to speak about freedoms.

In eighteenth-century America, the Committees of Correspondence were one of the most important loci of the public sphere in the years of revolution and constitution-building. If you look closely at the roots of the American Revolution, it becomes evident that a text-based, horseback-transported version of networking was an old American tradition. In their book *Networking*, Jessica Lipnack and Jeffrey Stamps describe these committees as

> a communications forum where homespun political and economic thinkers hammered out their ideological differences, sculpting the form of a separate and independent country in North America. Writing to one another and sharing letters with neighbors, this revolutionary generation nurtured its adolescent ideas into a mature politics. Both men and women participated in the debate over independence from England and the desirable shape of the American future. . . .

> During the years in which the American Revolution was percolating, letters, news-sheets, and pamphlets carried from one village to another were the means by which ideas about democracy were refined. Eventually, the correspondents agreed that the next step in their idea exchange was to hold a face-to-face meeting. The ideas of independence and government had been debated, discussed, discarded, and reformulated literally hundreds of times by the time people in the revolutionary network met in Philadelphia.

> Thus, a network of correspondence and printed broadsides led to the formation of an organization after the writers met in a series of conferences and worked out a statement of purpose—which they called a "Declaration of Independence." Little did our early networking grandparents realize that the result of their youthful idealism, less than two centuries later, would be a global superpower with an unparalleled ability to influence the survival of life on the planet.

As the United States grew and technology changed, the ways in which these public discussions of "matters of general interest," as Habermas called them—slavery and the rights of the states versus the power of the federal government were two such matters that loomed large—began to change as well. The text-based media that served as the channel for discourse gained more and more power to reshape the nature of that discourse. The communications media of the nineteenth century were the newspapers, the penny press, the first generation of what has come to be known as the mass media. At the same time, the birth of advertising and the beginnings of the public-relations industry began to undermine the public sphere by inventing a kind of buyable and sellable phony discourse that displaced the genuine kind.

The simulation (and therefore destruction) of authentic discourse, first in the United States, and then spreading to the rest of the world, is what Guy Debord would call the first quantum leap into the "society of the spectacle" and what Jean Baudrillard would recognize as a milestone in the world's slide into hyper-reality. Mass media's colonization of civil society turned into a quasi-political campaign promoting technology itself when the image-making technology of television came along. ("Progress is our most important product," said General Electric spokesman Ronald Reagan, in the early years of television.) And in the twentieth century, as the telephone, radio, and television became vehicles for public discourse, the nature of political discussion has mutated into something quite different from anything the framers of the Constitution could have foreseen.

A politician is now a commodity, citizens are consumers, and issues are decided via sound-bites and staged events. The television camera is the only spectator that counts at a political demonstration or convention. According to Habermas and others, the way the new media have been commoditized through this evolutionary process from hand-printed broadside to telegraph to penny press to mass media has led to the radical deterioration of the public sphere. The consumer society has become the accepted model both for individual behavior and political decision making. Discourse degenerated into publicity, and publicity used the increasing power of electronic media to alter perceptions and shape beliefs.

The consumer society, the most powerful vehicle for generating short-term wealth ever invented, ensures economic growth by first promoting the idea that the way to be is to buy. The engines of wealth depend on a fresh stream of tabloids sold at convenience markets and television programs to tell us what we have to buy next in order to justify our existence. What used to be a channel for authentic communication has become a channel for the updating of commercial desire.

Money plus politics plus network television equals an effective system. It works. When the same packaging skills that were honed on automobile tail fins and fast foods are applied to political ideas, the highest bidder can influence public policy to great effect. What dies in the process is the rational discourse at the base of civil society. That death manifests itself in longings that aren't fulfilled by the right kind of shoes in this month's color or the hot new prime time candidate everybody is talking about. Some media scholars are claiming a direct causal connection between the success of commercial television and the loss of citizen interest in the political process.

Another media critic, Neal Postman, in his book *Amusing Ourselves to Death*, pointed out that Tom Paine's *Common Sense* sold three hundred thousand copies in five months in 1776. The most successful democratic revolution in history was made possible by a citizenry that read and debated widely among themselves. Postman pointed out that the mass media, and television in particular, had changed the mode of discourse itself, by substituting fast cuts, special effects, and sound-bites for reasoned discussion or even genuine argument.

The various hypotheses about commodification and mode of discourse focus on an area of apparent agreement among social observers who have a long history of heated disagreements.

When people who have become fascinated by BBSs or networks start spreading the idea that such networks are inherently democratic in some magical way, without specifying the hard work that must be done in real life to harvest the fruits of that democratizing power, they run the danger of becoming unwitting agents of commodification. First, it pays to understand how old the idea really is. Next, it is important to realize that the hopes of technophiles have often been used to sell technology for commercial gain. In this sense, CMC enthusiasts run the risk of becoming unpaid, unwitting advertisers for those who stand to gain financially from adoption of new technology.

The critics of the idea of electronic democracy have unearthed examples from a long tradition of utopian rhetoric that James Carey has called "the rhetoric of the 'technological sublime.'" He put it this way:

> Despite the manifest failure of technology to resolve pressing social issues over the last century, contemporary intellectuals continue to see revolutionary potential in the latest technological gadgets that are pictured as a force outside history and politics. . . . In modern futurism, it is the machines that possess teleological insight. Despite the shortcomings of town meetings, newspaper, telegraph, wireless, and television to create the conditions of a new Athens, contemporary advocates of technological liberation regularly describe a new postmortem age of instantaneous daily plebiscitary democracy through a computerized system of electronic voting and opinion polling.

Carey was prophetic in at least one regard—he wrote this years before Ross Perot and William Clinton both started talking about their versions of electronic democracy during the 1992 U.S. presidential campaign. If the United States is on the road to a version of electronic democracy in which the president will have electronic town hall meetings, including instant voting-by-telephone to "go directly to the people" (and perhaps bypass Congress?) on key issues, it is important for American citizens to understand the potential pitfalls of decision making by plebiscite. Media-manipulated plebiscites as political tools go back to Joseph Goebbels, who used radio so effectively in the Third Reich. Previous experiments in instant home polling and voting had been carried out by Warners, with their Qube service, in the early 1980s. One critic, political scientist Jean Bethke Elshtain, called the television-voting model an

> interactive shell game [that] cons us into believing that we are participating when we are really simply performing as the responding "end" of a prefabricated system of external stimuli. . . . In a plebiscitary system, the views of the majority . . . swamp minority or unpopular views. Plebiscitism is compatible with

authoritarian politics carried out under the guise of, or with the connivance of, majority views. That opinion can be registered by easily manipulated, ritualistic plebiscites, so there is no need for debate on substantive questions.

What does it mean that the same hopes, described in the same words, for a decentralization of power, a deeper and more widespread citizen involvement in matters of state, a great equalizer for ordinary citizens to counter the forces of central control, have been voiced in the popular press for two centuries in reference to steam, electricity, and television? We've had enough time to live with steam, electricity, and television to recognize that they did indeed change the world, and to recognize that the utopia of technological millenarians has not yet materialized.

An entire worldview and sales job are packed into the word *progress*, which links the notion of improvement with the notion of innovation, highlights the benefits of innovation while hiding the toxic side-effects of extractive and lucrative technologies, and then sells more of it to people via television as a cure for the stress of living in a technology-dominated world. The hope that the next technology will solve the problems created by the way the last technology was used is a kind of millennial, even messianic, hope, apparently ever-latent in the breasts of the citizenry. The myth of technological progress emerged out of the same Age of Reason that gave us the myth of representative democracy, a new organizing vision that still works pretty well, despite the decline in vigor of the old democratic institutions. It's hard to give up on one Enlightenment ideal while clinging to another.

I believe it is too early to judge which set of claims will prove to be accurate. I also believe that those who would prefer the more democratic vision of the future have an opportunity to influence the outcome, which is precisely why online activists should delve into the criticisms that have been leveled against them. If electronic democracy advocates can address these critiques successfully, their claims might have a chance. If they cannot, perhaps it would be better not to raise people's hopes. Those who are not aware of the history of dead ends are doomed to replay them, hopes high, again and again.

The idea that putting powerful computers in the hands of citizens will shield the citizenry against totalitarian authorities echoes similar, older beliefs about citizen-empowering technology. As Langdon Winner (an author every computer revolutionary ought to read) put it in his essay "Mythinformation,"

> Of all the computer enthusiasts' political ideas, there is none more poignant than the faith that the computer is destined to become a potent equalizer in modern society. . . . Presumably, ordinary citizens equipped with micro-computers will be able to counter the influence of large, computer-based organizations.

Notions of this kind echo beliefs of eighteenth-century revolutionaries that placing fire arms in the hands of the people was crucial to overthrowing entrenched authority. In the American Revolution, French Revolution, Paris Commune, and Russian Revolution the role of "the people armed" was central to the revolutionary program. As the military defeat of the Paris Commune made clear, however, the fact that the popular forces have guns may not be decisive.

In a contest of force against force, the larger, more sophisticated, more ruthless, better equipped competitor often has the upper hand. Hence, the availability of low-cost computing power may move the baseline that defines electronic dimensions of social influence, but it does not necessarily alter the relative balance of power. Using a personal computer makes one no more powerful vis-à-vis, say, the National Security Agency than flying a hang glider establishes a person as a match for the U.S. Air Force.

The great power of the idea of electronic democracy is that technical trends in communications technologies can help citizens break the monopoly on their attention that has been enjoyed by the powers behind the broadcast paradigm—the owners of television networks, newspaper syndicates, and publishing conglomerates. The great weakness of the idea of electronic democracy is that it can be more easily commodified than explained. . . .

What should those of us who believe in the democratizing potential of virtual communities do about the technological critics? I believe we should invite them to the table and help them see the flaws in our dreams, the bugs in our designs. I believe we should study what the historians and social scientists have to say about the illusions and power shifts that accompanied the diffusion of previous technologies. CMC and technology in general [have] real limits; it's best to continue to listen to those who understand the limits, even as we continue to explore the technologies' positive capabilities. Failing to fall under the spell of the "rhetoric of the logical sublime," actively questioning and examining social assumptions about the effects of new technologies, [and] reminding ourselves that electronic communication has powerful illusory capabilities are all good steps to take to prevent disasters.

If electronic democracy is to succeed, however, in the face of all the obstacles, activists must do more than avoid mistakes. Those who would use computer networks as political tools must go forward and actively apply their theories to more and different kinds of communities. If there is a last good hope, a bulwark against the hyperreality of Baudrillard or Forster, it will come from a new way of looking at technology. Instead of falling under the spell of a sales pitch, or rejecting new technologies as instruments of illusion, we need to look closely at new technologies and ask how they can help build stronger, more humane communities—and ask how they might be obstacles to that goal. The late 1990s may eventually be seen in retrospect as a narrow window of historical opportunity, when people either acted or failed to act effectively to regain control over communications technologies. Armed with knowledge, guided by a clear, human-centered vision, governed by a commitment to civil discourse, we the citizens hold the key levers at a pivotal time. What happens next is largely up to us.

REFLECTING AND DISCUSSING

1. Rheingold believes in "the democratizing potential of virtual communities." Given this text and your own observations, is the Internet a valuable forum for democracy? Why or why not?

2. How has technology evolved since this essay was published in 1994? What changes have occurred? Have they been for good—or ill?
3. Which of Rheingold's arguments are attributed to Jurgen Habermas? How would you critique Rheingold's use of Habermas's work to make his points about authenticity and open access?

CONNECTING AND WRITING

1. Does the invention of new technologies such as the smartphone and the tablet and social media opportunities such as Facebook, Instagram, Snapchat, and others refute or support Rheingold's contention that there is a risk of a "direct assault on personal liberty" and the "erosion of old social values"? (And what are these old social values?) Write an essay in which you argue a point of view on this issue.
2. Reread Rheingold's final paragraph, in which he states that "we the citizens hold the key levers at a pivotal time." Remember that this piece was published in 1994. How might you argue that we still live in a pivotal time when it comes to the intersection of politics and technology? Use Rheingold's article and other credible sources to argue your point of view.

QUESTION

Overall, what is being proposed by the pieces in this section? "Civil Disobedience" is serious in tone, while the other selections in this section use a very different tone. Compare Thoreau's essay to one of this chapter's satiric pieces, and analyze the ways in which these works' purpose, tone, language (or image), and audience make their propositions effective.

This chapter essentially presents a "mixed bag" of essays and speeches that, whether contemporary or not, touch on issues that trouble or define us.

The Paranoid Style of American Policing

Ta-Nehisi Coates (1975–   )

MacArthur Genius Grant recipient (2013) and prolific author Ta-Nehisi Coates has produced work ranging from political journalism to the Black Panther series of comics for Marvel. Born and raised in Baltimore, he attended Howard University in Washington, D.C., and first worked as a reporter for the Washington City Paper, *an alternative newspaper in Washington. He has published a memoir,* The Beautiful Struggle: A Father, Two Sons, and an Unlikely Road to Manhood *(2008), followed by* Between the World and Me *(2015), which won the National Book Award for Non Fiction. The following essay appeared in the* Atlantic *in 2015.*

When I was around 10 years old, my father confronted a young man who was said to be "crazy." The young man was always too quick to want to fight. A foul in a game of 21 was an insult to his honor. A cross word was cause for a duel, and you never knew what that cross word might be. One day, the young man got into it with one of my older brother's friends. The young man pulled a metal stake out of the ground (there was some work being done nearby) and began swinging it wildly in a threatening manner. My father, my mother, or my older brother—I don't recall which—told the other boy to go inside of our house. My dad then came outside. I don't really remember what my father said to the young man. Perhaps he said something like "Go home," or maybe something like, "Son, it's over." I don't really recall. But what I do recall is that my dad did not shoot and kill the young man.

That wasn't the first time I'd seen my father confront the violence of young people without resorting to killing them. This was not remarkable. When you live in communities like ours—or perhaps any community—mediating violence between young people is part of being an adult. Sometimes the young people are involved in scary behavior—like threatening people with metal objects. And yet the notion that it is permissible, wise, moral, or advisable to kill such a person as a method of de-escalation, to kill because one was afraid, did not really exist among parents in my community.

The same could not be said for those who came from outside of the community.

This weekend, after a Chicago police officer killed her 19-year-old son Quintonio LeGrier, Janet Cooksey struggled to understand the mentality of the people she pays to keep her community safe:

"What happened to Tasers? Seven times my son was shot," Cooksey said.

"The police are supposed to serve and protect us and yet they take the lives," Cooksey said.

"Where do we get our help?" she asked.

LeGrier had struggled with mental illness. When LeGrier attempted to break down his father's door, his father called the police, who apparently arrived to find the 19-year-old wielding a bat. Interpreting this as a lethal threat, one of the officers shot and killed LeGrier and somehow managed to shoot and kill one of his neighbors, Bettie Jones. Cooksey did not merely have a problem with how the police acted, but with the fact that the police were even called in the first place. "He should have called me," Cooksey said of LeGrier's father.

Instead, the father called the Chicago Police Department. Likely he called them because he invested them with some measure of legitimacy. This is understandable. In America, police officers are agents of the state and thus bound by the social contract in a way that criminals, and even random citizens, are not. Criminals and random citizens are not paid to protect other citizens. Police officers are. By that logic, one might surmise that the police would be better able to mediate conflicts than community members. In Chicago, this appears, very often, not to be the case.

It will not do to note that 99 percent of the time the police mediate conflicts without killing people anymore than it will do for a restaurant to note that 99 percent of the time rats don't run through the dining room. Nor will it do to point out that most black citizens are killed by other black citizens, not police officers, anymore than it will do to point out that most American citizens are killed by other American citizens, not terrorists. If officers cannot be expected to act any better than ordinary citizens, why call them in the first place? Why invest them with any more power?

In America, we have decided that it is permissible, that it is wise, that it is moral for the police to de-escalate through killing.

Legitimacy is what is ultimately at stake here. When Cooksey says that her son's father should not have called the police, when she says that they "are supposed to serve and protect us and yet they take the lives," she is saying that police in Chicago are police in name only. This opinion is widely shared. Asked about the possibility of an investigation, Melvin Jones, the brother of Bettie Jones, could muster no confidence. "I already know how that will turn out," he scoffed. "We all know how that will turn out."

Indeed, we probably do. Two days after Jones and LeGrier were killed, a district attorney in Ohio declined to prosecute the two officers who drove up, and within two seconds of arriving, killed the 12-year-old Tamir Rice. No one should be surprised by this. In America, we have decided that it is permissible, that it is wise, that it is moral for the police to de-escalate through killing. A standard which would not have held for my father in West Baltimore, which did not hold for me in Harlem, is reserved for those who have the maximum power—the right to kill on behalf of the state. When police cannot adhere to the standards of the neighborhood, of citizens, or of parents, what are they beyond a bigger gun and a sharper sword? By what right do they enforce their will, save force itself?

When policing is delegitimized, when it becomes an occupying force, the community suffers. The neighbor-on-neighbor violence in Chicago, and in black communities around the country, is not an optical illusion. Policing is (one) part of the solution to that violence. But if citizens don't trust officers, then policing can't actually work. And in Chicago, it is very hard to muster reasons for trust.

When Bettie Jones's brother displays zero confidence in an investigation into the killing of his sister, he is not being cynical. He is shrewdly observing a government that executed a young man and sought to hide that fact from citizens. He is intelligently assessing a local government which, for two decades, ran a torture ring. What we have made of our police departments in America, what we have ordered them to do, is a direct challenge to any usable definition of democracy. A state that allows its agents to kill, to beat, to tase, without any real sanction, has ceased to govern and has commenced to simply rule.

REFLECTING AND DISCUSSING

1. What is Coates's central argument? How does he make this argument? Is it effective? Why or why not?
2. "In America, we have decided that it is permissible, that it is wise, that it is moral for the police to de-escalate through killing." Why do you think that Coates uses so forceful a statement? How do you respond to this quote? What are the reasons for your response?
3. How does Coates move between personal narrative and political commentary? What is the effect of this rhetorical strategy?

CONNECTING AND WRITING

1. Coates's essay asserts that instances of police brutality have increased in recent years. There are many perspectives on this argument, which has been frequently debated in the media. Research other credible sources as a way to expand the conversation and to argue your own point of view. For instance, has police brutality increased—or is it just being reported more frequently than before? Is this a longstanding issue or something new? Again, be sure to back up your arguments.

2. How does Coates delineate the relationship between the community and the police force, both as it exists now and as he feels it should exist? How would you articulate Coates's overall point about the community and the police? Use examples from the essay to back up your sense of this argument.

Baby Boomers are Taking on Ageism—and Losing

Lydia DePillis (1987–   )

Lydia DePillis was born in Seattle and later attended Columbia University in New York City. She became a well-known blogger while in college and now writes for the Houston Chronicle. *DePillis previously wrote for the* Washington Post, *in which this article appeared in 2016, and the* New Republic.

By and large, Dale Kleber had a pretty straightforward trip up the economic ladder. He went to law school and worked his way up to general counsel of a major food distributor in Chicago and then chief executive of a dairy trade organization. He is putting his third and fourth kids through private college.

"Our generation was pretty spoiled," says Kleber, 60. "We had it good. The economy was in a huge growth spurt. Some dips here and there, but nothing severe."

But a couple of years ago, Kleber hit a roadblock. He'd left the dairy group and started looking for another job; he and his wife didn't have quite enough saved to retire comfortably. He didn't think he'd have trouble finding work.

Scores of applications later, with few callbacks and no offers, Kleber is close to admitting defeat—and admitting that age discrimination might be one of the biggest challenges his generation has faced.

One job posting, from a medical device company called CareFusion, seemed to suggest Kleber's lack of success wasn't just due to a tough job market: The ad called for a maximum of seven years of legal experience. He applied anyway and, after being passed over, filed a complaint with the Equal Employment Opportunity Commission alleging age discrimination. The case is in the discovery phase in federal court in Illinois.

"They expressed concerns with an older person being less likely to take supervision from someone that's younger than they are," Kleber says, paraphrasing the company's response to his suit. "If I felt like I was going to be dissatisfied in the position, I wouldn't be pursuing it."

That disagreement goes to the heart of the awkwardness that baby boomers are now feeling as they enter the last years of their working lives. Often needing to stay in jobs longer than they anticipated to shore up savings depleted during the Great Recession, or simply wanting to remain active further into their lengthening life spans, they're coming up against a strong preference in America for youthful "energy" and "innovation."

That bias is so common we frequently don't recognize it. Todd Nelson, a psychology professor at California State University at Stanislaus, has singled out birthday cards for portraying advancing age as something to be ashamed of, with a tone that would never be used with race or religion. ("'Ha-ha-ha, too bad you're Jewish' . . . wouldn't go over so well," he noted.)

Internet memes like the "Scumbag Baby Boomer" and "Old Economy Steve," which lambast boomers for transgressions from failing to adopt technology to causing the wars and recessions that millennials have weathered, channel resentment against an entire category of people in ways that might not be tolerated if they were members of another protected class.

The whiteness and maleness of Silicon Valley and the tech industry have been the subject of numerous magazine cover stories, but with rare exceptions such as Dan Lyons's hilarious 2016 memoir about being a 50-something at a Cambridge, Mass., start-up, its youth passes without comment.

This cultural backdrop has horrifyingly real consequences for many on the wrong side of 40. Formal age discrimination cases like Kleber's spiked during the most recent recession and haven't fully subsided. Long-term unemployment, defined as being jobless for 27 weeks or longer, is markedly worse for workers over age 55 than for the general population.

In contrast to the respect often accorded to the generation that fought World War II, their progeny are facing relative hostility in their senescence.

At a time when conditions have vastly improved for women, gay people, disabled people and minorities in the workplace, prejudice against older workers remains among the most acceptable and pervasive "isms." And it's not clear that the next generations—ascendant Gen Xers and millennials—will be treated any better.

Ageism, of course, is as old as age itself. Even while venerating elders for their wisdom, cultures across the world have disparaged the weakness and unattractiveness of those past the bloom of youth. "Senectus morbidus est," wrote Roman philosopher Seneca in the 1st century A.D.: "Old age is a disease."

In modern times, there are more formal protections: The advent of Social Security in the 1930s ensured older people wouldn't be entirely penniless when they could no longer work. The Age Discrimination in Employment Act of 1967 ended some of the most egregious forms of prejudice, such as age limits for flight attendants and mandatory retirement ages for factory and mine workers.

At the same time, structural, economic and demographic changes have created new types of ageism that are more subtle and widespread.

One change is the presence of two large, culturally distinct generations— millennials and boomers, both about 75 million strong—that have found themselves in the workforce with less and less formal authority.

Older workers have the misfortune of wanting to work longer just as a new generation is trying to get an economic foothold. In a weak economy, companies are sometimes all too happy to dump veteran employees, with their higher health-care costs and legacy pensions, for younger ones who expect neither.

(And this isn't just an American thing: Faster-aging societies with low birthrates in Asia and Europe face an even larger demographic "bulge" of older citizens who will have to be supported by fewer wage earners, feeding into an image of the elderly as a drain on society. A 2013 meta-analysis found East Asian countries had even more negative attitudes toward their older populations than some Western ones—grimly punctuated by climbing suicide rates in China, South Korea and Taiwan.)

All of that underpins tensions in the workplace and has spawned a cottage industry of consultants who specialize in intergenerational relations.

In a 2015 survey by the Harris Poll, for example, 65 percent of boomers rated themselves as being the "best problem-solvers/troubleshooters," and only 5 percent of millennials agreed. Fifty-four percent of millennials thought boomers were the "biggest roadblocks." Sometimes these perceptions come straight from the top: Facebook founder Mark Zuckerberg once said "young people are just smarter."

Those attitudes apply not just to perceptions of "old" people, but also to expectations: A 2013 experiment found that young people looked more favorably upon older adults who "act their age" by listening to Frank Sinatra over the Black Eyed Peas, or by being more generous with their money. One of the researchers, Michael North, an assistant professor at New York University's Stern School of Business, says younger people tend to resent it when older workers don't "get out of the way" and retire.

Yet human resource consultants and the media have often placed the onus on older workers to overcome these biases, which surface in job postings for "recent college graduates," applicants who "enjoy the pressures of the job" and those who can "fit in with a young team." Over-50 job seekers are advised to update their wardrobes and hairstyles, purge their résumés of positions held during the Reagan administration and, above all, "show enthusiasm." Projecting "energy" is another common tip, as if lethargy kicks in only after 40.

And what of the legal protections for older workers? Federal anti-age-discrimination laws haven't proved to be an effective deterrent, says University of Houston professor emeritus Andrew Achenbaum. Proving you were passed over because of your age is devilishly difficult, and the EEOC has a large backlog of complaints that it hasn't had the resources to deal with.

"I wouldn't mess around with [gender bias] if I were a university," Achenbaum says. "But I'm willing to take my chances on age discrimination, because there are so many [cases] that are unsolved."

Efforts to battle ageism have cropped up now and then, but they can be stymied by the sheer force and fluidity of culture.

Margery Leveen Sher, 68, a former corporate consultant and nonprofit executive in the District, says she internalized the unspoken code of ageism long ago and was for many years a "closeted old person." "I thought, Nobody is going to want to work with me to start up a nonprofit because they will think I will want to retire shortly," she says. She never lied about her age; she just didn't mention it. And "thanks to good genes, good health and a wad of money thrown regularly at my hair salon," she could easily pass for a decade younger. Sher says only since she retired and started her own business, the Did Ya Notice? Project, writing and speaking about the importance of mindfulness, has she felt ready to "come out." "I am not a trailblazing anti-ageism fighter. I have been a closeted coward," she says. "But here goes: I am 68. I am full of energy and ideas, and I ain't done yet."

Multiply that sentiment by 74.9 million and maybe something will finally give. Ashton Applewhite, creator of the blog *Yo, Is This Ageist?*, says the size of the boomer generation should be an advantage when shifting the discourse around aging.

"Silicon Valley is finally getting some attention, and you know why? Educated, skilled, non-disabled white guys faced discrimination for the first time in their lives," Applewhite says. "Baby boomers are starting to realize that we are actually going to have to get old. So there is this sudden awareness—we have an unusual sense of demographic weight."

Nobody knows this better than AARP, which has appropriated the language of Silicon Valley in its "Disrupt Aging" campaign. It takes aim at common stereotypes and features stories about older people living unconventional lives, like a 55-year-old YouTube entrepreneur and a 64-year-old record-breaking long-distance swimmer.

But Applewhite thinks it's more important to examine the source of ageist attitudes. "They come from corporate interests that want to medicalize aging so they can sell you s— to cure it, or they want to treat it as a problem so they can sell you s— to fix it," she says. "Capitalism is a problem."

Capitalism has to be part of the solution too, says North, of the Stern School of Business. He contends successful companies will find ways to accommodate the needs of people nearing the end of their working lives, such as part-time schedules to help them transition rather than drop out. "Companies really should be taking stock of these demographic trends," North says. "There's tremendous value to be had there, and most companies aren't doing that."

For his part, Dale Kleber thinks he's a better hire than he was 20 years ago, when he was in the middle of raising kids and climbing the corporate ladder. He's had time to keep up on professional reading and stay in better shape. "I think the stereotypes [about older workers] are a little misleading, because the reverse might be true," Kleber says. "I've got a good 15 years in me at least."

REFLECTING AND DISCUSSING

1. What is ageism? Why is awareness of it important?
2. DePillis's article centers on baby boomers. Who are they, and why are they the focus of this particular article and conversation?
3. DePillis writes, "At a time when conditions have vastly improved for women, gay people, disabled people and minorities in the workplace, prejudice against older workers remains among the most acceptable and pervasive 'isms.'" What examples of this prejudice does DePillis provide? Are you surprised by them? Why or why not?
4. How is ironic that DePillis writes about ageism—and yet has managed to make it difficult to find her own birth year on the Internet? Is this obscuring of her age perhaps consistent with the point of the article? How so?

CONNECTING AND WRITING

1. This article focuses primarily on the tech industry. Find other articles about the problems faced by older workers (defined as those over forty years of age!) in job hunting. What other industries are implicated in these problems? How does age-related prejudice correlate with increased attention to gender and other forms of discrimination? How bad does this problem seem to be?

2. DePillis references the Age Discrimination in Employment Act of 1967 as one of the formal protections against this type of discrimination. Research the act itself. Using that as context, explain why age discrimination is so difficult to detect and fight.

Islam in Two Americas

Ross Douthat (1979–   )

A graduate of Harvard University, Ross Douthat is an essayist, blogger, and regular contributor to the *New York Times. Prior to joining the* Times, *he was a senior editor for the* Atlantic. *Douthat has published several books, including* Privilege: Harvard and the Education of the Ruling Class *(2005),* Grand New Party: How Republicans Can Win the Working Class and Save the American Dream *(2009), and* To Change the Church: Pope Francis and the Future of Catholicism *(2018). This essay appeared in 2010 in the* New York Times.

There's an America where it doesn't matter what language you speak, what god you worship, or how deep your New World roots run. An America where allegiance to the Constitution trumps ethnic differences, language barriers and religious divides. An America where the newest arrival to our shores is no less American than the ever-so- great granddaughter of the Pilgrims.

But there's another America as well, one that understands itself as a distinctive culture, rather than just a set of political propositions. This America speaks English, not Spanish or Chinese or Arabic. It looks back to a particular religious heritage: Protestantism originally, and then a Judeo-Christian consensus that accommodated Jews and Catholics as well. It draws its social norms from the mores of the Anglo-Saxon diaspora—and it expects new arrivals to assimilate themselves to these norms, and quickly.

These two understandings of America, one constitutional and one cultural, have been in tension throughout our history. And they're in tension again this summer, in the controversy over the Islamic mosque and cultural center scheduled to go up two blocks from ground zero.

The first America, not surprisingly, views the project as the consummate expression of our nation's high ideals. "This is America," President Obama intoned last week, "and our commitment to religious freedom must be unshakeable." The construction of the mosque, Mayor Michael Bloomberg told New Yorkers, is as important a test of the principle of religious freedom "as we may see in our lifetimes."

The second America begs to differ. It sees the project as an affront to the memory of 9/11, and a sign of disrespect for the values of a country where Islam has only recently become part of the public consciousness. And beneath these concerns lurks the darker suspicion that Islam in any form may be incompatible with the American way of life.

This is typical of how these debates usually play out. The first America tends to make the finer-sounding speeches, and the second America often strikes cruder, more xenophobic notes. The first America welcomed the poor, the tired, the huddled masses; the second America demanded that they change their names and drop their native languages, and often threw up hurdles to stop them coming altogether. The first America celebrated religious liberty; the second America persecuted Mormons and discriminated against Catholics.

But both understandings of this country have real wisdom to offer, and both have been necessary to the American experiment's success. During the great waves of 19th-century immigration, the insistence that new arrivals adapt to Anglo-Saxon culture—and the threat of discrimination if they didn't—was crucial to their swift assimilation. The post-1920s immigration restrictions were draconian in many ways, but they created time for persistent ethnic divisions to melt into a general unhyphenated Americanism.

The same was true in religion. The steady pressure to conform to American norms, exerted through fair means and foul, eventually persuaded the Mormons to abandon polygamy, smoothing their assimilation into the American mainstream. Nativist concerns about Catholicism's illiberal tendencies inspired American Catholics to prod their church toward a recognition of the virtues of democracy, making it possible for generations of immigrants to feel unambiguously Catholic and American.

So it is today with Islam. The first America is correct to insist on Muslims' absolute right to build and worship where they wish. But the second America is right to press for something more from Muslim Americans—particularly from figures like Feisal Abdul Rauf, the imam behind the mosque—than simple protestations of good faith.

Too often, American Muslim institutions have turned out to be entangled with ideas and groups that most Americans rightly consider beyond the pale. Too often, American Muslim leaders strike ambiguous notes when asked to disassociate themselves completely from illiberal causes.

By global standards, Rauf may be the model of a "moderate Muslim." But global standards and American standards are different. For Muslim Americans to integrate fully into our national life, they'll need leaders who don't describe America as "an accessory to the crime" of 9/11 (as Rauf did shortly after the 2001 attacks), or duck questions about whether groups like Hamas count as terrorist organizations (as Rauf did in a radio interview in June). And they'll need leaders whose antennas are sensitive enough to recognize that the quest for inter-religious dialogue is ill served by throwing up a high-profile mosque two blocks from the site of a mass murder committed in the name of Islam.

They'll need leaders, in other words, who understand that while the ideals of the first America protect the e pluribus, it's the demands the second America makes of new arrivals that help create the unum.

REFLECTING AND DISCUSSING

1. As the article's title indicates, and as Douthat explains in its first two paragraphs, there are two Americas. What are the two Americas he describes, and how does he distinguish between them?
2. How effective is Douthat's argument? How does he make this argument? What are the reasons for your perspective?
3. While the article is critical of these two Americas, Douthat suggests that they also serve a purpose, and that each has "real wisdom to offer." How does he argue that both Americas have been integral to the success of our country? Is this a good thing? Why or why not?

CONNECTING AND WRITING

1. Douthat writes, "These two understandings of America, one constitutional and one cultural, have been in tension throughout our history." Do some historical research and consider the ways in which these two Americas have been defined at other times. For instance, Michael Harrington's book *The Other America* (1962) articulates the divide between the haves and the have-nots. How does Harringon's argument compare to Douthat's? Alternatively, how have others articulated or described "two Americas"? Choose one such portrayal and compare and contrast its perspective with Douthat's.
2. Douthat articulates the contrasts in America's receptiveness to a variety of religious traditions. What is his argument, and what examples does he use to make it? What conclusions does he draw about religious conformity?

The Charmer

Henry Louis Gates, Jr. (1950–   )

Henry Louis Gates, Jr., is both a public intellectual and a prominent scholar of African American literature. He is also credited with locating, authenticating, and publishing the first known novel by an African American: Our Nig, *by Harriet Wilson (1859). In 1999, Gates wrote and hosted a public television series on Africa called* Wonders of the African World. *A professor at Harvard University and director of its Hutchins Center for African and African-American Research, Gates has also hosted a series about genetic heritage and "finding one's roots" entitled* Who Do You Think You Are? *The following rather editorial piece—commenting on a personality very much in the news at the time—originally appeared in the* New Yorker *in 1996.*

The drive to Louis Farrakhan's house, on South Woodlawn Avenue, took me through the heart of black Chicago—past campaign billboards for a hot city-council race, past signs for Harold the Fried Chicken King and Tony's Vienna Beef

Hotdogs. Much of the area is flecked with housing projects and abandoned lots, but when you turn the corner at Woodlawn and Forty-ninth Street things abruptly look different. You can see why the late Elijah Muhammad, who led the Nation of Islam—the Black Muslims—for almost four decades, built his house in this little pocket of opulence. It's a street of large brick houses, enshrining the vision of black-bourgeois respectability, and even grandeur, that has always been at the nostalgic heart of the Nation of Islam's creed. The neighborhood, known as South Kenwood, is integrated and professional. In 1985, Farrakhan bought Elijah Muhammad's house—a yellow-brick neo-Mediterranean structure—and he has lived there ever since; the creed and the neighborhood remain intact.

It was a warm spring morning the week after Easter, 1996, and everything was peaceful, quiet, orderly, which somehow made matters all the more unsettling. I wasn't expecting the Death Star, exactly, but I wouldn't have been surprised to see a formidable security detail: the Fruit of Islam patrolling the roof and gates with automatic weapons; perhaps a few attack dogs roaming the grounds. In fact, the only security measure in evidence was a rather elegant wrought-iron fence. After I spent a minute or so fumbling around, trying to find a hinge, a baby-faced young man with close-cropped hair and gleaming black combat boots came over and flicked the gate open. Together, we walked up a short, curved driveway, past two marble lions flanking the front door, and into the house that Elijah Muhammad built.

People in the Nation of Islam refer to the house as the Palace, and it does have an undeniable, vaguely Orientalist splendor. There is a large center hall, two stories high, filled with well-tended tropical plants, some reaching up between ten and twenty feet. Sunlight floods in from a huge dome of leaded glass; at its center, Arabic characters spell out "Allahu Akbar," or "God Is Great." To the right is a large and vibrant triptych: the Nation's founder, Wallace D. Fard; his prophet, Elijah Muhammad (with a set of gold keys in his hands); and Elijah's successor as the head of the Nation, a very youthful-looking Louis Farrakhan. The walls are spanking white, the floors are tiled in white and gray marble. A C-shaped sofa is upholstered in white fabric and covered with clear vinyl—the same stuff my mother put on to protect *her* good furniture, back in Piedmont, West Virginia.

Farrakhan's wife, Khadijah, came down to check on me, and to make sure everything was tidy now that company had arrived. Khadijah Farrakhan has a soft brown face and a warm smile. I had a bad cold that day, and she offered me some advice on how to unblock my ears, which still hadn't recovered from the flight to Chicago. "Open your mouth wide, and shift your jaw from side to side," she said, helpfully demonstrating the motion. We stood facing each other, our mouths contorted like those of a pair of groupers.

That is about when America's great black Satan himself came gliding into the room. Farrakhan was resplendent in a three-button suit of chocolate-brown silk, a brown-and-beige bow tie, and a matching pocket square. Only then did I notice that my own trousers did not match my suit jacket. Moments later, I referred to his wife as "Mrs. Muhammad," and there was a glint of amusement in his eyes. The truth is, I was having a bad case of nerves that morning. For good reason. After I criticized Farrakhan in print three years ago, a few of his more impetuous followers had shared with me their fervent hope for my death. Now that I was face to face with Farrakhan, I did feel, in fact, pretty deathly. "I'm a wounded warrior," I admitted.

Farrakhan, relaxed and gracious, made sure I was supplied with hot tea and honey. "Get the battlefield ready," he said, laughing. For the rest of a long day, we sat together at his big dining-room table, and it became clear that Farrakhan is a man of enormous intelligence, curiosity, and charm. He can also be deeply strange. It all depends on the moment and the subject. When he talks about the need for personal responsibility or of his fondness for Johnny Mathis and Frank Sinatra, he sounds as jovial and bourgeois as Bill Cosby; when he is warning of the wicked machinations of Jewish financiers, he seems as odd and obsessed as Pat Robertson.

Not long after we began talking, Farrakhan told me about an epiphany he had recently about the waning of white cultural supremacy. Farrakhan takes moments of revelation very seriously; one of his most profound occurred, he has said, while he was aboard a giant spacecraft. This particular revelation, less marvelously, took place at a Lionel Ritchie concert. There Farrakhan saw a beautiful young blond woman and her little daughter, who both clearly idolized this black performer. And when Ritchie told the mostly white crowd to raise their hands in the air almost everyone joined in. Farrakhan saw this as something not only amazing but telling.

"I see something happening in America," he said. "You go into white folks' homes, you see Michael Jackson on the wall, you see Michael Jordan on the wall, you see Hank Aaron on the wall. Their children are being influenced by black faces. And I say to myself, 'Where is this leading?' And what I see is that white supremacy is being challenged in so many subtle and overt ways, and gradually children are losing that thing about being superior."

The myths of black superiority are also going by the wayside. Someone might believe that a white cannot play the horn, he said, "then Kenny G. blows that all away." (Joe Lovano, maybe, but Kenny G.?) It used to be that white people listened to the blues but could never sing it. Now, though, "white people are experiencing that out of which the blues came," he said. "White people are suffering. Now you drive your streets and you see a white person with stringy hair sitting by the side of the road plucking his guitar, like we used to do in the South. Now *they're* into that." What people must do is "outgrow the narrowness of their own nationalistic feelings," Farrakhan declared. "When we outgrow the color thing, outgrow the race and the ethnic thing, outgrow the religious thing to see the oneness of God and the oneness of humanity, then we can begin to approach our divinity."

I scratched my head: we'd gone from Kenny G. to God in a matter of seconds; "the blue-eyed devils"—Elijah Muhammad's favorite designation for white folk—are learning the blues, and we're mightily impressed.

It turns out that there is in Farrakhan's discourse a strain that sounds awfully like liberal universalism; there is also, of course, its brutal opposite. The two tendencies, in all their forms, are constantly in tension. Pundits like to imagine that Farrakhan is a kind of radio program: the incendiary Louis Farrakhan Show. In fact, Farrakhan is more like a radio station: what you hear depends on when you tune in. His talk ranges from far-fetched conspiracy theories to Dan Quayle-like calls for family values. Farrakhan really does believe that a cabal of Jews secretly controls the world; he also suspects, I learned later in our conversation, that one of his own grandparents was a Portuguese Jew. Apologists and detractors alike feel free to decide which represents the "real" Farrakhan. The result may score debating points, but it has little to do with the man who lives at South Woodlawn and Forty-ninth Street.

Much is made of Farrakhan's capacity to strike fear into the hearts of white liberals. And it does seem that for many of them Farrakhan represents their worst nightmare: the Nat Turner figure, crying out for racial vengeance. As Adolph Reed, Jr., writes of Farrakhan, "he has become uniquely notorious because his inflammatory nationalist persona has helped to center public discussion of Afro-American politics on the only issue (except affirmative action, of course) about which most whites ever show much concern: What do blacks think of whites?"

A subject that receives far less attention is the fear that Farrakhan inspires in blacks. The truth is that blacks—across the economic and ideological spectrum— often feel astonishingly vulnerable to charges of inauthenticity, of disloyalty to the race. I know that I do, despite my vigorous efforts to deconstruct that vocabulary of reproach. Farrakhan's sway over blacks—the answering chord his rhetoric finds— attests to the enduring strength of our own feelings of guilt, our own anxieties of having been false to our people, of having sinned against our innermost identity. He denounces the fallen in our midst, invokes the wrath of heaven against us: and his outlandish vitriol occasions both terror and a curious exhilaration. . . .

The truly paranoid heart of Farrakhan's world view has been revealed in recent speeches in which he has talked about a centuries-old conspiracy of international bankers—with names like Rothschild and Warburg—who have captured control over the central banks in many countries, and who incite wars to increase the indebtedness of others and maximize their own wealth. The Federal Reserve, the I.R.S., the F.B.I., and the Anti-Defamation League were all founded in 1913, Farrakhan says (actually, the I.R.S. was founded in 1862 and the F.B.I. in 1908, but never mind), and then he poses the favorite rhetorical question of all paranoid historians: "Is that a coincidence?"

What do you do with a religious demagogue who promulgates the theory that Jewish financiers have manipulated world events for centuries? Well, if you're a Republican contender for the presidency, and the demagogue's name is Pat Robertson, you genuflect. It turns out that Farrakhan's conspiracy theory of Jewish cabals is essentially identical to Robertson's. "Rest assured, there is a behind-the-scenes Establishment in this nation, as in every other," Robertson writes in *The New World Order*, his recent best-selling book. "It has enormous power. It has controlled the economic and foreign policy objectives of the United States for the past seventy years, whether the man sitting in the White House is a Democrat or a Republican, a liberal or a conservative, a moderate or an extremist." Robertson goes on to inveigh against the tentacular Rothschilds and Warburgs. Michael Lind, who has analyzed Robertson's conspiracy theories at length, suggests that not since the days of Father Coughlin[1] has the grassroots right been as overtly anti-Semitic as it is now.

---

1 Charles Edward Coughlin (1891–1979), a Catholic priest famous for his vitriolic radio addresses in the 1930s.

And Farrakhan? He, too, believes all this conspiracy stuff, and thinks he's just telling it like it is. He must realize that such talk goes down well with inner-city audiences hungry for secret histories that explain how things went wrong. He turns mainstream criticism to his advantage, winning ovations by representing himself as the persecuted truth-teller. But turnabout isn't always fair play: and the fact that Farrakhan is a black American only makes his deafness to historical context all the more dismaying. Within his own lifetime, one of every three Jews on the face of the earth died at the hands of a regime suffused by the same language about nefarious Jewish influence. Ultimately, Farrakhan's anti-Semitism has the characteristics of a psychological obsession, and once in a while he shows signs of recognizing this. "I would prefer that this whole conflict would go away, in truth," he said to me. His voice sounded husky, and a little tired. "But it's like I'm locked now in a struggle. It's like both of us got a hold on each other, and each of us is filled with electricity. I can't let them go, and they can't let me go."

Farrakhan's peculiar mixture of insight and delusion would be a matter of mainly academic interest if it weren't for his enormous populist appeal among black Americans—an appeal that was clearly demonstrated in the 1995 Million Man March. That occasion has been widely seen as an illustration both of Farrakhan's strengths and of his weaknesses. "If only somebody else had convened it," the liberal-minded are prone to say. But nobody else—not Colin Powell, not Jesse Jackson—could have.

Some of the most heartfelt tributes to the event's success are also the most grudging. There's little doubt, after all, that the Farrakhan phenomenon owes much to a vacuum of radical black leadership. (Jesse Jackson has emerged over the past decade as the leading spokesman of the American left, one could argue, rather than of black America.) "We have the worst leadership in the black community since slavery," Eldridge Cleaver maintains. "Farrakhan saw that vacuum, saw nothing motivating the people, no vision being projected to the people, and he came up with the defining event for a generation of people, this Million Man March."

Timing had a lot to do with the event's success, of course. As Roger Wilkins likes to say, Newt Gingrich was one of the main organizers of the march. "If the white middle class feels it's losing ground, the black working class and unskilled working class are being slaughtered—hit by a blitzkrieg that no one notices," Wilkins points out. "And their plight is not on anyone's agenda anymore. Farrakhan supplies an answer, and an emotional discharge."

Farrakhan's people have won some real credibility in the black community. "It's as if Malcolm was having a march on Washington," Robert Moses, the civil-rights activist and education reformer, says. And Wilkins says, "Nobody else can go into the prisons and save souls to the degree that they have. Nobody else is able to put as many neat and clean young people on the streets of the inner city as they are. You think about the fellows who are selling their papers as opposed to those fellows you see standing around the liquor stores. Their men have this enviable sense of discipline, orderliness, and human purpose." (The Nation of Islam continues to have very conservative sexual politics, and Farrakhan is vehemently anti-abortion, but he has also inveighed against domestic violence, and—in a sharp break from tradition—even named a woman to be a Nation of Islam minister.) Hugh Price, the president of the National Urban League, calls the march "the largest family-values rally in the history of the United States." Indeed, another sign of its success was the number of mainstream civil-rights leaders who were present. Whatever their discomfort with Farrakhan's extremist rhetoric, they calculated that their absence might well imperil their legitimacy with the black public.

Attendance or nonattendance was a delicate decision. General Colin Powell was prominent among those blacks who decided that they could not afford to appear. When I asked Farrakhan if he would consider supporting a future Powell presidential bid, he said, "I don't want to support anybody because he's black—I think I have outgrown the need to support somebody because of the color of his skin. What is in the best interest of our people is really in the best interest of the country. So if General Powell had an agenda that is good for the totality of our people—the American people first—and in that package is something that can lift our people, he's got our support."

Farrakhan's level of support among black Americans is vigorously debated. If you gauge his followers by the number who regularly attend mosques affiliated with the Nation of Islam and eschew lima beans and corn bread, they are not very numerous. Estimates range from twenty thousand to ten times that. On the other hand, if you go by the number of people who consider him a legitimate voice of black protest, the ranks are much larger. (In a recent poll, more than half the blacks surveyed reported a favorable impression of him.) The march was inspired by the Muslims but not populated by them. Farrakhan knows that the men who came to the march were not his religious followers. They tended to be middle class and college-educated and Christian. Farrakhan is convinced that those men came "to a march called by a man who is considered radical, extremist, anti-Semitic, anti-white" because of a yearning "to connect with the masses."

Not everyone, to be sure, was quite so deeply impressed. "This was an opportunity for the black middle class to feel this symbolic connection, but what were the solutions that were proposed, except atonement?" Angela Davis asks. Julian Bond says bluntly, "You know, that Negro didn't even vote until 1984. He's the leader in the sense that he can gather people to him, but they don't go anyplace when they leave him." And Jesse Jackson, who addressed the marchers, now views the march as fatally flawed by its failure to reach out to Capitol Hill. "The 1963 March on Washington was connected to public policy—public accommodations," he says, and notes that the result was the signing into law of the Civil Rights Act the following year. By contrast, he argues, the Million Man March had "essentially a religious theme—atonement—disconnected from public policy," so it brought no political dividends in its aftermath. "On the very next day—the very next day, *the very next day*—there was the welfare bill," he said, referring to the House and Senate conferences to work out a final draft of a bill excusing the federal government from a degree of responsibility toward the poor. "The next day was the vote on the unfair sentence guidelines. The next day was the Medicare bill," another hostile measure. "The big debates in Congress took place between that Wednesday and Thursday. And so those who were taking away our rights and attacking us did not see any connection between the gathering and public policy." The lesson he draws is straightforward: "The march was essentially disconnected from our political leadership. Any mass action must be connected to the public-policy leaders."

Some critics express a sense that the mass mobilization may itself be a relic of a bygone era. It was an arena where Farrakhan was able to stake a claim for mass black leadership, in part because of the near-sacralization of the 1963 precursor; but its continued political viability has not been demonstrated. Indeed, the growing fragmentation of black leadership—the irrelevance of the old-fashioned notion of a "head nigger in charge"—is one sign that an elite now exists in black America that does enjoy an unmediated relation to power. Privately, many black leaders say that Farrakhan's moment has passed. Such remarks inevitably carry an air of wishful thinking. White liberal allies sometimes worry that pressure is required to keep black leaders from being "soft on Farrakhan": in reality, no love is lost among those who would compete for the hearts and souls of black America. At the helm of the mainstream black-advocacy groups are men and women who may say conciliatory things about the Nation of Islam, but their jaws are tense and their smiles are tight. They reassure themselves that Farrakhan is bound to remain a marginal phenomenon because of his extremism. Yet the organic leaders of the disenfranchised are seldom moderate in tone; and since, from all indications, the underclass is continuing to expand, Farrakhan's natural power base will only increase.

In the months following the march, Farrakhan dropped out of public view, and he spoke of having suffered from depression, in part because he was still being misrepresented by the press. This response highlights Farrakhan's paradoxical relation to the wider public—that of a pariah who wants to be embraced. "Both Malcolm and Farrakhan had a very tough ideology but at the same time wanted a degree of public acceptance in the white community," Ron Walters, a political scientist and an adviser to Jackson, says. "To me, that's a tremendous contradiction. I don't know whether it's a personality thing or just what happens to you when you reach a certain level of prominence—that you do want a sort of universal acceptance."

Such acceptance has been elusive so far. A few weeks before the Million Man March, Farrakhan gave an interview to make it clear that when he referred to Jewish "bloodsuckers" he didn't mean Jews in particular—he meant all non-black shopkeepers in the inner city, some of them Jewish but these days more often Koreans or Arabs. He must have found it galling when many newspapers wrested his remarks out of context, leaving the impression that he had merely repeated the original accusation: Farrakhan calls Jews bloodsuckers. Farrakhan's image also suffered when, early last year, the *Chicago Tribune* published an investigative series, by David Jackson and William Gaines, revealing financial disarray among Nation-owned businesses. Farrakhan's calls for economic self-sufficiency, it appeared, were not matched by his organization's performance.

Farrakhan hurt himself yet again, with his so-called World Friendship Tour, in January and February. He claims that his decision to make this trip to Third World capitals was a matter of divine inspiration, but it isn't hard to imagine human motivations as well. Public figures who feel that they have been badly used by the local papers often find that solace awaits them in admiring throngs overseas: call it the

Jerry Lewis syndrome. Besides, how better to shore up your position as the leader of black America than by being received as such by foreign potentates?

The domestic fallout, however, has lingered. Even many of those who supported Farrakhan were chagrined to find him holding friendly meetings with some of the world's worst dictators: Nigeria's Sam Abacha, Libya's Muammar Qaddafi, Zaire's Mobutu, and Sudan's Omar al-Bashir. Ron Walters observes, "He gave all those people who wanted an opportunity not to have to deal with him the golden reason. The tremendous political capital of the march had been dissipated." Black nationalists were among those who were the most horrified. Molefi Kete Asante, the Afro-centric scholar, says, "What Farrakhan did, in my judgment, was to take the legitimacy of the march and put it in his back pocket, and march around to these terrible governments, as if somehow he were the leader of a million black people. That upset me."

It is a sore subject with Farrakhan. Sure, he met with dictators, he said to me, but when you are dealing with atonement, sin, and reconciliation you don't travel to the blameless. "It's all right for Jesse to sit down with George Wallace in Alabama and for them to pray together—and there's applause," he went on. "But I can't go sit down with my brother who is a sinner? Nixon died a hero, but I cannot forgive a black man?" There was a surge of anger in his voice. "That's the damnable thing that I hate about this whole damned thing," he said. "If I go to a black man to retrieve him, all of a sudden I'm cavorting with a damned dictator, but Jesus could sit down with the sinners and you give him honor and credit. And Reagan can sit down with Gorbachev, and he gets honor and credit. He sits with the evil empire, but I can't sit with my own brother. To hell with you for that. That's why I am not a politician."

"Has the tour compromised the achievement of the march?" I asked him.

He sounded subdued when he said, "If I lost momentum, I believe it's only temporary."

Farrakhan lays much stress on the imagery of dialogue and conciliation these days. Certainly the Farrakhan I met was a model of civility and courtesy. I was reminded of Eric Lincoln's account of the last couple of visits he had paid to Farrakhan at his home: "Louis insisted on getting down on his hands and knees on the floor to take my shoes off. You know, I'm overweight and it's a difficult task to get shoes and socks off. And so Louis said, 'I will do that.' And I said, 'No, no.' And Louis said, 'No, I want to do it.' He took my shoes off and rubbed my feet to get the blood circulating."

If the Farrakhan phenomenon remains disquieting, the man himself seems oddly, jarringly vulnerable. I met someone who was eager, even hungry, for conversation; someone of great intelligence who seemed intellectually lonely. In fiery speeches before packed auditoriums, Farrakhan speaks of plots against his life, and does so in alarmingly messianic tones. ("I don't care nothing about my life," he told his audience on Saviour's Day in 1995, his voice breaking. "It's your life that I want to save!") To me he spoke of his mortality in a quieter mode. He spoke movingly of watching the funeral of Yitzhak Rabin—about the tragedy of a wise and tempered elder statesman assassinated by a callow extremist. He spoke about having a growing appreciation for compromise, about coming to see the value in the positions of his ideological antagonists within the civil-rights tradition. And he told me about a fight of his own, against prostate cancer, over the past several years.

"At first, it was frightening to me—how could I have cancer? I've eaten well, I've tried to live clean. Then I fasted and I prayed and I went into the desert, and after a month I went and had an M.R.I, and one of those rectal ultrasounds, and all they could find was a little scar." He paused, and added quietly, "But then it came back." He looks in splendid health: he is sixty-three, and his skin remains soft and almost unlined. He recently made a health-and-exercise video, which shows him going through an arduous regimen of weight-training. And he *is* remarkably fit. He has undergone seed-implantation radiation-therapy for his cancer, and remains optimistic about the results. "I've never had to take a pain pill, and I hope and pray that God will bless me ultimately to overcome it. At least, all accounts up to date, the P.S.A."—the blood-screening test for prostate cancer—"has been normal. And so I'm going on with my life, but warning all of us that this is such a hell of a killer of our people. And when you reach your early forties, many of us won't like somebody poking around in our rectum, but we have to encourage our young men and our middle-aged brothers, and the population as a whole, to do that for themselves, because all we have is our health."

We all know that the world isn't divided between saints and sinners. And yet the private Farrakhan's very humanness—those traits of kindness, concern, humor—makes his paranoia all the more disconcerting. He rails against the way the mainstream has demonized him, and yet he refuses to renounce the anti-Semitic conspiracy theories that have made him anathema: to him, it would be like denying the law of gravity. And so he is trapped, immobilized by his contradictory desires. His ongoing calls for dialogue are seemingly heartfelt; he genuinely wants a seat at the table, craves the legitimation of power. Yet he will not engage in the compromises and concessions that true dialogue requires. He cannot afford to. This is a man whose political identity is constituted by antagonism to the self-image of America. To moderate his stance of unyielding opposition would be to destroy the edifice he has spent his life constructing. Moreover, Farrakhan knows that there are people around him whose militancy puts his to shame. Some of them are former lieutenants of his in the Nation of Islam, such as Khalid Muhammad, whom Farrakhan suspended after judging him to have been *too* intemperate in his public pronouncements. Others have established an independent base of support, such as Silas Muhammad, another Elijah loyalist who split with the organization, and whose sect is now based in Atlanta. For leaders whose appeal is based on intransigence, outrage, and wrath, there is always the danger of being outflanked by those even more intransigent, more outrageous, more wrathful. This, in part, is why Farrakhan could not truly atone even at his own day of atonement.

In the end, however, it isn't Farrakhan but Farrakhan's following that demands explanation. We might start by admitting the moral authority that black nationalism commands even among those blacks who ostensibly disapprove of it. In the village where I grew up, there was a Holiness Church, where people spoke in tongues and fell down in religious ecstasy. It was not my church; my family and I shunned the Pentecostal fervor. And yet, on some level, we believed it to be the real thing, realer than our own, more temperate Episcopal services. It was the place to go if you really needed something—if you got desperately sick, say—because the Holy Ghost lived there. (There are Reform Jews who admit to a similar attitude toward their Hasidic brethren.) In this same vein, the assimilated black American, who lives in Scarsdale and drives a Lexus, responds to Farrakhan and Farrakhanism as a presence at once threatening and exhilarating, dismaying and cathartic. Though blackness isn't exactly a religion, it has become invested with a quasi-religious structure. Black nationalism is a tradition extending at least back to Martin R. Delany, in the nineteenth century. Cross it with the black messianic tradition—which spawned the legendary likes of Father Divine, Daddy Grace, and Prophet Jones—and you have the Nation of Islam.

Hard as it is to take stock of the organization's membership, it's harder to take stock of Farrakhan's place in the mind of black America. For his dominion is, in a sense, a dominion of metaphor, which is to say that it is at once factitious and factual. The political theorist Benedict Anderson has defined nations as "imagined communities," and the black nation is even more imaginary than most. We know that thirty-six million sepia Americans do not a collective make, but in our minds we sometimes insist upon it.

The Million Man March had all the hallmarks of a watershed event, yet a march is not a movement. I asked Farrakhan at one point what the country would look like if, by magic, he could turn his hopes into reality. The answer he gave me was long and meandering, but it centered on things like "revamping the educational system" to make it less Eurocentric—proposals of the sort debated by the New York State Board of Regents, rather than something that was radically transformative in any obvious way.

That was, in a sense, the most dismaying response I'd heard all day. Farrakhan is a man of visions. Just weeks before the march, he told congregants in a Washington, D.C., church about the "Mother Wheel"—a heavily armed spaceship the size of a city, which will rain destruction upon white America but save those who embrace the Nation of Islam. ("Ezekiel saw the wheel, way up in the middle of the air," in the words of the old spiritual.) What gave me pause was the realization that such visions coexist in Farrakhan's mind with a real poverty of—well, vision, which is to say a broader conception of the human future.

Farrakhan is a man of unhealthy fixations, but the reciprocal fixation on Farrakhan that you find in the so-called mainstream is a sign of our own impoverished political culture. Thirteen decades have passed since Emancipation, and half of our black men between twenty-four and thirty-five are without full-time employment. One black man graduates from college for every hundred who go to jail. Almost half of black children live in poverty. People say that Farrakhan is now the leading voice of black rage in America. One day, America will realize it got off easy.

REFLECTING AND DISCUSSING

1. What is the tone of this piece? How do you know? Look specifically at Gates's language and descriptions to articulate and make an argument about what you believe his attitude is toward his subject, Louis Farrakhan.

2. The title of the piece is "The Charmer," yet later in the essay, Gates calls Farrakhan "America's great black Satan." How is Farrakhan able to be persuasive to one group and appalling to another? How does the essay help you understand this? How do we still see this kind of dichotomy in our perception of public figures? How does that make this decades-old essay relevant, especially as Farrakhan has once again been in the news?

3. As mentioned, Farrakhan was a highly recognized figure when this essay was written. Comment on Gates's contentions that the black community is an "imagined" community and that "Farrakhan's anti-Semitism has the characteristics of a psychological obsession."

CONNECTING AND WRITING

1. Gates ends the essay by articulating the harsh realities of the lives of black men in America. Remembering that this article was published in 1996, research any of the social discrepancies Gates highlights (e.g., unemployment, mass incarceration) and analyze ways in which those social contexts have or haven't changed since the article's publication. Craft a thesis that argues a point of view and use Gates and your resources as evidence.

2. Write an essay that compares Farrakhan—using Gates's examples as evidence—to a more contemporary figure who might also be considered a "demagogue." What more global lessons can we learn by looking carefully at such figures? Articulate a point of view and use examples, drawing on research about the contemporary person, to support your points.

The Trouble with Fries

Malcolm Gladwell (1963–   )

Well-known writer, journalist, and speaker Malcolm Gladwell regularly produces stories for the New Yorker. *Gladwell is also the author of numerous books, many of them best-sellers, including* The Tipping Point: How Little Things Make a Big Difference *(2002),* Outliers: The Story of Success *(2011), and* Blink: The Power of Thinking Without Thinking *(2007). A Canadian American, Gladwell was appointed to the Order of Canada, and his work has been acknowledged with awards such as the American Sociological Association's Award for Excellence and an honorary degree from the University of Waterloo, Canada. His work is lauded for grappling with issues of race, bias, consumerism, and success. This article was published in the* New Yorker *in 2001.*

In 1954, a man named Ray Kroc, who made his living selling the five-spindle Multimixer milkshake machine, began hearing about a hamburger stand in San Bernardino, California. This particular restaurant, he was told, had no fewer than eight of his machines in operation, meaning that it could make forty shakes simultaneously.

Kroc was astounded. He flew from Chicago to Los Angeles, and drove to San Bernardino, sixty miles away, where he found a small octagonal building on a corner lot. He sat in his car and watched as the workers showed up for the morning shift. They were in starched white shirts and paper hats, and moved with a purposeful discipline. As lunchtime approached, customers began streaming into the parking lot, lining up for bags of hamburgers. Kroc approached a strawberry blonde in a yellow convertible.

"How often do you come here?" he asked.

"Anytime I am in the neighborhood," she replied, and, Kroc would say later, "it was not her sex appeal but the obvious relish with which she devoured the hamburger that made my pulse begin to hammer with excitement." He came back the next morning, and this time set up inside the kitchen, watching the griddle man, the food preparers, and, above all, the French-fry operation, because it was the French fries that truly captured his imagination. They were made from top-quality oblong Idaho russets, eight ounces apiece, deep-fried to a golden brown, and salted with a shaker that, as he put it, kept going like a Salvation Army girl's tambourine. They were crispy on the outside and buttery soft on the inside, and that day Kroc had a vision of a chain of restaurants, just like the one in San Bernardino, selling golden fries from one end of the country to the other. He asked the two brothers who owned the hamburger stand if he could buy their franchise rights. They said yes. Their names were Mac and Dick McDonald.

Ray Kroc was the great visionary of American fast food, the one who brought the lessons of the manufacturing world to the restaurant business. Before the fifties, it was impossible, in most American towns, to buy fries of consistent quality. Ray Kroc was the man who changed that. "The french fry," he once wrote, "would become almost sacrosanct for me, its preparation a ritual to be followed religiously." A potato that has too great a percentage of water—and potatoes, even the standard Idaho russet burbank, vary widely in their water content—will come out soggy at the end of the frying process. It was Kroc, back in the fifties, who sent out field men, armed with hydrometers, to make sure that all his suppliers were producing potatoes in the optimal solids range of twenty to twenty-three per cent. Freshly harvested potatoes, furthermore, are rich in sugars, and if you slice them up and deep-fry them the sugars will caramelize and brown the outside of the fry long before the inside is cooked. To make a crisp French fry, a potato has to be stored at a warm temperature for several weeks in order to convert those sugars to starch. Here Kroc led the way as well, mastering the art of "curing" potatoes by storing them under a giant fan in the basement of his first restaurant, outside Chicago.

Perhaps his most enduring achievement, though, was the so-called potato computer—developed for McDonald's by a former electrical engineer for Motorola named Louis Martino—which precisely calibrated the optimal cooking time for a batch of fries. (The key: when a batch of cold raw potatoes is dumped into a vat of cooking oil, the temperature of the fat will drop and then slowly rise. Once the oil has risen three degrees, the fries are ready.) Previously, making high-quality French fries had been an art. The potato computer, the hydrometer, and the curing bins made it a science. By the time Kroc was finished, he had figured out how to turn potatoes into an inexpensive snack that would always be hot, salty, flavorful, and crisp, no matter where or when you bought it.

This was the first fast-food revolution—the mass production of food that had reliable mass appeal. But today, as the McDonald's franchise approaches its fiftieth anniversary, it is clear that fast food needs a second revolution. As many Americans now die every year from obesity-related illnesses—heart disease and complications of diabetes—as from smoking, and the fast-food toll grows heavier every year. In the fine new book *Fast Food Nation*, the journalist Eric Schlosser writes of McDonald's and Burger King in the tone usually reserved for chemical companies, sweatshops, and arms dealers, and, as shocking as that seems at first, it is perfectly appropriate. Ray Kroc's French fries are killing us. Can fast food be fixed?

Fast-food French fries are made from a baking potato like an Idaho russet, or any other variety that is mealy, or starchy, rather than waxy. The potatoes are harvested, cured, washed, peeled, sliced, and then blanched—cooked enough so that the insides have a fluffy texture but not so much that the fry gets soft and breaks. Blanching is followed by drying, and drying by a thirty-second deep fry, to give the potatoes a crisp shell. Then the fries are frozen until the moment of service, when they are deep-fried again, this time for somewhere around three minutes. Depending on the fast-food chain involved, there are other steps interspersed in this process. McDonald's fries, for example, are briefly dipped in a sugar solution, which gives them their golden-brown color; Burger King fries are dipped in a starch batter, which is what gives those fries their distinctive hard shell and audible crunch. But the result is similar. The potato that is first harvested in the field is roughly eighty per cent water. The process of creating a French fry consists, essentially, of removing as much of that water as possible—through blanching, drying, and deep-frying—and replacing it with fat.

Elisabeth Rozin, in her book *The Primal Cheeseburger*, points out that the idea of enriching carbohydrates with fat is nothing new. It's a standard part of the cuisine of almost every culture. Bread is buttered; macaroni comes with cheese; dumplings are fried; potatoes are scalloped, baked with milk and cheese, cooked in the dripping of roasting meat, mixed with mayonnaise in a salad, or pan-fried in butterfat as latkes. But, as Rozin argues, deep-frying is in many ways the ideal method of adding fat to carbohydrates. If you put butter on a mashed potato, for instance, the result is texturally unexciting: it simply creates a mush. Pan-frying results in uneven browning and crispness. But when a potato is deep-fried the heat of the oil turns the water inside the potato into steam, which causes the hard granules of starch inside the potato to swell and soften: that's why the inside of the fry is fluffy and light. At the same time, the outward migration of the steam limits the amount of oil that seeps into the interior, preventing the fry from getting greasy and concentrating the oil on the surface, where it turns the outer layer of the potato brown and crisp. "What we have with the french fry," Rozin writes, "is a near perfect enactment of the enriching of a starch food with oil or fat."

This is the trouble with the French fry. The fact that it is cooked in fat makes it unhealthy. But the contrast that deep-frying creates between its interior and its exterior—between the golden shell and the pillowy whiteness beneath—is what makes it so irresistible. The average American now eats a staggering thirty pounds of French fries a year, up from four pounds when Ray Kroc was first figuring out how to mass-produce a crisp fry. Meanwhile, fries themselves have become less healthful.

Ray Kroc, in the early days of McDonald's, was a fan of a hot-dog stand on the North Side of Chicago called Sam's, which used what was then called the Chicago method of cooking fries. Sam's cooked its fries in animal fat, and Kroc followed suit, prescribing for his franchises a specially formulated beef tallow called Formula 47 (in reference to the forty-seven-cent McDonald's "All-American meal" of the era: fifteen-cent hamburger, twelve-cent fries, twenty-cent shake). Among aficionados, there is general agreement that those early McDonald's fries were the finest mass-market fries ever made: the beef tallow gave them an unsurpassed rich, buttery taste. But in 1990, in the face of public concern about the health risks of cholesterol in animal-based cooking oil, McDonald's and the other major fast-food houses switched to vegetable oil. That wasn't an improvement, however. In the course of making vegetable oil suitable for deep frying, it is subjected to a chemical process called hydrogenation, which creates a new substance called a trans unsaturated fat. In the hierarchy of fats, polyunsaturated fats—the kind found in regular vegetable oils—are the good kind; they lower your cholesterol. Saturated fats are the bad kind. But trans fats are worse: they wreak havoc with the body's ability to regulate cholesterol. According to a recent study involving some eighty thousand women, for every five-per-cent increase in the amount of saturated fats that a woman consumes, her risk of heart disease increases by seventeen per cent. But only a two-per-cent increase in trans fats will increase her heart-disease risk by ninety-three per cent. Walter Willett, an epidemiologist at Harvard—who helped design the study—estimates that the consumption of trans fats in the United States probably causes about thirty thousand premature deaths a year.

McDonald's and the other fast-food houses aren't the only purveyors of trans fats, of course; trans fats are in crackers and potato chips and cookies and any number of other processed foods. Still, a lot of us get a great deal of our trans fats from French fries, and to read the medical evidence on trans fats is to wonder at the odd selectivity of the outrage that consumers and the legal profession direct at corporate behavior. McDonald's and Burger King and Wendy's have switched to a product, without disclosing its risks, that may cost human lives. What is the difference between this and the kind of thing over which consumers sue companies every day?

The French-fry problem ought to have a simple solution: cook fries in oil that isn't so dangerous. Oils that are rich in monounsaturated fats, like canola oil, aren't nearly as bad for you as saturated fats, and are generally stable enough for deep-frying. It's also possible to "fix" animal fats so that they aren't so problematic. For example, K. C. Hayes, a nutritionist at Brandeis University, has helped develop an oil called Appetize. It's largely beef tallow, which gives it a big taste advantage over vegetable shortening, and makes it stable enough for deep-frying. But it has been processed to remove the cholesterol, and has been blended with pure corn oil, in a combination that Hayes says removes much of the heart-disease risk.

Perhaps the most elegant solution would be for McDonald's and the other chains to cook their fries in something like Olestra, a fat substitute developed by Procter & Gamble. Ordinary fats are built out of a molecular structure known as a triglyceride: it's a microscopic tree, with a trunk made of glycerol and three branches made of fatty acids. Our bodies can't absorb triglycerides, so in the digestive process each of the branches is broken off by enzymes and absorbed separately. In the production of Olestra, the glycerol trunk of a fat is replaced with a sugar, which has room for not three but eight fatty acids. And our enzymes are unable to break down a fat tree with eight branches—so the Olestra molecule can't be absorbed by the body at all. "Olestra" is as much a process as a compound: you can create an "Olestra" version of any given fat. Potato chips, for instance, tend to be fried in cottonseed oil, because of its distinctively clean taste. Frito-Lay's no-fat Wow! chips are made with an Olestra version of cottonseed oil, which behaves just like regular cottonseed oil except that it's never digested. A regular serving of potato chips has a hundred and fifty calories, ninety of which are fat calories from the cooking oil. A serving of Wow! chips has seventy-five calories and no fat. If Procter & Gamble were to seek F.D.A. approval for the use of Olestra in commercial deep-frying (which it has not yet done), it could make an Olestra version of the old McDonald's Formula 47, which would deliver every nuance of the old buttery, meaty tallow at a fraction of the calories.

Olestra, it must be said, does have some drawbacks—in particular, a reputation for what is delicately called "gastrointestinal distress." The F.D.A. has required all Olestra products to carry a somewhat daunting label saying that they may cause "cramping and loose stools." Not surprisingly, sales have been disappointing, and Olestra has never won the full acceptance of the nutrition community. Most of this concern, however, appears to be overstated. Procter & Gamble has done random-ized, double-blind studies—one of which involved more than three thousand people over six weeks—and found that people eating typical amounts of Olestra-based chips don't have significantly more gastrointestinal problems than people eating normal chips. Diarrhea is such a common problem in America—nearly a third of adults have at least one episode each month—that even F.D.A. regulators now appear to be convinced that in many of the complaints they received Olestra was unfairly blamed for a problem that was probably caused by something else. The agency has promised Procter & Gamble that the warning label will be reviewed.

Perhaps the best way to put the Olestra controversy into perspective is to com-pare it to fibre. Fibre is vegetable matter that goes right through you: it's not ab-sorbed by the gastrointestinal tract. Nutritionists tell us to eat it because it helps us lose weight and it lowers cholesterol—even though if you eat too many baked beans or too many bowls of oat bran you will suffer the consequences. Do we put warning labels on boxes of oat bran? No, because the benefits of fibre clearly outweigh its drawbacks. Research has suggested that Olestra, like fibre, helps people lose weight and lowers cholesterol; too much Olestra, like too much fibre, may cause problems. (Actually, too much Olestra may not be as troublesome as too much bran. Accord-ing to Procter & Gamble, eating a large amount of Olestra—forty grams—causes no more problems than eating a small bowl—twenty grams—of wheat bran.) If we had Olestra fries, then, they shouldn't be eaten for breakfast, lunch, and dinner. In fact, fast-food houses probably shouldn't use hundred-per-cent Olestra; they should cook their fries in a blend, using the Olestra to displace the most dangerous trans and saturated fats. But these are minor details. The point is that it is entirely possible, right now, to make a delicious French fry that does not carry with it a death sentence. A French fry can be much more than a delivery vehicle for fat.

Is it really that simple, though? Consider the cautionary tale of the efforts of a group of food scientists at Auburn University, in Alabama, more than a decade ago to come up with a better hamburger. The Auburn team wanted to create a leaner beef that tasted as good as regular ground beef. They couldn't just remove the fat, because that would leave the meat dry and mealy. They wanted to replace the fat. "If you look at ground beef, it contains moisture, fat, and protein," says Dale Huffman, one of the scientists who spearheaded the Auburn project. "Protein is relatively constant in all beef, at about twenty per cent. The traditional McDonald's ground beef is around twenty per cent fat. The remainder is water. So you have an inverse ratio of water and fat. If you reduce fat, you need to increase water." The goal of the Auburn scientists was to cut about two-thirds of the fat from normal ground beef, which meant that they needed to find something to add to the beef that would hold an equivalent amount of water—and continue to retain that water even as the beef was being grilled. Their choice? Seaweed, or, more precisely, carrageenan. "It's been in use for centuries," Huffman explains. "It's the stuff that keeps the suspension in chocolate milk—otherwise the chocolate would settle at the bottom. It has tremendous water-holding ability. There's a loose bond between the carrageenan and the moisture." They also selected some basic flavor enhancers, designed to make up for the lost fat "taste." The result was a beef patty that was roughly three-quarters water, twenty per cent protein, five per cent or so fat, and a quarter of a per cent seaweed. They called it AU Lean.

It didn't take the Auburn scientists long to realize that they had created something special. They installed a test kitchen in their laboratory, got hold of a McDonald's grill, and began doing blind taste comparisons of AU Lean burgers and traditional twenty-per-cent-fat burgers. Time after time, the AU Lean burgers won. Next, they took their invention into the field. They recruited a hundred families and supplied them with three kinds of ground beef for home cooking over consecutive three-week intervals—regular "market" ground beef with twenty per cent fat, ground beef with five per cent fat, and AU Lean. The families were asked to rate the different kinds of beef, without knowing which was which. Again, the AU Lean won hands down—trumping the other two on "likability," "tenderness," "flavorfulness," and "juiciness."

What the Auburn team showed was that, even though people love the taste and feel of fat—and naturally gravitate toward high-fat food—they can be fooled into thinking that there is a lot of fat in something when there isn't. Adam Drewnowski, a nutritionist at the University of Washington, has found a similar effect with cookies. He did blind taste tests of normal and reduced-calorie brownies, biscotti, and chocolate-chip, oatmeal, and peanut-butter cookies. If you cut the sugar content of any of those cookies by twenty-five per cent, he found, people like the cookies much less. But if you cut the fat by twenty-five per cent they barely notice. "People are very finely attuned to how much sugar there is in a liquid or a solid," Drewnowski says. "For fat, there's no sensory break point. Fat comes in so many guises and so many textures it is very difficult to perceive how much is there." This doesn't mean we are oblivious of fat levels, of course. Huffman says that when his group tried to lower the fat in AU Lean below five per cent, people didn't like it anymore. But, within the relatively broad range of between five and twenty-five per cent, you can add water and some flavoring and most people can't tell the difference.

What's more, people appear to be more sensitive to the volume of food they consume than to its calorie content. Barbara Rolls, a nutritionist at Penn State, has demonstrated this principle with satiety studies. She feeds one group of people a high-volume snack and another group a low-volume snack. Even though the two snacks have the same calorie count, she finds that people who eat the high-volume snack feel more satisfied. "People tend to eat a constant weight or volume of food in a given day, not a constant portion of calories," she says. Eating AU Lean, in short, isn't going to leave you with a craving for more calories; you'll feel just as full.

For anyone looking to improve the quality of fast food, all this is heartening news. It means that you should be able to put low-fat cheese and low-fat mayonnaise in a Big Mac without anyone's complaining. It also means that there's no particular reason to use twenty-per-cent-fat ground beef in a fast-food burger. In 1990, using just this argument, the Auburn team suggested to McDonald's that it make a Big Mac out of AU Lean. Shortly thereafter, McDonald's came out with the McLean Deluxe. Other fast-food houses scrambled to follow suit. Nutritionists were delighted. And fast food appeared on the verge of a revolution.

Only, it wasn't. The McLean was a flop, and four years later it was off the market. What happened? Part of the problem appears to have been that McDonald's rushed the burger to market before many of the production kinks had been worked out. More important, though, was the psychological handicap the burger faced. People liked AU Lean in blind taste tests because they didn't know it was AU Lean; they were fooled into thinking it was regular ground beef. But nobody was fooled when it came to the McLean Deluxe. It was sold as the healthy choice—and who goes to McDonald's for health food?

Leann Birch, a developmental psychologist at Penn State, has looked at the impact of these sorts of expectations on children. In one experiment, she took a large group of kids and fed them a big lunch. Then she turned them loose in a room with lots of junk food. "What we see is that some kids eat almost nothing," she says. "But other kids really chow down, and one of the things that predicts how much they eat is the extent to which parents have restricted their access to high-fat, high-sugar food in the past: the more the kids have been restricted, the more they eat." Birch explains the results two ways. First, restricting food makes kids think not in terms of their own hunger but in terms of the presence and absence of food. As she puts it, "The kid is essentially saying, 'If the food's here I better get it while I can, whether or not I'm hungry.' We see these five-year-old kids eating as much as four hundred calories." Birch's second finding, though, is more important. Because the children on restricted diets had been told that junk food was bad for them, they clearly thought that it had to taste good. When it comes to junk food, we seem to follow an implicit script that powerfully biases the way we feel about food. We like fries not in spite of the fact that they're unhealthy but because of it.

That is sobering news for those interested in improving the American diet. For years, the nutrition movement in this country has made transparency one of its principal goals: it has assumed that the best way to help people improve their diets is to tell them precisely what's in their food, to label certain foods good and certain foods bad. But transparency can backfire, because sometimes nothing is more deadly for our taste buds than the knowledge that what we are eating is good for us. McDonald's should never have called its new offering the McLean Deluxe, in other words. They should have called it the Burger Supreme or the Monster Burger, and then buried the news about reduced calories and fat in the tiniest type on the remotest corner of their Web site. And if we were to cook fries in some high-tech, healthful cooking oil—whether Olestrized beef tallow or something else with a minimum of trans and saturated fats— the worst thing we could do would be to market them as healthy fries. They will not taste nearly as good if we do. They have to be marketed as better fries, as Classic Fries, as fries that bring back the rich tallowy taste of the original McDonald's.

What, after all, was Ray Kroc's biggest triumph? A case could be made for the field men with their hydrometers, or the potato-curing techniques, or the potato computer, which turned the making of French fries from an art into a science. But we should not forget Ronald McDonald, the clown who made the McDonald's name irresistible to legions of small children. Kroc understood that taste comprises not merely the food on our plate but also the associations and assumptions and prejudices we bring to the table—that half the battle in making kids happy with their meal was calling what they were eating a Happy Meal. The marketing of healthful fast food will require the same degree of subtlety and sophistication. The nutrition movement keeps looking for a crusader—someone who will bring about better public education and tougher government regulations. But we need much more than that. We need another Ray Kroc.

REFLECTING AND DISCUSSING

1. This piece declares that we've already had one fast-food revolution and that we need a second. How does Gladwell characterize the first revolution, and what are his hopes for the second? Is this piece a call to action? How so?
2. What, exactly, is "the trouble with fries"? As Gladwell asks, "Can it be fixed?"
3. What is Gladwell's overall argument? How does he make it? In what ways does he integrate information and data with other sources to support his overall point of view? Are these methods effective?

CONNECTING AND WRITING

1. At the time that this piece was published, many other voices were expressing concern about our "fast-food nation," among them authors Eric Schlosser and Michael Pollan. Look at the arguments of these or other authors either agreeing or disagreeing with Gladwell and compare and contrast them. To what conclusion do you come?
2. This 2001 publication argues with a sense of urgency that America is in the midst of a health crisis that is due largely to our overconsumption of fast food. Explore federal and more local attempts to legislate healthier eating—or at least to promote awareness of food content. Explore evidence to determine whether these attempts have been effective and argue a point of view on the issue.

The "Busy" Trap

Tim Kreider (1967–   )

Tim Kreider is a well-known cartoonist-turned-essayist. His work has appeared in the New York Times, Al-Jazeera, Men's Journal, *and the* New Yorker. *Kreider's book series* Banta Graphics *catalogs his cartoon work. His first collection of essays, published by Simon and Schuster (2012) and called* We Learn Nothing, *showcased his witty and often irreverent view of pop culture. This essay was originally published in 2012 in the opinion pages of the* New York Times.

If you live in America in the 21st century you've probably had to listen to a lot of people tell you how busy they are. It's become the default response when you ask anyone how they're doing: "Busy!" "*So* busy." "*Crazy* busy." It is, pretty obviously, a boast disguised as a complaint. And the stock response is a kind of congratulation: "That's a good problem to have," or "Better than the opposite."

It's not as if any of us wants to live like this; it's something we collectively force one another to do.

Notice it isn't generally people pulling back-to-back shifts in the I.C.U. or commuting by bus to three minimum-wage jobs who tell you how busy they are; what those people are is not busy but *tired. Exhausted. Dead on their feet.* It's almost always people whose lamented busyness is purely self-imposed: work and obligations they've taken on voluntarily, classes and activities they've "encouraged" their kids to participate in. They're busy because of their own ambition or drive or anxiety, because they're addicted to busyness and dread what they might have to face in its absence.

Almost everyone I know is busy. They feel anxious and guilty when they aren't either working or doing something to promote their work. They schedule in time with friends the way students with 4.0 G.P.A.'s make sure to sign up for community service because it looks good on their college applications. I recently wrote a friend to ask if he wanted to do something this week, and he answered that he didn't have a lot of time but if something was going on to let him know and maybe he could ditch work for a few hours. I wanted to clarify that my question had not been a preliminary heads-up to some future invitation; this *was* the invitation. But his busyness was like some vast churning noise through which he was shouting out at me, and I gave up trying to shout back over it.

Even *children* are busy now, scheduled down to the half-hour with classes and extracurricular activities. They come home at the end of the day as tired as grown-ups. I was a member of the latchkey generation and had three hours of totally unstructured, largely unsupervised time every afternoon, time I used to do everything from surfing the World Book Encyclopedia to making animated films to getting together with friends in the woods to chuck dirt clods directly into one another's eyes, all of which provided me with important skills and insights that remain valuable to this day. Those free hours became the model for how I wanted to live the rest of my life.

The present hysteria is not a necessary or inevitable condition of life; it's something we've chosen, if only by our acquiescence to it. Not long ago I Skyped with a friend who was driven out of the city by high rent and now has an artist's residency in a small town in the south of France. She described herself as happy and relaxed for the first time in years. She still gets her work done, but it doesn't consume her entire day and brain. She says it feels like college—she has a big circle of friends who all go out to the cafe together every night. She has a boyfriend again. (She once ruefully summarized dating in New York: "Everyone's too busy and everyone thinks they can do better.") What she had mistakenly assumed was her personality—driven, cranky, anxious and sad—turned out to be a deformative effect of her environment. It's not as if any of us wants to live like this, any more than any one person wants to be part of a traffic jam or stadium trampling or the hierarchy of cruelty in high school—it's something we collectively force one another to do.

Our frantic days are really just a hedge against emptiness.

Busyness serves as a kind of existential reassurance, a hedge against emptiness; obviously your life cannot possibly be silly or trivial or meaningless if you are so busy, completely booked, in demand every hour of the day. I once knew a woman who interned at a magazine where she wasn't allowed to take lunch hours out, lest she be urgently needed for some reason. This was an entertainment magazine whose raison d'être was obviated when "menu" buttons appeared on remotes, so it's hard to see this pretense of indispensability as anything other than a form of institutional self-delusion. More and more people in this country no longer make or do anything tangible; if your job wasn't performed by a cat or a boa constrictor in a Richard Scarry book I'm not sure I believe it's necessary. I can't help but wonder whether all this histrionic exhaustion isn't a way of covering up the fact that most of what we do doesn't matter.

I am not busy. I am the laziest ambitious person I know. Like most writers, I feel like a reprobate who does not deserve to live on any day that I do not write, but I also feel that four or five hours is enough to earn my stay on the planet for one more day. On the best ordinary days of my life, I write in the morning, go for a long bike ride and run errands in the afternoon, and in the evening I see friends, read or watch a movie. This, it seems to me, is a sane and pleasant pace for a day. And if you call me up and ask whether I won't maybe blow off work and check out the new American Wing at the Met or ogle girls in Central Park or just drink chilled pink minty cocktails all day long, I will say, what time?

But just in the last few months, I've insidiously started, because of professional obligations, to become busy. For the first time I was able to tell people, with a straight face, that I was "too busy" to do this or that thing they wanted me to do. I could see why people enjoy this complaint; it makes you feel important, sought-after and put-upon. Except that I hate actually being busy. Every morning my in-box was full of e-mails asking me to do things I did not want to do or presenting me with problems that I now had to solve. It got more and more intolerable until finally I fled town to the Undisclosed Location from which I'm writing this.

Here I am largely unmolested by obligations. There is no TV. To check e-mail I have to drive to the library. I go a week at a time without seeing anyone I know. I've remembered about buttercups, stink bugs and the stars. I read. And I'm finally getting some real writing done for the first time in months. It's hard to find anything to say about life without immersing yourself in the world, but it's also just about impossible to figure out what it might be, or how best to say it, without getting the hell out of it again.

Idleness is not just a vacation, an indulgence or a vice; it is as indispensable to the brain as vitamin D is to the body, and deprived of it we suffer a mental affliction as disfiguring as rickets. The space and quiet that idleness provides is a necessary condition for standing back from life and seeing it whole, for making unexpected connections and waiting for the wild summer lightning strikes of inspiration— it is, paradoxically, necessary to getting any work done. "Idle dreaming is often of the essence of what we do," wrote Thomas Pynchon in his essay on sloth. Archimedes' "Eureka" in the bath, Newton's apple, Jekyll & Hyde and the benzene ring: history is full of stories of inspirations that come in idle moments and dreams. It almost makes you wonder whether loafers, goldbricks and no-accounts aren't responsible for more of the world's great ideas, inventions and masterpieces than the hardworking.

"The goal of the future is full unemployment, so we can play. That's why we have to destroy the present politico-economic system." This may sound like the pro-nouncement of some bong-smoking anarchist, but it was actually Arthur C. Clarke, who found time between scuba diving and pinball games to write "Childhood's End" and think up communications satellites. My old colleague Ted Rall recently wrote a column proposing that we divorce income from work and give each citizen a guar-anteed paycheck, which sounds like the kind of lunatic notion that'll be considered a basic human right in about a century, like abolition, universal suffrage and eight-hour workdays. The Puritans turned work into a virtue, evidently forgetting that God invented it as a punishment.

Perhaps the world would soon slide to ruin if everyone behaved as I do. But I would suggest that an ideal human life lies somewhere between my own defiant indolence and the rest of the world's endless frenetic hustle. My role is just to be a bad influence, the kid standing outside the classroom window making faces at you at your desk, urging you to just this once make some excuse and get out of there, come outside and play. My own resolute idleness has mostly been a luxury rather than a virtue, but I did make a conscious decision, a long time ago, to choose time over money, since I've always understood that the best investment of my limited time on earth was to spend it with people I love. I suppose it's possible I'll lie on my deathbed regretting that I didn't work harder and say everything I had to say, but I think what I'll really wish is that I could have one more beer with Chris, an-other long talk with Megan, one last good hard laugh with Boyd. Life is too short to be busy.

REFLECTING AND DISCUSSING

1. How does Kreider argue that busyness is a "trap"? Do you agree or disagree? Why?
2. Comment on the irreverence of Kreider's language. How does it influence—or not—your point of view regarding his argument? Is the language effective? Why or why not?

3. Kreider says, "If you live in America in the 21st century you've probably had to listen to a lot of people tell you how busy they are." Are you one of those people? How do you see yourself represented in this essay? Is this representation accurate? Why or why not?

CONNECTING AND WRITING

1. This is a rather tongue-in-cheek critique of American culture. Find examples, analyzing your own experience, that substantiate Kreider's claim that we keep busy as a "hedge against emptiness." Do you agree or disagree? Be sure that your examples—even if they are personal ones—support your claims.
2. "Even *children* are busy now, scheduled down to the half-hour with classes and extracurricular activities." Much has been written about the overscheduling of young people. Find articles that either refute or support Kreider's point of view and craft an argument that compares and contrasts them.

The Shawl

Cynthia Ozick (1928–   )

Cynthia Ozick's work often centers on the plight of the immigrant, but it spans many genres: short story, translation, critique, essay, novel, and poetry, including The Pagan Rabbi, and Other Stories *(1995) and* The Puttermesser Papers: A Novel *(1998). She uses language that is marked, in the words of one critic, by "eloquence and intricacy." Ozick is the recipient of numerous awards, including the Edward Lewis Wallant Award, the Diamonstein-Spielvogel Award for the Art of the Essay, and the National Book Critics Circle Award. This story, written in 1980, is among her most famous, and it moved famed writer Elie Wiesel to comment, "Non-survivor novelists who treat the Holocaust ought to learn from Ozick the art of economy and what the French call* pudeur."

Stella, cold, cold, the coldness of hell. How they walked on the roads together, Rosa with Magda curled up between sore breasts, Magda wound up in the shawl. Sometimes Stella carried Magda. But she was jealous of Magda. A thin girl of fourteen, too small, with thin breasts of her own, Stella wanted to be wrapped in a shawl, hidden away, asleep, rocked by the march, a baby, a round infant in arms. Magda took Rosa's nipple, and Rosa never stopped walking, a walking cradle. There was not enough milk; sometimes Magda sucked air; then she screamed. Stella was ravenous. Her knees were tumors on sticks, her elbows chicken bones.

Rosa did not feel hunger; she felt light, not like someone walking but like someone in a faint, in trance, arrested in a fit, someone who is already a floating angel, alert and seeing everything, but in the air, not there, not touching the road. As if teetering on the tips of her fingernails. She looked into Magda's face through a gap in the shawl: a squirrel in a nest, safe, no one could reach her inside the little house of the shawl's windings. The face, very round, a pocket mirror of a face: but it was not Rosa's bleak complexion, dark like cholera, it was another kind of face altogether, eyes blue as air, smooth feathers of hair nearly as yellow as the Star sewn in to Rosa's coat. You could think she was one of their babies.

Rosa, floating, dreamed of giving Magda away in one of the villages. She could leave the line for a minute and push Magda into the hands of any woman on the side of the road. But if she moved out of line they might shoot. And even if she fled the line for half a second and pushed the shawl-bundle at a stranger, would the woman take it? She might be surprised, or afraid; she might drop the shawl, and Magda would fall out and strike her head and die. The little round head. Such a good child, she gave up screaming, and sucked now only for the taste of the drying nipple itself. The neat grip of the tiny gums. One mite of a tooth tip sticking up in the bottom gum, how shining, an elfin tombstone of white marble gleaming there. Without complaining, Magda relinquished Rosa's teats, first the left, then the right; both were cracked, not a sniff of milk. The duct-crevice extinct, a dead volcano, blind eye, chill hole, so Magda took the corner of the shawl and milked it instead. She sucked and sucked, flooding the threads with wetness. The shawl's good flavor, milk of linen.

It was a magic shawl, it could nourish an infant for three days and three nights. Magda did not die, she stayed alive, although very quiet. A peculiar smell, of cinnamon and almonds, lifted out of her mouth. She held her eyes open every moment, forgetting how to blink or nap, and Rosa and sometimes Stella studied their blueness. On the road they raised one burden of a leg after another and studied Magda's face. "Aryan," Stella said, in a voice grown as thin as a string; and Rosa thought how Stella gazed at Magda like a young cannibal. And the time that Stella said "Aryan," it sounded to Rosa as if Stella had really said "Let us devour her."

But Magda lived to walk. She lived that long, but she did not walk very well, partly because she was only fifteen months old, and partly because the spindles of her legs could not hold up her fat belly. It was fat with air, full and round. Rosa gave almost all her food to Magda, Stella gave nothing; Stella was ravenous, a growing child herself, but not growing much. Stella did not menstruate. Rosa did not menstruate. Rosa was ravenous, but also not; she learned from Magda how to drink the taste of a finger in one's mouth. They were in a place without pity, all pity was annihilated in Rosa, she looked at Stella's bones without pity. She was sure that Stella was waiting for Magda to die so she could put her teeth into the little thighs.

Rosa knew Magda was going to die very soon; she should have been dead already, but she had been buried away deep inside the magic shawl, mistaken there for the shivering mound of Rosa's breasts; Rosa clung to the shawl as if it covered only herself. No one took it away from her. Magda was mute. She never cried. Rosa hid her in the barracks, under the shawl, but she knew that one day someone would inform; or one day someone, not even Stella, would steal Magda to eat her. When Magda began to walk Rosa knew that Magda was going to die very soon, something would happen. She was afraid to fall asleep, she slept with the weight of her thigh on Magda's body; she was afraid she would smother Magda under her thigh. The weight of Rosa was becoming less and less; Rosa and Stella were slowly turning into air.

Magda was quiet, but her eyes were horribly alive, like blue tigers. She watched. Sometimes she laughed—it seemed a laugh, but how could it be? Magda had never seen anyone laugh. Still, Magda laughed at her shawl when the wind blew its corners, the bad wind with pieces of black in it, that made Stella's and Rosa's eyes tear. Magda's eyes were always clear and tearless. She watched like a tiger. She guarded her shawl. No one could touch it; only Rosa could touch it. Stella was not allowed. The shawl was Magda's own baby, her pet, her little sister. She tangled herself up in it and sucked on one of the corners when she wanted to be very still.

Then Stella took the shawl away and made Magda die.

Afterward Stella said: "I was cold." And afterward she was always cold, always. The cold went into her heart: Rosa saw that Stella's heart was cold. Magda flopped onward with her little pencil legs scribbling this way and that, in search of the shawl; the pencils faltered at the barracks opening, where the light began. Rosa saw and pursued. But already Magda was in the square outside the barracks, in the jolly light. It was the roll-call arena. Every morning Rosa had to conceal Magda under the shawl against a wall of the barracks and go out and stand in the arena with Stella and hundreds of others, sometimes for hours, and Magda, deserted, was quiet under the shawl, sucking on her corner. Every day Magda was silent, and so she did not die. Rosa saw that today Magda was going to die, and at the same time a fearful joy ran in Rosa's two palms, her fingers were on fire, she was astonished, febrile: Magda, in the sunlight, swaying on her pencil legs, was howling. Ever since the drying up of Rosa's nipples, ever since Magda's last scream on the road, Magda had been devoid of any syllable; Magda was a mute. Rosa believed that something had gone wrong with her vocal cords, with her windpipe with the cave of her larynx; Magda was defective, without a voice; perhaps she was deaf; there might be something amiss with her intelligence; Magda was dumb. Even the laugh that came when the ash-stippled wind made a clown out of Magda's shawl was only the air-blown showing of her teeth. Even when the lice, head lice and body lice, crazed her so that she became as wild as one of the big rats that plundered the barracks at daybreak looking for carrion, she rubbed and scratched and kicked and bit and rolled without a whimper. But now Magda's mouth was spilling a long viscous rope of clamor.

"Maaaa—"

It was the first noise Magda had ever sent out from her throat since the drying up of Rosa's nipples.

"Maaaa . . . aaa!"

Again! Magda was wavering in the perilous sunlight of the arena, scribbling on such pitiful little bent shins. Rosa saw. She saw that Magda was grieving for the loss of her shawl, she saw that Magda was going to die. A tide of commands hammered in Rosa's nipples: Fetch, get, bring! But she did not know which to go after first, Magda or the shawl. If she jumped out into the arena to snatch Magda up, the howling would not stop, because Magda would still not have the shawl; but if she ran back into the barracks to find the shawl, and if she found it, and if she came after Magda holding it and shaking it, then she would get Magda back, Magda would put the shawl in her mouth and turn dumb again.

Rosa entered the dark. It was easy to discover the shawl. Stella was heaped under it, asleep in her thin bones. Rosa tore the shawl free and flew—she could fly, she was only air—into the arena. The sunheat murmured of another life, of butterflies in summer. The light was placid, mellow. On the other side of the steel fence, far away, there were green meadows speckled with dandelions and deep-colored violets; beyond them, even farther, innocent tiger lilies, tall, lifting their orange bonnets. In the barracks they spoke of "flowers," of "rain": excrement, thick turd-braids, and the slow stinking maroon waterfall that slunk down from the upper bunks, the stink mixed with a bitter fatty floating smoke that greased Rosa's skin. She stood for an instant at the margin of the arena. Sometimes the electricity inside the fence would seem to hum; even Stella said it was only an imagining, but Rosa heard real sounds in the wire: grainy sad voices. The farther she was from the fence, the more clearly the voices crowded at her. The lamenting voices strummed so convincingly, so passionately, it was impossible to suspect them of being phantoms. The voices told her to hold up the shawl, high; the voices told her to shake it, to whip with it, to unfurl it like a flag. Rosa lifted, shook, whipped, unfurled. Far off, very far, Magda leaned across her air-fed belly, reaching out with the rods of her arms. She was high up, elevated, riding someone's shoulder. But the shoulder that carried Magda was not coming toward Rosa and the shawl, it was drifting away, the speck of Magda was moving more and more into the smoky distance. Above the shoulder a helmet glinted. The light tapped the helmet and sparkled it into a goblet. Below the helmet a black body like a domino and a pair of black boots hurled themselves in the direction of the electrified fence. The electric voices began to chatter wildly. "Maamaa, maaamaaa," they all hummed together. How far Magda was from Rosa now, across the whole square, past a dozen barracks, all the way on the other side! She was no bigger than a moth.

All at once Magda was swimming through the air. The whole of Magda travelled through loftiness. She looked like a butterfly touching a silver vine. And the moment Magda's feathered round head and her pencil legs and balloonish belly and zigzag arms splashed against the fence, the steel voices went mad in their growling, urging Rosa to run and run to the spot where Magda had fallen from her flight against the electrified fence; but of course Rosa did not obey them. She only stood, because if she ran they would shoot, and if she tried to pick up the sticks of Magda's body they would shoot, and if she let the wolf's screech ascending now through the ladder of her skeleton break out, they would shoot; so she took Magda's shawl and filled her own mouth with it, stuffed it in and stuffed it in, until she was swallowing up the wolf's screech and tasting the cinnamon and almond depth of Magda's saliva; and Rosa drank Magda's shawl until it dried.

REFLECTING AND DISCUSSING

1. What do you know about the Holocaust? How does this story situate itself within what you already know? How does it add new knowledge?

2. What indications are there that this is a story of the Holocaust? What are the events that occur during it? When do you realize what is happening?

3. What is the struggle within Rosa? What are the ethical implications of situations in which people are forced to struggle with ethical decisions within completely unethical contexts?

CONNECTING AND WRITING

1. Comment on the tragedy of the ending. Why does the story end as it does, and what is the irony of Rosa's cramming the shawl down her throat? Use evidence from the story to support your contentions.

2. Although this is a work of fiction, Rosa represents people who are still forced to make decisions within unethical contexts. Do some research to find a contemporary example of Rosa's dilemma, even if it does not involve genocide. Use your research—and aspects of the story, as appropriate—to argue a point of view comparing the dilemma in Ozick's story to the dilemma in the example(s) you find.

Your Brain on Poverty: Why Poor People Seem to Make Bad Decisions

Derek Thompson (1986–   )

*Derek Thompson is a well-known blogger, writer, and Twitter personality. (*Time *magazine named Thompson's feed one of the 140 best Twitter feeds worth following.) Thompson graduated from Northwestern University in 2008. As a blogger for* Atlantic.com, *he often writes about the intersections of technology, business, and culture. His work has also been published in* Business Week, Slate, *and the* Daily Beast; *his first book,* Hit Makers: The Science of Popularity in an Age of Distraction, *was published in 2017.*

In August, *Science* published a landmark study concluding that poverty, itself, hurts our ability to make decisions about school, finances, and life, imposing a mental burden similar to losing 13 IQ points.

It was widely seen as a counter-argument to claims that poor people are "to blame" for bad decisions and a rebuke to policies that withhold money from the poorest families unless they behave in a certain way. After all, if being poor leads to bad decision-making (as opposed to the other way around), then giving cash should alleviate the cognitive burdens of poverty, all on its own.

Sometimes, science doesn't stick without a proper anecdote, and "Why I Make Terrible Decisions," a comment published on Gawker's Kinja platform by a person in poverty, is a devastating illustration of the *Science* study. I've bolded what I found the most moving, insightful portions, but it's a moving and insightful testimony all the way through.

I make a lot of poor financial decisions. None of them matter, in the long term. I will never not be poor, so what does it matter if I don't pay a thing and a half

this week instead of just one thing? It's not like the sacrifice will result in improved circumstances; the thing holding me back isn't that I blow five bucks at Wendy's. It's that now that I have proven that I am a Poor Person that is all that I am or ever will be. It is not worth it to me to live a bleak life devoid of small pleasures so that one day I can make a single large purchase. I will never have large pleasures to hold on to. There's a certain pull to live what bits of life you can while there's money in your pocket, because no matter how responsible you are you will be broke in three days anyway. When you never have enough money it ceases to have meaning. I imagine having a lot of it is the same thing.

Poverty is bleak and cuts off your long-term brain. It's why you see people with four different babydaddies instead of one. You grab a bit of connection wherever you can to survive. **You have no idea how strong the pull to feel worthwhile is. It's more basic than food.** You go to these people who make you feel lovely for an hour that one time, and that's all you get. You're probably not compatible with them for anything long-term, but right this minute they can make you feel powerful and valuable. It does not matter what will happen in a month. Whatever happens in a month is probably going to be just about as indifferent as whatever happened today or last week. None of it matters. **We don't plan long-term because if we do we'll just get our hearts broken. It's best not to hope. You just take what you can get as you spot it.**

When neuroscientists Joseph W. Kable and Joseph T. McGuire studied time, uncertainty and decision-making, they found that virtues like patience and self-control weren't as simple [as] previous studies suggested. In the ubiquitous Marshmallow study, for example, kids who ate the treat quickly were deemed impatient and kids who waited had self-control and, on the whole, went on to lead more productive lives, the study found.

But rational self-control in the real world, Kable says, isn't so black-and-white. Perhaps you have enough patience to wait an hour for a train, or to lose one pound each week with exercise and dieting. That sounds responsible. But what happens if the train isn't there in 90 minutes? If you never lose weight and you're making yourself miserable with your diet? Maybe you *should* give up! "In this situation, giving up can be a natural—indeed, a rational—response to a time frame that wasn't properly framed to begin with," Maria Konnikova summed it up for the *Times*.

As Andrew Golis points out, this might suggest something even deeper than the idea that poverty's stress interferes with our ability to make good decisions. The inescapability of poverty weighs so heavily on the author that s/he abandons long-term planning entirely, because the short term needs are so great and the long-term gains so implausible. The train is just not coming. What if the psychology of poverty, which can appear so irrational to those not in poverty, is actually "the most rational response to a world of chaos and unpredictable outcomes," he wrote.

None of this is an argument against poorer families trying to save or plan for the long-term. It's an argument for context. As Eldar Shafir, the author of the *Science* study, told the *Atlantic Cities'* Emily Badger: "All the data shows it isn't about poor people, it's about people who *happen to be in poverty*. All the data suggests it is not the person, it's the context they're inhabiting."

REFLECTING AND DISCUSSING

1. The tagline for the article when it initially ran suggested that these "bad decisions might be more rational than you think." How would Thompson characterize—and perhaps rationalize—such "bad decisions"? Do you agree with such a characterization? Why or why not?

2. Thompson structures the essay as a response to scientific research and social commentary. How is this approach effective? Why?

3. Thompson has written that "sometimes science doesn't stick without a proper anecdote." What does he mean? Why do we need these personal stories?

CONNECTING AND WRITING

1. Thompson's article is explicitly about the ways in which poverty has an impact on the brain. What is another example of an explanation of a scientific phenomenon that benefits from personal stories, specific instances, or graphic images? How does this type of information make scientific evidence more accessible? (Think of global warming, public health, or another issue.)

2. In his essay, Thompson quotes a comment published in response to another, similar article entitled, "Why I Make Terrible Decisions." The comment notes, "Poverty is bleak and cuts off your long-term brain. It's why you see people with four different babydaddies instead of one. You grab a bit of connection wherever you can to survive. . . . It's more basic than food." Read one of the articles Thompson cites and compare and contrast the two pieces. How are the arguments similarly made? How are they different? What effect do they have?

QUESTION

Choose one of the pieces in this section and connect it with a piece in the grouping on ethics (e.g., Ozick's "The Shawl" and Wiesel's "The Perils of Indifference"). How does one piece shed light on the other? Be sure to formulate an argument with your point of view, using the essays or stories to back up your points.

CREATE YOUR OWN CONNECTIONS

1. Select at least two of the pieces (essay, article, image) in this volume, ideally from different time periods and different thematic groups. Compare and contrast the overall point of each, arguing a point of view regarding what makes them similar or different and using examples from each to support your argument.

2. Looking at the essays, stories, poems, and images in this volume, find a concept or historical reference with which you are not familiar. Research that concept or reference and explain how this historical or other context is important to the work. How does it make a difference in your understanding of the work? Why is the context important?

3. Given your understanding of classical structures of argument, select one of the essays in this volume and analyze it according to those structures. How does the essay follow these guidelines? How does it depart from them? With what effect?

CREDITS

CHAPTER 1:

Excerpted from *Borderlands/La Frontera: The New Mestiza.* © 1987, 1999, 2007, 2012 by Gloria Anzaldua. Reprinted by permission of Aunt Lute Books. www.auntlute.com

Sam Louie, I Don't See Color: Then You Don't See Me!, *Psychology Today,* February 22, 2016

Bharati Mukherjee, Two Ways to Belong in America, *New York Times,* September 22, 1996

Staples: From "A Black Man Ponders His Ability to Alter Space" by Brent Staples. Published in Scholastic Literary Cavalcade, September 1998. Copyright © 1998 by Scholastic Inc. Used by permission.

Melissa R. Sipin, "Filipineza" doesn't mean "servant": Notes of witness from an immigrant daughter, *Salon,* June 18, 2017

Dinosaurs in the Hood, a poem, Danez Smith. Poetry [magazine] (Dec 2014)

Justin Reed, Killing Like They Do in the Movies, *Catapult,* October 30, 2015

CHAPTER 2:

Jane McGonigal, Be a Gamer, Save the World, *Wall Street Journal,* January 22, 2011

Harris: By permission of Tristan Harris

Gopnik: By permission of Adam Gopnik

Marche: © 2012 The Atlantic Media Co., as first published in *The Atlantic Magazine.* All rights reserved. Distributed by Tribune Content Agency, LLC

Atwood: © by O.W. Toad, Ltd.

CHAPTER 3:

Sameer Pandya, The Picture for Men: Superhero or Slacker, *Pacific Standard,* August 17, 2010

Mary E. Wilkins Freeman, A New England Nun, 1891

Copyright © 1985 by Barbara Ehrenreich Reprinted by permission of ICM Partners

Anna Howard Shaw, The Fundamental Principle of a Republic, 1915

Mary Wollstonecraft, Vindication of the Rights of Women, 1792

Mary McCarthy, Cruel and Barbarous Treatment, Southern Review, 1939

CHAPTER 4:

John F Kennedy, Inaugural Address, January 1961 From The New York Times, January 24, 1961 © 1961 The New York Times. All rights reserved. Used by permission and protected by the Copyright Laws of the United States. The printing, copying, redistribution, or re-transmission of this Content without express written permission is prohibited

MLK: © 1963 Dr. Martin Luther King Jr © renewed 1991 Correta Scott King

Franklin Roosevelt, The Four Freedoms

Sonia Sotomayor, Pappas v. Giuliani

"Shooting an Elephant" from A Collection of Essays, by George Orwell. Copyright 1950 by Sonia Brownell Orwell. Copyright © renewed by Sonia Pitt-Rivers. Reprinted by permission of Houghton Mifflin Harcourt Publishing Company. All rights reserved.

From TYRANNY OF THE MAJORITY by Lani Guinier. Copyright © 1994 by Lani Guinier. Reprinted with the permission of The Free Press, a division of Simon & Schuster, Inc. All rights reserved

CHAPTER 5:

Published by permission of David Brooks c/o Writers Representatives LLC, New York, NY 10011, www.writersreps.com/permissions. All rights reserved.

"The Guest" from EXILE AND THE KINGDOM by Albert Camus, translated by Justin O'Brien, copyright © 1957, 1958 by Penguin Random House LLC. Used by permission of Alfred A. Knopf, an

imprint of the Knopf Doubleday Publishing Group, a division of Penguin Random House LLC. All rights reserved.
Steve Lopez, Doin' Time with a New Ticker, Los Angeles Times, January 28, 2002
Garrett Hardin, Lifeboat Ethics, Psychology Today, September 1974
Chapter 10: pp. 118-32 from Words That Heal by Rabbi Joseph Telushkin. Copyright © 1996 by Joseph Telushkin. Reprinted by permission of HarperCollins Publishers.
Nathaniel Hawthorne, The Birthmark, 1843

CHAPTER 6:
Jonathan Swift, A Modest Proposal, 1729
Reprinted with permission of The Onion. Copyright © 2018, by Onion, Inc. www.theonion.com
Henry David Thoreau, Civil Disobedience, 1849
By permission of Howard Rheingold

CHAPTER 7:
Coates: © 2015 The Atlantic Media Co., as first published in The Atlantic Magazine. All rights reserved. Distributed by Tribune Content Agency, LLC
Depillis: From The Washington Post, August 4, 2016 © 2016 The Washington Post. All rights reserved. Used by permission and protected by the Copyright Laws of the United States. The printing, copying, redistribution, or retransmission of this Content without express written permission is prohibited.
Douthat: From The New York Times, August 15, 2010 © 2010 The New York Times. All rights reserved. Used by permission and protected by the Copyright Laws of the United States. The printing, copying, redistribution, or retransmission of this Content without express written permission is prohibited.
Henry Louis Gates, Jr., The Charmer, New Yorker, April 29, 1996
By permission of Malcolm Gladwell
Kreider: The New York Times, June 30, 2012 © 2012 The New York Times. All rights reserved. Used by permission and protected by the Copyright Laws of the United States. The printing, copying, redistribution, or retransmission of this Content without express written permission is prohibited.

'The Shawl' by Cynthia Ozick. Published by The New Yorker, 1980. Copyright © Cynthia Ozick. Reproduced by permission of the author c/o Rogers, Coleridge & White Ltd., 20 Powis Mews, London W11 1JN.

Thompson: © 2013 The Atlantic Media Co., as first published in The Atlantic Magazine. All rights reserved. Distributed by Tribune Content Agency, LLC

PHOTOS

CHAPTER 3:

Coffee ad – Chase & Sanborn

Orkin image: American Girl in Italy, Florence, 1951. Copyright 1952, 1980 Ruth Orkin

CHAPTER 5:

University of Arizona Class of 1898–1899: Special Collections, The University of Arizona Libraries

CHAPTER 6:

Boersma image: The Art Institute of Chicago/Art Resource, NY. Reprinted by permission of Jay Boersma

WWF ad: TBMA France/WWF

Image from Onion article: Pool photo/Newsmakers/Getty Images